The
Complete Book
of American Fish
and Shellfish
Cookery

The
Complete Book
of American Fish
and Shellfish
Cookery

Elizabeth Bjornskov

With Illustrations by the Author

WEATHERVANE BOOKS
NEW YORK

To Andre With Love

Copyright © 1984 by Elizabeth Bjornskov
All rights reserved.
This 1989 edition is published by Weathervane Books distributed by
Crown Publishers, Inc., 225 Park Avenue South, New York,
New York 10003, by arrangement with Alfred A. Knopf, Inc.

Manufactured in the United States of America

Library of Congress Cataloging-in-Publication Data
Bjornskov, Elizabeth.
The complete book of American fish and shellfish
cookery / Elizabeth Bjornskov : with illustrations
by the author.
Reprint. Originally published: New York : A. A. Knopf,
1984.
Includes index.
ISBN 0-517-67955-8
1. Cookery (Fish)   2. Cookery (Shellfish)   I. Title.
TX747.B5   1989   89-5265
641.6'92—dc19   CIP

ISBN 0-517-67955-8
h g f e d c b a

Contents

PART III

FISHING DOWN THE ATLANTIC COAST
FROM BORDER TO BORDER

PART VI

SAUCES AND MARINADES

Acknowledgments

FIRST, I would like to express my gratitude to my three daughters, all excellent cooks, who have cooked from the manuscript as it was being written, and also to my husband and son, often fishing partners, who took the roles of taster and critic.

My deepest thanks to Colleen Dibert for her encouragement, and to Orley Kelly for her assistance in bringing this book into being.

Lucille Wetzel and Mrs. Forbes Norris and the many fishing friends we have made during these five years have graciously shared their recipes. I send you my warmest greetings and sincere thanks.

I am indebted to the National Marine Fisheries Service, the Fish and Wildlife Service, and various state Departments of Fisheries that have generously provided information.

Lastly, I want to express my gratitude to my editor, Nancy Nicholas, for her enthusiastic support and encouragement, and to Edith Leavitt for superb copy editing, and to all who have helped in the production of this book.

Introduction

ON A COOL, crisp Saturday in September, just after rain had set the northern rivers afloat, half the population of Tillamook went fishing. Anglers lined Oregon's Trask River that early afternoon, from the mouth of the bay to the edge of town. Every six feet or so, another fisherman caught a toehold and plunked in his line. Each one had his tackle down to a science —sand shrimp, salmon eggs, nets and rods, weights and floats. Old Ernie settled down in his camp chair for the thirty-seventh year in a row.

I was the newcomer. I'd driven through a cow pasture to get to this spot in time for the cresting tide. Preparing for this adventure, I'd read how to attract a creature that doesn't eat on its upstream journey. I had studied all there was to know about coaxing it, surprising it, romancing it with the right bait.

I found my spot at the first bend in the river. Baiting my hook with freshly preserved salmon eggs, I cast upstream and glued my eyes to the bobber. Disappointed after the first five minutes of no action, I reeled in and cast in again. Then, settling down like the rest of the anglers, I waited. Now and then the bobber disappeared, my heart leapt, and nothing happened. Fishing jokes bounced around. The river inched down on the outgoing tide.

Snap! My rod went double. The line hissed as it played out up the river.

"Hold on! Jerk it fast!"

"Tighten your drag!"

"Get up on the bank so you won't tangle!"

Orders burst at me from every direction.

"FISH ON, FISH ON!" I shouted, trying not to slip into the water. Scrambling up the bank, reeling in, tightening my drag, I was beside myself.

"That's a big one! Watch out! It's heading for the stump!"

Every fisherman on the bank reeled in to give me room to fight. I struggled, leaning backward to counter the monster's strength. I thought I couldn't pull much harder when—suddenly—the pole straightened up and my line went loose.

To the Reader

IN THIS VOLUME, popular edible fish are introduced according to their geographical location; methods of preparing them and recipes for your enjoyment follow each.

In case a fish isn't available in your area or at the time of year the recipes strike your fancy, at the end of the recipes suggestions for other fish which might successfully be substituted have been added.

Each of these recipes, unless it is specifically noted, serves four.

Good fishing, get hungry, and bon appétit!

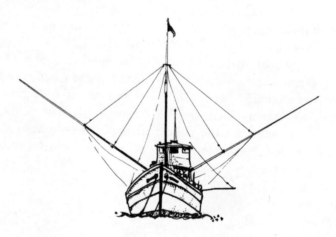

I

Basic Handling

FROM THE WATER TO THE KITCHEN

Choosing Fish

WHEN I CHOOSE a fresh fish at the market it is cool, translucent, firm to the touch, and beautiful. Its eyes are full, clear, and bright. Its gills are pinkish red, free from slime and any odor but its own characteristic good clean smell.

Keeping fish absolutely fresh until they go into the pan can be a problem—they deteriorate quickly out of water and should be cleaned, or at least have their gills slit, immediately after they are caught to prevent the flesh from becoming fishy tasting. Veteran fishermen carry a gunnysack. Wet-down, it acts as a cooler, keeping fish moist and out of the sun. A fish is at its best when eaten the day it is caught.

Icing-Down to Preserve Fish

Packing fish in crushed ice, from the water through marketing, is the professional method of preserving freshness, firmness, and flavor. On your next fishing trip, with a little preplanning, you can keep your catch fresh, without loss of quality, for up to seven days. The right proportion of rock salt mixed with crushed ice makes the difference, so you can maintain a temperature of about 28°F. (colder than the refrigerator but not cold enough to freeze the fish).

Bring with you on your trip an insulated ice chest, some rock salt (ice-cream salt), and aluminum foil or thick plastic wrap. Crushed ice (or tiny ice cubes) should be purchased just before you head out fishing. If possible, bring your ice chest aboard and place the fish on ice as you catch them. The sooner fish are gutted, bled, and degilled, the fresher they will remain.

Fillets and steaks must be wrapped tightly in foil or plastic wrap

3

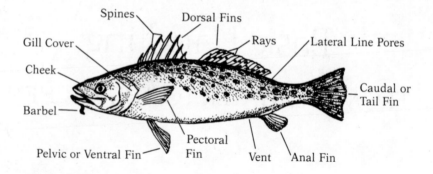

before icing-down. Whole fish must be cleaned and degilled before wrapping.

Open the bottom drain of the ice chest and leave it open to drain out the water. Pour in four inches of crushed ice. Place a single layer of wrapped fish on the ice. Then mix salt and ice well in a bucket, using one pound of rock salt for each twenty pounds of crushed (or tiny cube) ice. Cover the fish packages with a generous layer of ice-salt mixture. Alternate layers of wrapped fish and ice-salt until the ice chest is full. The top layer, however, must be ice-salt. The ice chest should be kept tightly closed except when you are adding more ice-salt or more fish.

At home, fish may be unwrapped, rinsed in salted ice water, drained on toweling, and rewrapped in airtight packages for freezing.

Cleaning Fish

The first handling of the catch is cleaning—as soon as possible.

Cleaning small fish such as smelts or anchovies is done simply by cutting off their heads with kitchen scissors; snip the belly to the vent and scoop out the innards with your thumb. Rinse well in salted water and dry on toweling.

CLEANING LARGER FISH
ENTAILS THE FOLLOWING STEPS:

Remove the scales. This is accomplished more easily when the fish is wet. Many fishermen make their own scraper, using a small block of wood with bottle caps nailed upside down to one side of it. A knife will do the trick as well. Put the fish flat on the cleaning board. With one hand hold the fish's head firmly. If you salt your hands you can get a better grip.

Then scrape, with the back edge of the knife or your scraper, from the tail toward the head. You can scale either before or after cleaning the fish.

Split the belly from vent to head and remove the innards and any clotted blood that clings to the backbone. The fish is now drawn or gutted. Rinse in 1 part vinegar to 3 parts cold water and pat dry. If you intend to bake the fish whole, cut out the gills which impart a disagreeable flavor. Pectoral (side) and pelvic fins are attached to large bones that are most easily removed after the fish is cooked. The dorsal (back) fin also is often left intact on large fish for a more attractive appearance when served. Otherwise,

Remove the head, gills, and pectoral fins together by cutting above the collarbone and through the backbone. If the backbone is very large, cut down to it on each side of the head and snap the bone over the edge of the board.

Trim off any remaining flesh holding the head to the body and cut off the tail. Save the head and tail to make fish stock, which is the basis for sauces and soup.

Remove the dorsal (back) fin and ventral (underside toward the tail) fins by cutting the flesh along each side of the fin; then, using pliers if need be, give a quick pull forward toward the head of the fish, which

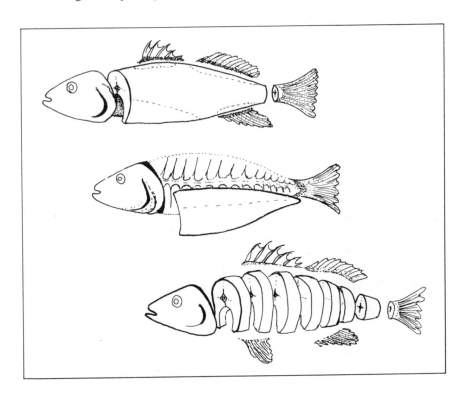

removes the fin with root bones attached. This is better than trimming the fins with shears.

Wash fish in cold salted water and pat it dry.

The fish is now *dressed* or *pan dressed*. Large fish can be crosscut into steaks, thin or thick as you like, or into chunks.

Filleting Fish

FISH UNDER 10 POUNDS

Lay fish (whole, but scaled and gutted) on a cutting board. With a razor-sharp knife cut down through the meat along the back from the tail to just behind the head. Then cut down to the backbone just above the collarbone. Turn the knife flat against the backbone and, using the ribs as a guide, cut along the backbone to the tail. Turn the fish over and repeat the process. Feel for any bones you may have missed in the two fillets.

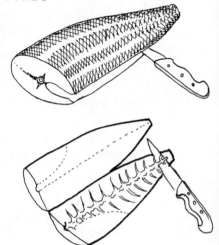

FISH OVER 10 POUNDS

Cut behind the gills and pectoral stub to the backbone. Cut the skin around the periphery of the fillet near the fins. (It is easier to slide your knife tip along under the skin, sharp edge facing out.) Starting at the gill cover top, lift a bit of the skin, using pliers if need be and cutting the flesh away if it clings. Then fillet the fish using the ribs as a guide for your knife. Feel for any bones that may have been missed. Turn the fish over and repeat the process.

FLATFISH
(such as halibut, flounder, or sole)

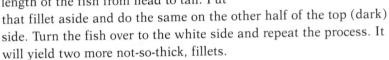

Start on the top (dark) side. Cut behind
the gills from the top of the head to the
center backbone. Then cut down to
the backbone from head to tail. Turn
the knife flat. Using the spines as a
guide, cut toward one periphery, the
length of the fish from head to tail. Put
that fillet aside and do the same on the other half of the top (dark)
side. Turn the fish over to the white side and repeat the process. It
will yield two more not-so-thick, fillets.

SKINNING A FILLET

Lay the fillet skin side down on a cutting board with the tail end toward
you. Grasp the fish by the tail end and hold it tightly. Cut through the flesh
to the skin about ½ inch from the tail end. Turn the knife flat against the
skin and slide the blade forward until the skin and meat have been
separated. Wipe the fillet with a damp towel only. Large fillets can be
crosscut into 1-inch steaks.

Cleaning Mollusks

Cleaning Abalone. First give a stunning
blow with a mallet to the top of the
abalone. Put it on a solid surface with the
spiral end down, the row of holes facing up.
Jam an abalone iron down inside against the shell
to pry, or pop, the meat loose. Pull the innards away
from the round muscle and discard. (Trimmings make
good bait. They can be put in a jar, capped, and kept in the
freezer.) Wash the abalone well in cold water. Cut off the head
and tentacles. Wait until the muscle flattens out before trimming it. This
could be immediately or could take overnight. Trim off the heel, all skin,
dark meat, and the cap. Keep trimming until your nail can pierce the tough
meat and there is only white muscle. Rinse, dry, and pound it lightly with
a mallet until the meat is soft but not broken up. The abalone may be cut
crosswise into ⅜-inch slices, then each one pounded into separate steaks.

Cleaning and Opening Clams. Cover fresh-dug clams with seawater, or cold salted water (1/3 cup to a gallon of water), and set them aside for 30 minutes so they can rid themselves of sand. A piece of iron in the bottom of the bucket seems to help clams discharge sand. Do this two or three more times, changing the water after each soaking. Then scrub shells clean under cold running water. Live clams in the shell will stay alive for several days if kept at a maximum temperature of 40°F.

Discard any partly opened shells that don't close when touched. Throw away any long-siphon clams that don't contract the siphon (neck) when touched. After clams have been thoroughly washed, put them on a cookie sheet and chill them in the freezer for an hour or two. Chilled clams offer less resistance to opening.

Open Pacific Coast clams with a knife and *remove all black portions, which during red tide months (May 15 to October 15) contain a lethal poison.*

Open hard-shell clams (i.e., all short-siphon clams that can close their shells completely) and Eastern soft-shell clams over a bowl to collect the juice. A thin, broad clam knife also makes shucking easier. Hold a clam in your hand with the shell hinge against your palm, then insert the blade between the shell halves. Cut around the rim with a twisting motion until you cut the adductor muscle, which is down toward the hinge. Remove the top shell, then run your knife under the clam to sever it from the bottom shell. (The bottom shell is a deeper and more curved shell. Meat is left in this deeper shell when raw clams are served on the half shell. Pick out any shell fragments.) Remove the shucked clam and rinse it briefly. If you are cleaning Eastern soft-shell clams, pull off the filmy sheath from the siphon and trim off the black siphon tip. Properly covered and refrigerated shucked clams will stay fresh for a week. Frozen clams must be defrosted in the refrigerator and used immediately once thawed.

Alternatively, to open clams, put them in a strainer, and dunk them in boiling water; leave them for a few seconds, then, draining, plunge them immediately in ice water, and drain again.

If clams are to be cooked, you may steam the shells open. Put 1/2 cup water and the clams in a large pot. Cover the pot tightly and steam until shells just open. Discard any that don't open.

It is easier, and much less messy, to put clams through the chopper when they are frozen almost hard.

Razor Clams. Soak clams and open shells the same as for hard-shell clams. Then, slit the neck, opening up both tubes of the siphon and cut along the length of the body and foot — enough so that the clam can be flattened into one large piece. Remove all black portions from the body, then rinse well. Scrape off all brown skin on the neck and trim off the siphon tip.

Gapors (blue clams, horse clams, summer clams, or Empires). Scrub clams under cold running water, then sever the muscle holding the shells together. Cut meat from the shell. Soak it in a bucket of cold water for an hour or two, changing the water several times. Slit the neck, opening up both tubes of the siphon. Slit open the body, then cut off the siphon and put it back in the water to soak. Remove all dark portions and the green gland. Rinse the body well and set it aside for cooking. Let the neck soak until it becomes limp and the brown skin peels off easily. Alternatively, trim off the tip of the siphon, cover it with scalding water for a minute or so, until the skin will pull right off. Skin the neck, then dry it on toweling and pound the neck meat with a mallet until it is tender and limp or grind it.

Pismo Clams. Wash shells well under cold running water. Cut the muscle holding shells together and pry open the clam. Cut the meat from the shell and place it on a plate. Remove and discard all black and soft portions. The firm light meat and clam liquor that are left are ready for ceviche or cooking.

Cleaning and Opening Mussels. Mussels will remain alive for up to 24 hours if kept cool and covered with damp sacks. Discard all broken shells and any open shells that don't close when touched. Scrape off all barnacles and debris under cold running water and remove as much of the beard as possible. Try sliding the shell halves sideways in opposite directions to see if you have a real mussel or a shell loaded with sand. Scrub mussels with a stiff-bristled brush (you can buy a special metal-bristled one), then soak for 1 or 2 hours in cold water to get rid of sand and some of the salty flavor. To open, cut the muscle that holds the shells together and separate the shells. Cut meat loose around the rim and pull it away from the beard and tough muscle attached to it. You may trim out the soft center dark part of large ocean mussels. Rinse meat under running water and dry it. Alternatively, steam the mussels open and pull off the beard and tough muscle attached to it. *To be safe, do not eat mussels gathered along the Pacific Coast from May 15 through October 15,* which is the quarantine period for red tide.

Cleaning Octopus. Trim out the beak and center head section. Using both hands, turn body inside out and remove all innards, including the ink sac, leaving only snowy white meat. Rinse the cavity well and turn it right side out again. Tenderize the meat by pounding with a rolling pin or mallet for at least 5 minutes, until quite limp. If not tenderized sufficiently, octopus is the toughest of meat. Rinse well and drop into a pot with just enough boiling salted water to cover. Add 1/4–1/2 cup vinegar and simmer for 5 minutes, then drain. Peel off the tough skin and trim off the tips of tentacles.

Cleaning and Opening Oysters. Scrub oyster shells clean under cold running water. With pliers or hammer, chip off a piece of the thin end to make an opening. Place oyster (cup or rounded side down) on a solid surface, with the hinge toward your hand. Force the shucking knife into the opening. Slide the blade from side to side along the flat top shell to sever the adductor muscle, then discard the top shell. Slide the blade under the oyster and cut the muscle loose from the center of the bottom shell. Lift out the shucked oyster.

Oyster liquor should be clear. If the juice is cloudy or milky, discard both the oyster and its liquor.

If you shuck oysters over a strainer placed in a bowl, the liquor collected will be strained free of shell fragments.

Cleaning Squid. Wash squid under cold running water. Gently separate the head-tentacle section from the long body by pulling apart. Remove the ink sac at the base of the head, if you want to use it. Cut off the tentacles close to the eyes, wash and rub off as much of the skin as will come off; dry and reserve them and discard the rest of the head section. Reach for and extract the long translucent sword-shaped shell from the body. Squeeze out the remaining contents, discard them, and rinse the inside well. Pull off the purplish, transparent membrane covering the body, leaving the snow white meat to use. Drain squid and dry on toweling.

Cleaning Crustaceans

Cleaning and Shelling Crab (Dungeness or rock crabs). Crabs should be actively alive until cooked, or cooked within 15 minutes of killing. To kill a crab, lay it on its back and strike it on the underside of the body, between the claws, with a heavy utensil. Scrub it under cold running water with a brush, then clean by pulling off the back shell and ventral placque (apron) and then the spongy gills. Rinse away all soft matter and break body in half vertically.

Plunge live crabs, head first, into rapidly boiling salted water to cover. Use fresh seawater or 1 tablespoon salt to each quart fresh water. Crab boil spices or vinegar may be added to the water. When the water resumes a boil, simmer crab for 15–20 minutes in a covered kettle. Immerse cooked crabs in cold water to cause meat to separate from the shell. Strike the edge of the back shell against a solid object and pull it off. Remove the apron and break the crab in half vertically. Shake out the viscera from each half, pull off the spongy gills, and rinse briefly. Twist and pull legs and claws from the body section. Crack the leg and claw shells with a mallet or nutcracker, then cut the body into 4 pieces. The delicious white meat picked from the cracked claws, legs, and body is now ready to eat. Fresh crab meat picked from the shell can be wrapped airtight for freezing. Keep crab meat chilled and no longer than 24 hours.

Cleaning Lobster. Lobster should be actively alive until it is cooked. Turn antennae back to the tail and bind them (and claws) with a rubber band. Bring a large quantity of salted water (1 tablespoon salt for each quart water) to a full boil and drop lobsters in headfirst. Cover, return to a boil, then simmer for 15 minutes for the first pound, 3 minutes for each additional pound. Drain, then drop them into cold water until cool enough to handle. Split lobster in half lengthwise down the back through the shell. Remove the black intestinal vein that runs lengthwise down the middle of the tail meat. You may lift the meat out of the tail shell or leave it in. Discard the hard food sac found near the back of the head. Retain any red coral (roe); you may also want to keep the grayish green liver for sauce. Crack the claws of American lobster.

To kill lobster without cooking, sever the spine by inserting a sharp pointed blade at the joint where body and tail section join. Then split the shell lengthwise down the back from head to tail. Remove and discard the black intestinal vein and hard food sac, located near back of the head. Save red coral and gray liver for garnish or sauce.

Cleaning Shrimp. Wash shrimp under cold running water and remove the legs. Use a sharp knife or scissors to make a shallow cut through the shell, the length of the curved back, to expose the black vein.
Rinse or lift the vein out with a toothpick.

Freezing Fish

Store fresh fish in your freezer at 0°F. or lower. High-fat-content fish and crab should not be stored more than three months. Lean fish and other shellfish (shelled) may be stored six months or more.

All fish should be eviscerated. Wash your fish in salted water, then wipe the skin of whole fish with 1 part vinegar to 2 parts water before freezing. Glazing is the best method of preserving a whole fish. It is done by first freezing the fish, then dipping it in water chilled with ice cubes, then refreezing it. Repeat this procedure several times. A thick glaze of ice builds up to preserve the fish indefinitely, as long as it is not allowed to thaw. Wrap the fish tightly in waxed paper to store.

Dip lean fillets and steaks in a salt solution (2/3 cup salt to 1 gallon water for lean fish; 1/3 cup salt to 1 gallon for oily fish) for 30 seconds before freezing. Be sure to remove the dark meat of the fish, especially around the rib cage, for these areas tend to taste most fishy and are the most perishable. Wrap each fillet or steak in a separate sheet of waxed paper (this keeps the fish from freezing stuck together), then seal in airtight freezer paper, label, and date.

Small fish can be put in a milk carton of water and frozen into a solid block of ice.

The process of freezing and thawing breaks down delicate fish tissue because of the expansion and contraction of ice crystals. This causes a slight change of taste and loss of moisture when cooked; it also speeds up spoilage.

It is best to thaw fish on the bottom shelf of the refrigerator, allowing a day (about 18 hours) for a pound package. However, to thaw quickly, put fish, in its package, in cold water for an hour or so. Don't thaw fish at room temperature or in warm water. Thawing at warm temperature causes a greater loss of protein- and mineral-containing fish fluids. Diminished food value and taste changes, due to damaged tissue and faster growth of dangerous spoilage bacteria, will result. Don't store thawed fish for more than one day. *Never refreeze fish.*

Basic Cooking Methods

AN AVERAGE SERVING of fish is: 1/3 pound of steak or fillet; 1/2 pound of dressed (bone in) fish; or 1 pound of whole fish, per person. This portion would yield about half of the daily requirement of protein and give you vitamins B, thiamine, niacin, riboflavin, iodine, iron, and copper. At most, fish has only moderate fat, is low in cholesterol, and is excellent diet food.

Basically, you can broil, bake, barbecue, deep fry, pan fry, poach, or steam fish. Fish vary in fat content, which influences the way they should be cooked. Those with higher fat content, such as salmon, mackerel, shad, and sablefish, lend themselves especially well to baking, broiling, and barbecuing. On the other hand, lean fish such as cod, flatfish, and rockfish need the moisture of poaching, steaming, or an extra application of fat to keep them from becoming dried out.

Rule of Thumb for Cooking Time

Allow 10 minutes cooking time for each 1-inch thickness, measured in the thickest part, when the piece of fish is lying flat. For example, a 1 1/2-inch-thick whole fish, fillet, or steak will require 15 minutes of cooking, whether it is baked, broiled, poached, or steamed; a 3 1/2-inch-thick piece of fish will require 35 minutes of cooking. This rule-of-thumb cooking guide can be followed for all fish except shellfish (mollusks and crustaceans).

Frozen fish should not be thawed before broiling, baking, poaching, or steaming. Instead, cook unthawed fish for twice the normal cooking time, allowing 20 minutes per inch thickness of fish.

A fish is cooked when the meat becomes opaque, flakes, and falls easily away from the bone when prodded. Because fish becomes fragile with cooking, careful handling and support with a wide spatula or cheesecloth are necessary to prevent the flesh from breaking or flaking when moving and serving.

To rid your hands and utensils of fish odors, wash them with a solution of 3 tablespoons baking soda to 1 quart water.

Basic Oven Broiling or Grilling

Oven broiling or grilling is a quick and nongreasy way to cook fillets, steaks, split or dressed medium-size fish. Those 1/2–1 1/2 inches thick broil best — these thicker pieces have more time to brown.
Lean fish may be broiled if they are kept moist by basting several times during cooking or by a covering of bacon.

Example:

2 pounds fish	4 Tablespoons (1/2 stick) butter, melted
Flour	1 teaspoon salt
4 Tablespoons lemon juice	1/4 teaspoon pepper

Preheat the broiler and pan 10 minutes before cooking.

Rinse and dry whole fish, or wipe steaks with damp toweling and blot them dry. Cut large fillets into serving pieces. Dust fish with flour and shake off the excess. Combine lemon juice with melted butter and, using a pastry brush, coat both sides of fish. Arrange fish, without crowding, in single layer on the hot greased broiler pan and return it to the oven at the proper distance from the heat (see chart below). Baste fish when you turn them, or more often.

Use the ratio of 10 minutes per inch thickness of fish to estimate cooking time. Broil frozen fish (without thawing) using the ratio of 20 minutes per inch thickness of fish.

Season cooked fish with salt and pepper and transfer it, using a fish server or wide spatula, to a warm platter. Garnish and serve sizzling hot.

OVEN BROILING CHART

Type	Thickness	Distance from Heat	Minutes per Side Side 1	Side 2
Steaks	1/2 inch	2 inches	3	3
Steaks	1 inch	2 inches	5	5
Fillets	1/2–1 inch	2 inches	5–10	Don't turn
Split Fish	1–1 1/2 inches	3 inches	10–14	Don't turn
Whole Flatfish		3 inches	8–10	Don't turn

Basic Baking

BAKING A WHOLE FISH

Baking a fish with its head on keeps juices in the fish. Clean, trim, rinse, and dry fish, then dust with flour and shake off the excess. Brush it with butter (oil or sauce) inside and out, and season with salt and pepper (herbs and/or spices). Place fish in a greased baking dish to bake uncovered and pour in ¼ cup water or wine for moisture. If more than one fish is baked at a time, arrange them so they don't touch.

Preheat the oven to 450°F. and bake fish 10 minutes per inch thickness at the thickest point when fish is lying flat. Double the cooking time for unthawed frozen fish to 20 minutes per inch thickness of fish.

Allow 5 minutes extra cooking time for heat to penetrate foil-baked fish and 10 minutes extra time for foil-baked frozen fish.

Lean fish must be kept moist—by basting; or draping with bacon, or other fat; or covering the pan; or baking in sauce; or baking in foil.

BAKING WHOLE STUFFED FISH

Preheat the oven to 425°F. Rub fish with lemon juice, season with salt and pepper, and set it aside while you make stuffing.

A 3–4-pound fish takes about 2½ cups of stuffing.

A 6–7-pound fish takes about 1 quart of stuffing.

Example:

SIMPLE DRESSING

¼ cup chopped onion	½ teaspoon salt
6 Tablespoons (¾ stick) butter	Pepper to taste
½ cup minced celery	1 egg, beaten
2 Tablespoons minced parsley	1½ cups unflavored bread crumbs
¼ teaspoon thyme	

Sauté onion in butter until lightly browned, add celery, parsley, and seasonings, and cook 2 more minutes. Remove from heat, mix in beaten egg and crumbs, then stuff fish loosely—two-thirds full. Close cavity and fasten with skewers, or sew the fish closed, or truss with twine or dental floss. If fish are small, use (nonplastic) cocktail picks.

Brush fish with oil (or with lemon-butter or cover with bacon strips), then place it in a buttered baking dish and add ¼ cup water or wine to the dish. Bake, uncovered, allowing 10 minutes cooking time per inch thickness of fish. Baste as needed with butter (herbed butter, wine, sauce, or fish stock).

BAKING SPLIT FISH
FILLETS, CHUNKS, AND STEAKS

Preheat the oven to 425°F. Fish may be cut into
serving pieces for ease of handling. Season with
salt and pepper (spices, herbs) and arrange pieces
in a buttered baking dish. Brush fish with butter
(oil, sauce), then cover baking dish with foil so fish can
bake in its own steam. Use a ratio of 10 minutes baking time per inch
thickness of fish, to estimate cooking time. Remove from oven and let
fish stand, covered, for several minutes before serving.

Fish baked in foil require an extra 5 minutes of cooking time to allow
heat to penetrate foil.

Frozen fillets should be baked without thawing. Wrap them in foil and
put them in a preheated 450°F. oven for twice the normal cooking time;
i.e., allow 20 minutes per inch thickness of fish and an extra 10 minutes
for heat to penetrate foil.
Example:
A ¾-inch-thick frozen foil-wrapped fillet will cook for 25 minutes.

When fish is baked, it is ready for a topping. Topping may be a sauce,
grated cheese, shrimp, sautéed mushrooms, tomatoes or onions, to name a
few.

Sauces That Go Well with Baked Fish
(Sauces in each group have a similar taste):

Cream Sauce, Egg Sauce, or Parsley White Sauce

Curry Sauce, Mushroom Sauce, or Shrimp Sauce

Hollandaise Sauce or variations of Hollandaise Sauce

Tomato Sauce or Creole Sauce

Brown Butter Sauce or Hot Herbed Butter

BAKING PLANKED FISH

A platter of fish surrounded by colorful vegetables all rimmed with fluffy
mashed potatoes is very elegant. Whole fish, pan-dressed butterflied fish,
steaks, or fillets may be planked. Bake and serve fish on a 1½-inch-thick
seasoned, grooved oak or hickory plank or a metal oven-to-table platter.
Put the plank or metal platter in a cold oven, turn oven to 425°F., and
preheat plank for 10 minutes. Grease the hot plank or platter before
placing fish on it.

Correlate cooking time for vegetables and mashed potatoes with cooking time for the fish. When the fish is baked, potatoes should be mashed, seasoned, and hot. Vegetables should be firmly cooked, hot, and seasoned, with at least two kinds ready for planking. Some suitable vegetables are: carrots, broccoli, onions, peas, cauliflower, tomatoes, mushrooms, string beans, and asparagus.

Season *whole cleaned, trimmed fish* with salt and pepper, brush with butter and oil (half of each), and bake at 425°F. for 10 minutes per inch thickness of fish, when it is lying flat. Don't baste.

Season *pan-dressed fish* with salt and pepper, center it on greased plank, brush with lemon-butter (2 tablespoons each), and bake at 425°F. until cooked (3 inches thick takes about 30 minutes).

Place *fillet or butterflied fish* skin side down on greased plank. Brush with lemon-butter (2 tablespoons each), season, and sprinkle with paprika. Bake at 425°F. for 10 minutes per inch thickness of fish, measured butterflied.

When fish is cooked, remove it from the oven and preheat the broiler while arranging a border of mashed potatoes around the fish on the plank. Slide the plank under the broiler, 4 inches from the heat, until potatoes brown lightly. Arrange hot seasoned vegetables around the fish, garnish with parsley and lemon wedges. Serve very hot.

Basic Barbecuing

Full-flavored fish with higher fat content are ideal for barbecuing, because the smoke enhances their flavor. Marinades and bastes keep fish moist while they are grilling, at the same time adding taste. Fish absorbs more flavoring from a marinade than from basting. You can vary the intensity of the flavoring by the 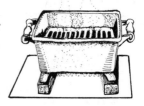 length of time you leave the fish in marinade. Every form and variety of fish must be brushed with a butter, oil, marinade, sauce, or other baste, while cooking on the grill. A rough estimate of charcoal broiling time is:

Small split fish:	8–10 minutes
Small whole fish:	12–18 minutes
Large split fish:	20–40 minutes
Large whole fish:	30–60 minutes

BARBECUING STEAKS, FILLETS,
OR WHOLE FISH, 1½ INCHES THICK OR LESS

Light 2–2½ dozen briquettes (for 2–3 pounds of fish) about 30–45 minutes before starting to cook. When coals are covered with white ash, spread them closely and evenly under the cooking area. Knock the white ash off the briquettes and let the glowing coals burn down again for another 5–10 minutes. The fire should now be moderately hot. Place the grill 4–6 inches above the coals.

The fish should be cut into serving pieces, and if it is not already marinating, prepare a baste, then dip fish in it. All your cooking tools, such as basting brush, spatula, condiments, etc., should be at your fingertips. Place fish pieces less than ¾ inch thick in a greased hinged wire broiler to cook. Otherwise, grease the grill with a solid fat like lard, margarine, or Pam, to keep the fish from sticking. Remove fish from marinade (or baste) and place pieces on the grill, arranging them so they don't touch. Brush the fish frequently with baste or marinade as they grill and turn them as needed. Cooking time for a ½-inch fillet is 2½ minutes on each side.

BARBECUING A LARGE 3–5-POUND
FILLET OR BUTTERFLIED FISH

Use 2½–3 dozen briquettes. Always let the coals burn down to white before starting to cook. Adjust the grill to 6 inches from the coals. Wrap the skin side of a fillet in heavy-duty foil, pressing it to mold around the fish. Place the fish on the grill foil side down and baste. Put the lid over the barbecue and adjust the dampers to maintain high heat. Or, cover the grill completely with aluminum foil. Press foil over the edges of the barbecue to seal in the heat and smoke. Grill the fish without turning for about 20 minutes. Raise the lid (foil) occasionally to baste and check on cooking. If the fish flakes when prodded, it is cooked. Slide the cooked fish onto a platter, cut down to the skin, and lift out the chunks carefully with a wide spatula or fish server.

BARBECUING A WHOLE 3–9-POUND PAN-DRESSED FISH

Light 3–4 dozen briquettes, depending on the size of the fish, and burn them down until white. Meanwhile, place the grill 6 inches above the coals, then prepare the fish. Season the cavity with salt and pepper, and place in it a green onion (split) and some lemon slices. Wrap one side of the fish in a double layer of foil. Press the foil smoothly around the fish so that it is well supported from head to tail. Use extra foil to support the tail if necessary.

When coals are white, rearrange them in 2 long, narrow parallel rows, about the length of the fish, leaving an empty space the width of the fish down the center of the barbecue. Place your fish on the grill. Put the lid over the barbecue and adjust the damper to maintain high heat. Or, cover the grill with foil to seal in the heat and smoke.

Lift the lid occasionally to baste. If the fish is 3 inches thick, test for doneness in 30 minutes, by probing the thickest part with a sharp thin knife.

Slide the cooked fish onto a warm platter. If you like, remove the skin from the top half. Start at the base of the tail and gently pull the pieces toward the head. To serve, cut the upper half away from the backbone, then slice into 1- or 2-inch chunks, cutting only to the bones. Lift out each chunk with a fish server or spatula. When the first side is consumed, disjoint and lay aside the backbone. Cut the other side the same way.

Basic Deep Frying

Deep frying is suitable for fillets, chunks, pan-dressed small fish, steaks, croquettes, and fish balls. Fried fish is best when brought sizzling to the table. So all garnishes, sauces, other food, people, etc. should be ready and waiting when the fish is done.

A deep fryer, electric skillet, wok, or any deep pan may be used. A pan that can hold a wire basket is convenient for small pieces and fish balls. Put in enough good vegetable oil or lard (2–4 inches) to cover generously the food to be cooked. Don't fill the pan more than two-thirds, because fat bubbles up when food is added and it could go over the pan. Use a deep-fry thermometer and heat fat slowly to 375°F. Prepare the fish for frying.

Example:

2 pounds fish	1 egg, lightly beaten
1 Tablespoon milk or water	1 cup fine dry bread crumbs, cracker
1 teaspoon salt	crumbs, or cornmeal
1/4 teaspoon pepper	

Wipe fish, then cut it into cubes or serving pieces. Combine milk or water and salt and pepper with beaten egg. Dip fish into beaten egg (which keeps fish from absorbing fat), then press the pieces into crumbs, coating the fish well. Crumbs adhere to fish better if the coated fish is left to dry for 30 minutes before frying.

Cook only a few pieces at a time to maintain high temperature of the oil, and also to keep fish from sticking together. Put fish directly into the oil, one piece at a time, or in a frying basket and lower slowly into the oil. Nudge and turn the pieces until they become evenly golden brown. Lift cooked fish out with tongs to drain a moment or two on paper toweling, then serve as quickly as possible.

BATTER

There are many different types of batter. The following beer batter may be used for fish and chips.

BEER BATTER

1 egg	1 teaspoon baking powder
3/4 cup beer	1 teaspoon salt
1 cup all-purpose flour	Pepper to taste

Beat the egg lightly, using a whisk. Beat in the beer, then flour, baking powder, salt and pepper, and beat until batter is smooth. Let the batter stand, covered, at room temperature, for 30 minutes before using.

LIGHT BATTER FOR FISH

1/2 cup all-purpose flour	1 teaspoon salt
1/2 cup cornstarch	1 egg
2 teaspoons baking powder	2/3 cup milk

Sift together dry ingredients. Beat egg lightly with milk, then combine with dry ingredients and beat with a whisk until batter is smooth.

Sauces That Go Well with Deep-fried Fish

Tartar Sauce	Horseradish White Sauce
Malt Vinegar	Sweet-and-Sour Sauce (p. 116)
Chili Sauce	Sesame-Vinegar Sauce (p. 81)
Catsup and mustard	Tempura Sauce (dipping) (p. 397)

Basic Oven Frying

Oven frying is suitable for fillets, steaks, or small whole fish that are ½–1½ inches thick. As in pan frying, fish are coated with flour or crumbs, which form a crispy crust. The end result is just about the same as pan frying.

Example:

1½ pounds fish

1 teaspoon salt

⅛ teaspoon pepper

½ cup milk

Flour or dry crumbs*

4 Tablespoons (½ stick) butter

4 Tablespoons vegetable oil

Parsley

Lemon

*Fish may be coated with flour, dry bread or cracker crumbs, cornmeal, half nuts/half crumbs, half cornmeal/half flour, or half crumbs/half cheese.

Preheat the oven to 500°F. Put a large, shallow baking pan in the oven to heat for 10 minutes. Wipe fish dry and cut into serving pieces. Add salt and pepper to milk and mix well. Spread flour or crumbs on waxed paper. Dip the fish into the milk and then roll in flour or crumbs. Remove hot pan from oven and put in enough butter and oil (olive oil, lard, etc.) to cover the bottom of the pan ⅛ inch deep. Tilt the pan to spread butter and oil around. Lay fish in the pan and spoon butter and oil over them. Alternatively, place pieces in the pan long enough to coat them with butter and oil, then turn them over so both sides will be buttered. Return the pan to the oven to bake, uncovered, until fish is brown and done. Use the ratio of 10 minutes per inch thickness in the thickest part of the fish to estimate the cooking time. Fish is done if it flakes when prodded with the tip of a knife. Serve fish at once on a warm platter, garnished with parsley and lemon.

Sauces That Go Well with Oven-fried Fish

Tartar Sauce

Herbed butters

Hollandaise Sauce

Mushroom Sauce

Basic Pan Frying

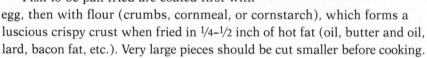

Fillets, steaks, and small whole fish 1 1/2
inches thick or less may be pan fried.
Whole fish should be cleaned and dressed.
    Fish to be pan fried are coated first with
egg, then with flour (crumbs, cornmeal, or cornstarch), which forms a
luscious crispy crust when fried in 1/4–1/2 inch of hot fat (oil, butter and oil,
lard, bacon fat, etc.). Very large pieces should be cut smaller before cooking.

Example:

2 pounds fish	Pepper to taste
1 egg, beaten	1 cup fine dry crumbs
1/4 cup milk	Butter and oil
1 teaspoon salt	Lemon slices

Combine beaten egg, milk, salt and pepper. Spread crumbs on a sheet of
waxed paper. Dip fish in egg mixture, then roll pieces in crumbs, covering
them evenly. If using half oil/half butter, heat until it foams; if using only
oil or lard, heat until it ripples. Place a single layer of fish in the pan,
without crowding, and fry, uncovered, until golden brown. Turn carefully
with a wide spatula and brown the other side. Thin fish (5/8 inch or less)
can be cooked on medium-high heat (375°F.); thicker are cooked on
medium (350°F.).
    Remove cooked fish to a warm platter and place, uncovered, in a low
oven to keep warm until all fish are cooked. Serve at once, garnished with
slices of lemon.

Basic Butter Sautéing

Fillets, steaks, small whole fish, and shellfish may be butter sautéed.
    Sautéing is cooking in a skillet, greased with just enough butter (oil,
lard, etc.) to keep food from sticking to the pan.
    Cooking in butter "à la meunière" means cooking in clarified butter. All
butter, when it gets near the perfect temperature for sautéing (a golden tan
color), has a tendency to stick and burn. The same delicious buttery-
cooked flavor, without the problem, is achieved by using half butter/half
vegetable oil.
    To sauté, first wipe fish dry with toweling, then dip it briefly in milk
and dust it lightly with flour, shaking off the excess. Heat butter and oil

(about ⅛ inch deep) in a heavy skillet or electric fry pan at 350°F., until it foams but doesn't brown. Place fish in pan (if more than one, don't crowd) and sauté until golden brown on one side. Turn carefully with a wide spatula and cook the other side. Remove fish to a warmed platter, salt and pepper it to taste. Garnish with parsley and lemon wedges and serve immediately.

Sauce Recipes for Butter-Sautéed Fish

Hot Butter Sauces	*White Butter*
Brown Butter	*Tartar Sauce*

Basic Poaching

Fish is poached by immersing it in boiling liquid, then simmering it either in the oven or on top of the stove, covered, until cooked. Simmering means keeping the liquid barely trembling. If the liquid is allowed to boil, fish will disintegrate. Poaching liquid flavors the fish while it cooks and supplies the basis for sauce after cooking. Poaching liquids are discussed later, but the following example is a flavorful, quick-to-make broth in which to cook your fish.

Example:

2–3 cups water	Sprig parsley
2 Tablespoons lemon juice, vinegar, or dry wine	½ teaspoon salt
	½ bay leaf
¼ cup grated carrot	3 peppercorns
1 green onion, minced	Pinch of thyme

Combine ingredients, bring to a boil, simmer for 15 minutes, then strain. If more than 3 cups of water are needed, double the amounts of other ingredients.

POACHING FILLETS, STEAKS, AND SMALL FISH UP TO 2 POUNDS

Preheat the oven to 425°F. Cut large fillets into serving pieces. Thin fillets may be folded or rolled. Sprinkle with salt and pepper, then place fish in single layer and barely touching in a buttered baking dish or buttered heavy skillet. Pour enough boiling liquid over fish barely to cover. Cover baking dish tightly with foil and place it in the preheated oven. Otherwise, cover the skillet and simmer slowly on top of the stove, over low heat, cooking the fish 10 minutes per inch of thickness measured when fish is lying flat.

Thin or fragile pieces of fish may be poached in a stove-to-table skillet to avoid breaking while handling. Remove fish carefully, using a wide spatula.

Poached fish may be left to cool in poaching liquid only if cooking time is shortened, so fish will not overcook.

Poached fish may be served hot with a sauce made with poaching liquid. Transfer fish to a platter and keep warm while making sauce.

Example:

Poaching liquid from cooked fish   Salt and pepper to taste
1 teaspoon cornstarch   Parsley
4 Tablespoons cream or evaporated
  milk

Pour poaching liquid into a saucepan and boil it down until the liquid is reduced to one-third its original volume. Blend cornstarch with half the cream, then add it to the reduced liquid and cook until sauce thickens. Add the remaining cream and salt and pepper to taste. Pour some of the sauce over the fish, garnish the platter with parsley, and serve the remaining sauce at the table.

POACHING CHUNKS AND SMALL FISH

Preheat the oven to 425°F. Any chunk larger than the width of the spatula should be double-wrapped in cheesecloth before cooking. If poaching on the stove top, place fish on the rack of a poacher or in a wire basket, cover with boiling liquid, and cook. Small fish may be put on a plate, then the plate tied in cheesecloth. Lower fish-on-plate into a kettle of boiling liquid. When the water returns to a simmer, use the ratio of 10 minutes per inch thickness of fish to estimate the cooking time.

POACHING A LARGE FISH OR CHUNK, 3–8 POUNDS

Have poaching liquid ready. Use a poacher, a large, deep roasting pan with a lid, or any pan that is deep enough to have the poaching liquid cover the fish by at least 1 inch when it is lying flat.

Rinse fish, wipe with a damp cloth, then wrap in a double layer of cheesecloth that is about 6 inches longer than the fish at each end. Twist these extended ends and tie them with string. Place fish on the rack of a poacher or roasting pan. If the roasting pan has handles, tie the strings at the end of the cheesecloth to the handles of the roaster; otherwise, fold the ends up on top of the fish. Pour in cool poaching liquid, enough to cover fish by about 1 inch. If you don't have enough liquid, add more water. When liquid comes to a boil, reduce heat to simmer. If oven poaching, place covered roaster in a preheated 425°F. oven to cook 10 minutes for each inch thickness of fish, measured when it is lying flat. When done, the flesh should be opaque and come away from the bone easily. If not, cover the pan again and cook longer.

Using the ends of the cheesecloth as handles, lift the fish from the pan. The extra support of a spatula underneath would help, if you can find a helper. Lay the fish on a platter or board large enough to accommodate it. Open the cheesecloth. At this point, you can 1) garnish the fish and serve it immediately; 2) cover the fish with foil to keep it warm while making a velouté or other sauce; 3) skin the fish. If you decide to skin it, use a sharp knife to cut the skin at the base of the tail and gently pull off the skin in strips, from the tail to the gill. Holding both ends of the cheesecloth, carefully lift and turn the fish onto a serving platter. Remove the skin on the upturned side.

If fish is to be served cold, let it stand and cool at room temperature, then cover it with foil or plastic wrap and refrigerate until it is thoroughly chilled, about 4 hours.

POACHING LIQUIDS

Fish may be poached in many kinds of liquids, such as chicken broth, cream, a mixture of half milk/half salted water, a wine-fish stock, mixtures of wine-fish stock and court bouillon. Court bouillon is a broth made of vegetables, herbs, and spices, with an acid base, such as lemon, vinegar, or wine.

SALTED WATER

To each quart boiling water add 1 tablespoon salt.

ACIDULATED WATER

To each quart boiling water add 1 tablespoon salt and 3 tablespoons vinegar, lemon juice, or wine.

BASIC COURT BOUILLON

2 Tablespoons (¼ stick) butter
1 onion, sliced thin
1 carrot, sliced thin
8 cups water
3 sprigs parsley
4 whole peppercorns, crushed

1 bay leaf
1 clove
Pinch of thyme
1 cup dry white wine or ½ cup lemon
    juice or vinegar

In a large saucepan, melt butter and sauté onion and carrot until tender. Add all other ingredients, bring to a boil, and simmer for 30 minutes. Strain the broth and discard the vegetables. Pour boiling court bouillon over fish.*

*All poaching liquids should be boiling when poured on fish.

SIMPLE FISH STOCK

To each quart cold water add 1 pound lean white-flesh fish trimmings—heads, bones, tails (tied in cheesecloth, if you like)—and ½ teaspoon salt. Bring to a boil and simmer for 30 minutes, skimming when necessary. Strain the stock and discard the solids.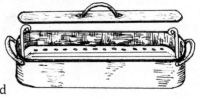

    Fish stock is used for making velouté sauce, which is the basis of many classic fish sauces. It is also used as a flavor booster in making soups, stews, and aspics. As a poaching liquid it may be reused many times. Boiling down just increases its strength. Keep it stored in the freezer.

WHITE WINE FISH STOCK
FOR SAUCES AND POACHING

2 pounds fish trimmings (heads,
    bones, tails, etc.)
Cold water to cover fish
1 onion, chopped
1 stalk celery, with leaves

2 sprigs parsley
1 slice lemon
1 cup dry white wine
5 whole peppercorns
½ teaspoon salt

Wash fish trimmings, then place all ingredients in a large kettle and bring to a boil. Simmer, uncovered, skimming when necessary, for 30 minutes. Strain the stock, discard the solids, and use for poaching. Or you can boil down the stock until reduced to 3 cups and use for sauces.

FISH STOCK-WINE POACHING LIQUID

To 2 parts White Wine Fish Stock (preceding recipe), add 1 part dry white wine.

WINE POACHING LIQUID

Mix half dry white wine and half water, or use dry white wine only.

Basic Steaming

Fillets, steaks, and cleaned whole fish may be steamed. The advantages of steaming are that none of the flavor or vitamin content is simmered out of the fish and that it is foolproof for retaining moisture.

Fish to be steamed are handled much the same as fish for poaching. Wipe fillets or steaks with a damp towel. Cut large thick fillets into serving pieces; thin fillets may be rolled or folded. Salt fish lightly, then place it in a greased vegetable steamer or colander (fish must be at least 2 inches above the boiling water with enough room allowed for steam to circulate 2 inches above the fish), cover tightly, and steam.

If fish is to be steamed in sauce, arrange the fish pieces in a bowl (or high-rimmed plate) in a single layer and pour sauce over it. Cover the bowl with a double thickness of waxed paper and place it on a perforated (or cake) rack, in a large enough pan, cover, and steam. Fillets and steaks an inch or less thick take 5–10 minutes of steaming to cook. Those 2 inches thick take about 15–20 minutes.

STEAMING A WHOLE CLEANED FISH
OR LARGE CHUNK

First rinse fish and wipe it with toweling. Sprinkle the cavity with salt and place in it slivers of green onion, lemon, and parsley; place slivers on top of fish too. Put fish, double-wrapped in cheesecloth, on a rack that will fit inside a roaster or wok. Alternatively, place fish on a platter that will fit on a rack (above the water) inside the wok or roaster. Wrap the fish and the platter in a double layer of waxed paper so the steaming moisture will not collect on the platter. Fill roaster with an inch or two of boiling water, then cover the pan tightly to steam. For added flavor place a bouquet garni of herbs and spices in the water. Allow 10 minutes for each inch thickness of fish, measured when fish is lying flat.

When testing or removing fish, lift the lid so the steam is released away from you. Fold back a corner of the waxed paper to test the thickest part of the fish. Lift the hot platter from the pan, remove the waxed paper, and wipe the plate. Serve fish hot with sauce and garnish, or set it aside to cool to room temperature before chilling it.

II

FISHING UP
THE PACIFIC COAST
FROM BORDER
TO BORDER

Tuna

ALBACORE (long-fin tuna) use the great ocean currents as inter-continental highways, migrating from Alaska, Japan, and Hawaii to Southern California. They are pelagic, that is, they swim near the surface. Their torpedolike bodies are shaped for speed. Fins fold down into slots, eyes are flush with their head, bodies are smooth and lubricated to slide easily through the water. Their strong tails vibrate ten to twenty times per second, each beat pushing them ahead a length.

These long-distance swimmers visit the West Coast from July through October. They forage around the Southern California offshore islands and follow the warm (65°–70°F.) currents twenty to sixty miles offshore, near the continental shelf.

During the season, albacore fishing from charter boats is popular from border to border. Anglers bait their line with a single anchovy placed to swim through a school of tuna. Tunas hit hard and line zips off the reel before the fish turn. Striking and feeding is frenzied. Albacores are hauled aboard, and the fury stops only when the school dives or moves on to another feeding ground.

BLUEFINS are the largest of the tunas—some are ten feet long and weigh three-quarters of a ton. They migrate between Japan and Southern California, appearing off the West Coast in May and staying until the water cools in late September. Unlike albacore that are fished up and down the entire coast, bluefin tunas are seldom seen north of Santa Barbara. They remain in deep blue water and are often found near the kelp beds of Santa Catalina, San Clemente, and Los Coronados islands.

Bluefins usually don't take trolled bait, but when one does strike, the

battle to land it is spectacular. These powerful giants are strong enough
to leap twenty feet in the air, doing gyrations that would put an acrobat to
shame.

West Coast tuna clippers fish bluefins by purse seine, which is hauled-
net fishing. The Japanese land most of the world's tuna catch. They have
huge factory trawlers that roam the seas in search of tuna. They catch the
fish on multiple-hook longlines that stretch many miles from the boat, and
the haul they bring in is processed and canned right on the ship.

YELLOWFINS are deep blue on top,
matching the water they swim in,
and silver beneath, resem-
bling the water surface reflected
against the sky, as seen from below.
Their smaller size (up to 150 pounds)
and brilliant yellow fins and tail distinguish them from bluefin tunas.

Yellowfins follow the warmer currents that flow south and north, from
the tropics to Southern California, usually reaching our shores in June.
Through August, schools of them are apt to be seen close inshore or far out
in the open ocean. Many gather around Los Coronados, San Clemente, and
Santa Catalina islands.

Most of the canned tuna we eat is yellowfin. Sportsmen troll for them,
using light or medium tackle and live bait. The commercial catch is made
with purse seine haul net gear.

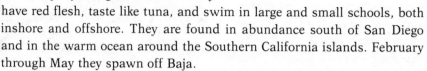

BONITO, also known as skipjack,
look different from other tunas.
Dark green-blue to purple stripes
run obliquely along their backs. They
have red flesh, taste like tuna, and swim in large and small schools, both
inshore and offshore. They are found in abundance south of San Diego
and in the warm ocean around the Southern California islands. February
through May they spawn off Baja.

Most inshore bonito are young; one to two year olds weigh three to twelve
pounds. They are heavily preyed upon by all predators. The older fish (up
to twenty-five pounds) are usually offshore and too large for most predators.

Chumming (scattering scoops of ground fish or oily bait) will attract
bonito schools to your fishing area. Party boats and commercial fishermen
chum routinely. When bonito are aroused, they bite on almost any bait or
lure. Just about all of the commercial bonito catch is canned as tuna.

About Tuna Meat

Albacore, bluefin tuna, yellowfin tuna, and bonito are the four tuna-meat fish taken on the West Coast. Albacore has the whitest meat of all and is considered by canners the premium tuna; however, all four varieties are canned.

All tunalike fish have a dark red meat streak running down either side that is oily and fishy tasting. Remove it before cooking and feed it to the cat—he'll love it. Tuna has moderate fat content. The bellies smoke admirably because they are oilier than the rest of the fish.

Tuna meat is sold fresh in the market during the summer season as whole fish, in chunks, and, rarely, in steak form.

Whole fish generally weigh 10–45 pounds. A whole fish can be filleted into four separate loins.

Loin fillets can be wrapped in foil and baked or broiled, or they can be poached.

Chunks cut from the filleted loin can be marinated and broiled or barbecued, or boiled to be served cold; small chunks can be deep fried or smoked.

Steaks should be trimmed of dark meat and boned at the same time. Raw tuna is very soft meat, but the steak pieces can be held together with toothpicks until they firm up during cooking. Steaks are good fried, broiled, or barbecued.

Thin slices of tuna can be butter sautéed or brushed with olive oil and grilled. Thin slices make delicious ceviche or sashimi.

TUNA SASHIMI

Sashimi is a Japanese dish of thinly sliced raw fish, garnished and served with dipping sauce.

1 pound raw tuna	Cucumber slices, carrot rounds,
1 cup finely shredded lettuce, daikon,*	celery sticks, or sliced orange or
cabbage, or watercress	grapefruit sections

*See Glossary.

Remove all skin, bones, and any dark meat from fish. Pour boiling water over the fish, then immediately dunk it into ice water. Use a very sharp knife to slice fish diagonally into pieces 1½–2 inches wide and ⅛–¼ inch thick. Prepare vegetables or fruit for garnish. Chill fish and vegetables or fruit until ready to serve.

Arrange fish slices overlapping attractively, on a bed of shredded lettuce. Garnish plate with a combination of raw vegetables or fruit.

Any firm-fleshed saltwater fish may be used, such as tuna, seabass, snapper, cod, or even squid, but it must be very fresh. Striped marlin may be used, but the dark meat should be removed.

HORSERADISH DIPPING SAUCE

2 teaspoons dry wasabi*   2 teaspoons hot water

*See Glossary.

SOY DIPPING SAUCE

¼ cup soy sauce   1 green onion, minced
2 Tablespoons rice vinegar   ½ teaspoon monosodium glutamate
1 clove garlic, pressed   ½ teaspoon pepper
1 teaspoon sugar   Few sesame seeds, toasted

Combine ingredients and serve sauces in individual small, shallow dishes. Dip each piece of fish in each of the sauces as you are eating.

MARINADE FOR GRILLING TUNA

¼ cup oil   ½ cup dry white wine
½ teaspoon rosemary   1 Tablespoon lemon juice
½ teaspoon garlic powder   Salt and pepper to taste

Combine ingredients and mix well. Let stand for an hour at room temperature before using. Marinate tuna for 30 minutes.

OVEN-BROILED TUNA TERIYAKI

2 pounds tuna, sliced thin   ½ teaspoon grated ginger
1 cup soy sauce   1 cup sake or dry sherry
⅓ cup sugar

Mix sauce, pour over fish, and marinate for 30 minutes. Preheat the broiler and pan. Drain off marinade, and heat it in a saucepan. Then broil fish on the oiled broiler pan for 3 or 4 minutes on each side. When nicely browned, remove to a warm platter, sprinkle with warm marinade, and serve.

Any firm lean fillet listed on page 447 (III A2) may be used.

CHARCOAL-BROILED TUNA TERIYAKI

Marinate tuna (see page 34). Spit 3 skewers through each piece of fish to keep it flat while grilling. If using bamboo skewers, soak them in water for 10 minutes before broiling. Broil 7 inches from the fire and baste frequently. Soy sauce tends to burn easily, so if fish gets dark too fast, move the grill farther from the fire. Heat remaining marinade and serve with fish.

Salmon may be used.

BAKED TUNA STEAKS WITH BACON

4 thick tuna steaks
8 strips lean bacon
2 green onions, minced
1/2 cup dry white wine

Generous milling of pepper
1 teaspoon paprika
1 Tablespoon minced parsley

Fry bacon until half cooked. Remove 4 strips and set them aside. Cook remaining bacon until crisp, drain on toweling, and reserve. Discard all but 2 tablespoons bacon fat; in it sauté green onions until soft. Remove from heat and stir in wine.

Preheat the oven to 425°F. Wrap each tuna steak in a slice of half-cooked bacon and secure it with a wooden cocktail pick. Sprinkle generously with pepper, and with paprika. Arrange steaks in single layer in a buttered baking dish or casserole. Heat wine-onion mixture to a boil and pour it over the steaks. Scatter in crumbled crisp bacon, cover with lid or foil, and bake for 10 minutes per inch thickness of the fish. Remove cocktail picks, sprinkle with parsley, and serve.

PLAIN BAKED TUNA
FOR VARIOUS RECIPES

3 pounds tuna fillet
2 green onions, sliced
2 Tablespoons olive oil
1 Tablespoon vinegar

1 teaspoon salt
1/2 teaspoon white pepper
1/8 teaspoon garlic powder
1/4 cup water

Preheat the oven to 425°F. Pour boiling water over tuna and let it stand for 7 or 8 minutes. Drain and wipe dry. Place onions in a buttered baking dish and lay fish on top. Mix remaining ingredients, then pour mixture over fish. Cover dish tightly with foil and bake for 10 minutes per inch thickness.

TUNA IN TOMATO-WINE SAUCE
WITH MUSHROOMS

2 pounds tuna slices
Salt and pepper to taste
7 Tablespoons butter
1 onion, chopped
1 Tablespoon flour
1/3 cup dry white wine

1/3 cup water
3 Tablespoons tomato paste
2 Tablespoons lemon juice
1/2 pound mushrooms, quartered
Sprig parsley, minced

Remove skin, dark meat, and bone, wipe dry, and sprinkle tuna with salt and pepper. Heat 3 tablespoons of the butter over high heat and brown slices quickly on both sides, then remove from pan and set aside while making sauce.

Preheat the oven to 325°F. In a clean skillet, sauté onion in 2 tablespoons of the butter until onion browns lightly. Stir in flour, blend in wine and water, and simmer slowly, uncovered, for 10 minutes. Add tomato paste and lemon juice, mix well, season with salt and pepper, then add tuna. Cover skillet and put in oven for 35 minutes.

Meanwhile, sauté mushrooms in the remaining 2 tablespoons of butter until cooked. Transfer tuna to warm serving platter. Mix mushrooms into the sauce, heat to a boil, and pour over and around fish. Sprinkle with minced parsley and serve.

SMALL BONITO

May be cooked in the same manner as mackerel (see pages 93–6 and 245–52).

BAKED WHOLE BONITO

4-6-pound bonito, pan dressed
3 cloves garlic, sliced
Juice of 1/2 lemon
6 Tablespoons (3/4 stick) butter, melted
Salt and pepper to taste

1/2 teaspoon marjoram
1 lemon, sliced
Paprika
1/4 cup water

Cover fish with cold salted water, soak for 15 minutes, and drain. Wash cavity and soak again for 15 minutes, drain and dry on toweling. Cut several diagonal slashes on both sides of fish.

Preheat the oven to 425°F. Combine sliced garlic and lemon juice with melted butter. Place bonito in a shallow buttered baking dish, brush it inside and out with lemon-butter, and season with salt, pepper, and marjoram. Place half of lemon and garlic slices in the cavity and a half-slice of lemon and some garlic slivers in each slash. Sprinkle with paprika, pour the 1/4 cup water in the dish, and bake for 10 minutes, then reduce heat to 350°F. and cook for 25–35 minutes, depending on thickness of fish.

MARINATED BAKED BONITO
WITH FRESH TOMATO SAUCE

2 pounds bonito slices	1/2 cup dry white wine
3 cloves garlic, sliced	2 cups peeled and chopped tomatoes
1/3 cup olive oil	1/4 teaspoon thyme
Juice of 1 lemon	1/4 teaspoon marjoram
1 onion, minced	Salt and pepper to taste
2 Tablespoons (1/4 stick) butter	Sprigs parsley

Mix garlic, oil, and lemon together and marinate fish in it 4–24 hours, turning occasionally. In a skillet, heat the marinade over high heat and brown tuna quickly on both sides, then remove fish and set aside. Preheat the oven to 425°F.

In a clean ovenproof pan, sauté onion in butter until tender and golden. Add wine, tomatoes, seasoning, and fish. Cover and bake for 10 minutes per inch thickness of fish. Transfer cooked fish to a warm platter, pour sauce around it, and garnish with parsley.

DEEP-FRIED TUNA WITH
SWEET-AND-SOUR PINEAPPLE SAUCE

1 1/2 pounds tuna fillet	Pepper to taste
2 eggs	Cornstarch
1 teaspoon salt	Oil for deep frying

Trim off dark meat and cut tuna into bite-size, 1/2-inch-thick pieces. Beat eggs with salt and pepper. Dip tuna into egg, then roll pieces in cornstarch. Deep fry a few pieces at a time in hot (375°F.) oil, then drain and keep warm until all are cooked.

Prepare Sweet-and-Sour Pineapple Sauce.

Sweet-and-Sour Pineapple Sauce

8-ounce can unsweetened pineapple
2 teaspoons cornstarch
1 Tablespoon dry sherry
1 Tablespoon soy sauce
4 Tablespoons vinegar
2 Tablespoons sugar

3 Tablespoons catsup
1/4 cup chopped green onion
2 Tablespoons chopped green pepper
1 clove garlic, pressed
Salt and pepper to taste

Cut pineapple into 1/2-inch pieces. Mix juice with cornstarch and combine all ingredients except salt and pepper in a saucepan. Bring to a boil, stirring, and cook until thickened. Season with salt and pepper and serve hot with deep-fried fish.

Bluefish, mahi mahi, yellowtail, or any firm lean fillet listed on page 447 (III A2) may be used.

DEEP-FRIED TUNA BALLS

1 pound tuna
1 package tofu, rinsed in boiling water
  and mashed
1 Tablespoon white miso bean paste
1 teaspoon sugar
1/4 teaspoon salt
1 teaspoon soy sauce

1 teaspoon minced ginger
2 Tablespoons sake or dry sherry
1 egg
2 teaspoons cornstarch
1 Tablespoon sesame seeds (optional)
2 cups oil for deep frying

Skin, bone, trim, then grind tuna twice, using the finest meat grinding blade of food processor. Now beat until fluffy with spoon attachment. Beat in tofu, bean paste, sugar, salt, soy, ginger, and sake, blending in each ingredient well before adding the next. Mix egg with a fork until blended but not frothy and add slowly to mixture, beating until light and increased in volume; then beat in cornstarch and optional sesame seeds. Cover and refrigerate for 1 hour.

Heat oil to 375°F. Form fish into balls and deep fry them until golden.

BOILED TUNA OR BONITO

Tuna or bonito may be poached to serve cold with a mayonnaise, in sandwiches, casseroles, or other recipes.

Skin, trim, bone, and cut fish into chunks. Cover chunks with boiling salted water (1 tablespoon salt for each quart water), bring to boil, lower heat, and simmer 6–8 minutes, then drain. Repeat the process, simmering another 6–8 minutes and draining. Let the fish cool to room temperature, then chill until ready to use.

PIMIENTO SAUCE FOR COLD TUNA

4-ounce can pimientos
4 hard-boiled egg yolks
⅔ cup cream
1 Tablespoon lemon juice

½ teaspoon wine vinegar
Salt and pepper to taste
⅓ cup stuffed olives

Purée pimiento and egg yolks with cream in a blender until smooth and creamy. Add lemon juice, wine vinegar, and salt and pepper. Slice stuffed olives, stir them into the sauce, and chill for an hour before serving.

Ideas for Leftover Tuna or Bonito

COOKED TUNA BALLS

1 cup cooked tuna, flaked
½ cup bread crumbs
1 egg, lightly beaten
1 teaspoon onion flakes

Sprig parsley, minced
2 Tablespoons olive oil
¾ of a 6-ounce can tomato paste
2 cups water

Mix tuna, crumbs, egg, onion flakes, and parsley, then form into small balls. Fry balls in olive oil until browned. Remove from pan and keep warm. Mix tomato paste and the 2 cups of water with pan drippings and cook slowly, uncovered, for 10 minutes. Add fish balls to the sauce and simmer another 10–15 minutes, then serve over rice.

TOASTED ENGLISH MUFFINS
WITH TUNA AND CHEESE SAUCE

1½–2 cups cooked tuna chunks
4 English muffins, halved

Cheese Sauce (p. 437)

Toast muffin halves, then place them on a cookie sheet, mound each with tuna bits, and put them in a slow oven to warm. When heated through, serve them smothered with hot cheese sauce.

COOKED TUNA CHUNKS IN SICILIAN SAUCE

1½–2 cups cooked tuna chunks
2 cloves garlic, minced
2 Tablespoons olive oil
8 anchovy fillets, cut in pieces
1 large (28-ounce) can tomatoes
1 teaspoon basil

Dash of cayenne pepper
¼ cup sliced black olives
¼ cup sliced stuffed green olives
2 teaspoons capers
1 pound vermicelli

Sauté garlic in oil until it yellows, add anchovies, stir in tomatoes, breaking them up with a spoon, and simmer for 10 minutes. Stir in spices, olives, and capers and simmer until sauce is thickened, about 10 minutes. Add tuna chunks to sauce and warm them through. Cook and drain the vermicelli, serve it in large bowls; spoon tuna chunks and sauce over.

COOKED TUNA CASSEROLE

1½–2 cups cooked tuna, flaked
1 large onion, chopped
2 Tablespoons (¼ stick) butter
1 can condensed mushroom soup
Sprig parsley, chopped
1 teaspoon thyme

1 teaspoon paprika
1 teaspoon dry sherry
1 teaspoon Worcestershire sauce
3 cups mashed potatoes
3 eggs, separated
Salt and pepper to taste

Preheat the oven to 400°F. Sauté onion in butter until soft and yellow, add soup, flaked tuna, parsley, seasonings, sherry, and Worcestershire sauce, bring to boil, then remove from heat. Mash potatoes until fluffy, add beaten egg yolks, then stir in mushroom-tuna. Beat egg whites with salt and pepper until they are stiff, then fold them into potato mixture. Pour it into a buttered casserole and bake until brown.

TUNA SALAD BOWL

Line individual bowls with crisp torn lettuce and on top arrange chunks of cold cooked tuna, cucumber, quartered hard-boiled eggs, a scattering of minced celery, and 2 or 3 anchovy fillets. Serve with a sauceboatful of Louis or Basic French Dressing (pp. 426 and 427).

SLICED TUNA SALAD

Place a serving-size slice of cold cooked tuna on individual lettuce-lined salad plates. Arrange fresh tomato wedges and thin-sliced small white onion rings around tuna. Place several pitted black olives on each. Spoon on Guacamole Sauce (p. 437).

TUNA GARBANZO SALAD

2 cups cooked tuna chunks
¼ cup chopped green onion
1 cup garbanzo beans, drained

2 tomatoes, peeled and cubed
¼ cup Basic French Dressing (p. 427)

Gently toss all ingredients together. Chill, allowing the salad to marinate for 30 minutes. Serve in crisp lettuce cups.

California Yellowtail

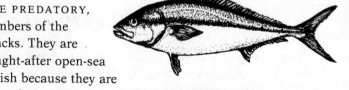

YELLOWTAILS ARE PREDATORY, fast-swimming members of the tropical family of jacks. They are one of the most sought-after open-sea warm-water game fish because they are excellent fighters, good eating, and a worthy size to hunt—ten to twenty pounds average, but can weigh over seventy-five. They are identified by their shape, as well as the dark streak that runs along the soft gray green body from eye to yellow tail.

During midsummer and early fall, these fish migrate into Southern California currents from the Cedros Island area. Small groups swim near the surface around the offshore islands and feed in kelp beds close inshore. The majority locate near floating plankton patches in deep blue water, as do albacore. When the water turns cool, yellowtail head south until next season.

About Yellowtail Meat

Yellowtail is a rich-flavored, moderately firm-textured meat, pinkish when raw, but white when cooked. Before it is cooked, it should be skinned and trimmed of the thick layer of dark oily meat just under the skin along the midside. It is best barbecued, broiled, baked, fried, or smoked.

MARINADE FOR YELLOWTAIL

¼ cup bottled tempura sauce
½ teaspoon sesame oil

Juice of 2 small limes
1 Tablespoon rice vinegar

Make a marinade by mixing together tempura sauce, sesame oil, lime juice, and rice vinegar, then marinate yellowtail for 1 hour.

GARLIC MARINATED YELLOWTAIL

2 pounds yellowtail fillet, cut into
  4 thick steaks
4 cloves garlic, sliced

Vegetable oil
Salt to taste
1/4 teaspoon pepper

Place yellowtail steaks in a bowl just large enough to hold them. Slice garlic over the steaks, cover them with oil, then cover the bowl and refrigerate for 24 hours, turning occasionally to marinate evenly.

Season with salt and pepper just before barbecuing over hot coals. If you wish, you can baste the steaks with the marinade as they are cooking.

OVEN-BROILED YELLOWTAIL
WITH SAUCE MONICA

2 pounds yellowtail fillet, cut into
  4 thick steaks
Salt

Juice of 1/2 lemon or 1 small lime
2 Tablespoons oil

Wipe steaks, sprinkle them with salt, place them in a flat dish, and pour the mixture of citrus juice and oil over them. Let them stand for 30 minutes. Preheat broiler and pan, then arrange steaks on it and broil, turning once, according to the thickness of the fish.

Serve the broiled steaks immediately, with a bowl of Sauce Monica. (Prepare the sauce several hours in advance.)

Sauce Monica

1/4 cup filberts
1/2 cup minced parsley
1 teaspoon grated onion
2 Tablespoons capers
1/4 cup chopped black olives

1/2 cup fine bread crumbs
1 small chili, seeded and chopped
3 Tablespoons wine vinegar
Salt and pepper to taste

Shell, blanch, and remove skin from filberts, then chop. Combine all ingredients, mixing thoroughly, and let stand at room temperature until served.

King mackerel, cero, or bluefish may be used.

SAUTÉED YELLOWTAIL
WITH MUSHROOMS AND TOMATO

2 pounds yellowtail fillet
2 cloves garlic, crushed
6 Tablespoons oil
Juice of 2 small limes
Salt and pepper to taste
Flour

½ cup sliced green onion
1½ cups sliced mushrooms
1 Tablespoon vinegar
2 large tomatoes, cut in wedges
Sprig parsley, minced

Make garlic oil by crushing garlic into oil; the longer it stands, the stronger it becomes. Cut fillet into serving pieces, sprinkle with lime juice, salt and pepper, and let it stand for 30 minutes. Drain, pat fish dry and dust lightly with flour, then sauté fish in 3 tablespoons of the garlic oil until nicely brown on both sides. Remove to a serving platter and keep warm while making sauce.

In a clean pan, heat 2 tablespoons of the garlic oil and sauté onion and mushrooms until tender. Add vinegar, season with salt and pepper, then pour mushroom mixture over fish.

In the remaining 1 tablespoon of garlic oil, over high heat, warm the tomatoes, then serve them on the fish platter. Scatter minced parsley over all and serve.

King mackerel or cero may be used for this dish.

YELLOWTAIL IN COCONUT MILK CURRY

2 pounds yellowtail, cut in 1-inch slices
2½ cups canned coconut milk*
4 cloves garlic, pressed
1 teaspoon grated ginger
4 pecans, ground
2 onions, chopped coarse

1 small hot pepper, seeded
  and crushed
½ teaspoon turmeric
Juice of 1 lemon
½ lemon, cut in wedges
Salt to taste

*To make fresh coconut milk, combine 2½ cups milk with 2½ cups packaged grated coconut in a saucepan, bring to a boil, and cook for 2 minutes. Strain, squeezing as much flavor from coconut as possible. Discard solids.

In a large, heavy saucepan, combine coconut milk, garlic, ginger, pecans, onions, pepper, turmeric, and lemon juice. Heat, stirring, until broth boils, lower heat to simmer, and cook until sauce has reduced to 2 cups. Add yellowtail and lemon wedges and continue to simmer, stirring occasionally, for about 10 minutes, until fish barely flakes. Season with salt and serve with boiled rice.

ESCABECHE

Escabeche is fish in vinegar sauce. It is a Latin dish brought from Spain, where it was introduced by the Romans, who got it from the Greeks. This is one of the many local variations on the basic recipe and should be prepared 24 hours before it is served.

3 pounds yellowtail fillet
Flour
2 cups oil for frying
3 Tablespoons olive oil
1 onion, sliced
6 cloves garlic, sliced
1 carrot, sliced thin
1 chili, seeded and sliced

1/2 cup water
1 teaspoon sugar
1 cup vinegar
1 teaspoon whole peppercorns
2 bay leaves
1/4 teaspoon thyme
1 teaspoon salt

Trim away dark meat, bones, and rough edges, then cut fillet into 1/2-inch-thick pieces. Roll them in flour and deep fry in hot (375°F.) oil until nicely brown. Drain well on toweling and lay fish in a nonmetal bowl.

Heat olive oil and sauté onion, garlic, carrot, and chili until onion turns light brown. Add the 1/2 cup of water, the sugar, vinegar, and the spices, bring to a boil, reduce heat, and barely simmer for 10–15 minutes. Pour hot vinegar mixture over the fish, cover, and, when cool enough, refrigerate for 24 hours.

Tuna, halibut, white seabass, or red snapper may be used.

Ocean Whitefish

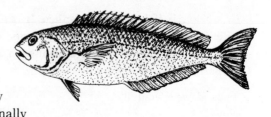

OCEAN WHITEFISH are not
white; they are olive green
and not related to the "salmon-
like" freshwater whitefish. They
are warm-water fish that seasonally
congregate around the islands off Santa Barbara, and they may be caught
from Monterey to the tropics in water 60–300-plus feet deep.

They are graceful fish, with long rippling rays. Their sinuous bodies
have very tiny scales. Mature fish average 3–6 pounds, but some reach
thirty. They feed on squid, shrimp, and small fish.

Whitefish are commonly used as bait for catching giant black seabass,
because they inhabit the same types of areas and are of a good size. They
are fished deep, on hook and line—initially, close to the bottom. But as the
school gets stirred up, fish grab for bait before the line is halfway down.
Fishing is excellent from spring through fall, but toward winter whitefish
move out into deep water.

About Ocean Whitefish Meat

Whitefish is lean, mild-flavored meat, with a taste similar to but a finer
texture than bass. Many fishermen prefer it to bass. Whitefish are marketed
fresh seasonally, whole or filleted. These excellent fish may be barbecued,
broiled, baked, fried, poached, or steamed.

OCEAN WHITEFISH BARBECUED IN FOIL

2 pounds whitefish fillets
4 Tablespoons (½ stick) butter, melted
¼ teaspoon thyme
⅛ teaspoon fennel seed

1 bay leaf
1 clove garlic, sliced
Salt and pepper to taste
2 Tablespoons flour

Heat butter with thyme, fennel seed, bay leaf, and garlic, then set aside for 30 minutes to allow flavors to meld. Wipe fillets, cut them into serving pieces, season with salt and pepper, and dust them lightly with flour.

Tear off 4 or 5 pieces of foil, each large enough to envelop a portion. Dip fillets in herbed butter, then place them on the foil and spoon remaining butter on each portion. Fold packages tightly (double fold the edges), then wrap the packages in another piece of foil. Barbecue them about 15-20 minutes, turning once.

Any bass may be used in this dish.

BAKED OCEAN WHITEFISH STUFFED WITH CRAB

4-5-pound whole whitefish	2 pimientos, minced
Salt and pepper to taste	Dash of nutmeg
2 Tablespoons (1/4 stick) butter	2 cups crab meat, picked over
2 cloves garlic, pressed	1 1/2 cups fresh bread crumbs
1 small hot pepper, seeded and crushed	2 sprigs parsley, chopped
1 Tablespoon lime juice	Flour
3 Tablespoons Madeira or dry sherry	Melted butter
	1/4 cup water

Trim and dry whole whitefish, then split it and remove the backbone, cutting it off near the tail and close to the head with poultry shears. Leave the fish whole, however. Season fish with salt and pepper, and set it aside while making stuffing.

Melt the 2 tablespoons butter with garlic and hot pepper, then remove from heat and stir in lime juice, wine, pimientos, and nutmeg. Combine crab, bread crumbs, and parsley, then moisten with the pimiento mixture. Mix ingredients well, season with salt, then use this mixture to stuff the fish. Fasten sides together with skewers or sew sides with unwaxed dental floss.

Preheat oven to 425°F. Flour fish lightly and brush with melted butter. Dip a piece of cheesecloth (large enough to hold fish) into melted butter, place the fish on it, and lift into a greased baking dish or roasting pan. Add the 1/4 cup water and bake for 25-35 minutes, 10 minutes per inch thickness of fish.

If whitefish is not available, use any lean whole fish for baking listed on page 447 (III A3).

BAKED SMALL OCEAN WHITEFISH

2 small whitefish, ¾ pound each
4 Tablespoons olive oil
Salt and pepper to taste
2 slices each of lemon and orange rind
Fennel
2 Tablespoons orange juice

2 teaspoons lemon juice
10 pitted black olives
¼ cup dry vermouth
¼ cup water
Parsley

Preheat the oven to 350°F. Trim and dry whitefish, brush inside and out with some of the olive oil, season them with salt and pepper, and place them in a buttered shallow baking dish. Put a slice of lemon and orange rind, a pinch of fennel, a spoonful of orange juice and squeeze of lemon juice, then 2 halved olives in each cavity. Pour remaining olive oil over the fish, add vermouth and water to the dish and bake, uncovered, for 15–20 minutes. During the last 5 minutes add the remaining olives. Serve on warmed plates, with pan juices and olives spooned over fish.

Bass, scrod, or snapper blues may be used.

OCEAN WHITEFISH FILLETS
WITH ONION SAUCE

1½ pounds whitefish fillets
Salt and pepper to taste
1 large onion, minced
2 Tablespoons butter
⅔ cup dry white wine
1 Tablespoon wine vinegar
1 clove garlic, pressed

1 Tablespoon flour
¼ cup water
2 Tablespoons cream
Flour for dusting
3 Tablespoons oil for frying
Parsley

Wipe fillets, sprinkle with salt and pepper, and let stand while making sauce.

Sauté onion slowly in butter until tender and brown. Add wine, vinegar, garlic, and salt and pepper. Mix 1 tablespoon flour with ¼ cup water, add it to the sauce, stirring until sauce begins to bubble and thicken. Reduce heat and simmer slowly for 10 minutes, stirring occasionally, then add cream. Keep sauce warm.

Dust fillets with flour, sauté in hot oil until brown, then serve fish on a warm platter, smothered in sauce and sprinkled with minced parsley.

Good for any lean white fillet listed on page 446 (III A1).

POACHED OCEAN WHITEFISH
WITH AIOLI SAUCE

2 pounds whitefish fillets
3 cups Basic Court Bouillon (p. 26),
    made with wine

1 teaspoon cornstarch
3 Tablespoons cream
Aioli Sauce (p. 424)

Preheat the oven to 425°F. Arrange fillets in a buttered baking dish (if the fillets are small, fold them), bring court bouillon to a boil and pour it over the fish. Cover baking dish tightly with foil and bake for about 7–10 minutes, or 10 minutes per inch thickness of fish. Transfer fish carefully to a platter, cover, and keep warm. Pour bouillon into a small saucepan and boil it down over high heat until it is reduced to 1 cup. Strain it, and then return it to the pan. Mix cornstarch with cream, add it to the strained bouillon and stir until the sauce thickens and boils. Stir a large spoonful of aioli into the sauce, then pour it over the fish. Pass a bowl of aioli sauce at the table.

Any firm lean fillet listed on page 447 (III A2) may be used.

OCEAN WHITEFISH CEVICHE

1 pound very fresh whitefish fillet
Juice of 6 small limes
2 tomatoes, peeled and chopped
1 onion (Bermuda), chopped
2 canned jalapeño chilis, seeded and
    chopped
2 Tablespoons minced cilantro

2 Tablespoons olive oil
1 Tablespoon vinegar
At least 1 teaspoon salt
Pepper to taste
1 avocado
Capers

Cut whitefish into bite-size pieces, place raw fish bits in a bowl, cover them with lime juice, and marinate them in the refrigerator for 6–7 hours, turning the fish occasionally.

An hour before serving, chop, combine, and chill the vegetables. To serve, mix a dressing of oil, vinegar, salt and pepper, and stir it into the vegetables, then combine vegetables with fish. Serve in sherbet glasses, garnished with sliced avocado and a few capers.

Flounder, tuna, seabass, red snapper, cod, or any firm fish on page 447 (III A2) may be used, but it must be very fresh.

Marlin may also be used.

STEAMED OCEAN WHITEFISH HUSSUNG

1 1/2 pounds whitefish fillets
2 Tablespoons oil
1 teaspoon grated lemon rind
1/8 teaspoon salt

1 teaspoon minced ginger
1/4 cup soy sauce
1/4 teaspoon cinnamon
1 green onion, sliced

Mix a sauce by combining oil, lemon rind, salt, ginger, soy sauce, and cinnamon. Dip fillets in the sauce (fold in half or roll, if small), and arrange them in a single layer on a heatproof dish. Pour remaining sauce over fish. Wrap dish in a double thickness of waxed paper and steam for 8-14 minutes, or 10 minutes per inch thickness of fish. When cooked, remove dish from steamer, unwrap and wipe dish, scatter green onion on fish and serve at once.

Greenling (red rock trout), pike, sea robin, walleye, or snapper may be used.

Idea for Leftover Ocean Whitefish

OCEAN WHITEFISH BALLS

2 cups cooked whitefish, flaked
2 Tablespoons minced green pepper
1 onion, chopped
2 Tablespoons (1/4 stick) butter
4 medium boiled potatoes
1/4 cup milk
2 eggs
1 teaspoon salt

Pepper to taste
1/2 teaspoon lemon juice
Flour mixed with water
Dry bread crumbs
2 cups oil for deep frying
Lemon wedges
Parsley White Sauce (p. 418)

Sauté green pepper and onion in butter. Mash potatoes with milk and sautéed vegetables until fluffy, then set aside to cool.

Stir in eggs, salt, pepper, lemon juice, and flaked fish, then refrigerate for 1 hour. Form into balls, dip them in a thick mixture of flour and water, then roll in bread crumbs.

Place several fish balls at a time in deep-fry basket and fry them in hot (375°F.) oil. Drain them on toweling, then serve on a warm platter with lemon wedges and accompany with a bowl of parsley white sauce.

Good for any lean white fish on page 446 (III A1).

California Barracuda

BARRACUDA, ALSO CALLED SCOOTS, are dark greenish black above and silver below the lateral line. The snout is long with a big mouth of fierce, dangerous teeth. They average three to ten pounds and are considered to be a number-one (but dangerous) sport fish. Scoots are fast, schooling predators that rely on their speed and strength to catch their prey. They are found near the surface, around the offshore islands and often close inshore, from Santa Monica south. In the early morning they may be on the prowl or hanging quietly in the water waiting for a school to come into range. When victims are spotted, the barracuda rush through the water, lunge swiftly, and chop the bait fish as clean as a cleaver. Too fast to stop, they circle back to swallow the chunks and lunge again. In the frenzy of feeding they will strike at anything.

About Barracuda Meat

Barracuda is lean white meat with distinctive flavor and flaky soft texture. During most of the year it is available fresh in local markets, whole, in steaks, or in chunks. It is also sold smoked, salted, and canned. It can be frozen and doesn't lose quality when thawed.

Barracuda is best barbecued, broiled, baked, fried, or braised. Dark meat should be trimmed from steaks and fillets.

FRIED BARRACUDA FILLET
WITH SWEET-AND-SOUR SAUCE

Dip pieces of barracuda in beaten egg and fine dry crumbs, then pan fry (p. 22).

Serve with Sweet-and-Sour Pineapple Sauce (p. 38).

BUTTERFLIED BARRACUDA BARBECUED

BASTE

Grated rind and juice of 1 lemon
1 onion, grated
4 thin slices ginger
1 teaspoon sesame oil

2 Tablespoons molasses
½–1 cup dry white wine
¼ cup soy sauce
½ teaspoon garlic powder

Stir all baste ingredients together and let stand for 1 hour before using.

Cut barracuda lengthwise, but not all the way through. Remove head, spread fish open, cut and lift out backbone, cutting bone off at tail. Carefully take out other bones along the sides. Place fish skin side down, on a support of foil. (See Basic Barbecuing suggestions, page 17.) Cook barracuda slowly over medium-hot coals without turning, brushing frequently with the baste.

BAKED BARRACUDA IN TOMATO SAUCE

2 pounds barracuda steaks, or the
    fillets of a small fish
1 large onion, chopped
1 stalk celery, chopped
¼ cup chopped green pepper
2 Tablespoons oil

Two 8-ounce cans tomato sauce
2 Tablespoons lemon juice
2 Tablespoons brown sugar
1 teaspoon chili powder
Salt to taste
1 bay leaf

Preheat the oven to 425°F. Arrange fish in a single layer on a shallow baking dish. Sauté onion, celery, and green pepper in oil until tender, then add the remaining ingredients and simmer, uncovered, for 10 minutes. Spoon sauce over fish and bake, uncovered, for 10 minutes per inch thickness of fish.

BRAISED BARRACUDA IN SOUR SAUCE

2 pounds barracuda fillet
Salt and pepper to taste
Flour
4 Tablespoons oil
1 onion, chopped

1½ Tablespoons minced garlic
2 green peppers, sliced in strips
2 bay leaves
5 Tablespoons vinegar
⅓ cup boiling water

Cut fillet into serving pieces, season with salt and pepper, dust lightly with flour, and brown fish quickly in 3 tablespoons of the oil, then set aside and keep warm.

In a clean skillet, sauté onion and garlic in the remaining tablespoon of oil. Add peppers, bay leaves, and vinegar, and cook until peppers are tender. Return fish to the skillet, add boiling water, and simmer slowly, allowing 10 minutes per inch thickness of fish. Serve at once, with boiled rice.

LEMON COOKED BARRACUDA

2 pounds barracuda fillet
Salt and pepper to taste
1/4 cup oil
2 onions, chopped
2 tomatoes, peeled and chopped

2 lemons, sliced
2 bay leaves
1/2 cup water
1 Tablespoon vinegar
2 teaspoons sugar

Cut fillet into serving portions (or remove skin from steaks) and sprinkle with salt and pepper. Heat oil in a heavy skillet and fry onions until brown. Place fish in a single layer on onions and add tomatoes, lemons, and bay leaves. Mix the 1/2 cup of water, vinegar, and sugar, and pour it over the fish. Cover the pan and cook, just below a simmer, for 30 minutes.

California Sheepshead

MALE SHEEPSHEADS are striking
looking, with black heads and
tails, crimson red bodies, and
white chins. Some people call them
"redfish," but they must be referring to
females, for those are solid dull red without any
black and white trim. All sheepsheads start out as females and change
their sex to male with age. During spawning season the male develops a
big lump on his forehead, which with his big blunt teeth and white chin
gives his profile a strong resemblance to a sheep's.

Sheepsheads can be found as far north as Monterey, but are abundant
south of Pt. Conception. They hang around the rocky bottom in kelp beds,
picking a certain rocky ledge or reef to inhabit. Spear fishermen do well
catching this piscatorial prize, but the angler finds fishing tricky. Hooked
fish tend to head for their protected ledge via all obstacles, tangling line
hopelessly in kelp. Sheepsheads relish lobster and often steal them from
the lobster traps. Paradoxically, sheepshead is the bait lobster fishermen
use in their lobster traps.

About Sheepshead Meat

Mild flavor and dense white meat make sheepshead an excellent choice for
chowder base or fish and chips or as a fine complement in lobster and
crab dishes. They bake well. They are marketed fresh in Southern California, whole drawn or dressed or as fillets, and are available year round.

FISH CHOWDER

2 pounds sheepshead trimmings
2½ quarts water
1 onion, sliced
1 carrot, sliced

¼ cup lime juice
1 Tablespoon salt
¼ teaspoon whole peppercorns
¼ teaspoon each thyme and oregano

Pour cold water into a large kettle, add all ingredients, bring to a boil, and simmer for 30 minutes. Cool a bit, then strain the broth, discarding solids. Return broth to a clean kettle (reserving ½ cup) and simmer slowly while preparing the following:

8 strips bacon	1 carrot, grated
1 onion, minced	½ green pepper, grated
½ cup flour	2 stalks celery, grated
4 medium potatoes, diced	2 Tablespoons dry white wine
1 bay leaf	
Pinch each of rosemary, basil, and thyme	

Fry bacon until crisp, then drain on toweling. Pour out all but 2 table-spoons bacon fat and sauté onion in that until tender and brown; add to the simmering broth. Dissolve the flour in the reserved ½ cup cool broth, then mix into the rest of the broth, stirring until broth boils. Add potatoes and continue cooking until they are soft, then add spices and crumbled bacon and simmer 5 minutes more. Stir in grated vegetables and wine, cover, remove from heat and let chowder rest for 1 hour, allowing flavors to mingle. Serve hot.

Any lean white fish listed on page 446 (III A1) may be used.

SPICY GRILLED SHEEPSHEAD STEAKS

2 pounds sheepshead, cut into 4 thick fillets	½ small dried, red, hot pepper, seeded
2 onions, chopped	2 Tablespoons lemon juice
4 cloves garlic, sliced	½ cup oil
1 teaspoon chopped ginger	½ teaspoon salt

Light coals. Wipe fillets with a damp cloth and set them aside while making a basting sauce. Combine all ingredients, except fish, in a blender container, and purée until smooth, then pour sauce over the fish.

When coals have burned down to medium-hot, place fish in a well-greased, hinged-wire grill. Cook 4 inches from the coals for 3–6 minutes on each side, or until fish flakes when tested. Baste fish frequently with sauce while cooking. Any sauce not used can be brought to a boil and served with fish.

Blackfish or California halibut may be used.

BROILED SHEEPSHEAD
GLAZED WITH SWISS CHEESE

2 pounds sheepshead fillet
3 Tablespoons butter
3 Tablespoons lemon
  juice

1/2 recipe (1 cup) Thick
  Béchamel Sauce (p. 417)
Salt and white pepper
2/3 cup grated Swiss cheese

Preheat the broiler and pan. Melt butter in a saucepan, stir in lemon juice, and set aside. Make béchamel sauce, using 2 tablespoons butter and flour and 1 cup hot milk seasoned with 1/4 teaspoon salt and white pepper, then set aside while broiling fish.

Cut fillet into serving pieces. Brush with or dip in melted lemon-butter. Arrange pieces on hot broiler pan and broil, basting often, for 10 minutes per inch thickness of fish.

Remove from oven, salt and pepper fish lightly, coat them with thick béchamel and sprinkle grated cheese evenly on top. Slide fish back under the broiler for a minute or two to melt and brown the cheese, then serve at once.

Good also for red snapper, ling cod, tilefish, or catfish.

BAKED SHEEPSHEAD
WITH CLAM–CILANTRO STUFFING

3-pound whole sheepshead, cleaned
  and trimmed
1/2 lemon
Flour
1 cup raw Pismo clams, or 1 can
  minced clams
1/2 cup fine cracker crumbs
1 1/2 Tablespoons chopped cilantro

2 Tablespoons minced onion
2 Tablespoons lemon or lime juice
1 egg, beaten
1 teaspoon salt
1/4 teaspoon pepper
1 tomato, peeled and diced
Melted butter
1/4 cup dry white wine

Rub fish with lemon, wipe it dry, then dust inside and out with flour, shaking off the excess; set aside. If using fresh clams, clean and chop them. Preheat the oven to 425°F.

To make stuffing, combine clams, crumbs, cilantro, onion, and citrus juice in a bowl, then add beaten egg, salt, pepper, and diced tomatoes. Mix all ingredients well, spoon stuffing into cavity, then close with skewers.

Place fish in a buttered baking dish, brush with melted butter, then salt and pepper it. Add wine to the dish and bake for 10 minutes per inch thickness of fish. Baste during cooking.

If sheepshead is not available, any lean whole fish for baking listed on page 447 (III A3) may be used.

SHEEPSHEAD-CRAB CASSEROLE

1 pound sheepshead fillet
1 cup crab meat, or 6½-ounce can
    crab meat
1 onion, chopped
2 stalks celery, chopped
1 Tablespoon butter
½ cup mayonnaise
5 slices crustless fresh bread, halved

2 eggs, beaten
1 cup milk
1 teaspoon salt
Pepper to taste
½ can condensed cream of mushroom
    soup, undiluted
¼ cup grated Parmesan cheese

Preheat the oven to 350°F. Wipe fillet, cut into 1½-inch cubes, and put them in a large bowl with picked-over crab. Sauté vegetables in butter until tender and add them to the fish. Stir in mayonnaise, mixing well. Generously butter a casserole and line it with bread. Spoon fish mixture into the casserole. Beat eggs with milk, add salt and pepper, and pour into casserole, nudging with a fork to allow liquid to seep under and all around.

Bake casserole for 10 minutes, then spread mushroom soup evenly and top with Parmesan. Return to oven and bake for 20 minutes more.

Ling cod, halibut, California black seabass, or red snapper may be used.

PAN-FRIED FILLETS OF SHEEPSHEAD

2 pounds sheepshead fillets
1 cup milk
1 teaspoon salt
½ teaspoon white pepper
Flour

2 eggs, beaten
Fine dry bread crumbs
1 cup oil for frying
Tartar Sauce (p. 426)

Season milk with salt and pepper. Cut fillets into portions and dry them on toweling. Dip pieces in milk, roll them in flour, then dip in beaten egg and press into crumbs. Let fish stand 30 minutes, turning once, before frying in hot oil.

Arrange cooked sheepshead on a hot platter, slices overlapping one another. Garnish attractively and serve with a bowl of tartar sauce.

POACHED SHEEPSHEAD FOR COLD BUFFET

5-6-pound whole or pan-dressed
  sheepshead
3 quarts cold water
1/2 cup lime juice
1 onion, sliced
2 stalks celery, sliced

2 cloves garlic, pressed
1 bay leaf
1 Tablespoon salt
1/4 teaspoon whole peppercorns
1 teaspoon oregano

Combine all ingredients except fish in the cold water, then bring to a boil and simmer for 15 minutes. Wrap the cleaned, degilled, trimmed sheepshead in a double thickness of cheesecloth. Pour boiling liquid over fish and poach as per instructions on page 23.

Skin fish, let it cool to room temperature, then wrap and chill it for several hours. Before serving, coat fish with avocado dressing.

If sheepshead is not available, striped bass, halibut, or Atlantic black seabass may be substituted.

Avocado Dressing

2 ripe avocados
2 Tablespoons lime juice
1 Tablespoon grated onion
1 clove garlic, pressed
1 teaspoon salt
Dash of hot pepper sauce

Dollop of mayonnaise
Pimiento strips
Hard-boiled eggs, sliced
Parsley snips
Black olives
Lime wedges

Mash avocados with lime juice, onion, garlic, salt, hot pepper sauce, and mayonnaise. Coat body of fish with dressing. Garnish with pimiento strips and thin slices of egg. Decorate platter with parsley, olives, and lime wedges.

Ideas for Leftover Sheepshead

SPRING SALAD

1 cup cooked sheepshead, flaked
1 cup crab meat, or 6 1/2-ounce can
  crab meat
Lettuce
2 pounds asparagus spears, cooked
  and chilled

2 tomatoes, cut in wedges
3 hard-boiled eggs
Thousand Island Dressing (p. 426)

Combine fish and picked-over crab. On individual salad plates place a bed of lettuce and on each arrange asparagus spears, a mound of fish, tomato wedges, and eggs, quartered lengthwise. Chill until ready to serve, then spoon half of the dressing over salads and serve the remaining dressing at the table.

SHEEPSHEAD–CRAB TOMATO CUPS

1 cup cooked sheepshead, flaked
1 cup crab meat or 6½-ounce can
　crab meat
2 hard-boiled egg yolks
3 Tablespoons butter, melted
2 Tablespoons lemon juice
1 teaspoon mustard

At least ¼ teaspoon salt
Pepper to taste
2 eggs, beaten
½ cup cream
Large ripe tomatoes
Grated Parmesan cheese

Preheat the oven to 350°F. Combine flaked fish and picked-over crab. Mash cooked egg yolks to a paste with butter, lemon juice, mustard, and salt and pepper. Beat eggs with cream, mix them with the paste and combine with fish. Remove insides from tomatoes and fill skins with fish. Place them on a buttered baking dish and bake for 10 minutes. Sprinkle grated cheese over tops and return to the oven until brown.

Croakers

CROAKERS ARE A LARGE FAMILY of fish common in warm ocean. They are so named because of the noises they make by using their air bladder as a resonating chamber. Noises increase when they are spawning or establishing territories.

They are distinguished by their rounded overhanging snouts and small mouths. Most are one- to two-pound fish that are found in loose aggregations in the surf of sandy beaches and shallow mud-bottom bays.

YELLOWFIN CROAKER AND SPOTFIN CROAKER are common from San Francisco south. Early-morning surf angling the sandy holes, on incoming tide, is a good way to get them. They bite on mussel or shrimp bait.

KINGFISH (white croaker) are abundant along the Central California shore. They congregate around underwater obstructions such as inshore reefs, inlets through ocean bars, and sunken wrecks. The old sunk cement ship on the beach at Seaside is one of their haunts.

BLACK CROAKER AND CORVINA inhabit the warmer ocean south of Pt. Conception. Night-fishing from piers, jetties, breakwaters, or wharves is the only way to get black croaker because they hide during the day in rocky crevices and come out to forage the sandy bottom at night.

Corvina closely resemble croakers, but they have chin whiskers (barbels) and no air bladder. They do make noises, though, by grinding their teeth together.

About Croaker, Kingfish,
and Corvina Meat

Croaker, kingfish, and corvina meat is white, soft, flaky, and very mild in flavor. These low-fat fish generally weigh between half a pound and two and a half pounds. They are best left whole—drawn, degilled, and trimmed—to deep fry, pan or oven fry, butter sauté, broil, or bake. Larger fish may be pan dressed or filleted.

BROILED CROAKERS
OR KINGFISH WITH SESAME SAUCE

4 whole croakers   Salt

Wipe cleaned fish dry, sprinkle lightly with salt, and set aside.

Sesame Sauce

1/4 cup sesame seeds   2 teaspoons bottled tempura sauce
1/4 cup salad oil   1/4 teaspoon pepper
1 1/2 Tablespoons lemon juice

Toast sesame seeds in a hot skillet, stirring them constantly until they turn brownish and pop and jump in the pan. Pulverize them in a blender for 30 seconds, add oil, lemon juice, tempura sauce, and pepper, then blend another 30 seconds. Roll fish in sesame sauce to coat them well, then place them on a greased grill, about 4 inches from the source of heat. Broil them about 6–9 minutes on each side, basting with sauce as needed during broiling, then serve at once.

SAUTÉED KINGFISH

Allow 1 pound, or about 3 fish per serving.

Clean and wipe tender little kingfish dry. Salt them and let stand for 10–15 minutes, then sprinkle them with garlic powder and roll them in flour. Sauté fish in butter and oil over medium heat (350°F.), covered, for 3–5 minutes on each side, until crispy and brown.

Transfer them to a warm platter, sprinkle them with parsley, and serve with halves of limes.

PAN-FRIED CROAKERS

4-8 whole croakers
Flour
2 eggs, beaten
1 teaspoon salt
1/2 teaspoon pepper

1/4 teaspoon each thyme and basil
Cornmeal
Salad oil
Olive oil
Tomato Sauce (p. 433)

Dust 4-8 fish, depending on size, with flour, dip them in eggs beaten with salt, pepper, thyme, and basil, then roll them in cornmeal. Pour half salad oil and half olive oil into a pan 1/8 inch deep, heat, then fry the fish to a golden brown. Serve with tomato sauce.

Good panfish recipe.

CRISPY CROAKER WITH ALMONDS

Serves 2

2 whole croakers, 1 pound each (1 fish per serving)
1 egg, beaten
1 teaspoon salt
1/4 teaspoon each pepper and monosodium glutamate
1 Tablespoon dry vermouth
2 teaspoons cornstarch

1 ounce slivered almonds
1/4 cup cold water
3 Tablespoons sugar
3 Tablespoons vinegar
1 teaspoon Worcestershire sauce
2 cups oil for frying
Parsley

Scale, clean, and wipe croakers dry. Score fish with pinecone-like cuts (i.e., short, forward-slanted cuts, deep enough to hold almond slivers) and place them on a platter. Combine egg, salt, pepper, monosodium glutamate, wine, and 1 teaspoon of the cornstarch, mix well, then pour over the fish. Roll the fish so every side is coated in mixture. Fill all of the cuts with slivered almonds—just stick them in.

Make sauce before frying fish, by stirring together the water, sugar, vinegar, Worcestershire sauce, the remaining teaspoon of cornstarch, and any remaining almond slivers, then set aside while frying fish.

In a large, deep skillet, heat oil to 375°F. (or until it begins to smoke) and fry fish until golden brown, about 4 minutes on each side. Remove croakers to a warm platter, pour off all but a spoonful of oil, and add sauce to the pan. Heat and stir until it thickens, then spoon sauce over the fish. Garnish with parsley and serve at once.

Whiting may be used.

DEEP-FRIED CROAKER OR CORVINA
WITH ONION SOY SAUCE

2 croakers, 1 pound each, or one 2-pound fish	1 Tablespoon dry sherry
Salt	1 teaspoon sugar
1/4 cup plus 1 teaspoon cornstarch	1/4–1/2 teaspoon chili powder
1/2 cup soy sauce	3 green onions
2 Tablespoons rice vinegar	1 clove garlic
	2 cups oil for deep frying

Slash fish with 2 or 3 diagonal cuts on either side, salt them lightly inside and out, and dust well with 1/4 cup of the cornstarch. (Reserve the remaining teaspoon.) Combine soy, vinegar, sherry, sugar, chili powder, and the remaining teaspoon of cornstarch in a bowl and set aside. Mince garlic and slice green onions.

Heat the oil to 375°F. (to smoking point), then fry fish until golden brown, about 4 minutes on each side for small fish. Larger fish can be fried in hot oil for 3 minutes, lifted out to drain, then put back in almost-smoking oil for another 3 minutes, repeating until fish is crisp and golden brown. Remove cooked fish to a platter and keep warm. Pour off all but 2 tablespoons of oil. Add onions and garlic and stir-fry for 1 minute. Add soy mixture and continue stirring until sauce thickens. Spoon it over the fish and serve.

Whiting may be used.

SPICY BAKED CROAKER OR CORVINA

4 croakers (1 pound fish per serving)	2 Tablespoons chopped fresh cilantro
3 tomatoes, peeled and chopped	Salt
2 onions, chopped coarse	Butter
1 clove garlic, chopped	
1/4 cup lime juice	

Preheat the oven to 425°F. Trim fins and dry fish. Slash them with several diagonal cuts on each side, then arrange them in a buttered shallow baking dish. Combine chopped tomatoes, onions, and garlic, lime juice, cilantro, and salt in a blender and purée into a sauce. Pour sauce on fish, then dab with butter. Bake for 10 minutes per inch thickness of fish. Serve on a warm platter with pan sauce poured over fish, accompanied by a crisp salad.

STUFFED KINGFISH

6 whole kingfish, cleaned
Salt to taste
¼ cup chopped green onion
½ cup chopped mushrooms
2 Tablespoons (¼ stick) butter
Dash of monosodium glutamate

Dash of garlic powder
2 eggs
Pepper to taste
¼ cup small peas
6 strips bacon

Trim and dry kingfish, salt them lightly, and set them aside while you make stuffing.

Sauté onion and mushrooms in butter until tender. Season with monosodium glutamate and garlic powder. Beat eggs with salt and pepper, toss in peas, then pour into the pan with cooked onion and mushrooms. Cook until eggs are scrambled, but moist, then turn eggs into a dish to cool.

Stuff fish with scrambled egg. Wrap a slice of bacon diagonally around each fish and secure it with a wooden cocktail pick. Place fish on a greased grill or broiler pan and cook slowly, turning once. Be sure to remove picks before serving.

Kelp, Rock, and Spotted Sand Bass

KELP BEDS are the forests of the sea
and are the protective shelters
and dwellings of many creatures of the sea animal kingdom.
Kelp bass are found only around kelp
beds, swimming singly or in loose groups.
Their brown backs, silver gray blotched sides, and the equal length of their
third, fourth, and fifth spines distinguish them. Like most bass they are
very slow growing—in five years they are only ten inches long and barely
mature.

Kelp bass is truly gourmet-quality fish and favored game for scuba
divers. Young one- to five-pound fish are known as "calicos." Big ten- to
fifteen-pounders—"bull bass"—are good fighters generally caught by slow
trolling the surface.

Due to overfishing, California prohibits commercial fishing and requires a bag and size limit of this sport fish.

ROCK BASS (cabrilla) inhabit rocky
areas south of Pt. Conception
down into Baja. Much of the
shore is protected from heavy
waves and strong ocean currents by
thick kelp beds. Cabrilla swim this sheltered
environment either singly or in loose schools, feeding on the many creatures that live on floating kelp streamers, on food washed off the rocks,
or on crustaceans, mollusks, and other small bottom animals (benthos).

Rock bass average two to three pounds, are green brown and technically identified by counting ten dorsal spines, followed by thirteen soft rays.

The water temperature drops to 57°F. in the winter and reaches a high
of 72°F. in August, yet despite this wide temperature range rock bass
remain in this area all year round.

Sport fishermen can catch them either off the rocks with light tackle or by still-fishing from dinghy or skiff. Rock bass are also fished commercially and generally found in markets as fillets.

SAND BASS, as the name suggests, live off the sandy-mud bottoms in bays, estuaries, and harbors. They are never far from shore and can be fished from piers, barges, or jetties.

Young bass are brightly colored with dark horizontal stripes. As they grow older the stripes disappear and their bodies, instead, become polka-dotted. Ten strong dorsal spines followed by eleven to fifteen soft rays, as well as their densely brown-spotted body, are sure identification.

These one- to three-pound bass are plentiful off Southern California, but rarely seen north of Monterey. They are a frequent catch for party boaters; however, it is unlawful to take them commercially.

About Kelp, Rock, and Spotted Sand Bass Meat

ALL THREE VARIETIES OF BASS have lean white flaky meat of delicate flavor. Small bass may be grilled, sautéed, pan fried, deep fried, or poached. Small rock bass are marketed whole, year round, larger rock bass are available filleted. Calicos (small kelp bass) are game fish and may be prepared like the others. Large kelp bass may be barbecued, baked with or without stuffing, poached, or braised.

GRILLED SMALL BASS

Serves 2–3

2 small bass, ¾–1½ pounds each | Juice of ½ lemon
Fennel sprigs or dried fennel seeds | ½ teaspoon salt
1 Tablespoon grated orange rind | ¼ teaspoon pepper
¼ cup oil | 2 ounces brandy

Cut 2 or 3 diagonal slashes on each side of fish and place a small piece of fresh fennel or a few fennel seeds in each slash and in the cavities. Mix a marinade of remaining ingredients except brandy, and marinate fish for 1 hour, turning occasionally. Grill over hot coals for approximately 6–9 minutes on each side, brushing with marinade while broiling.

Transfer cooked fish to a warm platter. Meanwhile, warm brandy in a ladle, set it alight, and spoon over fish until the flame dies, then serve at once. Wild rice with mushrooms complements this dish.

White perch or other bass-type fish may be used.

DEEP-FRIED SMALL BASS WITH TANGY SAUCE

Serves 2

2 whole bass, 3/4–1 pound each
Salt to taste
1/4 teaspoon pepper
3 Tablespoons cornstarch
2–3 Tablespoons dry sherry

2 Tablespoons each vinegar, sugar, and catsup
1 large green onion
1 teaspoon ginger
2 cups oil for deep frying

Trim and dry bass, season them with salt and pepper, and roll them in 2 tablespoons of the cornstarch. Lay them on a platter, spoon on just enough sherry to wet the fish, then let them dry for 15 minutes. Turn fish over and let the other side dry for 15 more minutes. Dust again with the remaining tablespoon of cornstarch. Mix vinegar, sugar, and catsup together and set aside. Chop onion and mince ginger.

Heat oil in skillet or electric fry pan to 375°F. (or to smoking point) and fry fish until golden brown, about 5 minutes, lifting and turning several times during cooking. Remove fish to a platter and keep warm. Pour off all but 1 tablespoon of oil, then add onions and ginger and stir-fry for 1 minute. Add the vinegar mixture, stir and cook for another minute, then spoon sauce over the fish and serve.

White perch, small snapper, or snapper blues may be used.

MARINATED DEEP-FRIED BASS

2 pounds bass fillet
2 eggs, beaten
1 1/2 cans (18 ounces) beer
Flour

1 teaspoon salt
Garlic powder
Pepper to taste
1 cup oil for frying

Cut fillet into serving pieces. Combine beaten egg and beer and marinate fish, covered, overnight in the refrigerator. Drain on toweling, then dust with flour and seasonings. Heat oil to 375°F. (until it ripples) and fry fish to a golden brown. Serve with Fish Cocktail Mayonnaise (p. 425) or Tartar Sauce (p. 426).

White seabass, tilefish, striped bass, grouper, redfish, or snapper may be used.

PAN-FRIED SMALL BASS
WITH RED WINE SAUCE

Serves 2

1½-2-pound bass, dressed, head and
  tail removed
Salt
1 onion, minced
1 Tablespoon olive oil
1 Tablespoon tomato paste
1 cup each red wine and water

1 bay leaf
2 cloves garlic, minced
¼ teaspoon thyme
Salt and pepper to taste
½ cup salad oil
Flour
Parsley

Rinse fish, pat it dry, sprinkle with salt inside and out, then set it aside.
Sauté onion in olive oil until tender. Mix in tomato paste, wine, and water.
Add bay leaf, garlic, and thyme, then heat to a boil. Simmer, uncovered,
and cook, stirring occasionally, until sauce has thickened. Season with salt
and pepper, and keep warm.

Heat salad oil in a heavy skillet. Roll fish in flour, and fry in hot oil,
over medium heat, until crispy golden brown on both sides. Transfer
cooked fish to a warm platter, pour steaming hot sauce over, sprinkle with
parsley, and serve immediately.

Or use snapper, ocean whitefish, white perch, or any bass-type fish.

POACHED SMALL BASS
WITH GROUND BEAN SAUCE

Serves 2

2 bass, ¾-1½ pounds each
4 dried black mushrooms
1 Tablespoon soy sauce
2 teaspoons ground bean sauce*
1 Tablespoon dry sherry
2 teaspoons vinegar
1 teaspoon sugar

1 Tablespoon cornstarch
1 green onion, chopped
¼ cup slivered water chestnuts
1 teaspoon minced ginger
2 cloves garlic, minced
2 Tablespoons oil
⅛ teaspoon salt

*See Glossary.

Arrange trimmed fish in a skillet and pour over enough boiling water
barely to cover them. Put a lid on the pan and bring to the boiling point,
then cook fish just below a simmer for 10 minutes per inch thickness of
fish as they are lying flat. Remove fish to a platter, cover, and keep warm.
Pour the broth into a small bowl and set it aside.

Meanwhile, rinse mushrooms, remove stems, cover with hot water, and soak them for 20 minutes. Combine soy sauce, ground bean sauce, sherry, vinegar, sugar, and cornstarch in a bowl and set aside. Cut softened mushrooms into several pieces, and put them in a dish with the onion and water chestnuts. Combine ginger and garlic in a small dish.

Heat oil in a wok or heavy skillet, over highest heat, and keep it high. Add salt and garlic-ginger bits to the oil, and stir-fry for a few seconds. Add the vegetables and stir-fry them for 1 minute, then add reserved fish broth. When fish broth comes to a boil, add soy mixture; stir and cook until the broth is thickened. Pour sauce over the fish and serve.

Good with small snapper, white perch, ocean whitefish, or striped bass.

STEAMED WHOLE BASS
WITH CHINESE PICKLES

1½-2½-pound whole bass, cleaned and degilled	¼ cup vinegar
	¼ cup sugar
Salt	2 Tablespoons dry sherry
2 green onions, split	2 Tablespoons cornstarch
⅓ jar Chinese Pickle	½ cup cold water

Trim bass, wipe dry, and salt lightly. Lay fish on a heatproof platter (fish may be pan dressed if too long), place a green onion in the cavity and one on top of fish. Wrap (see Basic Steaming, pp. 27–8), and when water boils, put platter on rack to steam for 10 minutes per inch thickness of fish.

Meanwhile, shred pickles and combine them with vinegar, sugar, and sherry in a small saucepan. Dissolve cornstarch in cold water and stir into sauce. Cook, stirring, until sauce thickens and becomes translucent, then pour it over the fish and serve.

BAKED BASS

4-pound whole kelp bass, dressed	Melted butter
Oil	Hot butter sauce
Salt and pepper to taste	Lemon wedges
Flour	

Preheat the oven to 425°F. Brush bass with oil, sprinkle with salt and pepper inside and out, then roll in flour. Place in a greased baking dish, add ¼ cup water, and bake for 10 minutes per inch thickness. Baste with melted butter during cooking. Serve with plain melted butter or one of the Hot Butter Sauces on pages 430–1, lemon wedges, and parsley boiled potatoes.

WHOLE BASS IN SOUR SOUP

3-4-pound calico, pan dressed
At least 2 teaspoons salt
6¼ cups cold water
1 onion, chopped
½ cup vinegar
½ teaspoon whole peppercorns

½ teaspoon monosodium glutamate
4 dried black mushrooms
1 fresh chili or dried red pepper
1 Tablespoon soy sauce
4 cloves garlic, pressed

Sprinkle pan-dressed bass with salt and set aside. Place fish head and tail, tied in cheesecloth for easy removal, in a large saucepan; then add 6 cups of the water, onion, vinegar, 2 teaspoons salt, and peppercorns. Cover, heat to a boil, then reduce heat and simmer stock for 30 minutes. Strain the broth, discarding solids, into a pan large enough to hold the fish.

Meanwhile, soak mushrooms in warm water for 20 minutes. Seed and purée chili or dried red pepper in blender with the remaining ¼ cup of water.

Bring strained broth to a boil, add bass, and return to boil, then simmer for 15–18 minutes, covered loosely. Add mushrooms (sliced, with their water), chili, soy sauce, monosodium glutamate, and garlic. Simmer for 5 minutes, then remove from heat and let stand for 5 minutes. Remove fish to a warm platter and serve soup in bowls.

Rockfish, Atlantic black seabass, or any bass-type fish may be used.

KELP BASS
WITH SALT PORK STUFFING

5-6-pound kelp bass, split and boned,
  not skinned
2 cloves garlic, pressed
¼ cup olive oil
Salt and pepper to taste
2 cups French bread, crumbled
Milk

¼ cup minced salt pork
½ cup chopped green onion
1 cup minced celery
½–1 small hot chili, seeded and
  crushed
½ cup minced parsley
¼ cup white wine or juice of 1 lemon

Preheat the oven to 425°F. Mix garlic with olive oil and brush the 2 fillets on both sides with it. Salt and pepper, then set aside while making stuffing.

Soak bread in enough milk to moisten. Fry salt pork bits until crispy, remove them from pan, and reserve. Add onion, celery, and chili to the drippings and sauté until soft. Mix in softened bread, pork bits, and parsley, season with salt and pepper, then spoon stuffing onto one of the fillets. Place other fillet on top of stuffing and either sew the two halves together, enclosing the stuffing, or tie the top and bottom together (dental floss is handy for trussing). Lift fish on cheesecloth into a greased shallow baking dish or roasting pan. Pour wine or lemon juice over fish and bake for about 35 minutes, or 10 minutes per inch thickness of fish. Baste while cooking.

If kelp bass is not available, use any lean whole fish for baking listed on page 447 (III A3).

KELP BASS
WITH MUSHROOM-CRAB STUFFING

6–7-pound kelp bass, dressed
Flour
Melted butter
Salt and pepper to taste
1 onion, chopped
4 Tablespoons (½ stick) butter
2½ cups finely
　chopped mushrooms

1 clove garlic, minced
1 cup fresh or 6½-ounce can
　crab meat
2 cups soft French bread crumbs
¼ cup minced parsley
4-ounce can pimiento, chopped
At least ⅓ cup Rhine wine to moisten

Preheat the oven to 425°F. Wipe bass dry and dust lightly all over with flour, shaking off the excess. Brush with melted butter both inside and out; then sprinkle with salt and pepper. Set prepared bass aside while making stuffing.

Sauté onion in the 4 tablespoons of butter until all the vegetables are tender, then add mushrooms and garlic; cover and cook until soft. Combine picked-over crab, bread crumbs, parsley, and pimiento, then mix into the mushrooms. Pour in enough wine to moisten mixture, season with salt and pepper, and stuff into fish. Skewer or sew fish closed and place it on greased roasting pan. Pour ⅓ cup wine into the pan and bake for 10 minutes per inch thickness of fish (about 40–50 minutes). Baste while baking.

If kelp bass is not available, use any lean whole fish for baking listed on page 447 (III A3).

Ideas for Leftover Bass

AU GRATIN BASS

2 cups cooked bass

2 Tablespoons (¼ stick) butter

2 Tablespoons flour

2 cups hot milk

½ teaspoon salt

Generous milling of pepper

1 Tablespoon Worcestershire sauce

¾ cup grated Swiss cheese

Preheat the oven to 350°F. Flake cooked bass with a fork. Melt butter and blend flour into it, then add hot milk, all at once, stirring constantly with a whisk, until sauce is thick and smooth. Stir in seasonings and add cheese. Cook over low heat until cheese melts, then stir in fish. Pour into individual greased ramekins or a casserole and bake until browned on top, about 15–20 minutes.

Good for any firm lean white fish listed on page 447 (III A2).

KELP BASS CANAPÉS

Kelp bass is especially fine-tasting fish, but any lean flaky fish may be used. It makes a good dip, canapé spread, or sandwich.

1 cup cooked bass, flaked

Dry, light Rhine-type wine

3-ounce package cream cheese

1 teaspoon grated onion

Dash of cayenne pepper

Mix enough wine with cheese to soften. Stir in onion, pepper, fish, and additional wine to desired consistency.

Ocean whitefish may be used.

California Black Seabass

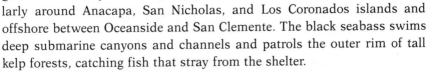

BLACK SEABASS, also called
jewfish, is *the* big member of
the bass family—150 to 250 pounds
is average size, but some reach 500. The
giants are solitary fish occurring particu-
larly around Anacapa, San Nicholas, and Los Coronados islands and
offshore between Oceanside and San Clemente. The black seabass swims
deep submarine canyons and channels and patrols the outer rim of tall
kelp forests, catching fish that stray from the shelter.

Giant black seabass is taken on hook and line even by commercial
fishermen all year round. However, fishing is best June through September.

About Black Seabass Meat

Small black seabass have deliciously delicate, firm meat, flaky and white.
Very large fish retain delicate flavor, but the meat is inclined to be coarse.

BLACK SEABASS BAKED IN MILK

2 pounds black seabass fillet
Lemon juice
1 cup milk
1 teaspoon salt
Sprig fresh fennel

1/4 teaspoon each fresh ground
    nutmeg and pepper
3 cups soft bread crumbs
8 Tablespoons (1 stick) butter, melted
Lemon wedges

Preheat the oven to 400°F. Cut seabass into 1-inch cubes, put them in a
buttered casserole, and sprinkle them with a little lemon juice. Simmer
milk, salt, fennel, nutmeg, and pepper together for 2 or 3 minutes, then
pour over fish. Toss crumbs in melted butter and scatter them on top of
fish. Bake for about 15–18 minutes, then serve with lemon wedges.

*Fluke, flounder, petrale, halibut, Atlantic black seabass, or snapper
may be used for this dish.*

GRILLED BLACK SEABASS

Choose an oil- or butter-base marinade (for selection, see pages 439–40) and marinate fillets for 1 hour before grilling, then baste with it while cooking.

BLACK SEABASS SAUTÉ FLAMBÉ

4 seabass fillets, 1 inch thick (about 2 pounds)
Salt and pepper to taste
Flour
3 Tablespoons butter
2 Tablespoons oil

2 small bay leaves
1/4 teaspoon each fennel seed, thyme, and savory
2 sprigs parsley, minced
1/3 cup brandy, warmed

Wipe fillets, sprinkle with salt and pepper, and dust with flour. Heat butter and oil in a skillet, add spices and then fish, and sauté for 5 minutes. Turn fillets over and cook until nicely brown. Pour brandy over the sizzling fish, set alight, and spoon sauce over the fillets as long as the flame burns, then serve immediately. Seasoned rice and cucumbers in lime juice complement this dish.

White seabass or tilefish may be substituted for black seabass.

BLACK SEABASS WITH CURRIED VEGETABLES

2 pounds seabass fillets
Salt and pepper to taste
Juice of 1/2 lemon
1 cup fish or chicken stock
1 teaspoon minced ginger
2 teaspoons sugar
1 Tablespoon soy sauce
1 Tablespoon dry sherry
4 carrots, slivered

1 green pepper, cut in large pieces
1 stalk celery, diced small
1/2 cucumber, peeled and diced
5 Tablespoons oil
1/2 cup dry white wine
2 teaspoons curry powder
At least 1 Tablespoon cornstarch
3 green onions, cut into 1 1/2-inch lengths

Wipe and cut fillets into portions, season with salt, pepper, and lemon juice; set aside. Combine stock, ginger, sugar, soy sauce, and sherry in a bowl and reserve. Combine the cut carrots, green pepper, celery, and cucumber. In a heavy skillet, heat 2 tablespoons of the oil until very hot, add vegetables and stir-fry for a minute until coated with hot oil. Pour in stock mixture, cover skillet, and cook about 5 minutes, until vegetables are crisply tender. Transfer them to a bowl and keep warm.

Combine wine, curry powder, and 1 tablespoon of the cornstarch and set it aside. Dust seabass with more cornstarch. Heat the remaining 3 tablespoons of oil in a clean skillet and sauté fillets with green onions until fish is crispy and cooked, then transfer them to a warm platter. Return vegetables to the skillet and over high heat stir in wine-curry mixture. Cook, stirring constantly, until sauce has thickened. Add salt if needed, then spoon vegetables and sauce around, not over, the fish. Serve at once with rice, if you like.

Any firm lean fillet listed on page 447 (III A2) may be substituted.

GEFILTE FISH

1 pound seabass fillet	1 teaspoon pepper
1/2 pound halibut fillet	1/4 teaspoon plus a pinch of sugar
1 pound sheepshead fillet	3 eggs, beaten
2 quarts cold water	3 Tablespoons matzo meal
3 onions, chopped	1/3 cup ice water
2 pounds fish trimmings from these three fish	2 carrots, sliced
	1 onion, sliced
4 teaspoons salt	Horseradish sauce

Pour cold water into a large kettle, add 2 chopped onions, fish trimmings, 2 teaspoons of the salt, 1/2 teaspoon of the pepper, and 1/4 teaspoon of the sugar. Bring to a boil and simmer for 30 minutes, then strain, discarding solids, and boil stock down until reduced by one-third.

Grind fillets and the remaining chopped onion together in a food processor, using the finest blade. Stir in beaten eggs, the remaining 2 teaspoons of salt, the remaining 1/2 teaspoon of pepper, and a pinch of sugar. Beat mixture for a few minutes and beat in matzo meal. Add ice water by the spoonful, beating each addition until well integrated.

With wet hands, form fish into 2-inch balls. Bring stock to a boil and carefully place balls in enough hot broth to cover, add sliced carrots and onion. Cover and bring back to a boil, then lower heat to simmer, covered loosely, for 1 1/2 hours.

Remove kettle from heat and let it stand 15 minutes, then transfer fish balls to a high-rimmed platter. Pour strained stock over them and place carrots decoratively around the fish. When they cool to room temperature, cover the platter and chill until stock jells. Serve with horseradish sauce.

Carp, pike, and whitefish may be used.

BLACK SEABASS MIZUTAKI

This is a Japanese stew, made of fish and vegetables, cooked in broth and served with a dipping sauce. Both fish and vegetables are cut into bite-size pieces and placed on a platter, ready for cooking in simmering broth. Stew should be cooked in a stove-to-table cooking vessel or in an electric skillet in which the food may be cooked at the table.

2 pounds seabass fillet, cut in 1-inch pieces	1/2 cup daikon (grated white radish)
8 dried mushrooms, soaked	1/4 cup soy sauce
1 package tofu, cut in 3/4-inch cubes	2 teaspoons lemon juice
1 bunch bok choy, sliced	1 Tablespoon dry sherry
1 can bamboo shoots, sliced	Dash of cayenne pepper
10 green onions, sliced	3 cups water
	1 dashi-no-moto bag*

*If dashi-no-moto is not available, chicken broth may be substituted.

Rinse and soak mushrooms in hot water for 20 minutes, then drain and slice them. Arrange fish, tofu, and vegetables decoratively in groups, on a large platter, then set it aside while making dipping sauce.

Put grated radish in a small bowl and combine with it soy sauce, lemon juice, sherry, and cayenne.

Heat 3 cups of water in the electric skillet and add dashi, which is packaged like tea bags. Make broth by boiling the dashi bag in the water for 10 minutes. Remove dashi bag, then add fish chunks and simmer for 5 minutes, put in vegetables and tofu to simmer until the vegetables are crisply cooked.

Serve from the cooking vessel into soup bowls. Dip cooked food into sauce.

This dish is good for any lean white fish listed on page 446 (III A1).

Idea for Leftover Black Seabass

SEABASS SALAD

Cut cooked black seabass into dice and marinate fish bits in Ravigote Sauce (p. 428) for 30 minutes. Remove bits from marinade and place them on lettuce beds lining salad plates. Garnish salads with hard-boiled eggs, gherkins, sliced beets, and anchovy strips. Mix marinade with a large dollop of mayonnaise and spoon it over the salads.

White Seabass

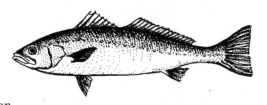

WHITE SEABASS is not really a bass at all; it is a croaker. Young white seabass are found close inshore, identified by their shape and the four to five vertical bars on their sides. They swim in sandy bottom areas in small groups and can be night-fished either from piers or small boats around Santa Monica, Oceanside, or Coronado Strand. Live anchovy or sardine bait brings the best results.

Mature white seabass are frequently thirty- to fifty-plus-pounders. They are found offshore, swimming in loose schools along the outer margin of kelp beds, from San Francisco to Baja.

In the summertime, sportsmen enjoy night-fishing from party boats (or skiffs) in the Southern California area. Commercially, they are one of our most marketable catches.

About White Seabass Meat

The meat of white seabass is mild-flavored, lean, and firm in texture. Small fish may be cooked whole and large fish are usually sold as thick fillets, allowing a variety of cooking methods—grilled thick steaks and broiled, poached, or steamed fillets.

BARBECUED WHITE SEABASS

Fillets may be marinated for 30 minutes in an oil, butter, tomato, or other marinade or brushed with a spicy baste while grilling. Select any of the recipes in the chapter on Sauces and Marinades, pages 439–40.

BAKED SEABASS
WITH CREAMED CLAM AND SHRIMP

2-3-pound whole white seabass
1/2 pound raw shrimp
6 Tablespoons (3/4 stick) butter
Juice of 1/2 lemon plus 1 teaspoon
Salt and pepper to taste
1/4 cup water
1 green onion, minced

1 Tablespoon oil
2 Tablespoons flour
1 cup hot milk
1 can minced clams, or 6-7 fresh
 clams, chopped
2 Tablespoons heavy cream

Preheat the oven to 425°F. Shell and devein shrimp. Melt 4 tablespoons of the butter and combine with lemon juice, reserving 1 teaspoon juice. Trim and dry the cleaned seabass, brush it with lemon-butter inside and out, sprinkle lightly with salt and pepper, and place it in a greased baking dish. Add 1/4 cup water to the dish and bake for 10 minutes per inch thickness of fish.

Sauté shrimp with green onion in hot oil, over medium heat, stirring until shrimp are pink and barely cooked. Add salt to taste, then remove from heat and cut shrimp into small pieces.

Melt the remaining 2 tablespoons of butter in a saucepan, add flour, and stir until bubbly. Add hot milk, beating with a whisk until sauce is thick and smooth. Stir in clam liquor (if using fresh clams, add them now) and cook for 2 minutes, add the reserved teaspoon of lemon juice, the clams, and shrimp to sauce. Adjust seasonings, stir in cream, heat to the boiling point, and serve sauce with bass.

If white seabass is not available, use any lean whole fish for baking listed on page 447 (III A3).

GARLIC-BAKED SEABASS FILLET

2 pounds seabass fillet, cut into
 4 thick steaks
Salt and pepper to taste
2 large cloves garlic, pressed

1/4 teaspoon rubbed oregano
1/4 cup olive oil
3 Tablespoons minced onion
2 Tablespoons minced parsley

Preheat the oven to 425°F. Wipe steaks, season with salt and pepper, and place them in a greased baking dish. Spread garlic purée on both sides of fish. Mix oregano with oil and drizzle on steaks, then scatter on onion and parsley. Bake, uncovered, basting several times during cooking, allowing 10 minutes per inch thickness of fish. Serve on warm plates with pan juices spooned onto the fillets.

Tilefish is also a good fish for this dish.

ORANGE-BAKED
WHITE SEABASS FILLET

2 pounds seabass fillet
Salt and pepper to taste
1 large orange, peeled
1 Tablespoon cornstarch
1 cup orange juice

1 green onion, chopped
1 clove garlic, minced
1 Tablespoon butter
1 teaspoon chicken bouillon grains, or
    1 bouillon cube, crushed

Preheat the oven to 425°F. Cut fillet into serving pieces, season with salt and pepper, and place them in a buttered baking dish large enough to hold them without crowding. Peel the membrane from the orange sections and cut them into several pieces. Dissolve cornstarch in orange juice. Sauté onion and garlic in butter until soft. To this, add bouillon grains, then orange juice–cornstarch mixture, stirring constantly while it cooks and thickens. Remove from heat and stir in orange bits. Spoon sauce over fillets and bake until meat barely separates when tested, then serve at once.

Also good with snapper or Atlantic black seabass.

BAKED SEABASS AND POTATOES
WITH WINE VINEGAR DRESSING

2 pounds thick seabass fillet
4-5 boiling potatoes
1½ cups minced parsley
Salt and pepper to taste

2 Tablespoons olive oil
2 Tablespoons water
Basic French Dressing (p. 427), made
    with red wine vinegar

Boil potatoes so they will be cooked shortly before fish is done. Peel cooked potatoes and cut into small dice, then mix them with half of the minced parsley. Cover and keep them warm. Preheat the oven to 425°F.

Wipe fillet on toweling, salt and pepper both sides, and place it in a buttered baking dish. Sprinkle with oil and water and bake, uncovered, for 10 minutes per inch thickness of the fillet. Baste several times during baking.

Drain and break cooked fish into large chunks. Scatter remaining parsley on fish, then combine with potatoes. Pour French dressing over, toss gently to mix, and serve hot. Otherwise, serve on individual plates with fish on top of potatoes and dressing poured on.

Any firm, thick, lean fillet listed on page 447 (III A2) may be used.

SEABASS BAKED IN
BUTTER AND WHITE WINE

2 pounds white seabass fillets
4 Tablespoons (½ stick) butter, melted
¼ teaspoon thyme

Salt and pepper
¼ cup white wine
Parsley White Sauce (p. 418)

Preheat the oven to 425°F. Cut fillets into 1½-inch strips, dip them in melted butter mixed with thyme, and place them in a buttered baking dish. Season with salt and pepper, pour on any remaining butter, add wine to the dish and bake, basting occasionally with pan juice, until fish barely separates when prodded with a knife. Accompany fillets with a bowl of parsley white sauce.

Tilefish fillets may be cooked the same way.

OVEN-FRIED SEABASS WITH NOODLES
AND MUSHROOM GRAVY

2 pounds white seabass fillets
Salt and pepper to taste
2 cloves garlic, minced
½ cup minced parsley
4 Tablespoons (½ stick) butter
4 Tablespoons olive oil

2 cups sliced mushrooms
2 Tablespoons flour
At least ½ cup water
1 package noodles
Flour for dusting

Wipe fillets, cut into serving pieces, season with salt and pepper, then set aside while making gravy.

Sauté garlic and parsley in 2 tablespoons each of the butter and olive oil for a few seconds over high heat, then add mushrooms and cook, stirring, for 1 minute. Lower heat and simmer, covered, for 8 minutes. Make a thin, smooth paste of the 2 tablespoons flour and the water, add it to the pan, stirring constantly, and bring to a boil. Season with salt and pepper; gravy should be of medium-thin consistency.

Meanwhile, cook and drain noodles. Preheat the oven and pan to 500°F. Dust seabass with flour. Remove pan from oven, add the remaining 2 tablespoons each butter and oil and shake it around. Put fillets in the pan, then turn them over so both sides of fillets will be covered with butter and oil. Return pan to oven and bake, uncovered, until fish is brown and flakes. Place noodles on a platter and arrange fillets on top. Pour pan juice over and spoon on mushroom gravy.

Tilefish may be used instead of seabass.

SESAME-VINEGAR SAUCE
FOR SAUTÉED WHITE SEABASS

¼ cup sesame seeds
2 Tablespoons bottled tempura sauce

2 Tablespoons sugar
2 Tablespoons white vinegar

Put sesame seeds in a heavy fry pan and heat them, stirring constantly, until seeds jump in pan and begin to turn light golden, then scoop them into a blender with the other ingredients and purée. Serve with sautéed or pan-fried seabass.

Good with sea robin or pike.

PAN-FRIED SEABASS
WITH MUSHROOMS AND PEA PODS

1½ pounds white seabass fillet
6 dried black mushrooms
1 egg
2 Tablespoons flour
1 teaspoon salt
Pepper to taste
1 cup peas in pod
½ cup green onions,
    cut in 1½-inch pieces
¼ cup sliced bamboo shoots

½ cup slivered celery
1 Tablespoon cornstarch
½ cup chicken broth
¼ cup soy sauce
1 Tablespoon dry sherry
1 teaspoon sugar
1 cup oil
½ cup slivered almonds
1 teaspoon minced ginger
1 clove garlic, minced

Rinse mushrooms, cover with hot water, and soak for 20 minutes, then drain and quarter them. Beat egg lightly with flour and salt and pepper. Cut fillet into strips and put them in the egg mixture. Combine peas, onions, bamboo shoots, and celery. Mix together cornstarch, broth, soy sauce, sherry, and sugar.

Heat oil in a skillet and fry fish until golden brown, then remove fish and keep them warm, uncovered, in a low oven. Put almonds in a strainer or deep-fry basket and fry in the oil until they begin to brown. Set them aside.

Pour off all but 1–2 tablespoons of oil. With high heat, stir-fry ginger and garlic for a few seconds. Add vegetables and stir-fry for 3 minutes, then add broth-soy mixture and cook until thickened. Serve vegetables on a platter, put fish on top, and scatter fried almonds over all.

Any lean white fillet listed on page 446 (III A1) may be used.

SEABASS FILLET IN COCONUT CREAM
AND LIME JUICE

1½ pounds white seabass fillet
¼ cup lime juice
1 large onion, sliced thin
2 Tablespoons oil

½ cup sweet cream of coconut (½ of
   a 9-ounce can)
Salt and pepper to taste
Cornstarch

Wipe fillet, cut into serving pieces, and marinate in lime juice at least
1 hour, turning occasionally. Remove fish with slotted spoon and set aside
both fish and marinade.

Sauté onion in oil until tender. Add coconut cream and lime juice
marinade to skillet and mix well. Season drained fillets with salt and
pepper and dust them with cornstarch. Arrange them in the skillet, cover,
and simmer them in sauce for 3–4 minutes. Turn fillets over and cook until
fish barely separates when tested. Serve with boiled rice.

Tilefish or snapper may be used for this dish.

Ideas for Leftover Bass

KEDGEREE

2 cups cooked white seabass, flaked
2 cups warm cooked rice
2 sprigs parsley, minced
4 hard-boiled eggs, chopped

½ cup cream
1 teaspoon salt
Salt and pepper to taste

Boil rice, add flaked seabass and the rest of the ingredients. Mix gently
and reheat in a double boiler. Serve when steaming hot.

Any lean white fillet listed on page 446 (III A1) may be used.

MOLDED SEABASS SALAD

2 cups cooked seabass, flaked
1 Tablespoon (1 envelope) gelatin
1½ teaspoons salt
1½ Tablespoons sugar
1 teaspoon dry mustard
1½ teaspoons flour
Dash of cayenne pepper

2 egg yolks
1½ Tablespoons butter, melted
¾ cup milk
¼ cup vinegar
¼ cup catsup
2 Tablespoons chopped green pepper

Soak gelatin in 2 tablespoons cold water. Combine dry ingredients in top of double boiler. Add egg yolks, melted butter, milk, and vinegar. Cook, stirring constantly with a whisk, until thickened. Stir in dissolved gelatin until incorporated, then add catsup, green pepper, and flaked fish. Rinse a mold in cold water, then pour in gelatin-fish mixture and chill until set.

Any lean white fillet listed on page 446 (III A1) may be used.

Sculpins

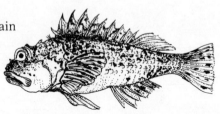

UGLY. "CABEZONIES" are just plain ugly. They have scaleless bodies with wrinkled skins, huge wide heads, big eyes popping out on top, and large mouths with skin flaps on their snouts. Males are mottled with deep brown, red, tan, or grayish green. Females, larger than males, are green— even their mouths are turquoise blue inside. Cabezons are the largest members of the sculpin family and are found along the entire coast. Their cousins, red-mottled Irish lords, second largest of the sculpins, occur in the cooler waters off Oregon and Washington.

Angling rocky pockets along the coast or poke hole fishing for sculpin is year-round sport.

About Sculpin Meat

Ugly as they are, the usually discarded sculpin is exceptionally fine eating. Many sculpins have white meat, but cabezon have blue green flesh that fades to white during cooking. The green coloring looks odd but is in no way harmful and has no effect on the flavor. The meat is light textured and tends to fall to pieces when broiled or baked. It has delicate flavor.

All sculpins should be skinned before cooking; larger fish should be filleted. WARNING: NEVER EAT THE ROE; IT IS POISONOUS.

SMALL SCULPINS SAUTÉED

Small 6–8-inch fish may be pan dressed and skinned, sprinkled with salt, and marinated in lemon juice for 30 minutes. Then, dust with flour and gently sauté in butter with a little garlic.

CABEZON CORONADOS

2 pounds cabezon fillets	4-ounce can pimientos
Juice of ½ lemon	12 green olives
Garlic powder	1 Tablespoon capers plus 1 Tablespoon
Salt and pepper to taste	caper liquid
½ cup chopped onion	1 cup vegetable oil
¼ cup olive oil	Flour
1 large (28-ounce) can tomatoes	Parsley

Wipe fillets, season with lemon juice, garlic powder, salt and pepper, then set aside while making sauce.

Sauté onion in olive oil until it begins to brown. Add tomatoes, break them up a little, then cover skillet and cook for 5 minutes. Cut 1 pimiento in strips and set it aside; chop the rest and stir them with olives into the tomatoes. Simmer, uncovered, for 15 minutes. Stir in capers and caper liquid and season to taste. Keep sauce warm while fish is cooking.

Heat vegetable oil in skillet or electric fry pan to 400°F. Dust fillets in flour and fry until fish is nicely brown. Transfer fillets to a warm platter, garnish with pimiento strips and snips of parsley, and serve with sauce and rice.

Any lean white fillet listed on page 446 (III A1) may be used.

BROILED SCULPIN BÉARNAISE
WITH ARTICHOKE

2 pounds cabezon fillets	Juice of ½ lemon
Béarnaise Sauce (p. 423)	Salt and pepper to taste
4 Tablespoons (½ stick) butter, melted	1 jar marinated artichoke bottoms

Preheat the broiler and broiling pan. Make Béarnaise sauce.

Mix melted butter and lemon juice. Dip fillets in lemon-butter, place them on hot broiler pan, season with salt and pepper, and pour the rest of the lemon-butter over them. Return pan to broiler and cook until meat barely separates when tested, basting several times during broiling.

Dip artichoke bottoms in Béarnaise, coating each heavily with sauce. Place one on top of each fillet and serve immediately on warm plates, with a bowlful of sauce.

Greenling (red rock trout), sea robin, or any perch may be used.

BAKED SCULPIN WITH MUSHROOMS

2 pounds cabezon fillets	2 Tablespoons minced parsley
1 teaspoon salt	Grated fresh nutmeg
Pepper to taste	Dash of cayenne pepper
1 cup sliced mushrooms	3 Tablespoons dry white wine
5 Tablespoons butter	2 Tablespoons brandy

Wipe fillets, season with salt and pepper, and arrange in single layer in a buttered baking dish (thin pieces may be folded).

Preheat the oven to 425°F. Sauté mushrooms in butter until tender, then add parsley, nutmeg, cayenne, wine, and brandy; mix well and remove from heat. Pour mixture over fish, cover tightly with foil, and bake for 10 minutes per inch thickness of fish. Serve with slices of warm toast.

Rockfish may be used.

Ideas for Leftover Sculpin

FLAKED SCULPIN IN GELATIN

1½ cups cooked sculpin, flaked	Salt and pepper to taste
1½ Tablespoons unflavored gelatin	2 hard-boiled eggs, sliced
¼ cup cold water	Pimiento, cut in strips
2 egg whites	At least 3 Tablespoons minced parsley
2 cups chicken broth	½ cup celery, cut in small dice
¼ teaspoon dried tarragon	¼ cup minced Bermuda onion
1 green onion, minced	Lettuce leaves
¼ cup grated carrot	Tomato slices
2 teaspoons brandy	Rémoulade Sauce (p. 426)
1 Tablespoon Port	

To get a sparkling clear molded gelatin, put gelatin in a saucepan with water and egg whites, and beat until frothy. Add cold broth, tarragon, green onion, and carrot. Heat, stirring, to the boiling point, lower heat immediately, then cook just under a simmer for about 15 minutes. Rinse a double layer of cheesecloth in cold water, line a strainer with it, and place the strainer in a bowl. Make a small hole in the cooked, coagulated egg whites, and without disturbing them, carefully pour gelatin into the strainer. Add brandy, and Port, and season with salt and pepper. Set the bowl of gelatin in ice water to chill.

Coat the bottom of a 3-cup mold with ¼ inch of cold gelatin. Lay slices of egg and pimiento alternately around the bottom of the mold, and put it in the freezer until set. Then mix 1 tablespoon of the parsley, the celery, the onion, and the fish into remaining gelatin, and pour into the mold. Cover, and refrigerate until set.

Unmold onto lettuce leaves, garnish with tomato slices dipped in chopped parsley, and serve with rémoulade sauce.

Good made with any lean white fish, shrimp, or crab.

FLAKED FISH SALAD

1 cup cooked sculpin, flaked
¼ cup mayonnaise
1 green onion, chopped
Juice of ½ lemon
Salt and pepper to taste
Dash of garlic powder

Lettuce
6 radishes
½ cucumber, sliced
6 black olives, pitted
Dash of paprika

Make a dressing by mixing mayonnaise, onion, lemon juice, salt, pepper, and garlic powder. Flake leftover sculpin and mix half of the dressing with it.

Arrange crisp lettuce leaves on 2 salad plates. Place a mound of fish mixture on each. Around the fish arrange radishes, cucumbers, and olives. Spoon remaining dressing on top, sprinkle with a dash of paprika, and serve chilled.

Any lean white fish listed on page 446 (III A1) may be used for this dish.

Mahi Mahi

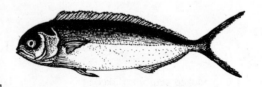

THERE ARE TWO DIFFERENT
KINDS of dolphins dwelling in
the same areas. The mammal
called dolphin was named by
ancient Greeks, who considered
the animal friendly and included it in their legends. The fish dolphin
was so named later by fishermen who confused the two because of their
similar shape and jumping habits. We eat only the fish dolphins.

Fish dolphins (dorado) are beautifully colored: predominantly turquoise blue, with silver bellies and yellow orange pectoral fins. When
threatened they light up, their colors changing in rapid succession. They
lose the color with death. Their foreheads are high, bodies long, slender,
and gracefully tapered with a dorsal fin that runs from head to forked tail.
Males are dominant, becoming twice the size of females. They grow very
rapidly throughout their short three- to four-year life-span, most reaching
twenty-five pounds, a few up to sixty-five pounds and five feet.

Dolphins are warm-water fish, fast swimmers who prefer blue water.
When jumping after flying fish, it is said they reach speeds of thirty-seven
miles an hour. In the late summer they are found at the water surface, in
warm currents, from Baja to Oregon, swimming singly or traveling in
groups of a dozen or two. They tend to congregate around floating kelp or
debris patches miles from shore.

About Mahi Mahi Meat

Mahi mahi (the Hawaiian name for fish dolphin) is a featured fish in
coast seafood restaurants. The meat is full flavored and moderately rich,
with firm, meatlike texture. During the season, it is marketed fresh, either
whole, cut into steaks, or filleted. Frozen steaks or fillets are generally
available.

There is a streak of dark meat along the midsides, just under the skin,
which should be removed before cooking. Fillet and skin small fish.

GRILLED MAHI MAHI

2 pounds mahi mahi, cut into steaks
   3/4 inch thick
Salt
1/4 teaspoon pepper
1 cup catsup

1 small onion, grated
Juice of 2 small limes
2 Tablespoons Worcestershire sauce
4 Tablespoons (1/2 stick) butter, melted

Remove skin and trim dark meat from steaks and sprinkle with salt and pepper. Mix catsup, onion, lime juice, and Worcestershire sauce with melted butter. Put fish into the sauce, then onto hot greased grill to barbecue for 3–4 minutes on each side, basting as needed with sauce.

Shark, swordfish, marlin, grouper, or snook may be used.

SKEWERED MAHI MAHI

1 pound mahi mahi fillet
3/4 cup lime juice
1/4 cup oil
2 Tablespoons grated onion
1/2 teaspoon salt

6 strips bacon
Button mushrooms
Pimiento-stuffed green olives
Lime wedges

Remove skin, trim off dark meat, and cut mahi mahi into 3/4-inch cubes. Mix a marinade of lime juice, oil, onion, and salt, add fish and marinate, covered, for several hours.

Partially cook bacon, drain on toweling, and cut strips into several pieces. Alternate cubes of fish, bacon, mushrooms, and stuffed olives on skewers. Grill over medium-hot coals, then serve with lime wedges.

Shark, swordfish, marlin, grouper, or snook may be used.

MAHI MAHI BALL SOUP

3/4 pound mahi mahi, ground
2 egg whites, beaten
1/2 teaspoon salt
2 Tablespoons cornstarch

1 can concentrated chicken broth
1 soup can water
2 green onions, minced
1 Tablespoon minced cilantro

Beat egg whites with salt until frothy, add cornstarch and fish, mixing well, then form into balls. Dilute broth with water and bring to a boil. Add fish balls, green onions, and cilantro. When broth returns to a boil, lower heat, simmer for 5 minutes, and serve hot.

BAKED MAHI MAHI
WITH ITALIAN SAUCE

2 pounds mahi mahi fillets
¼ pound lean salt pork
1 Tablespoon flour
2 Tablespoons tomato paste
½ cup beef consommé
1½ cups water
1 cup chopped mushrooms

1 green onion, minced
1 Tablespoon butter
1 large tomato, peeled, seeded,
   and diced
3 Tablespoons minced parsley
½ cup dry white wine (optional)
Generous milling of pepper

Cut salt pork into small dice and fry it slowly in a heavy skillet until crisp and brown. Remove pork bits with a slotted spoon and reserve them. Make a basic brown sauce by mixing flour with pan drippings, adding tomato paste, consommé, and water, stirring constantly until sauce thickens and boils. Simmer sauce, stirring frequently, until it has reduced to 1¼ cups.

Meanwhile, sauté mushrooms and onion in butter until they begin to brown. Add them, the pork bits, diced tomato, parsley, wine, and pepper to the reduced sauce and simmer for 3–4 minutes.

Preheat the oven to 425°F. Arrange fish in a buttered baking dish, dot them with butter, and bake, allowing them 10 minutes per inch thickness of fish. Remove cooked fish to a warm platter, spoon hot Italian sauce on fish, and serve at once.

Bluefish or any firm lean fish fillet listed on page 447 (III A2) may be used.

BAKED MAHI MAHI
WITH FILBERTS AND CHEDDAR

2 pounds mahi mahi (4 steaks)
Salt and pepper to taste
Juice of 1 lime
1 cup filberts, blanched
4 Tablespoons (½ stick) butter

3 Tablespoons milk
¼ cup dry sherry
1 cup grated sharp Cheddar cheese
½ cup bread crumbs
⅛ teaspoon nutmeg

Skin, bone, and trim, then salt and pepper mahi mahi, sprinkle with lime juice, and set aside for 1 hour. In a heavy skillet, roast filberts in 2 table-spoons of the butter until they turn straw color, then purée them to a powder. Mix ground nuts with milk and sherry, then stir in cheese. Preheat the oven to 425°F.

Melt the remaining 2 tablespoons butter and stir in bread crumbs.

Arrange fish in a buttered baking dish and spoon cheese-nut mixture onto them. Sprinkle with buttered crumbs and nutmeg, then bake, allowing 10 minutes per inch thickness of fish.

Yellowtail, black drum, catfish, redfish, or tilefish may be used.

MAHI MAHI IN SWEET AND PUNGENT SAUCE

2 pounds mahi mahi fillets, skinned
At least 1 teaspoon salt
3 Tablespoons salad oil
1 large onion, sliced
Flour
1 large green pepper, sliced thin

¾ cup vinegar
¾ cup water
½ cup sugar
1½ teaspoons ginger powder
2 teaspoons cornstarch

Cut fillets into serving portions, sprinkle with salt, and set aside. Heat oil in a large skillet and fry onion until lightly brown, then remove from the pan and reserve. Roll fish in flour, shake off the excess, and fry over medium heat, just to brown on both sides.

Scatter green pepper and reserved onion over fish. Mix together the vinegar, ½ cup of the water, the sugar, the salt, and ginger powder, and pour over fish. Simmer slowly until fish flakes when tested, then remove mahi mahi to a warm deep platter. Mix cornstarch with the remaining ¼ cup water, add it to the pan, and cook, stirring, until sauce thickens. Pour sauce over fish and serve.

SESAME-FRIED MAHI MAHI SLICES

1½ pounds mahi mahi fillet, cut ¼ inch thick
2 Tablespoons sesame seeds
¼ cup soy sauce
¼ teaspoon sesame oil

1 Tablespoon vegetable oil
½ cup minced green onion
¼ teaspoon pepper
2 Tablespoons oil for frying

Heat sesame seeds in a heavy skillet, stirring constantly, until they turn straw colored. Purée them in blender with soy sauce, sesame oil, and 1 tablespoon vegetable oil. Place mixture in a flattish bowl. Stir in green onions and pepper.

Heat oil for frying in a heavy skillet. Wipe fish on toweling, dip slices in sesame mixture, and fry them until golden brown on both sides. Serve immediately.

Tuna, white seabass, tilefish, or grouper may be used.

MAHI MAHI CEVICHE

1 pound mahi mahi (must be very
  fresh)
1 cup lime juice
2 large tomatoes, peeled and diced
1 pickled chili jalapeño, seeded and
  chopped

1 Tablespoon minced cilantro
1/2 teaspoon salt
1/4 teaspoon white pepper
1/4 cup minced onion
1/4 teaspoon rubbed oregano
1 Tablespoon olive oil

Skin, bone, and trim fish of dark meat, cut it into 1/2-inch cubes and put them in a nonmetal bowl. Cover fish with lime juice, then cover bowl and marinate in refrigerator for 4–6 hours until fish is opaque.

Mix together tomatoes, chili, and cilantro and chill. When ready to serve, mix a dressing of salt, pepper, onion, oregano, and olive oil and toss it with vegetables. Combine vegetables and fish mixture, spoon it into sherbet glasses and serve with cocktails, or as a first course of a meal.

Flounder or any firm flesh fish such as tuna, seabass, snapper, or cod may be used, but it must be very fresh.

Idea for Leftover Mahi Mahi
MAHI MAHI GRAPE SALAD

1 cup cooked mahi mahi, in small
  chunks
1/4 cup jicama, 1/4-inch dice*
1 cup large muscat grapes, halved and
  seeded

4 lettuce cups
2 avocados, cut in wedges
Lemon juice

*Jicama is a crisp root vegetable, similar in taste to water chestnuts.

DRESSING

1/2 cup sour cream
2 Tablespoons mayonnaise
1/2 teaspoon curry powder
1 teaspoon instant onion

Dash of cayenne pepper
2 teaspoons lemon juice
Salt to taste

Combine all dressing ingredients and chill for several hours before using.

Combine and chill mahi mahi, jicama bits, and halved grapes. Place a lettuce cup on each of 4 salad plates. Sprinkle avocado wedges with lemon juice and arrange them on lettuce. Combine fish mixture with dressing and toss gently to mix well. Spoon mixture into lettuce cups, across the wedges of avocado.

California black seabass, white seabass, or striped bass may be used.

California Jack Mackerel and Pacific Mackerel

JACK MACKEREL (horse mackerel) swim at the surface in schools, usually in open ocean near offshore banks or islands. When they come inshore, however, they often  team up with Pacific mackerel. They are sleek, streamlined, two- to four-plus-pound fish, with deeply forked tails. Their bodies are iridescent green on top, silvery below, with large scales on their forefront and bony scutes along their lateral line.

Jack mackerel leave the proximity of the California coast each year, March through July, swimming out past the continental shelf into very deep ocean to spawn. They have been sighted swimming as far as 600 miles off the coast. Like Pacific mackerel, they are fed upon by all large predators. They are an important food to albacore, dolphins, and other blue-water fish.

When they return to the coast, anglers take them on small hooks, using live anchovy bait. Market fishermen bring their catch into Monterey and harbors south.

PACIFIC MACKEREL are small pound-size ocean fish that travel in very large schools. They can be found along the entire coast, from Baja California to Alaska. Early in spring and summer they come inshore en masse, and at that time, you can catch them from piers or jetties, using small hooks and live anchovy bait. Commercially they are taken with round haul nets.

Suggested recipes for Pacific mackerel are in Mackerel chapter, pages 245-52.

About Jack Mackerel Meat

Jack, like other mackerel, is rich, firm-textured meat. It is high in oil content and consequently is extremely perishable. Avoid getting fishy-tasting mackerel by looking for fish that are straight and firm, fish with bright clear eyes and red gills—and smell the fish before you buy.

If you catch your own, slit the gills to bleed the fish when caught, then immediately place fish on ice; your mackerel will not be fishy-tasting.

JACK MACKEREL FILLETS GRILLED

2½-3-pound jack mackerel
Juice of ½ lemon
3 Tablespoons soy sauce

3 Tablespoons water
2 cloves garlic, pressed
Oil

Fillet and skin mackerel and remove dark meat layer along the midside. Mix a marinade of lemon juice, soy sauce, water, and garlic, then marinate fish for 30 minutes, turning occasionally. Drain and pat fish dry. Dip fillets in oil, place them in a hot greased hinged grill, and cook over hot coals; or, under the broiler, on a preheated, oiled pan, place the fillets 2 inches from the flame.

SAUCE

3 heaping Tablespoons fried onion
   flakes
2 Tablespoons soy sauce
2 Tablespoons lemon juice

2 Tablespoons water
1 teaspoon seeded and minced mild
   green chili

Heat all ingredients together and serve with grilled mackerel.
   Good for bluefish, bonito, or mullet.

BAKED JACK MACKEREL FILLETS

2½-3-pound jack mackerel,
   filleted
Salt and pepper to taste
1 lemon, sliced thin

Dijon-type mustard
Butter
Chopped parsley

Skin mackerel and remove the dark meat layer along the midsides. Cut the fillets in half crosswise to make 4 fillets, and sprinkle with salt and pepper. Preheat the oven to 425°F. Butter a baking dish and place all but 4 slices of lemon in the dish. Brush mackerel heavily with mustard, and arrange fillets on the lemon. Place a slice of lemon on each, dot with butter, and bake, uncovered, until done. Serve with parsley garnish. (Allow more cooking time if fillets are not completely thawed.)

Perch

PERCH ARE DISTRIBUTED along the entire West Coast, and each area — such as sandy beaches, rocky shores, kelp beds, jetties, or dock areas — has its own species. The greatest concentration of them is off Central and Southern California.

Here are a few general facts about perch. Their bodies are elliptical and their tails are forked. Two pounds or fifteen inches is about their maximum. They mature sexually soon after birth, and all species give birth to live young. They school in shallow water, five to twenty-five feet deep, usually feeding on incoming tide. In rocky areas they bite well on an outgoing tide also, because they eat what is washed down off the rocks. Their tiny mouths can just manage shrimp, worms, clam necks, and the like.

The following is a list of a few of the more commonly sought-after species, traveling from south to north.

From the Mexican border to Pismo Beach, you find:

Barred surfperch (silver perch). They have silver metallic bodies with green or brown vertical bars. They are caught off piers and along sandy beaches.

From Southern California to Central California, you find:

Black perch (buttermouth). They are brown with blackish vertical bars, yellow lips, and alternating blue and orange anal fins. The colors become more intense during breeding season. They school in rocky areas, in bays and estuaries from Baja to Ft. Bragg.

Rubberlip perch. They have silver metallic bodies with yellow, black-tipped fins. Their lips, naturally, are big and droopy. They are taken around jetties, piers, and rocky shores.

Walleye perch. When mating time comes (October to December), dense schools break up and males and females pair off.

From Central to Northern California, you find:

Calico perch. They abound north of San Simeon and around Monterey and San Mateo counties.

In Northern California, Oregon, and Washington, you find:

Redtail perch (pogie or pinkfin). They are dark green on top, silver underneath, with reddish blotched bars on each side and bright light red fins and tail. They are taken from sandy beaches, rocky areas, and jetties.

Pile perch (dusky). They are brown with dark blotches on top and sides, silver underneath, and a dark vertical bar at the midsection. These are one of the largest perches and one of the kinds most often caught.

Striped seaperch. These perch are the most beautiful of the northern species, copper colored with vibrant blue horizontal stripes. They are taken from sandy beaches and rocky areas.

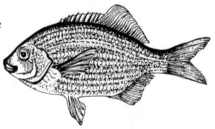

White seaperch. They are all silver and are commercially important fish.

Halfmoon, Opaleye, and Zebraperch. These perch-shaped fish are really members of the sea chub family. The different varieties look alike except for their spectacular colorings. Halfmoons are blue—deep blue on top, pale below. Opaleyes are dusky green with a white spot beneath the dorsal fin and have bright blue eyes. Zebras are light gray with a dozen vertical stripes. These lovely one- to three-pound fish are abundant south of Pt.

Conception, in rocky areas where the kelp is lush. They swim the midwater column alone or in schools, nibbling constantly on their vegetarian diet of algae. Anglers use green peas for bait, divers spearfish them, and the commercial catch is made with nets.

About Perch Meat

Perch is delicately flavored, lean white meat, with a rather coarse texture. Many varieties are small panfish, to be sautéed or pan fried. Larger sizes may be filleted and cooked with or without the skin on. Most of the commercial catch is filleted, flash frozen, and packaged within hours after unloading at the docks.

BROILED FILLETS OF PERCH
WITH TOPPING

Wipe fillets dry, season with lemon juice and salt and pepper. Spread on each a mixture of half mayonnaise/half prepared cream-style horseradish sauce. Place fillets on a hot oiled pan and slide it under the broiler until topping is bubbly and brown and fillets barely flake when tested.
Sole or panfish fillets may be used.

STUFFED PERCH TURBANS
WITH SMETANA SAUCE

2 pounds perch fillets
Juice of 1 lemon
4 Tablespoons (½ stick) butter, melted
1 cup chopped mushrooms
2 Tablespoons minced parsley
2 Tablespoons grated onion
¼ teaspoon monosodium glutamate

⅛ teaspoon thyme
2 Tablespoons fine dry bread crumbs
Salt and pepper to taste
1 cup sour cream
¼ cup minced green onion
1 teaspoon paprika

Mix juice of ½ lemon with melted butter. Cook mushrooms in 1 tablespoon of the lemon-butter until tender. Stir in parsley, onion, monosodium glutamate, and thyme, cook 1 minute and remove from heat. Add crumbs and salt and pepper to taste.

Preheat the oven to 425°F. Wipe fillets, season them with salt and pepper, and place a spoonful of mushroom dressing in the center of each.

Roll them and secure with wooden cocktail picks. Place perch turbans in a buttered casserole, brush with remaining lemon-butter, and bake for 10 minutes per inch thickness of turbans.

Meanwhile, combine sour cream, green onion, paprika, and 2 tablespoons water in a small saucepan. Cook, covered, over low heat for 15 minutes, stirring occasionally.

Transfer perch to a platter. Combine pan juices with sauce, correct seasoning with salt, pepper, and a drop or two of the lemon juice, then pour over fish and serve at once. This dish may be served over rice.

Sole may be used for this dish.

BAKED PERCH
WITH SPICED ALMOND COATING

1½-2 pounds perch fillets	2 teaspoons lemon juice
Salt and pepper	1 teaspoon soy sauce
½ cup almonds	1 teaspoon sugar
1 Tablespoon prepared mustard	4 Tablespoons heavy cream

Wipe fillets, sprinkle lightly with salt and pepper, and arrange them on an oiled broiler pan. Preheat the oven to 425°F. Grind almonds in blender until pulverized, then mix with the remaining ingredients. Spread mixture on the fillets and bake them for 7–10 minutes, or until fish flakes when prodded.

Good for sole or pompano.

PERCH WITH BANANAS
IN GRAPEFRUIT CURRY

1½ pounds perch fillets	Cornstarch
1 egg	1½ Tablespoons each butter and oil
2 Tablespoons milk	2 bananas, halved lengthwise
1 teaspoon salt	1 cup grapefruit juice
Pepper to taste	1 teaspoon curry powder

Beat egg with milk, salt, and pepper. Wipe fillets, dip them in egg mixture and roll them in cornstarch. Heat butter and oil until foamy and fry fillets quickly, browning both sides. Add bananas to the pan, then grapefruit juice mixed with curry. Bring to a boil, lower heat, and simmer for 5 minutes. Serve at once.

Good for any lean white fillet listed on page 446 (III A1).

PAN-FRIED REDTAIL PERCH
OR OPALEYE WITH MUSSELS

Serves 2

1–1½ pounds perch, cleaned
and trimmed
8–10 mussels
1 clove garlic, sliced
½ cup dry white wine
½ cup water
Salt and pepper to taste
Flour
3 slices fresh ginger

1 green onion, split
½ cup salad oil
1 egg
3 Tablespoons milk
1 teaspoon sesame oil
1 Tablespoon minced green onion
1 teaspoon minced ginger
1 Tablespoon vinegar

Scrub mussels, place them in a saucepan with sliced garlic, wine, and water. Cover and boil for about 5 minutes, until the shells open. Remove meat from shells, pull off beards and set them aside. (Strain juice for use another time. It makes good soup base.)

Wipe perch, cut several slashes on each side, season with salt and pepper, dust with flour, and place ginger slices and split green onion in the cavity.

Heat salad oil in a heavy skillet. Beat egg with milk and salt and pepper, dip fish in the egg mixture and fry it over medium-high heat, turning frequently, until it is nicely brown—about 10–14 minutes.

Remove cooked fish from pan and drain off all but 1 tablespoon of oil, then return skillet to the heat. Stir in sesame oil, minced onion, and minced ginger and cook them a few seconds. Dip mussels in egg mixture and put them in the pan, then add fish. Pour remaining egg mixture over the fish and heat, covered, for about 2 minutes, until mussels are warm. Transfer fish to a warm platter and arrange mussels around it. Mix vinegar into the pan juice, then spoon it over the fish and serve.

FRIED PERCH FILLETS

2 pounds perch fillets
3 egg whites
1½ teaspoons salt
1½ Tablespoons plus 2 teaspoons
cornstarch

3 Tablespoons salad oil
3 Tablespoons water
1 Tablespoon sherry
1 green onion, minced
2 teaspoons minced ginger

Cut fillets into 2½-inch pieces. Combine egg whites, 1 teaspoon salt, and 1½ tablespoons cornstarch. Beat with a whisk until frothy, and then dip fish in mixture. Heat oil in a large skillet and fry perch about 2 minutes on each side, until almost done.

Add water and sherry to remaining egg mixture, stir in the remaining 2 teaspoons of cornstarch, and ½ teaspoon salt, the onion, and the ginger. Pour mixture over fried fish, and cook 1 minute more on each side until the liquid becomes translucent.

Serve at once.

Flounder may be used for this dish.

PERCH POACHED IN WINE WITH BERCY SAUCE

2 pounds perch fillets	½ cup hot milk
¼ cup sliced onion	1 egg yolk
Salt and pepper to taste	¼ cup cream
1½ cups dry white wine	½ teaspoon lemon juice
1 bay leaf	1 Tablespoon minced parsley
2 shallots, minced	1-2 Tablespoons butter, softened
2 Tablespoons (¼ stick) butter	(optional)
2 Tablespoons flour	

Preheat the oven to 425°F. Butter a large shallow baking dish and scatter onions over the bottom. Wipe fillets, sprinkle with salt and pepper, and arrange them in single layer (thin fillets may be folded) on onions. Pour in wine, enough water or stock barely to cover fish, and a bay leaf. Cover tightly with foil and heat dish on the stove top, to the boiling point, then bake for 5–10 minutes, depending on thickness of fish.

Transfer fillets to a platter and keep warm. Strain poaching liquid into a saucepan and boil it down until reduced to 1 cup. Discard the solids.

Sauté shallots in the 2 tablespoons butter until tender, add flour, and cook a few seconds. Beat in hot reduced poaching liquid and milk, cooking until sauce thickens and boils. Remove it from heat; then mix an egg yolk with cream, stir it into a little of the hot sauce, then beat this mixture back into the rest of the velouté sauce. Add lemon juice and parsley, season with salt and pepper, and swirl in softened butter until melted, if desired. Drain any collected liquid from platter. Spoon hot sauce over fish and serve at once.

Any lean white fillet listed on page 446 (III A1) may be used.

PERCH FILLETS FLORENTINE

2 pounds perch fillets
At least 1 teaspoon salt
At least ⅛ teaspoon white pepper
⅔ cup dry white wine

Two 10-ounce packages frozen spinach
2 Tablespoons (¼ stick) butter
1½ cups Mornay Sauce (p. 420)
½ cup grated Cheddar cheese

Preheat the oven to 425°F. Sprinkle fillets with 1 teaspoon salt and ⅛ teaspoon pepper, then arrange them in single layer on a shallow buttered baking dish. Heat wine and enough water barely to cover fish to a boil and pour it over perch. Cover dish with foil and bake for 7–10 minutes, depending on thickness of fish. Drain cooked fillets on toweling. Reduce oven temperature to 400°F.

Cook and drain spinach, then add butter and season with salt and pepper. Spread spinach over the bottom of a baking dish and arrange fillets on top. Cover with mornay sauce, sprinkle with Cheddar cheese, and slide the baking dish into the oven to heat until cheese begins to brown.

Good for any lean white fillet listed on page 446 (III A1).

PERCH AND CRAB IN PATTY SHELLS

¾–1 pound perch fillet
Lemon rind
½ cup sliced mushrooms
2 Tablespoons minced green onion
4 Tablespoons (½ stick) butter
3 Tablespoons dry white wine
½ cup crab meat, picked over
2 Tablespoons flour

1¼ cups chicken broth, heated
¼ cup heavy cream
1 egg yolk
Salt and pepper to taste
¼ cup grated cheese (optional)
6 patty shells
Paprika

Poach perch in salted water with a slice of lemon rind (see Basic Poaching, p. 23), then drain and cut the fish into cubes. Sauté mushrooms and onions in 2 tablespoons of the butter until tender. Add wine and simmer a minute, then gently stir in perch and crab meat; set aside while making sauce.

In a saucepan heat the remaining 2 tablespoons butter, whisk in flour, then pour in hot chicken broth and beat until sauce boils. Reduce heat to very low. Mix cream with egg yolk and beat it into the sauce. Stir in fish mixture, season with salt and pepper, stir in cheese and heat through. Spoon mixture into patty shells, sprinkle a dash of paprika on top of each and serve.

Flounder, California sheepshead, haddock, cod, or walleye may be used.

Idea for Leftover Perch

POTATO SALAD WITH PERCH

1 1/2 cups perch, cooked and diced
1 1/2 cups potatoes, cooked and diced
1 teaspoon lemon juice
2 Tablespoons mayonnaise
1/2 teaspoon salt
2 Tablespoons minced green onion

1 Tablespoon minced green pepper
1/3 cup peeled and diced cucumber
1/3 cup finely diced celery
1 Tablespoon bacon chips
Italian seasoned dressing

Combine perch and potatoes. Mix lemon juice, mayonnaise, and salt with fish and potatoes. Add all other ingredients, toss lightly, and chill until served.

Good with catfish too.

Smelts, Silversides, and Whitebait

GRUNIONS ARE SMALL SILVER-
SIDES, five to six inches, that
inhabit shallow water south of Pt.
Conception. Their peculiar spawning
habits draw throngs to the sandy beaches to watch or gather a tasty meal.

Grunion runs occur at night during the new or full moon phase, two or three days after the highest tide. Shortly after the tide peaks, the beach becomes littered with thousands of wriggling, silvery forms. Females, flanked by males, jump out of the water, stranding themselves on the sand. The females bury themselves tail first in the sand so that only their heads are showing. Males curl around females, releasing their milt to fertilize the eggs. The grunions then flop back to the water and are carried out in receding waves.

The eggs remain in the sand until the next high tides two weeks later. Just minutes after the water touches them, they are hatched.

All you need to catch grunion are your two hands, a lantern, and a bucket.

About Smelt Meat

Smelt family fish are oily,
whether they are silversides
such as grunions, or true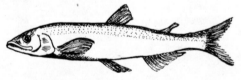
smelts like silver or surf smelts,
or whitebait. All are good broiled or baked, pan fried or deep fried for fish and chips. Jacksmelts, so common around piers and docks, are delicious charcoal grilled or pickled.

Smelts can be boned after cooking by merely opening up the belly cavity and lifting out the head, bones, and tail, all in one piece.

Whole smelts are marketed year round, but are most plentiful during spring or summer runs.

Every year, from May to September, sea-run silver smelts come to spawn in the sandy coves of Yachats, Oregon. Fishermen come from all over to dip their nets into the incoming waves for these tasty little fish. The smelt run is celebrated with a Community Smelt Fry in early July and has become a famous annual event.

GRILLED LARGE SMELTS

2-3 pounds smelts
Melted butter

Fresh fennel or rosemary

Clean, rinse, drain, and wipe smelts dry. Mix egg-vinegar-wine marinade (see below) and marinate for at least 1 hour. When coals are ready, arrange fish (or skewered fish) on the grill and drizzle them with butter as they broil about 2 minutes on each side. Place a sprig of fennel or rosemary that has been dipped in water onto the coals for flavor and aroma. Remove cooked fish from skewers, and serve plain or with barbecue sauce, or catsup.

Grill cisco the same way.

MARINADE FOR GRILLING LARGE SMELTS

2 eggs
1/3 cup vinegar
1 cup dry white wine

1 1/2 teaspoons salt
1/2 teaspoon pepper
2 Tablespoons cornstarch

Beat eggs until frothy, then whisk in the other ingredients. Add smelts and marinate for 1 hour or more.

BROILED JACKSMELT FILLETS

2 pounds smelts
Salt and pepper to taste
Prepared brown mustard

Juice of 1 lemon
Melted butter
Parsley

Clean, rinse, remove fins, and open up fish completely to remove bones. Rinse again and dry. Salt and pepper fillets, spread them with mustard, sprinkle with lemon juice, then set aside for 1 hour.

Preheat the broiler and pan. Place smelts on the oiled hot pan, drizzle with melted butter, and broil until delicately brown. Garnish with parsley.

SAUTÉED SMELT FILLETS WITH ALMONDS

Split fish and remove the fins, the head, and the bones and discard. Sprinkle fillets with lemon juice, salt and pepper, and let them stand for 15 minutes. Dip fillets into egg, then into fine crumbs, and sauté them in butter. Add 1/3 cup slivered almonds to the pan and cook until they turn straw colored. Sprinkle in 1 tablespoon parsley and pour over the smelt fillets.

PAN-FRIED PICKLED SMELTS

2-3 pounds smelts
At least 1 1/2 cups vinegar
4 Tablespoons (1/2 stick) butter,
  softened
4 Tablespoons minced parsley
1/2 cup bread crumbs
1 teaspoon salt

Pepper to taste
4 Tablespoons butter for frying
1 cup sugar
1 teaspoon whole peppercorns
1 clove garlic
1/2 medium onion, sliced
  into very thin rings

Split fish, remove head and bones, and marinate them for 15 minutes in vinegar. Wipe dry and spread open, skin side down, on waxed paper. Spread them with parsley butter (made by creaming softened butter with parsley). Refold the fish around the butter, then roll them in crumbs seasoned with salt and pepper. Fry fish in butter until crisp and brown on both sides.

Combine the 1 1/2 cups of vinegar, the sugar, peppercorns, and garlic in an enameled pan and bring to a boil, stirring to dissolve the sugar. Place fish in a nonmetal baking dish. Scatter onion rings around fish and pour the hot marinade over them. Cover and refrigerate for 24 hours before serving.

DEEP-FRIED PICKLED SMALL SMELTS

2 dozen small smelts
Salt
Flour
Oil for deep frying

1 cup rice vinegar
1/2 cup sugar
1/4 teaspoon monosodium glutamate
1 dried red pepper, crumbled

Clean smelts, sprinkle salt inside and out, and let them stand for 30 minutes, then wipe dry. Dust with flour and deep fry them in hot (375°F.)

oil until brown, then drain on toweling. Place fish in a shallow baking dish or nonmetal bowl.

Combine vinegar, sugar, monosodium glutamate, and crumbled hot pepper and bring to a boil, stirring until sugar is dissolved, then cool. Pour cool marinade over smelts, cover dish, and refrigerate for 24 hours. Turn fish occasionally. They taste best at room temperature.

DEEP-FRIED SILVER SMELT OR JACKSMELT FILLETS

2½ pounds smelts   Oil for deep frying
Vinegar

ONION BATTER

5 Tablespoons flour   ¼ teaspoon pepper
2 Tablespoons water   1 egg, beaten
1 teaspoon salt   2 green onions, minced

Make batter by mixing flour, water, salt, and pepper with beaten egg until smooth; stir in minced onions. Split smelts, remove fins, head, and bones and marinate fillets in vinegar for 15 minutes, then wipe dry.

Dip fillets in batter and deep fry several at a time in hot (375°F.) oil until golden brown. Drain on toweling and serve.

Cisco are delicious deep fried.

Variation: Try a combination of fish—smelts, oysters, shrimp, and rockfish—dipped in batter and deep fried.

DEEP-FRIED WHOLE SMALL SMELTS

3 pounds smelts   Generous milling of pepper
Vinegar   Flour
3 eggs   1 cup fine bread crumbs
½ cup milk   Oil for deep frying
2 Tablespoons oil   Tartar Sauce (p. 426)
1½ teaspoons salt

Clean fish but leave them whole—head and bones pull off easily after cooking. Marinate them in vinegar for 10 minutes, then wipe dry. Beat eggs with milk, the 2 tablespoons of oil, salt, and pepper. Dust smelts with flour, dip them in egg mixture, then roll them in bread crumbs. Deep fry fish in hot (375°F.) oil until nicely brown. Drain briefly on toweling and serve with tartar sauce.

ANCHOVY-STUFFED SMELTS

2½ pounds smelts   1 can anchovy fillets
At least 1 cup fine bread crumbs   2 Tablespoons (¼ stick) butter
Vinegar   Juice of ½ lemon

Generously butter a baking dish and scatter around enough bread crumbs to coat the bottom and sides. (These are in addition to the 1 cup.) Clean smelts, remove head and bones, then marinate them in vinegar for 15 minutes. Wipe fish dry.

Preheat the oven to 425°F.

Open the can of anchovies and reserve the oil for the sauce. Cut anchovies in half lengthwise and place a half inside each fish. Arrange fish in baking dish with backs up, in tight rows, then sprinkle with the 1 cup crumbs. Heat butter with lemon juice and drizzle it over the smelts. Bake them for 10 minutes per inch thickness of fish. Meanwhile, make sauce:

2 Tablespoons minced onion   At least ½ teaspoon salt
Reserved oil from anchovy fillets   ¼ teaspoon pepper
1½ Tablespoons flour   1 Tablespoon lemon juice
1⅓ cups half-and-half, scalding hot   1 Tablespoon chopped fresh dill, or ½
1 egg yolk   teaspoon dried dill

In a saucepan, sauté onion in anchovy oil until tender, then mix in flour. Pour scalding hot half-and-half in all at once, beating until sauce thickens and boils. Mix egg yolk with several spoonfuls of the hot sauce, then stir it into the rest of the sauce. Add salt, pepper, lemon juice, and dill, mix and serve hot with fish.

STUFFED SILVER SMELTS

2½ pounds smelts   2 teaspoons minced chives
Salt   2 eggs, beaten
3 Tablespoons butter   ½ cup rye-meal
2 teaspoons finely minced dill (or   Butter and oil for frying
  ½ teaspoon dried dill with
  1 teaspoon fresh minced parsley)

Split smelts and remove fins, head, and bones. Sprinkle generously with salt and set aside for 1 hour. Cream butter until very soft and mix in herbs.

Lay fish, skin side down, on waxed paper. Put a little herbed butter on each fillet, and brush the edges with egg. Re-form fish, pressing sides together well.

Mix rye-meal with crumbs. Dip smelts in egg, roll them in crumbs, and fry in butter and oil until brown and crunchy.

Rockfish

THERE ARE sixty-three varieties of Sebastes-family rockfish. Most of them are mistakenly called rock cod. They swim the cool-temperate ocean from Alaska to Baja. Some varieties live in the shallow intertidal zone, others at several hundred fathoms—always over the same kind of rubbly, rock bottom that is densely covered with seaweed or kelp. Technically the entire family is identified by the number of spines: thirteen to fifteen sharp spines in the dorsal fin, three in the anal fin, and one in the pelvic fin. All varieties have large heads and deep basslike bodies. All bear live young and are brightly colored. Their markings, depending upon the species, can be spotted or striped, speckled or mottled. Shallow-water varieties, weighing two to six pounds, vary from yellow to blue or black; deepwater species are usually orange to red.

Off Southern California rockfish are found around deep submarine reefs. The catch includes: vermilions—large rockfish called "reds"; bocaccio—up to twenty pounds; chilipeppers—pinky red; and pink-meat greenspots.

Along the Central California coast there are many rocky points jutting out into the surf where shore anglers take yellow-and-black rock cod. Small-skiff fishermen, jigging close to the cliffs and around small inshore rock islands, bring in good catches of gopher and olive rockfish.

Priest fish (blue rockfish) are blue black on top, silver white below. They inhabit shallow to moderately deep water along the entire coast.

Angling the rocky pockets of the Oregon coast can reward you with a bag of copper rockfish and black snapper (Oregonians call them black bass). Many are taken by lucky accident by fishermen trolling for salmon.

In addition to the many small rockfish that inhabit shallow water, there are large deep-water varieties that local commercial fishermen call the "red snapper" group. These are all red orange in color, and are taken around deep submarine reefs from Northern California to Alaska. Orange rock cod (three to twenty pounds) is gourmet-quality fish; yelloweye (turkey fish or red snapper) is the largest of all rockfish, weighing up to thirty pounds.

About Rockfish Meat

Rockfish is mild, flavorful, firm and lean, off-white meat, and is marketed year round. The "red snappers" are especially savored for delicious large, thick fillets. Small two- to five-pound fish are marketed whole locally, but most are filleted. Small whole fish may be stuffed and baked; fillets are best broiled, baked in foil, fried, poached, or steamed.

ROCKFISH MARINADE

2 pounds rockfish fillets	6 Tablespoons (¾ stick) butter, melted
3 Tablespoons lemon juice	Salt and pepper to taste
1 clove garlic, pressed and/or	
2 Tablespoons grated onion	

Mix lemon juice, garlic and/or onion with melted butter. Salt and pepper fillets, arrange them in a single layer in a shallow baking dish, pour butter marinade over them, and marinate for 1 hour. You may then choose the method of cooking.

Preheat the oven to 425°F. Bake marinated fillets in the marinade, allowing 10 minutes cooking time per inch thickness of fillets.

Cut thick marinated fillets in serving pieces and barbecue on a hot greased grill, about 4–6 inches above coals, for 14–18 minutes, basting with marinade and turning as needed.

Oven broil marinated fillets, on a preheated oiled broiler pan 2 inches from the heat, for 5–10 minutes, depending on the thickness of fillets.

ROCKFISH STEAMED IN MILK

1½ pounds rockfish fillet	Butter
Salt to taste	Minced parsley
1½ cups milk	2 teaspoons cornstarch
3 Tablespoons water	

Cut fillet into serving pieces. Sprinkle with salt and arrange them in a single layer in a heatproof bowl. Mix milk and water, season with salt, and pour into the bowl. Dot fish with butter and sprinkle with minced parsley. Cover bowl and steam 12–18 minutes until cooked (see Basic Steaming, page 27). Thicken milk gravy with cornstarch and serve at once.

CHINA BASIN WHOLE STEAMED ROCK COD

1½–2-pound rockfish, cleaned and degilled	1 Tablespoon dry sherry
	1 green onion, minced
1 Tablespoon fermented salted black beans	1 Tablespoon peanut oil
	½ teaspoon sesame oil
1 teaspoon minced fresh ginger	1 Tablespoon minced cilantro
1 clove garlic	1 Tablespoon minced green onion
1 Tablespoon soy sauce	

Trim, rinse, and dry rockfish. Cut several diagonal slashes, ¼ inch deep, on both sides of fish and place it on a heatproof platter.

Wash and drain black beans and, in a small bowl, mash with minced ginger and garlic. Stir in soy sauce and sherry. Brush fish with this mixture inside and out. Scatter minced onion over fish and steam for 15–20 minutes. (See Basic Steaming, page 27, for details.)

When fish is cooked, remove platter from steamer. Combine oils, heat them to smoking point, and pour sizzling over fish. Scatter over minced cilantro and 1 tablespoon minced onion and serve at once.

Good with Atlantic black seabass.

STEAMED FILLETS

Arrange serving pieces of rockfish in a heatproof serving dish. Sprinkle with sherry and soy sauce and scatter over the other ingredients from the preceding recipe. Place dish on rack and steam 7–10 minutes, depending on thickness of fillets (see Basic Steaming, page 27). Pour hot oil over cooked fish, as in preceding recipe, and garnish with onion and cilantro.

COULIBIAC

Coulibiac is Russian bread roll, stuffed with fish, usually salmon. Make dough 8–12 hours prior to baking.

DOUGH

1 package yeast	2 Tablespoons sugar
¼ cup lukewarm water	1 cup boiling water
4 Tablespoons (½ stick) butter	1 egg
1½ teaspoons salt	About 2⅔ cups all-purpose flour

Dissolve yeast in lukewarm water. Combine butter, salt, and sugar in a large bowl, pour boiling water over them, and stir with a whisk until dissolved. When mixture has cooled to lukewarm, stir in dissolved yeast, then beat in egg. Stir in flour, making a soft dough. Cover the bowl and chill dough 3–12 hours (no kneading). Dough will triple in bulk. Thirty minutes before baking, spread dough out thin, to cover a 15-inch-long sheet of plastic wrap. (Or line a 9 × 14-inch buttered baking dish with half of the dough.) Meanwhile, prepare:

FILLING

1 pound red snapper fillet	3 hard-boiled eggs
1½ Tablespoons oil	1 cup chopped green onion
Salt and pepper to taste	1 cup sliced fresh mushrooms
1¼ cups cooked rice	Pinch of fennel
8 Tablespoons (1 stick) butter	2 Tablespoons dry white wine
¼ cup chopped parsley	1 egg, beaten

Wipe fish, cut it into strips, and cook in oil for 2 or 3 minutes, until it turns white, then season with salt and pepper. Mix cooked rice with 2 tablespoons of the butter and the parsley. Slice hard-boiled eggs. Sauté onion and mushrooms seasoned with fennel in 4 tablespoons of the butter until tender. Season to taste and add wine.

Preheat the oven to 375°F. Melt remaining 2 tablespoons of butter, then brush them on dough. Layer filling on half of the dough, arrange the fish in a layer, then the rice, then the mushroom-onion mixture, and egg slices on top. Fold dough over the filling, tuck it in, and pinch the edges to seal. Transfer coulibiac carefully, rolling it off the plastic wrap, onto a buttered baking sheet. Brush dough with beaten egg and bake for 30–40 minutes. Serve hot or cold, with an herbed melted butter or Hollandaise Sauce (p. 422), if you like.

Any firm mild-flavored fillet, such as snapper and seabass, found on page 447 (III A2), may be used.

ROCKFISH FILLETS BAKED IN FOIL

2 pounds rockfish fillets
1 onion, minced
4 Tablespoons (½ stick) butter
1 cup sliced mushrooms
4 Tablespoons flour
1 cup dry white wine

1 cup half-and-half, scalding hot
½ teaspoon salt
Pepper to taste
½ teaspoon dried dill
1½ teaspoons dried tarragon
1 Tablespoon capers

Lightly salt and pepper serving pieces of rockfish, then set aside while making sauce.

Sauté onion in butter until tender, add mushrooms, and cook them until soft. Mix in flour, then add wine and scalded half-and-half, stirring while sauce becomes smooth, thickens, and boils. Season with salt, pepper, dill, tarragon, and capers, simmer a minute or two, then remove from heat and let cool.

Preheat the oven to 450°F. Tear off pieces of foil, about 9 × 12 inches, for each serving and butter foil to within 1½ inches of its edges. Place a spoonful of sauce on one-half of the foil, a piece of fish on it and another spoonful of sauce to cover the fish. Fold foil in half, then double fold the edges to seal the package tightly. Bake for 15 minutes, until each package is puffed.

Any lean white fillet listed on page 446 (III A1) may be used.

BAKED ROCK COD CURRY

3½–4-pound rock cod, cleaned,
   trimmed, and degilled
½ lemon
At least ½ teaspoon salt
1 onion, chopped
6 cloves garlic
4 slices fresh ginger
1½ teaspoons ground turmeric

½ teaspoon cumin
¼ cup water
⅓ cup oil
½ cup tomato paste
1 red pepper, seeded and crushed
½ cup chopped cilantro
Dash of pepper
Juice of ½ lemon

Rub skin of rock cod with half a lemon, sprinkle lightly with salt, and set aside while making sauce.

Combine onion, garlic, ginger, turmeric, cumin, and water in blender and purée to a smooth paste. Heat oil, add purée and cook, stirring constantly, for about 5 minutes. Add tomato paste, hot pepper, and cilantro and continue cooking and stirring until well integrated, then remove the curry paste from heat. Season with the 1/2 teaspoon salt, the pepper, and the lemon juice.

Preheat the oven to 400°F. Butter a piece of foil large enough to envelop the fish to within 1 1/2 inches of the foil's edges. Wipe fish, cut 4 diagonal slashes on each side, and brush evenly with curry paste, inside and out. Wrap fish in foil and bake for 30 minutes. Loosen foil to expose fish and place under broiler to brown and finish cooking, about 10 minutes. Baste while broiling.

Transfer fish to a platter and serve with pan juices, rice, and condiments, such as: chopped cucumbers and tomatoes, roasted peanuts, coconut shreds, chutney, sliced bananas, raisins, yogurt, and chopped green peppers.

Ling cod, striped bass, red snapper, redfish, or cod may be used.

POACHED ROCK COD DIEGO

2 rockfish, 1 pound each;	1 small chili
or 2 pounds red snapper fillet,	2 whole allspice berries
1 inch thick	1/2 teaspoon thyme
4 cups water	1/4 cup dry white wine
1/2 cup lime juice	Pepper to taste
At least 1 Tablespoon salt	2 Tablespoons minced parsley
3 cloves garlic, pressed	Lime wedges
1 onion, chopped fine	

Clean, trim, and degill rockfish or cut fillet into serving pieces.

Mix a marinade of 2 cups of the water, lime juice, 1 tablespoon of the salt, and 2 cloves of the garlic, stirring until salt is dissolved. Pour over fish; if not completely covered, add more water. Marinate fish, turning occasionally, for 1 hour, then drain and discard the marinade.

Pour the remaining 2 cups of water into a heavy skillet. Add onion, the remaining pressed garlic clove, the chili, allspice, and thyme. Cover skillet, bring to a boil, and simmer 5 minutes. Add rockfish, return broth to a boil, then simmer very slowly for 8-10 minutes, until fish is cooked. Remove fish to a deep platter and keep warm. Stir wine into broth, season with salt and pepper, and pour broth over fish. Scatter parsley over rockfish and garnish platter with several lime wedges. Serve at once, with boiled rice and/or fried bananas.

Red snapper may be used for this dish.

SWEET-AND-SOUR WHOLE ROCK COD

2–3-pound rockfish, cleaned and degilled	1 teaspoon salt
2 Tablespoons soy sauce	Flour
2 eggs, beaten	Cornstarch
	Oil for frying

Trim rockfish, rinse well, and pat dry. If your fish is too large for your wok or skillet, remove the head and tail. Cut 4 diagonal slashes on each side. Brush fish inside and out with soy sauce and let stand for 5–10 minutes. Dip fish in beaten egg mixed with salt, then roll it in flour. Set fish aside until sauce is made.

Sweet-and-Sour Sauce

2¼ Tablespoons cornstarch	3 Tablespoons dry sherry
1 cup water	4 slices fresh ginger
½ cup vinegar	4 Tablespoons instant dried onion
6 Tablespoons sugar	2 tomatoes, cut in large slices
4 Tablespoons soy sauce	1 green pepper, cut in large slices
½ teaspoon salt	

Dissolve 2¼ tablespoons cornstarch in water, then combine all other ingredients in a saucepan and stir while cooking the sauce, until it thickens and boils; set aside and keep hot.

Just before frying, dust fish with cornstarch. Deep fry to golden brown in hot (350°F.) oil. (Turn fish often while frying to assure even cooking and crispiness.) Transfer the cooked fish to a warm platter and pour steaming hot sauce over fried fish. At the table pass a bowl of thin-sliced canned Chinese Pickle Mixed Vegetables and red ginger.

Atlantic black seabass is delicious served this way.

CIOPPINO

Serves 6

2 pounds rockfish fillets	½ cup minced parsley
2 Dungeness crabs	¼ cup olive oil
2 dozen clams in shell	1 large (28-ounce) can tomatoes
At least 1 teaspoon salt	8-ounce can tomato sauce
Pepper to taste	2 cups red wine
1 cup chopped onion	1 bay leaf
1 Tablespoon minced garlic	½ teaspoon oregano
⅓ cup chopped green pepper	½ teaspoon basil

Cut fillets into 2-inch pieces, season with salt and pepper, and set aside. Clean crab, crack legs and claws, then cut body into 4 pieces. Scrub clams.

Sauté onion, garlic, green pepper, and ¼ cup of the parsley in olive oil until they brown lightly. Into a large enamel kettle, pour tomatoes (break them up with a spoon), tomato sauce, wine, sautéed vegetables, the 1 teaspoon salt, pepper to taste, and the bay leaf, oregano, and basil. Bring to boil and simmer 10 minutes, covered. Add clams, then fish, crab, and remaining ¼ cup parsley. Cover kettle again, bring to boil, lower heat, and simmer 8-10 minutes. Serve with garlic French bread.

Any firm lean white fillet listed on page 447 (III A2) may be substituted for rockfish. See also Crab Cioppino, page 371.

BOUILLABAISSE

Serves 6–8

1½ pounds red snapper fillet
1 pound seabass fillet
½ pound sole fillet
1 pound raw prawns in shell
1 onion, chopped
4 cloves garlic, pressed
2 leeks, sliced
½ cup olive oil
6 cups water
2 cups tomato purée

2 tomatoes, peeled and cut in wedges
1 teaspoon each salt, thyme, and
    grated lemon rind
¼–½ teaspoon saffron
Cayenne pepper to taste
2 potatoes, peeled, sliced, and
    precooked, but underdone
¼ cup dry white wine
2 sprigs parsley, minced

Cook onion, garlic, and leeks in olive oil until onion is lightly brown. Add water, tomato purée, tomatoes, and seasonings. Cover, bring to a boil, and simmer gently for 15 minutes. Meanwhile, wipe fish and cut it into serving pieces. Wash and slit shells of prawns to remove the vein. To the broth add potatoes, snapper, and seabass, then prawns and sole last. Cover kettle, bring to a boil, and simmer slowly for 10–12 minutes. Add wine and parsley, remove from heat, and serve with sourdough French bread.

Ideas for Leftover Rockfish

ROCKFISH HASH

2 cups rockfish, cooked and flaked
2 cups cold boiled potatoes, diced
1 green onion, minced

1 egg, beaten
Salt and pepper to taste
3 Tablespoons bacon fat or salt pork

Combine ingredients and fry in hot fat until brown. Serve with catsup.

STUFFED CELERY STALKS
OR SANDWICH FILLING

1 cup rockfish, cooked and flaked
1/2 cup minced celery
4 Tablespoons chopped pimiento
1/2 teaspoon grated onion
1/2 teaspoon curry powder

Few drops of lemon juice
2 Tablespoons sour cream or
  mayonnaise
Salt and pepper to taste

Mix ingredients and spoon onto crisp celery sticks or spread for sandwiches.

Flatfish

FLOUNDER, SOLE, AND SAND DABS

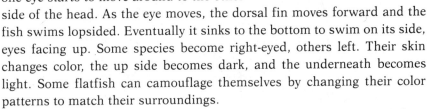

FLATFISH ARE A UNIQUE PHENOM-
ENON in the fish world. Sole,
flounder, turbot, and halibut—
all flatfish—start life swimming
in an upright position, with an eye
on either side of the head. Before long,
one eye starts to move around to the other
side of the head. As the eye moves, the dorsal fin moves forward and the
fish swims lopsided. Eventually it sinks to the bottom to swim on its side,
eyes facing up. Some species become right-eyed, others left. Their skin
changes color, the up side becomes dark, and the underneath becomes
light. Some flatfish can camouflage themselves by changing their color
patterns to match their surroundings.

Flounder have long, continuous, soft-rayed dorsal and anal fins.
Characteristically, they ripple through the water, glide to the bottom, flip
sand on their backs, and lie buried in sandy mud with only their eyes
sticking out. Most are deepwater fish living out of the range of anglers. The
market catch is made with trawl nets, and the bulk is filleted, flash frozen,
and sold either under its own name or the loose term "fillet of sole."

Nearly 200 species of flatfish inhabit the coastlines of the United
States, and the following are some of the most popular flounder.

On the Pacific Coast:

Petrale sole (brill) have excellent flavor, firm meat, and large thick
fillets. They grow to five or six pounds and are caught from Mexico
to Alaska in depths of sixty feet or more.

Pacific English sole (flounder) is firm, delicious meat. Fresh small
fillets (four inches or so) are marketed, usually skinned.

Butter sole are filleted and sold fresh or frozen. They are occasionally caught by sport fishermen, drift-fishing around silty soft bottom areas, but most are taken with trawl from California to Alaska.

Pacific Dover sole (flounder) have soft meat that tends to be mushy. Dover can weigh up to seven pounds, but smaller fish are best. Commercially important, they are caught from California to Alaska.

Curlfin sole are deep bodied fish with fine flesh. They are fished from California to Alaska and marketed all year.

Sand sole are taken on the northern coast. Fresh or frozen six-inch fillets are marketed skinned.

Starry flounder are shallow water game fish found from Central California to the Bering Sea. They are taken by still-fishing, throughout the year, and are marketed locally.

Rex sole are small, slender, excellent quality fish, marketed whole dressed with skin off or left on.

On the Atlantic Coast:

Winter flounder (blackback, blueback, mud dab, or lemon sole) are superb table and game fish, found in bays, channels, and inlets from the Gulf of St. Lawrence to Chesapeake Bay. They are still- or drift-fished on light tackle.

Witch flounder (gray sole or pole flounder) weigh from one to four pounds. They are thinner but otherwise nearly identical to blackback. They are caught with trawls in deep water.

Summer flounder (fluke) are excellent table fish and are the most important game and commercial catch of mid-Atlantic states.

Yellowtail flounder (rusty dab) are thin bodied and medium sized (one to two pounds). Taken in depths of thirty to three hundred feet from Labrador to Virginia, they are occasionally caught by party boaters, drift-fishing.

American plaice (Canadian plaice, dab) are ten- to eighteen-inch fish with firm, delicious flesh taken in cool, deep waters, from the Grand Bank to Rhode Island.

In the Gulf of Mexico:

Southern flounder are twelve- to twenty-inch fish very similar to summer flounder. They are found in shallow coastal water over sandy/mud bottom from North Carolina to Texas.

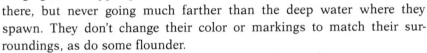

PACIFIC SAND DABS are found near harbors and around shrimping grounds
from Baja to the Northern coast
of Alaska. They are abundant
on sandy or mud bottoms in
water of between twenty and
fifty fathoms. Dabs collect in
congregations, rippling from here to
there, but never going much farther than the deep water where they
spawn. They don't change their color or markings to match their surroundings, as do some flounder.

Sand dabs are always left-eyed. They have thin scales and a nearly
straight lateral line. They average eight to ten inches and weigh about
a pound.

Anglers bottom-fish from skiffs, with ten to twelve hooked lines sus-
pended from a metal ring. Squid is used as bait because it holds to the
hooks well. In Southern California scuba divers catch all these fish with
nets.

To prepare delicate dabs (and also rex sole) for cooking, scale, clean,
remove head, and trim, rinse and pat fish dry on toweling. They may be
cooked with skin on or removed.

Dabs and rex sole may be grilled or sautéed meunière.

Both fish may be dipped in beaten egg, then dredged in flour, and
seasoned with salt, pepper, and garlic powder as they are sautéed in
butter and oil until golden crispy brown. Serve with Tartar Sauce (p. 426).

About Flounder and Sole Meat

Delicate texture and delicate flavor characterize the soft, lean, fine-grained
flounder and sole family meats. Flounder average a quarter pound to five
pounds and are marketed year round. Pacific sand dabs and rex sole are
among the smallest flounder. Small flounder are excellent panfish. After
cooking, most of their many bones can be lifted out intact during eating.
Instructions for filleting larger flounder are on page 6. The meat of petrale
sole and winter and summer flounder is fine and firm enough to be used in
making French fillet of sole dishes. Flounder may be barbecued, baked
in foil, butter sautéed, poached, or steamed. They adapt well to all kinds
of sauces.

GRILLED FLOUNDER FILLETS

4 thick flounder fillets, 1/2 pound each
Salt and pepper to taste
Flour
1 clove garlic, pressed
Juice of 1/2 lemon

6 Tablespoons (3/4 stick) butter, melted
1/2 cup oil, if charcoal broiling
Sprig parsley, minced
Lemon wedges

Wipe fillets, sprinkle with salt and pepper, dust lightly with flour and shake off the excess. Preheat the broiler and pan. Mix garlic and lemon juice into melted butter. Brush or dip fillets in butter and arrange them on an oiled broiler pan. (If charcoal broiling, mix garlic and lemon juice with oil and marinate fillets for 30 minutes.) See Oven Broiling Chart on page 14 for cooking time. Baste while cooking. Serve on a warm platter, garnish with parsley and lemon wedges.

GRILLED FILLET OF SOLE AMANDINE

Grill sole as in preceding recipe. Fry 1/4 cup sliced or slivered almonds in a little butter until light golden brown. Stir in a spoonful of minced parsley and a few drops of lemon juice. Spoon topping onto grilled fillets and serve.
Mahi mahi may be used.

GRILLED PACIFIC SAND DABS OR REX SOLE

Sand dabs or rex sole may be dipped in seasoned melted butter and grilled 2-4 minutes on a large electric sandwich grill, preheated to the highest heat.

Or arrange buttered fish on a hot broiler pan and broil them quickly, basting often. Serve them with Tartar Sauce (p. 426).

SOLE MEUNIÈRE

Dip fish briefly in milk, dust with flour, shake off the excess. Heat enough butter and oil to cover the bottom of a heavy skillet 1/8 inch deep. Heat until it foams, then sauté fish until brown and crisp on both sides.

Make a sauce by heating fresh butter until bubbly, squeeze in lemon juice, stir with a spoonful of minced parsley, and pour sizzling over the sautéed fish.

PAN-FRIED FLOUNDER
WITH MUSHROOMS AND ALMONDS

4 thick flounder fillets, ½ pound each
¼ cup slivered almonds
4 Tablespoons (½ stick) butter
1 cup sliced mushrooms
At least 1 teaspoon salt
½ cup milk

Flour
2 Tablespoons oil
¼ cup minced green onions
½ cup dry white wine
Pepper to taste

Sauté almonds in 2 tablespoons of the butter until lightly golden brown, then remove nuts from pan and set aside. In the same butter, sauté mushrooms quickly, until just tender, then remove from heat, set aside, and keep warm.

Dissolve 1 teaspoon of the salt in the milk. Wipe fillets dry, dip them in salted milk, and dust with flour. Heat the remaining 2 tablespoons of butter with oil in a large, heavy skillet and fry fillets until nicely brown on both sides. Transfer cooked fish to a warm platter.

Turn fire up to very hot and toss mushrooms and onions in the pan for about 30 seconds. Pour in wine, bring to a boil, then stir in almonds and season with salt and pepper.

Spoon topping over fillets and serve.

Good with pompano too.

DEEP-FRIED FILLETS OF SOLE

8 fillets of sole, skinned,
  ¼ pound each
1 teaspoon salt
¼ teaspoon pepper
2 Tablespoons lemon juice

Light Batter for Fish (p. 20)
Oil for deep frying
Sprig parsley, minced
Tomato Sauce (p. 433)

Wipe fillets, sprinkle with salt, pepper, and lemon juice, and set them aside while making batter.

Dip sole in batter, let it drip for a moment, then deep fry in hot (375°F.) oil until crispy brown. Drain on toweling and keep warm until all are cooked. Scatter minced parsley on fish and serve with a bowl of tomato sauce.

Pompano may be used.

BAKED FILLET OF SOLE ALLA ANDREAS

2 pounds fillet of sole
1/2 cup milk
1 teaspoon salt
1/4 teaspoon pepper
1 cup fine sourdough French bread
　crumbs
2 cans condensed cream of mushroom
　soup, undiluted

3/4 cup dry sherry
3/4 cup Chablis
1 teaspoon soy sauce
1 teaspoon bottled teriyaki sauce
1 teaspoon white vinegar
3 Tablespoons lemon juice

Combine milk with salt and pepper and stir until salt is dissolved. Dip sole in milk, then gently press each fillet in crumbs, coating both sides well. Dry them on waxed paper while making sauce.

Heat mushroom soup in a saucepan until it boils. Preheat the oven to 350°F. Combine sherry, Chablis, soy and teriyaki sauces, vinegar, and lemon juice and stir into mushroom soup. Heat, stirring, to a boil, then pour half of the sauce into a large shallow baking dish. Spread it over the bottom and arrange fillets on top. Bake for 7–10 minutes, or until coating turns golden brown. Remove from oven and pour over remaining sauce, then return dish to the oven to bake for another 10 minutes. Serve hot, with rice.

QUENELLES OF SOLE

Quenelles are little forcemeat rolls made of ground fish, cream, and panada (a binding paste that also gives body to the quenelles), beaten together, with the aid of a food processor. The beaten mixture is chilled, formed into sausagelike rolls, then dropped into hot stock or salted water, like a dumpling, to cook. After cooking they are served with a sauce, such as Velouté Sauce (p. 420), Shrimp Sauce (p. 420), or White Butter Sauce (p. 431), and often on rice.

1 1/2 pounds fillet of sole
1/2 cup milk
1 1/2 teaspoons salt
11 Tablespoons (1 stick plus
　3 Tablespoons) butter, softened

1/2 cup sifted all-purpose flour
2 egg yolks, beaten
1/4 teaspoon white pepper
1/4 teaspoon nutmeg
2 eggs

Combine milk, 1 teaspoon of the salt, and 3 tablespoons of the butter in a heavy saucepan, bring to the boiling point, and remove from heat. Add flour all at once, mix in beaten egg yolks, and beat vigorously with a wooden spoon for 1 minute. Return to heat and cook slowly, beating constantly, until mixture shrinks from the sides and bottom of the pan and forms a mass. Remove mixture to a buttered bowl and chill the panada thoroughly.

Cut sole into small pieces and put it through the meat grinder twice, using the fine blade. Add the remaining 1/2 teaspoon of salt, the pepper, and the nutmeg, and beat well (use pastry attachment). Beat in chilled panada and the remaining stick of butter, then 2 eggs, one at a time, integrating each completely before adding the other. Refrigerate mixture until thoroughly chilled.

Make a test by taking a rounded soupspoon of the mixture, shaping it into a 21/2-inch cylinder by rolling it in your hands. Drop the dumpling into salted water or broth, about 4 inches deep and barely simmering. (If the water boils, the quenelle might split.) Poach for 5–10 minutes. If the quenelle disintegrates, beat another egg yolk or two into the mixture. If it is too dry, beat in a little cream, a tablespoon at a time. Test after each addition. If the test is just right, shape the remaining mixture into little rolls and poach them.

Quenelles are cooked when they have doubled in size and roll over easily in the poaching liquid. As they are cooked, place them on a buttered plate and keep warm until sauced and served on rice; or sauce them, sprinkle with grated cheese, and brown under the broiler. If they are not to be used until later, dip them in melted butter and refrigerate in a covered bowl.

Shrimp Sauce for Quenelles

4 Tablespoons (1/2 stick) butter	1 teaspoon lemon juice
3 Tablespoons flour	1/2 teaspoon salt
1 cup White Wine Fish Stock (p. 26)	Pinch of sugar
1/2 cup heavy cream	Dash of cayenne pepper
2 Tablespoons Shrimp Butter (use 1/2	2 Tablespoons brandy
of recipe, p. 432)	1 Tablespoon Madeira

Melt 2 tablespoons of the butter in a saucepan and stir in flour. Add the fish stock and cream, and cook, stirring with a whisk, until thickened. Add the shrimp butter, the lemon juice, the salt, sugar, and the cayenne pepper. Stir in brandy and Madeira, then blend in the remaining 2 tablespoons of butter, bit by bit.

Preheat the oven to 350°F. Place a single layer of quenelles in a buttered baking dish, and spoon the shrimp sauce over them. Cover the dish tightly with foil and put in the oven to bake for 20 minutes. Don't uncover quenelles during baking or they will fall.

Pike may be used.

SOLE VÉRONIQUE

8 fillets of sole
2 cups muscat grapes
½ cup Liebfraumilch or other
    medium-dry white wine

Juice of ½ lemon
Salt and white pepper
1 cup White Wine Fish Stock (p. 26)

Peel, halve, and seed grapes, then marinate them in wine for 1 hour. Wipe fillets, press to flatten, and fold them in half, then sprinkle with lemon juice and salt and white pepper. Preheat the oven to 425°F. Arrange sole in a buttered baking dish and spoon grapes around the fish. Heat white wine fish stock to boiling point and pour over fillets. Cover baking dish with foil and poach in the oven for 10 minutes per inch thickness of fish.

Transfer cooked fish to a platter, cover, and keep warm. Remove grapes from poaching liquid and set them aside. Place liquid in a saucepan and, over high heat, reduce it to ¼ cup. Cool the concentrate and with it make a mousseline sauce.

SAUCE

3 egg yolks
¼ cup heavy cream
¼ cup reserved reduced stock
    concentrate

8 Tablespoons (1 stick) butter, softened
    and cut into ½-ounce pieces
Salt and pepper to taste
Lemon juice

Combine egg yolks, cream, and concentrate in the top of a double boiler and, over low heat, beat with a whisk until thickened enough to coat the whisk. (Don't overheat; it will scramble the eggs.) Remove from heat and beat in pieces of butter, one at a time, integrating each well before adding the next. Sauce should be as thick as hollandaise. Season with salt and pepper and a few drops of lemon juice.

Drain off any juices that have collected on the fish platter. Spoon some sauce and some grapes on each fillet and serve. The remaining sauce may be passed at the table.

Pompano may be used.

POACHED SOLE IN WINE SAUCE
WITH CHEESE

2 pounds fillet of sole	2 Tablespoons (¼ stick) butter
¼ cup chopped onion	3 Tablespoons flour
2 small bay leaves	¾ cup milk, scalding hot
Salt and pepper to taste	Pinch each of basil, thyme, and pepper
1 cup dry white wine	Mozzarella cheese, sliced

Preheat the oven to 425°F. Butter a large baking dish and scatter chopped onion and bay leaves over the bottom. You may fold very thin fillets in half, sprinkle them with salt and pepper, and arrange them on the onion. Pour in wine and enough boiling water or stock barely to cover fish. Cover dish tightly with foil and heat on the stove top to the boiling point, then bake for 10 minutes per inch thickness of fish.

Transfer cooked fillets to individual ovenproof plates or a broiler-to-table platter. Strain, then boil down poaching liquid to 1 cup.

Meanwhile, make a sauce. Heat butter with flour, beat in hot milk, stirring as it thickens. Add reduced poaching liquid and stir in seasonings.

Place thin slices of mozzarella cheese on fish, pour sauce on top to cover and put under the broiler until sauce browns. Fried tomatoes complement this dish.

POACHED FILLET OF SOLE WITH SHRIMP

1½ pounds fillet of sole	Tartar Sauce (p. 426)
Salt and pepper to taste	1 pound cooked shrimp, deveined and
¼ cup chopped onion	shelled
Sprig fresh fennel	Sliced oranges
½ cup dry white wine	Sprigs parsley
½ cup boiling water	Black olives

Preheat the oven to 425°F. Salt and pepper fillets, arrange them in a single layer on a buttered baking dish, and add onion, fennel, wine, and boiling water. Cover the dish and poach fillets in the oven for 10 minutes per inch thickness of fillets.

Drain cooked sole on toweling, then place on a platter. Mask each with a thick coating of tartar sauce and arrange cooked shrimp on top. Garnish platter with sliced oranges, parsley sprigs, and black olives and serve.

Good for pompano.

Idea for Leftover Flounder and Sole

CREAMED FLOUNDER OR SOLE

1 cup cooked flounder, flaked
5 Tablespoons butter
3 Tablespoons flour
2 cups hot milk
1/2 teaspoon salt
1/4 teaspoon white pepper

Dash of cayenne pepper
1 Tablespoon lemon juice
1 green onion, minced
1/2 cup cooked peas
2 hard-boiled eggs, chopped
1/2 cup bread crumbs

Preheat the oven to 350°F. Melt 2 tablespoons of the butter, stir in flour and cook until bubbly, then beat in hot milk, cooking until sauce thickens and boils. Remove from heat and season with salt, pepper, cayenne, and lemon juice. Stir in flaked fish, green onion, peas, and chopped eggs. Pour into a small buttered casserole and top with the remaining 3 tablespoons butter mixed with crumbs. Bake until the crumbs brown.

Monkfish may be used for this dish.

Sturgeon

PACIFIC GREEN and white
sturgeon, and Atlantic
sturgeon are game
fish. They start out
in freshwater, spend
most of their life in the ocean, but migrate back into freshwater to spawn
(as do shad, striped bass, etc.). They grow very large—some weigh over
300 pounds—and may live fifty years or more. Scientists determine the age
of fish by counting growth rings on scales or ear bones, like growth rings
on trees. In summer when growth is rapid the rings are wide, in winter
growth slows down, rings form closer together, completing the ring cycle
for the year.

Sturgeons have a long snout with four feelers (barbels) hanging. Their
mouths are underslung like sharks'. The feelers, just in front of the mouth,
feel out food as they swim along the bottom, and their mouth opens to
scoop it up. Their bodies are scaleless, covered with leathery hide and five
rows of sharp diamond-shaped bony shields on each side. These can be
dangerously abrasive for a person handling a hooked fish.

The Mississippi shovelnose and Great Lakes sturgeon are some of the
freshwater species. Pacific sturgeon range from Central California through
Washington. Atlantic range from Maine to the Gulf of Mexico. They are
found in bays, in tidewater of deltas, and in deep holes and pockets of
rivers. Large fish remain in deep main channels, smaller sturgeon can be
found in the sloughs.

Fishing season is year round, but early spring when they follow
herring runs into the bays is best (February–April, especially just after a
rain). Big sturgeon, however, are not caught every day even by delta or
river sportsmen specifically fishing for them, because sturgeon take bait
(grass shrimp or other) so gingerly their bite is often missed, and when a
bite is felt it takes a strong jerk to set the hook in that very tough mouth.
They are strong fighters when hooked and leap and run with incredible
stamina.

About Sturgeon Meat

Lean white sturgeon meat is rich in flavor but firm and dry in texture, like animal meat. It has no small bones. The meat may be broiled, baked in sauce, butter sautéed, fried, braised, or steamed. White sturgeon is considered more choice.

It is marketed fresh in the Northwest, in steak form or chunks, especially during spring and summer. Much of the canned smoked sturgeon comes from Astoria, Oregon and Ilwaco, Washington. Sturgeon roe makes the best Russian-type caviar.

GRILLED STURGEON SLICES

1½ pounds sturgeon slices	2 teaspoons grated lemon rind
Salt and pepper to taste	1 green onion, chopped
½ cup olive oil	¼ teaspoon thyme (optional)
⅔ cup dry white wine	Fennel Butter (see below)

Salt and pepper sturgeon slices. Mix a marinade of oil, wine, lemon rind, onion, and thyme, pour over steaks, and marinate for at least 1 hour. Baste with marinade while grilling and serve the steaks with Fennel Butter:

Fennel Butter

Remove 3 branches from a fennel bulb, trim off the ferny tops, then mince the stalks. Place fennel in a strainer and blanch in boiling water for a minute; drain, then douse in cold water for a few seconds. Drain fennel again, and empty the mince onto toweling to dry a little.

Sauté fennel in 4 tablespoons (½ stick) butter for about 15 seconds. Remove from heat, and stir in 1 tablespoon lemon juice and pepper to taste, or 1 teaspoon Anisette liquor.

STURGEON BAKED IN SOUR CREAM

2 pounds sturgeon steak	1 Tablespoon oil
Salt and pepper to taste	1 teaspoon paprika
1 onion, chopped	1 cup sour cream
1 carrot, minced	Parsley
1 stalk celery, minced	

Preheat the oven to 450°F. Cut sturgeon into serving slices, season with salt and pepper, and arrange them in a buttered baking dish. Sauté onion, carrot, and celery in hot oil until almost tender, then add cooked vegetables around fish. Mix paprika with sour cream, spread it over fish, then cover and bake for 10 minutes per inch thickness of fish. Serve sauced sturgeon and vegetables on a warm platter garnished with parsley.

STURGEON SAUTÉ
WITH BÉARNAISE SAUCE

Make Béarnaise Sauce according to recipe on page 423, then sauté flour-dusted sturgeon slices in butter and oil until brown and crisp. Serve them sizzling hot, sprinkled with parsley and accompanied with a bowl of Béarnaise.

STURGEON SLICES WITH BROCCOLI

1 pound sturgeon fillet	3 Tablespoons bottled oyster sauce
½ teaspoon salt	1 Tablespoon sherry
Pepper to taste	1 teaspoon sugar
3 Tablespoons cornstarch	4 Tablespoons oil
8 dried black mushrooms	1 clove garlic, minced
½ cup chicken broth or water	1 Tablespoon minced ginger
1 Tablespoon soy sauce	4 cups broccoli, cut in florets

Cut sturgeon into ½-inch-thick slices, 1½ inches wide. Salt, pepper, and dust them with 2 tablespoons of the cornstarch, then set them aside. Rinse and soak mushrooms in warm water for 20 minutes. Drain, reserving the water, cut caps into quarters and discard tough stems. Combine soy and oyster sauces, sherry, sugar, and the remaining tablespoon of cornstarch.

Heat oil in a heavy skillet or wok, add garlic and ginger, and stir-fry for a few seconds until garlic becomes straw colored. Add sturgeon. Fry fish over high heat about 2 minutes, then remove from pan and keep warm. Add broccoli to pan and stir-fry in hot oil for about 3 minutes. Add chicken broth, mushrooms, and mushroom water, then cover the pan, reduce heat, and simmer for 10 minutes. Stir in reserved oyster sauce mixture and, when it boils, add sturgeon. Cover and simmer slowly for several minutes, until fish flakes when tested and broccoli is done. Correct seasoning with salt and pepper, then serve at once.

MARINATED AND FRIED STURGEON

1 sturgeon slice, 2 inches thick
1/2 cup vinegar
2 Tablespoons (1/4 stick) butter, melted
Juice of 1/2 lemon
1/2 teaspoon salt

1/4 teaspoon pepper
1 Tablespoon milk
1 egg, beaten
3/4 cup dry bread crumbs
1/2 cup oil for frying

Pour boiling water over sturgeon slice, then drain. Combine vinegar, melted butter, lemon juice, salt, and pepper. Pour marinade over fish and marinate for 6 hours, turning occasionally.

Remove sturgeon and dry on paper toweling. Beat milk with egg, then dip fish in the egg and press it into crumbs, coating both sides well. Pan fry sturgeon in hot oil, over medium heat, about 10 minutes on each side. Serve with Mustard Sour Cream Sauce.

MUSTARD SOUR CREAM SAUCE

1/2 cup sour cream
2 teaspoons butter

1 Tablespoon Dijon-type mustard
Minced parsley

Combine all ingredients in a small suacepan, bring to the boiling point, and serve in a sauceboat.

PICKLED STURGEON

2 pounds sturgeon fillet
Salt
1/2 cup salad oil
1/4 teaspoon pepper
2 cloves

1/2 lemon, sliced thin
1/2 Bermuda onion, sliced thin
2/3 cup white vinegar
2/3 cup dry white wine
1/2 cup water

Cut sturgeon into 1/2 inch-thick, fingerlike pieces, 2 1/2 inches long, dredge them in salt, and let stand for 1 hour. Rinse under running water, then dry pieces on paper toweling. Preheat the broiler and pan. Dip in oil, place pieces on the hot greased broiler pan, and cook 2 inches from heat for 3 minutes. Turn fish, baste, and broil about 3 minutes more.

Sprinkle sturgeon with pepper and put it in a nonmetal bowl with cloves, lemon, and onion slices. Mix vinegar, wine, and water; pour it over sturgeon, then cover and refrigerate for 12 hours before using. Stir occasionally to marinate evenly.

SMOKED STURGEON

Home-smoked or canned in oil, smoked sturgeon is a delicacy. Serve it as:

Appetizer: Spread crackers with softened cream cheese and top with chopped onions and sturgeon.

Sandwich Filling: Finely chop ⅓ cup celery, 1 Tablespoon onion, 1 sweet gherkin, 1 cup smoked sturgeon, and mix with ½ teaspoon lemon juice and 2 Tablespoons mayonnaise.

Quick Hot Meal: Heat smoked sturgeon chunks in Parsley White Sauce (p. 418) and serve on toasted English muffins or baked potatoes.

Casserole: Preheat oven to 350°F. Place 2 cups smoked sturgeon in a buttered casserole,* season with pepper, add ⅔ cup milk and dot with 2 tablespoons butter. Bake uncovered for 10–15 minutes, depending on size of chunks. Remove from oven. Rim casserole with hot, seasoned mashed potatoes, then brown quickly under the broiler.

*If sturgeon was too heavily salted before smoking, freshen it just prior to baking by soaking in cold water for as long as 1 hour, then drain and dry on toweling.

Greenling

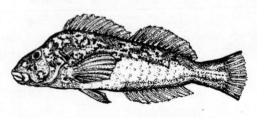

IT SEEMS ODD that the greenling, one of the most beautiful of the small fish, and the big, ferocious, ugly ling cod could be members of the same family. But they are. Greenling make up a goodly portion of Washington and Oregon's shore fish, but some are found as far south as Pt. Conception, California.

They weigh about a pound, are twelve to twenty inches long, and are easily recognized by their long dorsal fin and large fan-shaped pectoral fins. These agile little fish can dart swiftly when alarmed, but their spurts of speed are short. They stalk their prey, pounce on it, then return to their rocky retreats.

The "magic gyro" that enables fish to school or dive into crevices with accuracy is located along the fish's lateral line. Tiny sense organs lining the pores react to water pressure and direction. Greenlings have five lateral lines.

The Pacific hosts three kinds of greenlings:

Whitespot, so called because of their white-spotted body, are particularly prevalent in Washington.

Rock greenling are also known as red rock trout because of their appearance.

Kelp greenling are called seatrout by Californians. Male and female seatrout differ completely in color and pattern. Females are evenly speckled red and brown, but the males are spectacularly covered with sky blue blotches ringed in orange red on their forefront; dusky blue pelvic fins dress their sides.

Anglers fish them in rocky areas, kelp beds, and from jetties.

About Greenling Meat

Greenling meat is slightly greenish blue, finely textured, and delicate in flavor. The lean fine meat, recognized by its wavy grain, turns white when cooked. These fish may be broiled, grilled, butter sautéed, pan fried, poached, or steamed.

Greenling are available all year round, but only in local markets.

BROILING SAUCE FOR GREENLING

Greenling
4 Tablespoons (½ stick) butter, melted
Juice of ½ lemon
1 ounce vermouth
1 teaspoon salt

1 teaspoon Worcestershire sauce
Pepper to taste
Paprika
Minced parsley

Mix melted butter with lemon juice, vermouth, salt, Worcestershire sauce, and pepper; pour over fish and marinate for 30 minutes. Grill whole fish on the barbecue or split and broil them. Baste frequently while broiling. Sprinkle cooked fish with paprika and minced parsley.

BAKED GREENLING FILLETS WITH TOPPING

1½ pounds greenling fillets
At least ¼ teaspoon salt
Pepper to taste
Garlic powder
Juice of ½ lemon

4 Tablespoons (½ stick) butter, melted
½ cup mayonnaise
2 Tablespoons grated onion
3 Tablespoons grated cheese
2 egg whites, beaten stiff

Preheat the oven to 425°F. Wipe fillets, season with salt, pepper, and garlic powder and arrange them on a greased baking dish. Mix all but 1 teaspoon lemon juice with melted butter and pour it over the fish. Cover dish tightly and bake for 10 minutes per inch thickness of fish.

Meanwhile, combine mayonnaise, 1 teaspoon lemon juice, grated onion and cheese. Add a pinch of salt to beaten egg whites, beat stiff, then fold in mayonnaise mixture. Spread mixture thickly over cooked fillets and slide them under the broiler until nicely brown.

White perch, flounder, or small rockfish may be used in this dish.

GREENLING AU GRATIN

1½ pounds greenling fillets	⅓ cup dry white wine
¼ cup minced onion	⅓ cup water
¼ cup minced green pepper	2 Tablespoons tomato sauce
5 Tablespoons butter	2 sprigs parsley, minced
1 cup sliced mushrooms	Salt and pepper to taste
1 Tablespoon flour	½ cup soft bread crumbs

Preheat the oven to 350°F. Wipe fillets and arrange them in a baking dish. Sauté onion and pepper in 3 tablespoons butter until tender, add mushrooms, and cook 3 minutes more. Mix in flour, wine, water, tomato sauce, and parsley. Season with salt and pepper and pour boiling sauce over fish. Melt remaining butter, add crumbs; scatter them over sauce. Bake until crumbs brown and fish flakes when prodded.

Any lean white fish listed on page 446 (III A1) may be used.

POACHED GREENLING IN MUSHROOM SAUCE

1½ pounds greenling fillets	Basic Court Bouillon (p. 26)

BASIC SAUCE

3½ Tablespoons butter	1 teaspoon lemon juice
2 Tablespoons flour	2 Tablespoons minced parsley
¾ cup hot milk	Salt and pepper to taste
1½ cups diced mushrooms	1 egg yolk
2 Tablespoons minced green onion	¼ cup cream

Preheat the oven to 425°F. Have court bouillon boiling. Fold fillets in half and arrange them in a buttered baking dish. Pour in enough bouillon barely to cover fish. Poach, covered, for 3–8 minutes, or 10 minutes per inch thickness. Remove cooked fish to a platter, cover, and keep warm. Pour bouillon into a saucepan and reduce it to ¾ cup.

To make the sauce, heat 2 tablespoons of the butter with flour, beat in reduced bouillon and hot milk, cooking until sauce thickens and boils, then reduce heat to less than a simmer while cooking mushrooms.

Sauté mushrooms with green onion in remaining 1½ tablespoons butter and when tender add them to barely simmering sauce. Stir in lemon juice, parsley, and salt and pepper. Beat egg yolk with cream, then mix it into the sauce, pour over fish and serve.

Monkfish or rockfish may be substituted for greenling.

GREENLING-FILLED EGG ROLLS WITH SAUCE

2 Tablespoons plus ½ teaspoon
  vegetable oil

FISH FILLING

1 pound greenling fillet
⅓ cup minced green onions
2 teaspoons minced ginger
½ teaspoon salt
Dash of pepper

1 Tablespoon cornstarch
1 Tablespoon dry sherry
1 teaspoon sesame oil
1 egg white, beaten stiff

Cut fish into small ¼-inch strips. Combine with other filling ingredients, mixing well. Cover and chill while making skins.

EGG SKINS

6 eggs
¼ teaspoon salt
1 Tablespoon water

1 teaspoon cornstarch
1 teaspoon sesame oil

SAUCE

1 cup chicken broth
2 teaspoons cornstarch
1 Tablespoon cold water

2 teaspoons each sherry and soy sauce
1 teaspoon sesame oil
⅓ cup minced green onion

Put ingredients for skins in a blender and blend until smooth. Heat ½ teaspoon vegetable oil in an 8-inch pan and swirl it around. Ladle about ¼ cup egg mixture into pan and cook over medium-low heat until dry on top, but not brown on the bottom. Place cooked skin on a platter to cool and cook the rest the same. This should make 6 skins.

Divide filling equally on the 6 skins, then roll them. Heat 2 tablespoons oil and fry rolls, moving them often to assure an even golden brown. When brown, pour in chicken broth, cover, and simmer them slowly for 10 minutes. Remove rolls to a warm platter and cut them into serving pieces. Dissolve 2 teaspoons cornstarch in 1 tablespoon cold water, then add it and sherry, soy sauce, 1 teaspoon sesame oil, and green onion to the pan. Cook over high heat, stirring, until sauce thickens and boils, then pour over fish rolls and serve.

Small rockfish, perch, snapper, or other small lean white fillet listed on page 446 (III A1) may be used.

GREENLING TURBANS WITH CRAB SAUCE

1 pound greenling fillets
1 cup (or 6½-ounce can) crab meat
4 Tablespoons (½ stick) butter
Juice of ½ lemon
4 mushrooms, chopped

¼ cup minced green onion
2 Tablespoons minced parsley
1 Tablespoon fine dry crumbs
¼ teaspoon each salt, pepper,
  and thyme

Melt 4 tablespoons butter and combine with lemon juice. Cook mushrooms, onion, and parsley in 1 tablespoon lemon-butter until soft. Add crumbs, salt, pepper, and thyme. Preheat the oven to 425°F. Place a little crab meat and a spoonful of mushroom-crumbs on each fillet (reserve remaining crab for sauce), then roll and fasten with wooden cocktail picks. Dip rolls in remaining lemon-butter, place them in a baking dish, and pour the rest of the lemon-butter over. Bake them, uncovered, for about 15 minutes. Make sauce while rolls are baking.

SAUCE

2 Tablespoons (¼ stick) butter
2 Tablespoons flour
1 cup hot milk
2 Tablespoons minced parsley
¼ teaspoon salt

Dash of cayenne pepper
1 egg yolk
2 Tablespoons sherry
2 teaspoons lemon juice

Heat 2 Tablespoons butter and flour, add hot milk, and stir vigorously until sauce thickens and boils. Remove from heat and add reserved picked-over crab, parsley, salt, and cayenne. Beat egg yolk with sherry and 2 teaspoons lemon juice, and mix it into the sauce.

When rolls are cooked, transfer them to a warm platter. Pour pan juices into the sauce, mix well, and pour it over the fish rolls.

Sea robin, perch, sole, or rockfish may be used.

SAUTÉED GREENLING
WITH SAVORY HOT BUTTER SAUCE

1½ pounds greenling fillets
1 egg
2 Tablespoons milk
1 cup fine cracker crumbs
¼ teaspoon garlic powder

1 teaspoon salt
2 Tablespoons (¼ stick) butter
2 Tablespoons oil
Savory Hot Butter (p. 431)

Beat egg with milk, then dip fillets in egg and roll them in cracker crumbs seasoned with garlic powder and salt. Sauté fish in butter and oil until crunchy and brown. Have savory hot butter sauce ready to serve with sizzling sautéed fillets.

Small rockfish or any lean white fillet listed on page 446 (III A1) may be used.

Idea for Leftover Greenling

FISH AND RICE SOUP

1 cup cooked greenling
1 egg white, beaten
¼ teaspoon each salt and white
    pepper
2 teaspoons cornstarch
1 teaspoon minced ginger
1 green onion, minced

2 cans concentrated chicken broth
3 cans water
⅓ cup rice
2 teaspoons soy sauce
½ teaspoon sesame oil
1 Tablespoon minced cilantro

Cut cooked greenling into ½-inch slices. Beat egg white with a pinch of salt. Mix in pepper, cornstarch, minced ginger, green onion, and fish slices and set aside while cooking soup.

Dilute chicken broth with water, bring to a boil, and add rice. Simmer for 30–45 minutes.

Add fish mixture and cook, stirring, for 4–5 minutes. Stir in soy sauce, sesame oil, and cilantro. Serve hot.

Rockfish or any lean white fish listed on page 446 (III A1) may be used.

Herring

A HERRING SCHOOL is a shimmering, round, silvery mass that moves slowly along in a clockwise direction, from one patch of plankton to another. Herring spend their lives snacking on tiny plankton plants and animals that they filter through their toothless mouths.

During the winter they come inshore to spawn en masse—in bays, estuaries, and certain beaches. They tend to return each year to the same spawning ground. Their southernmost spawning range is San Francisco and Tomales bays.

During the run the bay is crowded with fishing boats. Nets are spread across the Golden Gate, almost from shore to shore, and the bay is littered with the white sticky spawn.

When hulls are filled, the boats return to harbor to unload. The fish are sucked up from the holds through vacuum tubes, directly into huge crates that are loaded onto waiting trucks that cart them away to be flash frozen and shipped to Japan. On the scene are the specialists who have flown in from Japan to evaluate and price each catch for the amount of its roe, which is processed into a high-priced delicacy in Japan.

When spring bursts out at sea, plankton starts growing again, the water gets dark green and opaque with new life, and the herring schools return to their offshore grazing grounds.

Herring are a vital link in the food chain, eaten by all the predators: birds, seals and other mammals, fish, and even man. However, their abundance enables them to survive.

(Atlantic herring occur on both sides of the Atlantic Ocean. They are taken from North Carolina to Greenland.)

About Herring Meat

Herring are oily fish with distinctive rich-flavored soft meat. Fresh herring are not often found in the markets, outside of the frozen food section, but salted, kippered, smoked, and pickled herring can be found in most delicatessens.

The time to get your supply for pickling, smoking, etc., is during herring runs, as the fishing boats come into harbor.

TO FILLET HERRING

Scale; clean; remove fins, head, and tail. Split the entire length of the belly, spread fish open—skin side up—and rub firmly up and down the backbone several times. Turn fish over. Pull out the tail end of the backbone, lifting gently up toward the head. It should lift away in one piece—with all the other little bones. Trim and cut fillets apart.

FRESH BROILED HERRING
WITH MUSTARD CREAM SAUCE

2 pounds (about 6) fresh herring	1 1/2–2 teaspoons prepared mustard
Salt	2 Tablespoons chopped parsley
Juice of 1 lemon	2 Tablespoons (1/4 stick) butter, melted
2 cups Cream Sauce (p. 419)	Boiled new potatoes

Fillet herring, sprinkle with salt and lemon juice, then set aside for 30 minutes. Meanwhile, prepare cream sauce and add to it the mustard and 1 tablespoon of the parsley.

Wipe fish dry and arrange them on a buttered broiler pan. Drizzle them with melted butter, then broil for 2 minutes on each side. Transfer herring to a hot platter, surround them with small boiled potatoes, and pour sauce on top. Sprinkle remaining tablespoon of parsley over all and serve.

Ciscos are also good for this dish.

FRIED FRESH HERRING

Clean and dress 6 herring, removing heads and tails. Brush with oil, sprinkle with salt and pepper, and set them aside for 1 hour. Dip herring in egg and press in bread crumbs, then pan fry in butter until crispy and brown. Accompany fish with broiled tomato halves topped with onion, boiled potatoes, and Brown Butter (p. 430).

MARINATED BAKED FRESH HERRING

6 fresh herring
Salt and pepper to taste
1/2 cup dry white wine
1/2 cup wine vinegar
1/4 cup each sliced carrots,
    green onion, and celery tops

Sprig parsley
1 small bay leaf
1/2 teaspoon whole peppercorns
1/4 teaspoon dried thyme
1 teaspoon olive oil

Clean and dress herring, removing both heads and tails. Sprinkle with salt and pepper and set them aside for 1 hour. Meanwhile, combine all other ingredients, except the oil, in a saucepan and simmer, covered, for 20 minutes.

Preheat the oven to 425°F. Arrange herring in a buttered baking dish. Pour the boiling marinade over the fish, sprinkle with oil, cover with foil, and bake for 5–7 minutes. Let fish cool in the marinade and serve cold.

MOLDED FRESH HERRING

6 fresh herring
Salt to taste
6 leeks (white part only)
2 cups water
2 bay leaves
1/2 onion

3 tomatoes, sliced
Snipped parsley
1 Tablespoon gelatin
1 chicken bouillon cube
1 teaspoon vinegar

Clean and dress herring (removing heads and tails), salt, and set them aside for 1 hour. Preheat the oven to 425°F. Cook leeks until tender in 2 cups water, to which bay leaves, onion, and salt have been added. Remove cooked leeks and set them aside, but save the broth.

Place herring in a single layer in a buttered baking dish. Pour boiling broth from leeks over herring, cover the dish with foil, and bake for 5–7 minutes, then let fish cool in the broth.

Arrange cold herring in a mold. Place tomato slices around them, snipped parsley here and there, and the leeks on top of the herring. Strain the cold broth and dissolve gelatin in a little of it. Add the gelatin, a bouillon cube, and vinegar to 2 cups broth. Bring to a boil, stirring to dissolve bouillon cube and gelatin. Pour about half of the gelatin broth over the fish. Chill until it begins to thicken, then pour on the rest of the gelatin broth. When set, unmold onto a bed of lettuce leaves.

PICKLED (FRESH) HERRING

5 pounds very fresh herring
2 cups salt
1 cup sugar
2 teaspoons whole peppercorns

1 teaspoon whole cloves
1½ quarts vinegar
1 quart water

Clean and fillet herring immediately, rinse in fresh water, and put them into an earthenware crock. Mix together salt, sugar, and spices. Layer the bottom of the crock with herring, cover with a layer of salt mixture, and repeat alternating layers. Combine vinegar and water and add enough to the crock to cover fish completely. Let herring stand in brine for 72 hours.

MARINADE

1 teaspoon mustard seed
¼ cup sugar
1 teaspoon whole cloves
3 bay leaves
2 red peppers, cut into strips

1 teaspoon whole allspice
2 teaspoons peppercorns
1 quart distilled vinegar
3 cups water
¼ cup slivered onion

Combine all ingredients, except onion, in an enameled pan. Bring to a boil, stirring until sugar is dissolved. Lower flame and simmer for 30 minutes (don't boil). Cool and let marinade stand for several hours. Have some sterilized jars ready to put fish in. Drain fish, discarding brine, and rinse briefly under fresh water. Cut fillets into strips about 1 inch wide, if you like. Put a few spices from the marinade in the bottom of each jar, some bay leaf, a scattering of onion, then a layer of cut herring. Repeat the layering until the jars are filled. Cover fish with the cold marinade. Cover jars and store in the refrigerator for a week before using. Keep refrigerated.

PICKLED (SALT) HERRING

2 salted herring
4 Tablespoons vinegar
2 teaspoons sugar
2 cloves

½ teaspoon allspice
½ teaspoon white pepper
2 Tablespoons minced onion

Remove the heads and clean herring under cold running water. Soak them overnight (no longer than 12 hours, refrigerated) in a large, covered bowl of water, then fillet, trim, and skin fish. Slice fillets crosswise into ½-inch strips. Mix a marinade of vinegar, sugar, and spices, pour it over herring, and let stand for several hours. Sprinkle with minced onion and serve chilled.

PICKLED HERRING SALAD I

1 cup pickled herring tidbits	1 cup sour cream
4 hard-boiled eggs, sliced	2 Tablespoons prepared horseradish
4 tomatoes, sliced	2 Tablespoons catsup
2-3 thin slices Bermuda onion	1/4 teaspoon salt
Snipped parsley	Dash of cayenne pepper
Sprigs watercress	1/4 onion, scraped for juice

Place a mound of herring in the center of a round platter. Surround herring with thin slices of hard-boiled eggs. Circle the platter with sliced tomatoes. Garnish here and there with onion rings, parsley or watercress sprigs. Chill until ready to serve.

Prepare dressing by mixing sour cream with horseradish, catsup, salt, cayenne, and a few drops of scraped onion juice. Chill until ready to serve with salad.

PICKLED HERRING SALAD II

1 cup pickled herring tidbits	1/4 teaspoon salt
1 cup heavy cream	2 hard-boiled eggs
2 teaspoons lemon juice	Lettuce leaves
1 teaspoon sugar	Black olives
1 teaspoon prepared mustard	Radishes
1 teaspoon onion juice, made by	Tomato wedges
scraping onion	

Make dressing by whipping cream until stiff and blending into it the lemon juice, sugar, mustard, onion juice, and salt. Chop hard-boiled eggs, drain herring fillets, then fold them into the whipped cream. Place lettuce cups on individual salad plates and mound herring salad in the center. Arrange a few black olives, radishes, and/or tomato wedges around it and serve chilled.

FRIED SALT HERRING

2 salted herring	4 Tablespoons (1/2 stick) butter
1/4 cup bread crumbs	1/2 cup cream
3 onions, sliced	

Clean, skin, fillet, and trim herring, then soak fillets overnight in cold water. (If salt herring is still too salty after soaking in fresh water overnight, soak it in milk for an hour or two, then wipe dry.) Drain on paper toweling and roll them in bread crumbs. Sauté onions in butter until tender, season, and when cooked remove them to a platter and keep warm. Sauté herring in the same butter. When golden brown, pour cream into the pan and simmer for a minute. Arrange fillets on the onions, spoon cream gravy over, and serve with baked potatoes.

SALT HERRING CASSEROLE

2 salted herring	Pepper
4 medium-size potatoes	3 eggs
2 onions	2 cups milk
Butter	Brown Butter (p. 430)
Bread crumbs	

Clean, skin, fillet, and trim herring. Soak fillets in cold water overnight, then drain and cut them into 1/2-inch pieces. Peel potatoes and slice them thin. Slice onions thin. Preheat the oven to 350°F. Butter and crumb a casserole dish and fill it with alternating layers of onion, herring, and potato, in that order. Sprinkle each layer generously with pepper, including the top layer of potatoes. Beat eggs well with milk, then pour into the casserole. Bake for 30–40 minutes, until potatoes are cooked. Serve hot in the casserole, accompanied with a bowl of brown butter sauce.

SALT HERRING WITH NEW POTATOES

2 salted herring	Dill
1 Tablespoon minced parsley	Butter
8–12 small new potatoes	1 cup sour cream with chives

Clean and soak herring in cold water overnight. Skin, fillet, trim, and cut into 1/2-inch slices. Put them on a plate large enough to fit on top of the kettle the potatoes boil in. Sprinkle fish with parsley. Peel potatoes, add a small sprig of dill, and boil in salted water. (A pot with a steamer is ideal.) When potatoes are half done put the plate of herring on top of the pot. Cover so that fish will steam while potatoes are cooking. In 15 or 20 minutes remove herring. Drain the potatoes, then put them back over heat to dry out for a minute. Transfer them to a serving bowl and sprinkle with chopped dill and melted butter. Serve with a bowl of sour cream mixed with chives.

SALT OR SMOKED HERRING SALAD

1 salt or smoked herring, diced
1 ½ cups diced boiled potatoes
1 ½ cups diced beets*
1 pickled gherkin, diced
2 tart apples, diced
¼ cup minced onion
4 Tablespoons vinegar

1 Tablespoon sugar
½ teaspoon white pepper
Lettuce
2 hard-boiled eggs, sliced
Snipped parsley
1 cup sour cream

*Reserve 2 tablespoons of the beet juice to color the sour cream.

Clean, skin, and fillet herring. Soak overnight in cold water. Drain, wipe dry, and trim. Mix together diced fish, potatoes, beets, gherkin, apples, and onion. Combine vinegar, sugar, and pepper, then mix with diced ingredients, stirring gently. Rinse a mold in cold water. Pack the fish mixture into it and chill. Unmold onto a plate lined with lettuce leaves. Garnish salad with sliced hard-boiled eggs and parsley. Serve with sour cream colored with the reserved beet juice.

Ling Cod

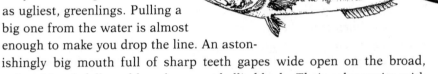

THE NAME LING COD is misleading,
because they are not cod at all.
They are the largest, as well
as ugliest, greenlings. Pulling a
big one from the water is almost
enough to make you drop the line. An aston-
ishingly big mouth full of sharp teeth gapes wide open on the broad,
pointed head, followed by a long, pot-bellied body. Their color varies with
locality from mottled black brown to greenish blue. Their blotches, edged
with yellow, blue, or orange, are subject to rapid color and pattern changes.

Ling cod are found from Alaska to Mexico. Around Puget Sound they
grow to five feet and can weigh eighty pounds and more; rock anglers there
fish them from shore. Down the coast, north of Eureka, skiff fishermen
work the kelp beds, rocky areas, and the deeper waters of the bays and
inlets. In the San Francisco area, fishermen go for them ten to thirty miles
out, around the Farelone Islands. Farther south smaller fish (four to
twelve pounds) are dragged from deep water.

The ling cod spawning routine is unusual. The male, puny (maximum
twenty-five pounds) compared to the female (up to three times that
weight), establishes a territory and within it sets up a nest where the
female can lay her eggs. Around December the female deposits her sticky
masses in the rocky nest and departs, leaving the male to guard the
nursery for the next two months, until the eggs hatch.

Newly hatched ling cod are delicate looking with big bright blue eyes.
That look changes quickly, however, because they are soon feeding on
anything and everything smaller than themselves, including each other.

About Ling Cod Meat

The color of raw ling cod flesh can vary from white to intense blue green.
This coloring is in no way harmful and fades to white during cooking.
Ling's delicately flavored meat is lean, flaky, and firm in texture. It is
marketed fresh all year, dressed, in chunks, steaks, or fillets.

STEAMED LING COD AND ASPARAGUS
WITH MALTAISE SAUCE

2 pounds ling cod fillet
1 bunch asparagus (20 stalks)
1/2 teaspoon salt
Pepper to taste

1 cup Hollandaise Sauce (p. 422)
2 Tablespoons orange juice
Grated rind of 1 orange

Cook asparagus and set aside to keep warm. Wipe fillet, cut it into portions, and season with salt and pepper. Arrange pieces close together on a heatproof plate. Double wrap plate in waxed paper and set it on a rack to steam (see page 27) for 8–12 minutes, depending on thickness of fish.

Meanwhile, make hollandaise sauce. Into hollandaise, beat orange juice and grated orange rind. This makes it maltaise sauce.

Serve ling cod fillets on warm plates, with asparagus spears and sauce spooned over both.

POACHED LING COD WITH VEGETABLES

2 pounds ling cod fillet
Poaching liquid (p. 27)
1 1/2 cups button mushrooms
2/3 cup carrot, in julienne strips
2/3 cup celery, in julienne strips
4 Tablespoons (1/2 stick) butter
3 Tablespoons flour

1 cup milk, hot
1/2 teaspoon salt
Pepper to taste
1 green onion, minced
1 egg yolk
1/4 cup cream
Grated cheese (optional)

Have poaching liquid ready. Preheat the oven to 400°F. Wipe fillet, cut it into serving pieces, arrange them in a buttered baking dish, and scatter mushrooms between. Bring poaching liquid to a boil and pour it over fish. Cover baking dish with foil and put it in the oven to poach, allowing 10 minutes per inch thickness of fish. When cooked, remove from oven, pour poaching liquid into a saucepan and boil it down until reduced to 1 cup. Cover and keep fish and mushrooms warm.

Meanwhile, cook carrot and celery in a little water and 1 tablespoon of the butter until tender. Then arrange them around the fish and mushrooms.

To make velouté sauce, cook the remaining 3 tablespoons of butter and the flour in a saucepan until bubbly, then beat in reduced poaching liquid, hot milk, salt, and pepper. Cook, stirring, until sauce is smooth and boils. Add minced green onion, simmer for a minute, then remove from heat. Beat egg yolk with cream, then whisk it into the hot sauce.

Preheat the broiler. Pour sauce over fish and vegetables, sprinkle with grated cheese, if you like, and place under broiler to glaze for 2–3 minutes, then serve.

Any lean white fillet listed on page 446 (III A1) may be used.

LING COD SOUFFLÉ

3/4 cup poached ling cod	1 teaspoon salt
3 Tablespoons butter	Pepper to taste
Fine bread crumbs	Dash of cayenne
4 eggs, plus 1 egg white	1 teaspoon paprika
3 Tablespoons flour	1 teaspoon lemon juice
1 cup hot fish stock (or milk)	1 green onion, minced

Flake ling cod, measure it out, and set it aside. Generously butter and crumb a 1 1/2-quart casserole. Separate eggs, placing the whites (including extra white) in a large bowl. Beat the yolks until thickened and lemon colored. Preheat the oven to 375°F.

Melt butter in a saucepan and stir in flour, cook until bubbly, then add hot stock or milk, beating with a whisk until thick. Remove from heat and whisk in beaten egg yolks. Season with 1/2 teaspoon salt, pepper, cayenne, paprika, lemon juice, and green onion. Stir in flaked fish.

Beat egg whites with 1/2 teaspoon salt until they stand in peaks. Gently fold fish mixture into egg whites. Pour into casserole and tap the bottom of the casserole several times on a table or counter to settle the mixture. Run the tip of a spoon around the rim to indent the top like a top hat. Place casserole in the center of the oven and cook for 35–45 minutes. Make sauce while soufflé is baking. When knife blade inserted into soufflé comes out clean, cook 5 minutes longer. Serve immediately.

Mushroom Hollandaise Sauce

1 cup (1/2 recipe) Thick Béchamel Sauce (p. 417)	Butter
	Salt and pepper to taste
1 cup sliced mushrooms	3 Tablespoons Hollandaise Sauce
1 green onion, minced	(p. 422)

Make béchamel sauce, using 2 tablespoons each of flour and butter and 1 cup of milk. Sauté sliced mushrooms with green onion in a little butter. Add them to the béchamel and season with salt and pepper. Stir in hollandaise and mix well. Serve warm sauce over (or with) the soufflé.

Pike, monkfish, and Pacific or red snapper may be used.

BAKED LING COD

3-pound ling cod chunk (tail section)	4 Tablespoons (1/2 stick) butter, melted
Vinegar	1/4 cup water
Salt and pepper to taste	Juice of 1/2 lemon

Preheat the oven to 425°F. Rub skin of ling with vinegar and wipe dry. Salt and pepper the piece, put it in a buttered baking dish, and brush with melted lemon-butter. (Fish may be split and placed skin side up in the dish.) Add 1/4 cup water to the dish, cover loosely with foil, and bake for 10 minutes per inch thickness of fish (in the thickest part), measured when fish is lying flat.

Baked ling may be served with Mornay Sauce (p. 420) or with Oriental Fish Sauce (p. 438) and boiled rice, or with other sauce.

BAKED LING COD SANTA CRUZ

2 pounds ling cod fillet	3 tomatoes, peeled, seeded, and diced
1/4 cup olive oil	1/3 cup dry white wine
Salt and pepper to taste	1/2 teaspoon sugar
1/4 cup chopped onion	2 Tablespoons minced parsley
1 clove garlic, pressed	

Cut fillet into thick steaks and put them in a buttered baking dish. Brush with half the olive oil and season with salt and pepper. Preheat the oven to 425°F. Sauté onion and garlic in remaining oil until tender. Add tomatoes and cook, stirring, until sauce is thickened, then stir in wine, sugar, and salt and pepper. Pour sauce over fish and bake for 10 minutes per inch thickness of fish. Serve cooked ling cod covered with sauce and sprinkled with parsley.

OVEN-FRIED LING COD FILLETS

2 pounds ling cod fillets, 1 1/2 inches thick	1 teaspoon salt
	Pepper to taste
1/4 cup olive oil	1 egg
2 cloves garlic, pressed	1 Tablespoon milk
3 Tablespoons minced onion	1/3 cup fine bread crumbs
1/4 teaspoon rubbed oregano	1/3 cup grated Parmesan cheese
Juice of 1/2 lemon	

Mix together oil, garlic, onion, and oregano. Cut fillets into 4 steaks, rub them with lemon juice, salt, and pepper, then marinate steaks in the oil for 1 hour.

Preheat the oven and pan to 500°F. Beat egg with milk. Mix crumbs and grated cheese. Drain fillets, dip in egg, then roll in crumbs, pressing them in well. Remove pan from oven, pour in marinade and enough oil to cover the bottom of the pan ⅛ inch deep. Place fillets in pan, then turn them over to coat both sides with oil. Return pan to oven. Bake until fish is brown and flakes. Fried ling cod is complemented by zucchini in tomato sauce or may be served with just tomato sauce.

Haddock, cod, pollock, tomcod, or hake may be used.

LING COD IN ISLAND CURRY

2 pounds ling cod fillet
Salt to taste
Cornstarch
3 Tablespoons oil
½–1 hot pepper, seeded and crushed
1 teaspoon powdered coriander
1 teaspoon powdered cumin seed
¼ teaspoon black pepper

2 cloves garlic, pressed
2 tamarind beans, peeled and cut in pieces
½ teaspoon powdered turmeric
1 cup coconut cream (or a 9-ounce can cream of coconut)
1 pound fresh bean sprouts

Wipe fish, cut in serving pieces, season with salt, and dust lightly with cornstarch. Heat oil in a large, heavy skillet, add spices, stir to mix, then cook for a minute. Stir in coconut cream, then add pieces of fish. Cook slowly, about 10 minutes, until fish barely flakes when tested.

Meanwhile, cook bean sprouts in a little oil until thoroughly hot.

Serve directly onto warmed plates. Place each portion of fish on a bed of bean sprouts and spoon curry over. Boiled rice is not necessary, but may be served along with the fish.

Tilefish, catfish, or cod may be used in this dish.

BRAISED LING COD

2½-pound chunk of ling cod, or a   Garlic powder
   small ling cod cut in chunks   4 strips bacon
Lemon   Cream-style horseradish
Salt and pepper to taste

A good-size chunk or a small pan-dressed ling cut in 2 or 3 pieces, to fit into a large, heavy skillet, may be used. Rub the skin with lemon, salt, pepper, and plenty of garlic powder.

Fry bacon slowly in skillet, then add fish. Cover the pan and cook fish slowly over low heat for 30 minutes. Serve with cream-style horseradish.

Cod family fish may be used.

Ideas for Leftover Ling Cod

LING COD SANDWICH

1 cup cooked ling cod, flaked   1 small green onion, minced
2 Tablespoons mayonnaise   2 sprigs parsley, minced
1 teaspoon lime juice   Salt and pepper to taste

Mix all ingredients and serve on buttered toast.

SCALLOPED LING COD

2 cups cooked ling cod, flaked   3 Tablespoons butter
2 cups plus 4 Tablespoons cold milk   ½ teaspoon salt and white pepper
¼ cup minced onion   2 Tablespoons flour
Sprig parsley, minced   About 15 crackers, crumbled

Pour 2 cups of the milk into top of double boiler; add to it onion, parsley, 2 tablespoons of the butter, and salt and pepper. Mix flour with the remaining 4 tablespoons milk to make a smooth liquid paste, then stir it into the warming milk. Bring to a boil and remove creamy sauce from heat.

Preheat the oven to 350°F. Butter a small casserole. Cover the bottom with a layer of flaked ling cod, then a layer of creamy sauce, and sprinkle over that some cracker crumbs. Repeat layers until casserole is full. The top layer should be cracker crumbs. Dot with the remaining tablespoon of butter and bake for about 30 minutes. Serve hot.

Any lean white fish listed on page 446 (III A1) may be used.

Halibut

ELUSIVE HALIBUT, as many fishermen call them, are primarily
offshore fish, but migrate into
bays (or close inshore) to spawn
May through July. The two important
species taken on the Pacific Coast are California halibut and giant Pacific halibut.

California halibut are warm-water fish and are plentiful from Pt.
Conception to the tropics. They average five to forty pounds inshore
and up to seventy-five pounds offshore. Unlike other flatfish, which
stay in one area buried in the sand, halibut are voracious predators
constantly prowling for small fish, which are, almost, their exclu-
sive diet. At the peak of their spawning season (June and July) they
can be fished from piers or dinghies over sandy bottoms in shallow
water, in kelp beds, and in open surf just behind the first waves at
the time of the grunion and smelt runs. Good fishing areas in
Southern California are around Oceanside, Coronado Strand, inside Morro Bay, and Newport Beach. Sometimes they are caught as
far north as Moss Landing and Seaside.

Pacific halibut can be caught from Northern California to Alaska.
The farther north you go, the more abundant they are. The Strait
of Juan De Fuca, which separates Washington from British Columbia,
is an excellent fishing ground where great concentrations of larger
migrating fish spawn from late May to June. Females grow to eight
feet in length and several hundred pounds; males seldom reach as
much as four feet or more than forty pounds. Large halibut are
hooked from boats, free-drifting with the tide, in 100–200-foot
depths. Squid, octopus, or herring, weighted down so it can bounce
along the bottom, is used as bait. A hooked halibut is a mean,
vicious creature. Its remarkably strong tail, whipping around, can
knock a small boat to pieces. Needless to say, a large fish is not

brought aboard, but is towed into shore. Oregon has good halibut fishing, especially around Pacific City and Sand Lake.

Atlantic halibut are similar in shape, size, and habits to their Pacific cousins. They, too, are cold-water fish, found in relatively deep water. Halibut grow slowly, and overfishing has greatly reduced the amount of the Atlantic halibut fishery. They are taken by longline fishing on sand/gravel or hard clay ocean floor, from New Jersey to Greenland.

About Halibut Meat

Mild-flavored halibut, always a favorite, is lean white meat, firm textured and tender.

Small "chicken halibut" should be scaled and pan dressed before preparing. Larger fish can be filleted or steaked. Fresh halibut is found in the market from May through September.

Halibut grills, fries, bakes, and poaches well, and may be prepared as stew, fish loaf, soup, or salad.

STEAMED HALIBUT WITH EGG SAUCE

Place a 2½-inch-thick halibut steak on a heatproof platter, season it with salt and pepper, put several slices of lemon and a sprig of parsley on top. Double wrap the fish and plate in waxed paper and steam it (p. 27) for about 20 minutes, until fish flakes.

When cooked, unwrap and wipe platter, garnish fish with fresh parsley and lemon wedges, and serve with Egg Sauce (p. 419).

HALIBUT POACHED IN COURT BOUILLON WITH MUSTARD SAUCE

Poach halibut chunk (next to the tail is best for poaching) in Basic Court Bouillon (p. 26), about 6 minutes per pound. When cooked, cover halibut and keep warm. Pour poaching bouillon into a saucepan and boil it down until reduced to 1 cup.

Make mustard sauce by whisking the reduced cup of poaching bouillon and 1 cup of hot milk into a roux of 3 tablespoons each butter and flour; stir-cook to a boil. Add 2 teaspoons prepared mustard. For rich sauce, beat an egg yolk with ½ cup cool cream, then whisk it into the sauce.

BAKED CHICKEN HALIBUT

4–5-pound chicken halibut,
  pan dressed
Salt
Vinegar
5 Tablespoons butter
Juice of 1 1/2 lemons
Flour

1/3 cup walnuts, ground in blender
  or processor
1 Tablespoon Worcestershire sauce
1/2 teaspoon sugar
1/4 teaspoon each garlic powder,
  ground nutmeg, and pepper
Scraped onion to taste

Rub fish with salt and vinegar, then score the skin several times on each side. Melt 4 tablespoons butter and combine with juice of 1/2 lemon. Preheat the oven to 425°F. Wipe fish dry, dust with flour, brush with lemon-butter, and season with salt and pepper. Lay fish on a dripping pan, add 1/4 cup water to the pan, and bake for 10 minutes per inch thickness of fish. Baste frequently with melted lemon-butter, mixed with warm water. When fish is brown and cooked, remove it to a platter and keep warm while making gravy.

In dripping pan combine walnuts, Worcestershire sauce, the remaining tablespoon of butter, juice of 1 lemon, the sugar, garlic powder, nutmeg, pepper, and onion, blending well with pan juices. Add a little boiling water, if necessary, and thicken gravy with flour mixed with cold water. Heat to a boil, stirring away any lumps, then serve in a bowl with halibut.

BAKED HALIBUT STEW

2 pounds halibut fillet
Salt and pepper
Juice of 1 lemon
3 onions, chopped coarse
2 cloves garlic, minced

1/4 cup minced parsley
1/4 cup olive oil
1/2 cup dry white wine
1 large (28-ounce) can tomatoes
1 teaspoon rubbed oregano

Cut halibut into serving pieces, season with salt, pepper, and lemon juice, then set aside while making sauce.

Preheat the oven to 350°F. In a large ovenproof skillet, sauté onion, garlic, and parsley in olive oil until vegetables are tender. Add wine, cook several minutes, then add tomatoes, breaking them up with a spoon while they heat to a boil. Add oregano and salt and pepper, mix well. Then, finally, add halibut. Put skillet in the oven to bake until fish is cooked.

BROILED HALIBUT
IN DEVILED CLAM SAUCE

2 pounds halibut fillet

2 Tablespoons (¼ stick) butter

2 Tablespoons flour

1 can minced clams, drained with juice
  reserved

½ cup or more hot milk

Juice of ½ lemon plus 2 Tablespoons

⅓ cup minced green onion

¼ cup sliced green olives

1 teaspoon prepared mustard

¼ cup mayonnaise

Salt and pepper to taste

In a saucepan, heat butter and flour until frothy, add clam juice from drained clams plus enough hot milk to make 1 cup. Cook, beating with a whisk, until sauce is smooth and boils. Stir in 2 tablespoons of the lemon juice, the onion, olives, drained clams, mustard, mayonnaise, and ½ teaspoon each of salt and pepper.

Preheat the broiler. Place halibut on a greased baking dish, season with salt, pepper, and the remaining juice of ½ lemon, dot with butter, and slide under the broiler for 5–6 minutes. Remove pan from broiler, turn fish over, and cover with clam sauce. Return dish to broiler and cook until fish is done and sauce is bubbly, about 5 minutes.

Good for ling cod, blackfish, or catfish.

BROILED HALIBUT
WITH SOUR CREAM AND MUSHROOMS

2 pounds halibut, in a steak
  1½ inches thick

Juice of 2 limes

Salt and pepper to taste

3 Tablespoons butter

1 cup sliced mushrooms

2 green onions, sliced

1 cup sour cream

Place halibut chunk in a shallow dish, squeeze on lime juice, season with salt and pepper, and let fish marinate for 1 hour, turning occasionally.

Preheat the broiler and pan. Transfer halibut to hot oiled pan, dot fish with 1 tablespoon of the butter, and cook 3 inches under broiler for 10–15 minutes, until it barely flakes. Don't turn, but do baste while cooking.

Meanwhile, sauté mushrooms and onions in the remaining 2 tablespoons of butter until cooked; salt and pepper them to taste. When fish is almost cooked, heat sour cream in mushroom and onions, mixing well. Transfer halibut to a platter and serve at once, with a bowl of sour cream–mushroom sauce.

BROILED HALIBUT STEAK

2 pounds halibut, in 4 steaks 1 inch
   thick
¼ teaspoon paprika
1 Tablespoon grated onion
2½ Tablespoons lemon juice

5 Tablespoons butter, melted
Salt and pepper to taste
Parsley
Lemon wedges

Mix paprika, onion, and lemon juice with melted butter. Arrange halibut in a baking dish, pour butter over steaks, and marinate for 1 hour, turning once.

Preheat the broiler and pan, then broil fish 2 inches from the heat for 5 minutes on each side, dabbing with marinade as needed. Salt and pepper cooked steak, garnish with parsley and lemon wedges, then serve at once.

ROLLED STUFFED HALIBUT FILLETS

1½ pounds halibut fillet
4–5 slices bacon, halved
¼ cup slivered almonds
2–3 green onions
3 Tablespoons vegetable oil
¼ cup water

At least 1 Tablespoon cornstarch
1 Tablespoon soy sauce
½ Tablespoon brandy
Salt and pepper to taste
1 Tablespoon bottled oyster sauce

Fry half-slices of bacon slowly, remove them from pan just before they crisp, and drain them on paper toweling. Fry almonds in bacon fat, stirring them as they cook. Remove and drain when they turn golden. Discard bacon fat and wipe pan. Split onions lengthwise, then cut them into 2-inch lengths. Heat oil in the skillet and add onions; when they become limp, remove them from pan. Combine water, 1 tablespoon cornstarch, soy sauce, and brandy in a bowl and set aside.

Cut fillet into 3 × 2 × ½-inch-thick strips. Flatten them out on waxed paper covered with cornstarch, and sprinkle with salt and pepper. Place some nuts, bacon, and green onion on each piece of fish, then roll and fasten with wooden cocktail picks.

Sauté halibut rolls gently for about 3 minutes, turning them carefully. Add oyster sauce and continue cooking for 2 minutes more. Pour in soy mixture and cook, turning and moving fish around in the pan until sauce thickens and the rolls are coated with sauce. Transfer cooked halibut rolls to a warm platter and remove the cocktail picks before serving.

Tilefish, white seabass, or snapper may be used.

FRIED HALIBUT SLICES
WITH SALT PORK

2 pounds halibut steak
Pepper to taste
Juice of ½ lemon
6 thin slices salt pork
Flour

¼ cup minced green onion
Parsley
Lemon wedges
Small boiled potatoes

Cut halibut into serving portions, sprinkle with pepper and lemon juice, then set aside.

Pour boiling water over salt pork, let stand for 2–3 minutes, then drain, wipe dry, and dust in flour. Fry pork slices slowly in a heavy skillet until brown and crisp, then remove to a platter and keep warm.

Roll fish in flour and fry in hot pork drippings. Add green onion to the pan when turning fish to brown the other side. Arrange alternate slices of cooked fish and pork on a platter, garnish with parsley and lemon wedges, and serve with small boiled potatoes.

HALIBUT SOUP WITH MATZO BALLS
OR FISH BALLS

3 pounds trimmings, head, and bones
  of 6–10-pound halibut
3 quarts water
1 large onion, chopped
1 cup celery, with leaves
1 carrot, grated
2 cloves garlic, minced

2 Tablespoons oil
1 bay leaf
10 peppercorns
⅓ cup tomato sauce
1 teaspoon rubbed oregano
Salt and pepper to taste

To make a rich stock, place fish trimmings (wrapped in cheesecloth, if you like, for easy retrieval) in a large kettle with 3 quarts of cold water. Sauté onions, celery, carrot, and garlic in oil until tender. Add them, bay leaf, and peppercorns to stock and simmer for 30 minutes. Strain stock, discard solids, then return stock to a clean kettle. Add tomato sauce, oregano, and salt and pepper. Simmer slowly while making either matzo or fish balls.

Matzo balls are made as directed on the package of matzo meal. Drop them into boiling broth and simmer them for 20 minutes.

FISH BALLS

1 pound boned, ground halibut
Salt and pepper to taste
1 egg, beaten

½ cup cornstarch
¼ teaspoon rubbed oregano

Season ground fish with salt and pepper, beat in egg, cornstarch, and oregano. When well integrated and smooth, chill for 1 hour. Form fish into walnut-size balls, drop them into boiling broth, and simmer for 20 minutes.

Idea for Leftover Halibut

FLAKED HALIBUT ON TOAST

1½ cups cooked halibut, flaked
2 cups water, plus trimmings
1 slice onion
Dash of cayenne pepper

1 teaspoon flour
1 teaspoon butter
1 drop of almond extract
Sprig parsley, minced

Place flaked halibut in a bowl in a steamer to heat. Put water and any skin and bones or trimmings of the halibut in a saucepan. Add onion and cayenne and simmer until reduced to 1 cup, then strain. Mix flour into butter, then beat it into the broth with a whisk and cook until thickened. Add almond extract and pour sauce over warmed halibut. Sprinkle with minced parsley and serve on toast.

Sablefish

SABLEFISH, also called black cod,
inhabit the entire West Coast,
but the bulk of the catch is
taken from Eureka, California,
north. They are deepwater fish that
school along the blue clay bottom by the
edge of the continental shelf. Commercial fishermen, fishing for market-valuable cod, etc., drag their nets over the ocean floor, scooping up everything in the net's path. The catch they net is too often sablefish, and it happens that more sablefish are brought in than are wanted by our marketers. A large proportion of our sablefish are taken to Japan and the U.S.S.R.

The life history of sablefish starts in late winter, when schools migrate into very deep water to spawn. The eggs float on the surface until they hatch. Young fish that are not eaten by albacore, salmon, or seal, etc., make their way inshore, where they spend their juvenile days. By the end of the first year they are about a foot long and resemble adults—gray black on top fading to silver underneath, rounded snout and fin placement that distinguish them from other fish. At five years males are double the size, weigh about six pounds, and are fully developed. Females mature a year later, but grow larger. As adults, they head for deep water and seldom, except for spawning migrations, roam many miles from their habitat.

Some years, during summer months, thousands of young black cods are caught off piers, jetties, and skiffs from Central California north.

About Sablefish Meat

Sablefish are among our richest, fattest fish. The meat is white, flaky, and soft, with a buttery quality and mild flavor. They are sold whole, in fillets and steaks, marketed as butterfish, black cod, or sablefish. Because of their high fat content they are excellent smoked.

Some of the best kippered black cod is processed and smoked in

160

Tacoma and Seattle, Washington, with quality that compares favorably with smoked salmon. You can find it at better delicatessens as kippered black cod, Alaska smoked cod, or smoked sablefish, and in the East just called smoked sable.

SMOKED SABLEFISH (KIPPERED)

10-15 pounds sablefish

BRINE

2 cups salt

3 cups brown sugar

3 quarts water

3 bay leaves

2 Tablespoons onion powder

1 teaspoon each black pepper, garlic powder, coriander seeds, and allspice

First make brine: Heat salt, sugar, and water together in an enamel kettle (use nonmetal containers for brine), stirring until salt is dissolved. Add spices, bring to a boil, then remove from heat and set aside until cool. The brine should float a whole raw egg in its shell.

Clean, dress, rinse, and drain fish. Split it into sides, remove backbone, and trim away thin belly flesh, which may be smoked as strips. Cut the rest into small fillets, no thicker than 1-1½ inches. Put fish into enough cold brine to submerge the pieces completely, and brine the fish for 3-3½ hours.

After brining, rinse fish well in cold fresh water and drain. At this point, commercially smoked black cod is dipped in a harmless orange kipper dye, which makes smoked fish look more attractive, but the dye might be difficult to obtain. Place fish, skin side down (if skin is left on) on wire racks, oiled to prevent fish from sticking. Allow fish to dry until it looks shiny and feels dry—an hour or so. Pieces should not touch and should be, as nearly as possible, the same size and thickness on each rack. Begin smoking at 75-100°F. for the first 2 hours or so. Raise the temperature to 150°F. until fish is cooked—about 2 hours, or when thermometer in the thickest part reads 140°F. and fish is deep brown and flaky. The degree of preservation depends on the length of time the fish is smoked. Alder, oak, hickory, or grape, etc., sawdust or chips, regularly applied, are used for smoke. For extra flavor place a sprig of bay leaves, rosemary, or other aromatic herbs on chips. After fish has cooled, wrap what is not to be eaten immediately and keep it refrigerated.

Kippered black cod can be warmed by steaming or broiling. Serve it with parsley butter sauce.

KIPPERED BLACK COD
WITH LEMON–MUSTARD SAUCE

Two 10-ounce packages frozen spinach
1½ pounds kippered black cod
4 Tablespoons (½ stick) butter
2 Tablespoons flour
1½ cups boiling water

3 egg yolks
Juice of 1 lemon
½ teaspoon Dijon-type mustard
Salt and pepper to taste

Cook frozen spinach in salted water as per directions, then drain and keep warm. Warm fish in a steamer or under the broiler.

Meanwhile, make sauce: Melt butter in a saucepan and stir in flour. Add boiling water all at once, beating with a whisk until sauce is thickened and boils, then reduce heat. Beat egg yolks with lemon juice and mustard, then beat them into the rest of the sauce. Cook 30 seconds over low heat, then remove and season with salt and pepper.

Serve kippered black cod on a bed of spinach and over it pour tangy lemon-mustard sauce.

SMOKED BLACK COD SANDWICH

Like kippered salmon, kippered sablefish makes good salads and sandwiches.

1 cup smoked Alaska black cod, flaked
2 Tablespoons sour cream
1 Tablespoon mayonnaise
1 teaspoon lemon juice
¼ teaspoon paprika

¼ teaspoon curry powder
1 tomato, sliced
4 slices toast
Alfalfa sprouts

Combine sour cream, mayonnaise, and lemon juice, then mix in paprika and curry powder. Stir flaked smoked fish into the mixture. Place a thin slice of tomato on each piece of toast. Spread alfalfa sprouts over tomato and put a big dab of fish mixture on top of each.

MISO MARINADE FOR BLACK COD

1½ pounds sablefish fillets
1 Tablespoon miso (white)*

¼ cup sake*
Pickled ginger, sliced thin*

*See Glossary.

Cut fillets in serving pieces. Mix together miso, sake, and several slices of pickled ginger, then marinate fish in it for 12 hours in the refrigerator, turning occasionally. Baste fillets with marinade while charcoal broiling; when cooked, garnish with pickled ginger. Serve with rice.

BAKED BUTTERFISH STEAKS

4 sablefish steaks, 1 inch thick
Salt to taste
Juice of ½ lemon
2 Tablespoons (¼ stick) butter, melted
Pepper to taste

½ teaspoon paprika
2 Tablespoons minced onion
¼ cup dry bread crumbs
½ cup dry white wine

Sprinkle steaks with salt and lemon juice and let stand for 30 minutes. Preheat the oven to 425°F. Arrange fish in a buttered baking dish, brush pieces with melted butter, sprinkle on pepper, paprika, onion, and crumbs, then pour in wine. Cover with foil and bake for 8 minutes, then remove cover and slide dish under the broiler to quickly brown and crisp steaks.

PAN-FRIED BUTTERFISH FILLETS

2 pounds sablefish fillets
Salt to taste
Juice of ½ lemon
1 egg, beaten
½ cup cornmeal

6 Tablespoons corn oil
Pepper to taste
Garlic powder
1 green onion, minced
Lemon wedges

Sprinkle butterfish with salt, squeeze on juice of half a lemon, and let stand for 30 minutes. Dip fish in beaten egg, then in cornmeal. Heat oil until it ripples and fry fish until golden brown, turning once. Season with salt, pepper, and garlic powder while cooking and serve with minced green onion and lemon wedges.

Pan-fried fillets may also be served with Creole Sauce (p. 434), White Wine Sauce (p. 422), or other sauce.

Salmon

PROBABLY THE MOST universally
popular fish is salmon. North
of the California–Oregon border, Indian tribes, commercial fishermen, sportsmen, and large lumber
corporations that have spread into the fishing
industry are all clamoring over this noble (and diminishing) fish.

It is part of their life cycle to return to the place where they begin life, whether this place is a hatchery or stream. However, as nature would have it, they start as an egg buried in an upstream gravel nest, hatch, and migrate to the sea where they disperse. The majority travel great distances. King salmon range as far south as Morro Bay. They mature and grow fat in the ocean. When spawning time comes, they travel back upstream, some-times with great hardship, to the grounds where they began. Here, after spawning, they complete their life cycle.

There are five species of Pacific Coast salmon:

Chinook (king or spring) are the largest. Big types weigh anywhere from thirty to a hundred pounds. Chinook go to sea shortly after birth and spend most of their three- to six-year life-span there. They spawn spring and fall.

Coho (silver) stay upstream a year before migrating, then remain in the ocean two years before spawning. The silver run starts in September. Puget Sound has especially good fishing; average catch is six to fifteen pounds.

Sockeye (red) spend several years in freshwater before going to sea. They turn red at breeding time.

Humpback (pink), the smallest of the salmon, go to sea soon after birth. Males develop a hump on their backs at spawning time.

Chum (dog salmon) are the least popular, probably because they don't readily take a baited hook.

About Salmon Meat

Salmon have firm-textured, orange pink meat, with rich, distinctive flavor. Red sockeye has the reddest meat and is the salmon most prized by canners. Coho and chinook, both high-priced, fine-quality salmon, are sold fresh in the markets, smoked, kippered, canned, salted, or frozen. Pink and chum salmon bring the lowest price from fish dealers and canners. Salmon meat freezes well, without much change after thawing.

During the summer, at Tillicum Indian Village, Blake Island, Washington, you can eat Northwest Indian-style barbecued salmon. Whole fresh salmon are opened up, spread out, and strapped onto alder stakes with cedar crosspieces, to bake over open wood-burning fire pits.

Summertime salmon bakes are held in many towns along the West Coast, from Sequim, Washington, to Depoe Bay, Oregon.

BARBECUED SALMON STEAKS

2 pounds salmon, in 4 thick steaks
4 Tablespoons (½ stick) butter
1 clove garlic, sliced thin

Juice of ½ lemon
Salt and pepper to taste

Melt butter with sliced garlic and lemon juice. Dip steaks into butter, then place them on a well-greased grill to broil over medium coals (p. 18). Baste with the garlic butter while broiling.

For smoky-wood flavor, add some alder or apple wood chips or sawdust to the coals. Chips and sawdust used for smoking can be purchased at most sporting goods stores.

SOY BASTE OR MARINADE
FOR BROILED SALMON STEAKS

¼ cup soy sauce
¼ cup sake or dry sherry
2 Tablespoons salad oil
1 teaspoon sugar

½ teaspoon dry mustard
¼ teaspoon garlic powder
¼ teaspoon grated ginger

Combine all ingredients and mix well, then pour sauce over salmon steaks. Leave steaks to marinate or put them directly on to broil, using sauce to baste while cooking.

BROILED SALMON STEAKS
WITH BÉARNAISE SAUCE

4 salmon steaks, ¾ inch thick
⅓ cup olive oil
1 green onion, minced
1 Tablespoon grated lemon rind

¼ teaspoon thyme
Salt and pepper
Béarnaise Sauce (p. 423)

Combine oil, onion, lemon rind, thyme, and salt and pepper, mix well and pour over salmon. Marinate steaks for 1 hour at room temperature, turning them occasionally. Preheat the broiler and pan. Then arrange steaks on the broiler pan (or grill) and broil 2 inches from the heat, for 3 minutes on each side. Baste while cooking. Have Béarnaise ready; when steaks are broiled, serve them at once with sauce.

FRIED SALMON SLICES
OR STEELHEAD FILLETS

2 pounds salmon fillets
6 slices bacon
1 egg, beaten
¼ cup milk

1 teaspoon salt
Pepper to taste
½ cup each flour and cornmeal

Fry bacon crisp, drain on toweling, and set aside. Beat egg with milk and salt and pepper. Dip serving pieces of salmon in egg, then in flour mixed with cornmeal. Fry in hot bacon fat over medium heat until golden brown; turn slices and adjust heat to allow fish to cook through, then raise heat to brown. Serve fillets with bacon slices, lima beans, and tomato.

FRIED SALMON BELLIES
WITH CURRANT SAUCE

Soak salted salmon bellies in a large amount of fresh water overnight. If still very salty, soak them in milk for 1-2 hours. Salted salmon bellies might be hard to find, for this old-time recipe, but fresh salmon, sautéed, is delicious with currant sauce.

Dust pieces of salmon with flour and sauté them in butter and oil until crisp and brown, season with pepper, and serve with sauce.

Currant Sauce

2½ cups currants
¼ cup Sauterne
¼ cup orange juice
2 Tablespoons sugar
Grated rind of 1 orange

Grated rind of 1 lemon
1 teaspoon ground cinnamon
Pinch of ground clove
1 Tablespoon fresh cilantro (optional)

Combine ingredients in a saucepan and bring to a boil. Reduce heat to simmer and cook until the mixture is reduced and thickened, about 15 minutes. Allow sauce to cool before serving.

WHOLE STUFFED SALMON DEL NORRIS

6-8-pound whole salmon
½ medium onion, minced
1 carrot, minced
2 stalks celery, minced
8 Tablespoons (1 stick) butter
1 cup sliced mushrooms
1 cup coarsely chopped water
  chestnuts
½ cup minced parsley
1 cup water

1 cup dry white wine
½ teaspoon tarragon
½ teaspoon basil
¼ teaspoon rosemary
Pinch of sage
Salt and pepper
2 cups Oroweat's (or other popular
  brand) Seasoned Cornbread
  Dressing
¼ cup more dry white wine

Sauté onion, carrot, and celery in butter over medium heat for 5 minutes, then add mushrooms, water chestnuts, and parsley. Sauté 2-3 minutes longer until mushrooms are limp. Pour in 1 cup water and wine, then cook it down, uncovered, until liquid is reduced to 1 cup. Add spices, and salt and pepper to taste. Stir in corn bread dressing. Mix until all liquid is absorbed. If corn bread is not moist enough, add more wine and water, then stuff fish and truss with prongs and dental floss or sew the sides closed.

Salt and pepper the salmon. Place a large piece of heavy-duty foil on a flat baking sheet and lay the fish on it. Brush salmon with melted butter and before wrapping, pour ¼ cup wine around the fish. Preheat the oven to 425°F. Double fold edges of foil to seal in moisture, then bake, allowing 5 minutes for heat to penetrate foil and 10 minutes per inch thickness of fish. Remove cooked fish from the oven, open foil and let it rest for several minutes before serving.

If salmon is not available, use any whole fish for baking listed on page 447 (III A3).

FOIL-WRAPPED BAKED JACK SALMON

3-5-pound whole salmon, cleaned   2 cloves garlic, slivered
Salt and pepper to taste   Very thin lemon slices
4 Tablespoons (½ stick) butter

A jack salmon is a small male salmon that enters freshwater along with the larger, older fish. Its meat is finer grained, with more delicate flavor than the big tyees.

Scale and clean, rinse and dry salmon. Sprinkle inside and out with salt and pepper. Dot the cavity generously with butter and sliced garlic.

Preheat the oven to 425°F. Tear off a piece of foil large enough to wrap the fish. Place several thin slices of lemon on foil and lay the fish on top. Then place several more lemon slices on top of fish. Wrap salmon, folding the edges and ends tightly. Bake, allowing 5 minutes for the heat to penetrate foil and 10 minutes per inch thickness of fish. Remove and unwrap cooked fish, discard garlic, lemon, and salmon skin before serving.

BAKED LARGE SALMON

10-20-pound salmon, pan dressed   Thyme
Vinegar   Butter
Salt and pepper   Lemon slices
Garlic powder   Horseradish Hollandaise Sauce (p. 423)

Preheat the oven to 425°F. Wipe fish skin with vinegar and pat dry. Sprinkle inside and out with salt, pepper, garlic powder, and a touch of thyme. Dot the cavity with small lumps of butter and place lemon slices around. Double wrap salmon in foil to hold in the moisture and lay fish on a large flat baking sheet. Bake for 10 minutes per inch thickness of fish (measured in the thickest part, when fish is lying flat), plus 5 minutes for heat to penetrate the foil.

When fish is cooked, lift it in the foil to a serving platter. Open and tear the foil down the middle, away from the fish on both sides, and remove it. Much of the skin will pull away with the ungreased foil; trim away the remainder. Decorate the platter and serve with a hollandaise sauce.

Horseradish hollandaise sauce is an especially good sauce to serve with baked salmon.

SALMON POTATO CASSEROLE

1 pound salmon, skinned and boned
4 medium potatoes
4 Tablespoons (½ stick) butter
1 onion, chopped coarse

¼ teaspoon garlic powder
Salt and pepper to taste
1 cup milk

Preheat the oven to 350°F. Boil potatoes in salted water until barely cooked and still firm. Heat butter in a heavy skillet and sauté onion until tender. Cut salmon into small pieces and add them, potatoes, seasonings, and milk to the sautéed onion. Mix them well, cover tightly, and bake for 20–25 minutes, until fish flakes.

Any lean white fillet listed on page 446 (III A1) may be used.

SALMON OR SALMON TROUT
IN COURT BOUILLON

2-3-pound salmon or salmon trout, dressed
⅔ cup each chopped onion, celery, and carrot

4 Tablespoons (½ stick) butter
6 cups water
2 cups dry white wine

Sauté vegetables in butter until tender. Combine water and wine in a kettle large enough to accommodate salmon and bring to a boil. Add sautéed vegetables and simmer for 5 minutes. Lower wrapped salmon (see page 26) into court bouillon, bring to boil, then reduce heat and simmer until fish is cooked.

If you are using 1-inch-thick steaks, wrap them in cheesecloth and tie the ends. Lower them into boiling bouillon, then remove kettle from heat, cover, and let steaks cook in hot bouillon for 10 minutes. Transfer salmon to a warm platter (remove cheesecloth) and keep warm, covered, while preparing sauce.

Strain the court bouillon, bring it to a boil in a pan, and reduce it over high heat to one-half the original amount. Use part of it to make a sauce and save the remaining for use another time. To make Velouté Sauce, or any of its variations (see pages 420–1), use 2 cups Basic Court Bouillon. To make White Wine Sauce for salmon (see recipe on page 422), use 1½ cups court bouillon. Poached salmon is elegant served with Mousseline Sauce (p. 422).

STOCK WITHOUT WINE
FOR POACHED SALMON OR SALMON TROUT

4-pound piece of the tail of salmon
6 cups water
4 Tablespoons white vinegar
2/3 cup chopped onion
2/3 cup chopped carrot
2 stalks celery, chopped

10 peppercorns
6 whole allspice
1 bay leaf
2 teaspoons salt
5 sprigs fresh dill

Wrap salmon in cheesecloth. Bring water to boil in a kettle large enough to accommodate salmon. Add all ingredients except salmon and dill. Cover and boil for 15 minutes, then add dill and salmon. Salmon should be covered, but just barely, by stock. Bring stock back to a boil, reduce heat, skim the top, and simmer until fish is cooked (see pages 24-5).

Poached salmon may be served with any number of sauces: Hollandaise Sauce (p. 422), Shrimp Sauce (p. 420), Caper White Sauce (p. 418), Horseradish White Sauce (p. 419), or Anchovy Butter (p. 432), to name a few choices.

GRAVLAX SALMON

2-2½-pound center cut salmon fillet
  (skin on)
2 teaspoons dill weed, or 1 Tablespoon
  minced fresh dill
3 Tablespoons salt

4 teaspoons brown sugar
¼ teaspoon ground pepper
¼ teaspoon ground allspice
4 Tablespoons white wine vinegar
1 clove garlic, sliced thin

Use very fresh salmon only. Sprinkle the bottom of a shallow glass baking dish with half of the dill and lay salmon in the dish, skin side down. Combine salt, sugar, pepper, and allspice and gently rub everywhere onto both sides. Pour vinegar on the fillets, place garlic slivers evenly on the fish, and scatter on the remaining dill. Cover the dish with a piece of plastic. Wrap a brick or two in plastic bags and lay them on top to weigh down the salmon. Refrigerate, bricks and all, for about 16-24 hours. Remove bricks occasionally and spoon juices over salmon.

The next day, remove weights and discard garlic—the salmon is ready to eat. Slice it thin, diagonally, across the grain. Serve on pumpernickel bread, accompanied with hard-boiled eggs, caviar, and sliced tomatoes.

SALMON IN ASPIC

2 pounds poached salmon
3 cups Basic Court Bouillon, or stock
  (p. 26)
1 egg white

1 1/2 envelopes (4 1/2 teaspoons)
  unflavored gelatin
2 Tablespoons chopped green onion
2 Tablespoons chopped fresh dill

Cut cold poached salmon into attractive, uniform-size pieces and place them in a mold. Heat to boiling all but 1/3 cup bouillon with egg white, then remove it from stove and let stand for 10 minutes. Meanwhile, dissolve and soak gelatin in the remaining 1/3 cup cold bouillon for 5 minutes. Strain cooling bouillon through a double thickness of cheesecloth. Heat it again, mix it well with gelatin, add onion and dill, then pour the gelatin over salmon. Chill aspic until firm. Unmold and serve with Sour Cream Cucumber Sauce (p. 429) or mayonnaise.

Good for any lean fish fillet listed on page 446 (III A1).

Ideas for Leftover Salmon

JELLIED SALMON

Cooked salmon glazed in gelatin makes a very attractive summertime meal. Glazing also prevents cooked fish from drying out or discoloring. Make a gel for salmon (or salmon trout) by dissolving 1 envelope unflavored gelatin in 1 3/4 cups boiling liquid such as: stock flavored with vinegar, grapefruit juice or lemon base, tomato base or wine base, or chicken broth base (see page 86).

SALMON BALL

2 cups cooked salmon, flaked
8-ounce package cream cheese
1 teaspoon Worcestershire sauce
1 Tablespoon chili sauce
1 Tablespoon lemon juice

2 Tablespoons grated onion
1 Tablespoon prepared horseradish
1/2 cup chopped nuts
3 Tablespoons minced parsley

Blend softened cheese with Worcestershire and chili sauce, lemon juice, onion, and horseradish. Mix in flaked salmon and chill. Form into a ball, roll it in chopped nuts mixed with parsley, and serve with crackers.

SALMON PIE

PASTRY

1 1/2 cups sifted all-purpose flour　　1/2 cup lard, chilled
1/2 teaspoon salt　　　　　　　　　3 Tablespoons ice water

Sift flour with salt into a large bowl that has been chilled and then cut in the lard with a pastry blender, until mixture resembles coarse sand. Sprinkle in water gradually, tossing the mixture with a fork to blend. Gather the dough into a ball, handling it as little as possible, then roll it out on a lightly floured board to 10 inches in diameter. Transfer the dough carefully to a 9-inch pie plate. Trim and flute the edges of the pastry. Preheat the oven to 450°F.

FILLING

1–1 1/2 cups cooked salmon, cut into　　4 eggs, beaten
　　very small pieces　　　　　　　　1 cup milk
1/2 cup chopped onion　　　　　　　1 teaspoon salt
1/2 cup green pepper　　　　　　　　1/2 teaspoon pepper
1 clove garlic, minced　　　　　　　1/2 cup shredded Monterey Jack
3 Tablespoons butter　　　　　　　　　cheese

Sauté onion, green pepper, and garlic in butter until tender. Beat eggs with milk, add sautéed vegetables, salt, and pepper, blending them well.

Put pie shell in oven for about 10 minutes, then remove shell and lower heat to 325°F.

Place salmon in the pie shell, scatter around shredded cheese, pour in egg mixture, and return pie to the oven to bake for 30 minutes or until knife comes out clean. Let pie rest for 5 minutes before serving.

SALMON LOAF

2 cups cooked salmon, flaked　　　　2 cups soft bread crumbs
4 strips bacon　　　　　　　　　　2 eggs, beaten
1 onion, chopped　　　　　　　　　1/4 teaspoon each dried rosemary,
1 green pepper, chopped　　　　　　　thyme, and garlic powder
1 teaspoon lemon juice　　　　　　　1 teaspoon salt
1 cup hot milk　　　　　　　　　　1/4 teaspoon pepper

Fry bacon crisp and drain on toweling. Pour off all but 2 tablespoons of bacon fat and sauté onion and green pepper until tender, then remove from heat and combine with flaked salmon. Sprinkle in lemon juice and crumbled bacon.

Preheat the oven to 350°F. Pour hot milk into bread crumbs and beat to a smooth paste, then whisk in beaten eggs, spices, salt, and pepper. Mix all ingredients together and pour into a buttered baking dish. Bake for about 45 minutes. Serve with Parsley White Sauce (p. 418).

Shad may be used instead of salmon.

SALMON TIMBALES

2 cups cooked salmon
3 eggs, separated
1 teaspoon grated lemon rind
1½ teaspoons lemon juice
¾ cup fine dry bread crumbs

¼ teaspoon ground fresh nutmeg
Salt and pepper to taste
½ cup heavy cream
Broccoli florets
Hollandaise Sauce (p. 422)

Flake cooked salmon very fine or put through a processor. Beat egg yolks and stir into bowl with salmon, lemon rind and juice, crumbs, nutmeg, and salt and pepper, mixing well.

Whip the cream until stiff, then separately whip egg whites with ¼ teaspoon salt until stiff. Fold whipped cream into salmon mixture, then fold in egg whites.

Preheat the oven to 325°F. Pour mixture into a large buttered mold (or individual buttered custard cups), filling two-thirds. Cover with waxed paper and hold paper on tightly with a rubber band. Place mold on a rack in a pan of hot water (water level as high as the fish mixture), and put pan in oven to steam for about 45 minutes (20 minutes for cups), or until a knife comes out clean.

Unmold onto a hot plate, garnish with broccoli florets, and serve with hollandaise sauce.

Also good made with shad.

SALMON BEET SALAD

Cut cooked salmon into uniform small slices. Dip them in tarragon French dressing and arrange slices, overlapping, to form a ring in the center of a bed of shredded lettuce. Place slices of beets and hard-boiled eggs around it. Scatter capers decoratively here and there and serve with mayonnaise.

SALMON CUCUMBER SALAD

Place serving-size slices of cold salmon on beds of crisp lettuce. Spoon over sour cream and top with overlapping thin slices of cucumber. Garnish with black olives and pimiento.

SALMON EGG ANCHOVY SALAD

Flake cooked salmon, moisten with lemon juice (or vinegar) and a few drops of oil, and refrigerate for an hour or so. Break lettuce leaves into a salad bowl, add salmon, quartered hard-boiled eggs, olives, and bits of anchovy. Serve with Green Goddess Dressing (p. 425).

Cured Salmon

The first manufactured product on the Pacific Coast was cured fish. Long before the "white man" appeared, the Indians had an established trade of dried salmon with the central plains tribes.

At the Dalles, stake gill nets were used to catch fish. At the Dalles, on the Columbia River, they caught salmon in a series of cylindrical baskets, each filling and opening into a smaller one. The series ended in a small tube, with a trap in the bottom, through which the women could remove the salmon to prepare them for drying.

At the beginning of the nineteenth century, the Russians, established at Fort Ross, California, were already shipping salt salmon to St. Petersburg. Then, the Northwest Fur Company started a salmon-salting business on the Columbia River. Soon, they merged with the Hudson's Bay Company, which shipped the salted salmon to the Orient, Australia, and eastern United States.

KIPPERED SALMON

Split a cleaned, dressed salmon, remove the backbone (don't remove skin), and chill for 2-4 hours. Cut backs into equal-size chunks, thinner parts in equal-size pieces, and the belly, which is the best kippered salmon, into strips.

BRINE

3 quarts water
2½ cups salt
3½ cups brown sugar
½ cup molasses

1½ teaspoons sage
1 teaspoon each allspice, pepper, and
  garlic powder

Mix brine in a nonmetal container. Submerge salmon completely in brine and soak ½–2 hours, depending on size (maximum 1 pound) and thickness of pieces.

Drain salmon. Rub smoker racks with lard and oil to prevent sticking. Sprinkle salmon with black pepper and place pieces of equal size on racks so they don't touch. Let fish dry for a few hours before smoking.

Use alder chips and sawdust in smoker. If possible, keep temperature at about 80°F. for 7–13 hours, then raise the temperature to 170°–80°F. to hot smoke for 1 hour.

Remove salmon from smoker to cool. When cold, kippered salmon should be wrapped and kept in the refrigerator until ready to use.

Shad may be used.

SALTED SALMON BELLIES
WITH SPLIT PEAS

2 cups salted salmon bellies,* soaked
  and poached
4 cups hot water
1 cup split peas
½ medium onion, grated
1 cup chopped celery
1 small carrot, grated

1 clove garlic, pressed
1 bay leaf
At least 1 teaspoon salt
4 peppercorns
Minced parsley
Lemon wedges

*Salted salmon bellies might be hard to find. Substitute with 2 cups cooked salmon, cut or broken into chunks. This is an old-time recipe, from the days when salmon was so plentiful that only the rich bellies were considered worth eating or salting. The rest of the fish was discarded.

Combine the water, peas, onion, celery, carrot, and garlic in a large pot. Add bay leaf, salt, and peppercorns; cover, and heat to a boil. Simmer for 1 hour and 15 minutes, remove the bay leaf, then purée until smooth. Return the soup to the pot, add salmon chunks, and heat to a boil. Garnish steaming hot bowls of salmon-pea soup with parsley. Serve with lemon wedges and warm sourdough French bread and butter.

BROILED SMOKED SALMON

Pour melted butter over kippered or smoked salmon and heat it under the broiler. Serve with boiled new potatoes, Parsley White Sauce (p. 418), and lemon wedges.

SMOKED SALMON ASPARAGUS SALAD

Arrange smoked or kippered salmon slices, asparagus spears, and tomato wedges on a bed of shredded lettuce. Spoon mustard French dressing over all and garnish with olives and lemon.

SMOKED OR KIPPERED SALMON SALAD

Arrange slices of kippered or smoked salmon on beds of lettuce.

DRESSING

1 cup whipped cream   1 cup cooked shrimp, chopped
1 Tablespoon prepared horseradish

Combine ingredients and spoon them over salmon.

SMOKED SALMON–CREAM CHEESE SNACKS

Soften cream cheese with milk and spread it on rye crisps or dark bread. Put a slice of smoked (or kippered) salmon on top and dab with prepared horseradish.

SMOKED (OR KIPPERED) SALMON–BROCCOLI CREPES

2 eggs   Broccoli
1/2 teaspoon salt   Mornay Sauce (p. 420)
1 cup flour   Smoked salmon
1 cup milk   Grated Parmesan or Swiss cheese
Oil or butter

For 15–18 crepes: Beat eggs, then whisk in salt, flour, and milk to make a smooth batter, just thick enough to coat a spoon. Cover and let stand for several hours or overnight. Then heat oil (or butter) in a 6-inch crepe or frying pan. Pour in enough batter to form a thin layer, tilting pan to spread it evenly. Brown on one side, then the other. As crepes are cooked, stack them with a piece of waxed paper between each.

Cook broccoli until tender, drain, then chop coarsely. Combine enough Mornay with broccoli to bind it together.

Preheat the oven to 350°F. Place a slice of salmon on each crepe, spoon on some broccoli, and roll the crepe. Spread a spoonful of Mornay over the bottom of a buttered baking dish that is just big enough to hold the crepes, one against the other. When all are rolled and in the pan, pour Mornay sauce over the crepes and heat in the oven until bubbly. Sprinkle a little cheese on top and glaze under the broiler before serving.

III

FISHING DOWN THE ATLANTIC COAST FROM BORDER TO BORDER

Codfish

CODFISH HISTORICALLY HAVE
been the most important fish in
the world, both as a food and as a
resource in world trade and wealth.
The bounteous cod supply off the North
Atlantic seaboard led to the colonization of both New England and the
Canadian maritime provinces. Since that time, commercial fishing boats
have left snug harbors and challenged the rugged sea to ply their trade
along the continental shelf from the Grand Bank off Newfoundland to
Georges Bank east of Massachusetts and south to Block Island and
Montauk Point, Long Island.

Cod are bottom dwellers, inhabiting the submarine plateaus on the
continental shelf, where the water is cool and rich in food. At certain
seasons, they leave their offshore grounds and migrate around the coast to
spawn. The cod runs start around December on the New England, New
York, and New Jersey coasts and last until late March. They are popular
game fish. Young cod are caught in the shellfish beds. When weather
permits, anglers bottom-fish at anchor or drift-fish in ten to twenty fathoms
of water, frequently getting forty and fifty pounders.

In the 1860s the presence of cod off the coast of Alaska was well
known, and the possibility of developing a prosperous salt cod industry
there was a major consideration by Congress for the purchase of Alaska.
Pacific codfish are found from Oregon north. Scrod (cod less than two and
a half pounds) are abundant in Puget Sound and can be fished from piers
and wharves.

Cod, like many other fish, have a swim bladder, or "maw," an organ
that allows them greater buoyancy without having to use their fins—the
maw adjusts to give the fish the same weight as the surrounding water. A
substance produced in the maw is called isinglass, a kind of gelatin. This
was used long ago for preserving eggs and in clarifying wines and beers.
The maw itself is edible and considered a delicacy by many.

Cod tongues are also eaten as a delicacy. The following is an 1890s recipe for Cod Tongues: "Blanch 18 cod tongues and put them in a saucepan with half a gill of the liquor that they were blanched in, heat, but do not boil. Drain, dress on a hot dish and pour over 1 pint of black butter sauce."

Pollocks (Boston bluefish), northern Atlantic cousins of cod, are not found on the West Coast. They are abundant along the Maine coast, down to Cape Cod. Surf, skiff, and party boat anglers crowd coastal areas during April and May, when pollock move inshore from deep water. Commercially important, they are almost as versatile and often less expensive than true cod.

Haddock are found in deeper water than codfish, and only in the northern Atlantic.

Two members of the cod family inhabiting both the Atlantic and Pacific Northwest coasts are tom-cod (as shown) and hake. Tomcod are silvery white, foot-long fish that range from Labrador to Virginia and from Alaska to Central California. Hake are plentiful, but have not been commercially valuable until the recent development of flash-freezing methods. Both are very edible fish.

About Codfish Meat

Cod is mild-flavored, snowy white meat, very lean, with firm but tender texture. It flakes easily when cooked. Fresh cod is available year round and locally is marketed whole, in steaks, or fillets. Frozen fillets and strips are sold in most supermarkets, as are salted, smoked, and dried forms. Most recipes for codfish, pollock, haddock, tomcod, and hake may be used interchangeably. All are excellent fish for chowder, casseroles, or stews and may be baked, sautéed, fried, poached, steamed, or smoked.

BAKED CODFISH WITH OYSTER STUFFING

4–5-pound whole codfish, degilled and
  drawn
Salt and pepper to taste
Oyster Stuffing (p. 230)

6 strips lean bacon
Melted butter
2 cups fish or chicken stock or water

Season cleaned, trimmed cod with salt and pepper, then set aside while making oyster stuffing. Stuff the fish with the dressing.

Preheat the oven to 425°F.

Put 3 slices of bacon on the bottom of a greased baking pan and place cod on top. Brush with melted butter, then lay 3 slices of bacon across the top of the fish. Add 1 cup boiling stock or water to the pan and bake for 10 minutes per inch thickness of fish. Baste often with a mixture of the remaining cup of stock and melted butter.

Bluefish or any whole fish for baking listed on page 447 (III A3) may be used.

BAKED COD FILLETS IN TOMATO-WINE SAUCE

2 pounds codfish fillets	6 Tablespoons (¾ stick) butter
1 onion, chopped	1 Tablespoon tomato paste
2 sprigs parsley, minced	1 Tablespoon flour
4 tomatoes, peeled and diced	Salt and pepper to taste
⅓ cup dry white wine	½ cup soft bread crumbs

Preheat the oven to 425°F. Wipe fillets with damp toweling and cut into serving pieces. Put chopped vegetables in a buttered baking dish, arrange fish slices on top, pour wine over, and dot with 2 tablespoons of the butter. Bake, uncovered, allowing 10 minutes per inch thickness of fish.

Remove cooked cod to a heatproof platter, cover, and keep warm. Pour juice from baking dish into a saucepan and boil it down until reduced to half the original amount. Blend tomato paste, flour, salt and pepper, and 2 more tablespoons of the butter; mix into reduced juices and cook, stirring, until sauce boils and thickens, then pour over cod. Mix crumbs with the remaining 2 tablespoons butter melted, sprinkle them over the top, and slide the platter under the broiler to brown. Serve at once.

Ocean perch fillets may also be used.

SAUTÉED WHOLE SCROD

Pan dress one or several ¾–1-pound scrod and butter sauté according to the directions on page 22.

FRIED SCROD NIÇOISE

4 scrod, 3/4 pound each	1 clove garlic, pressed
Juice of 1/2 lemon	1 dozen black pitted olives
Salt and pepper to taste	3 tomatoes, peeled and diced
Flour	4 anchovy fillets
2 Tablespoons (1/4 stick) butter	Sprig parsley, minced
2 Tablespoons oil	

Rub cleaned, trimmed fish with lemon juice, season with salt and pepper, then roll each in flour. Heat butter and oil in a heavy skillet and fry scrod until golden brown. Transfer to a platter and keep warm.

Add garlic, olives, and tomatoes to the skillet, cook 4–5 minutes, then season to taste with salt and pepper, and spoon sauce around fish. Place an anchovy fillet on each fish, sprinkle with parsley, and serve at once.

Croaker, snapper blues, speckled seatrout, or panfish may be used.

CODFISH FILLETS MAÎTRE D'HÔTEL

2 pounds codfish fillets	1 Tablespoon lemon juice
Salt and pepper	1 Tablespoon minced parsley
Flour	1/8 teaspoon ground nutmeg
1 egg, beaten	4 Tablespoons (1/2 stick) butter,
1 Tablespoon milk	softened
1 cup fine cracker crumbs	Lard for frying

Cut fillets into serving pieces, season with salt and pepper, and dust with flour. Beat egg with milk, dip fillets in it, press them in cracker crumbs, and let them dry for 30 minutes.

Make sauce by stirring lemon juice, parsley, and nutmeg into softened butter. Fry cod in hot lard until golden brown. Spread sauce over the fish and serve at once.

Good for ocean perch fillets or any lean white fillet listed on page 446 (III A1).

CODFISH AND OYSTERS
IN LEMON-CHEESE SAUCE

Poach cod fillets in salted water, flavored with 2 whole cloves, 4 crushed peppercorns, and a small piece of lemon peel. Drain and keep warm while making sauce.

Whiting may be substituted for cod.

OYSTERS IN LEMON-CHEESE SAUCE

1 cup oysters	Pepper to taste
Juice of ½ lemon	Pinch of dry mustard
2 Tablespoons (¼ stick) butter	½ teaspoon Worcestershire sauce
2 Tablespoons flour	Grated rind of ½ lemon
1 cup hot milk	⅓ cup grated American cheese
¼ teaspoon salt	Few sprigs watercress or parsley

Cook oysters in their liquor until they become plump and the edges curl. Cut each oyster into several pieces and sprinkle the pieces with lemon juice.

Heat butter, blend in flour, add hot milk, stirring until sauce thickens and boils. Add seasoning, lemon rind, and grated cheese. Stir in oysters and juice, bring to the boiling point, then spoon sauce over codfish. Garnish with watercress or parsley and serve.

POACHED COD FILLETS

Cut fillets into serving pieces and poach them.

Recipes for poaching liquids are on pages 23-27.

The following are a few ideas for poaching cod fillets:

Poach fillets in acidulated water, drain, and flake. Sprinkle with lemon juice and cover with melted butter and minced parsley. Serve with mashed potatoes and broiled tomatoes.

Tomato Sauce. Poach fillets in acidulated water, then drain. Smother fish in Tomato Sauce (p. 433) and serve with fingers of toast spread with Anchovy Butter (p. 432).

Mornay Sauce. Poach fillets in Basic Court Bouillon (p. 26), then drain. Place fish on a heatproof platter (or ovenware dishes), cover with Mornay Sauce (p. 420), and slide under a preheated broiler to glaze.

Florentine. Poach fillets in Poaching Liquid (p. 23), then proceed with ingredients and directions for Perch Fillets Florentine (p. 102).

Egg Sauce. Poach fillets in Basic Court Bouillon (p. 26) or stock, then drain. Place fish on a warm platter, surrounded with a border of parsley snips, and serve with Egg Sauce (p. 419).

COD AND SHELLFISH CHOWDER

1 pound codfish fillets
1¼ cups fresh oysters
1 can (6½ ounces) minced clams
1 can (4 ounces) shrimp
4 Tablespoons (½ stick) butter
½ cup thinly sliced leek
½ cup finely diced celery
¼ cup finely diced carrot
¼ cup minced green pepper
1 clove garlic, minced
2½ cups boiling water
⅓ cup dry white wine
1 teaspoon powdered chicken bouillon

1 bay leaf
½ teaspoon thyme
Dash each of cayenne pepper and
  mace
1 teaspoon salt
½ teaspoon pepper
¼ cup flour
⅓ cup water
1 cup macaroni shells
1 cup half-and-half
2 Tablespoons chopped pimiento
2 Tablespoons minced green onion

Melt butter in a large heavy-bottomed enamel saucepan and sauté leek, celery, carrot, green pepper, and garlic until soft. Add boiling water, wine, and liquid from shellfish. Stir in chicken base and seasonings, then simmer, covered, for 15 minutes. Mix flour and ⅓ cup water to a paste and add to the pan, stirring constantly, until thickened.

Cut codfish into 1-inch cubes, add them and oysters to the pan. Bring to a boil, reduce heat and simmer, uncovered, for 7–8 minutes.

Meanwhile, boil macaroni shells in salted water until cooked, then drain. Add them, shellfish, half-and-half, pimiento, and green onion. Stir gently, heat thoroughly, and serve.

Any lean white fillet listed on page 446 (III A1) may be substituted for cod.

OLD–FASHIONED CODFISH CHOWDER

2 pounds cod fillet
⅓ pound salt pork
2 large onions, chopped
Summer savory
Pepper
Crackers

½ cup minced parsley
3 Tablespoons butter
1 Tablespoon flour
1 lemon, sliced
2 dill pickles, diced
2 cups stewed tomatoes, hot

Slice salt pork, put it in a small bowl, pour boiling water over to freshen it for 5 minutes, then drain and dry on toweling. Fry slices slowly in a heavy skillet and, when brown and rendered, remove and chop them. Cut codfish into 2-inch slices.

Preheat the oven to 325°F. In the skillet, place a layer of onion, then a layer of pork bits, then fish, sprinkle with a little summer savory and pepper. Make a layer of crackers, moistened in warm water, then scatter a layer of parsley over them. Repeat layers—onion, pork, fish, seasoning (not too much), crackers, and parsley, until all ingredients are used. Let the top layer be crackers, dotted with 2 tablespoons of the butter. Pour in enough water barely to cover ingredients. Cover the skillet, bring to a boil, and place in the oven for 45 minutes. Check occasionally to see that liquid covers the top layer; if not, add water.

When cooked, transfer with a skimmer or slotted spoon to a tureen. Thicken the gravy with flour blended with the remaining tablespoon of butter, bring to a boil, and pour back over the chowder. Serve hot with sliced lemon, diced pickles, and a bowl of stewed tomatoes to add to your own dish, if desired.

Black drum, blackfish, sheepshead, or ling cod are fine for this dish.

MANHATTAN-STYLE CODFISH CHOWDER

1 pound cod fillets	2 cups boiling water
5 slices bacon	4 Tablespoons catsup
1 onion, chopped	1 Tablespoon Worcestershire sauce
1 cup finely diced celery	1 teaspoon salt
1 carrot, diced fine	1/4 teaspoon each pepper and thyme
1 large potato, diced	1 Tablespoon chopped parsley
1 large (28-ounce) can tomatoes	

Fry bacon until crisp, then drain on paper toweling and crumble. Pour off all but 3 tablespoons fat. Add onion to the pan and sauté until brown. Stir in celery, carrot, and potato, then add tomatoes, water, catsup, Worcestershire sauce, salt, pepper, thyme, and bacon. Cover and simmer about 30 minutes, until vegetables are tender. Cut cod in 1-inch cubes, add them to the pan, and cook 7–10 more minutes. Correct seasonings and serve hot, garnished with parsley.

Good with pollock, tomcod, or hake.

BRINE-PACKED COD,

from Puget Sound and Alaska areas, is superior to dry salt cod. It rehydrates more readily and has better flavor and texture. Soak it for 3 hours in cold water, then drain. Pour in boiling water to cover and simmer until fresh enough, up to 20 minutes.

BRANDADE OF SALT COD (MORUE)

1 pound brine-packed cod	1/2 cup heavy cream
1/4 cup milk	2/3 cup olive oil
1 clove	Generous milling of pepper
2 large cloves garlic, pressed	Crouton triangles

Soak cod in cold water for 3 hours, then drain. Place pieces of fish in a saucepan with milk, clove, and enough boiling water to cover. Heat to the boiling point, then simmer for 10 minutes. Drain the fish, pick it over for bits of bone, and flake it. Press 2 cloves garlic into the flaked fish and put it through the grinder (or food processor), using the finest blade.

Beat cod in the mixer until it is smooth—almost a paste. In separate pans, heat cream to scalding and oil to very hot. Beat them alternately into the fish, being sure that cream and oil are absorbed after each addition. When all has been added and the brandade has the consistency of mashed potatoes, add freshly ground pepper. The taste should be slightly peppery.

Serve brandade lukewarm or cold, mounded on a round platter, surrounded with triangles of buttered, slowly toasted bread.

DRIED SALT COD CREAMED WITH EGGS AND POTATOES

1 pound dried salt cod	Paprika
4–5 large baked potatoes	4–5 hard-boiled eggs
Salt and pepper to taste	2 cups Parsley White Sauce (p. 418)
Bacon fat	Snipped parsley
1 Tablespoon grated onion	

Remove skin and bones from salted dried codfish. Wash in cold water, tear into small pieces, and soak overnight in just enough cold water to cover. Drain. Place cod in a saucepan, barely covered with fresh water, heat slowly (but never allow to boil) until fresh enough, then drain. Pick over and shred; there should be about 2 cups of fish.

Cut baked potatoes in half, scoop out, mash, and season them with salt, pepper, bacon fat, and onion. Spoon back into the shells, sprinkle with paprika and keep warm in the oven.

Meanwhile, shell eggs and slice them. Heat codfish in parsley white sauce. Pour it into a hot dish, lay sliced eggs on top, garnish with parsley snips, and serve with potatoes.

SMOKED OR BARBECUED COD,

orange red in color, is ready to eat as is, just out of the package. It may be served cold with Rémoulade Sauce (p. 426) or may be steamed to serve hot.

SMOKED CODFISH CREAM

1 pound smoked cod	2 gherkins or pickled ginger, minced
2 cups Parsley White Sauce (p. 418)	Lettuce
1 envelope unflavored gelatin	Mayonnaise
1/4 cup cold water	Juice of 1/2 lemon
2 green onions, minced	

Flake cod and chop fine. Add parsley white sauce, a small amount at a time, beating with a wooden spoon until well integrated. Soak gelatin in cold water, dissolve it over hot water, then let it cool. Mix cool gelatin into fish, then stir in minced onions and pickles. Wet a mold with cold water, pour in fish mixture, and chill until set. Unmold onto a bed of lettuce and serve with mayonnaise flavored with lemon juice.

FINNAN HADDIE

Finnan Haddie is made of cod, hake, ling cod, large flounder, or haddock that is brined, then smoked for a short time. It is saffron yellow in color. The fish should not be eaten as is from the package because it is only cured, not cooked.

Poach it in a saucepan, barely covered with water. Heat slowly to a boil and simmer it 20 minutes. Serve with melted butter, Mustard White Sauce (p. 418), etc.

A variation on the method described above is to simmer for only 10 minutes, then drain and put in casserole, cover with Egg Sauce (p. 419), and bake at 350°F. for 15–20 minutes.

Bake finnan haddie in a baking dish, partly covered with milk or cream, seasoned with chopped green peppers and onions, at 350°F. for 40 minutes.

Steam finnan haddie, previously rinsed with cold water, in a steamer until it flakes. Serve with Parsley White Sauce (p. 418) or Mustard White Sauce (p. 418).

Hake, ling cod, large flounder, or haddock may be used.

Ideas for Leftover Codfish

DEVILED COD

2 cups cooked codfish
2 Tablespoons (¼ stick) butter
2 Tablespoons flour
1½ cups hot milk
1½ teaspoons Dijon-type mustard
1 Tablespoon minced green onion

½ teaspoon salt
2 teaspoons Worcestershire sauce
2 teaspoons lemon juice
1 egg, beaten
½ cup cracker crumbs

Preheat the oven to 350°F. Cut cooked cod into small pieces. Heat butter, mix in flour, and cook a few seconds. Pour in hot milk and beat until mixture boils, then remove from heat. Stir in mustard, green onion, salt, Worcestershire sauce, and lemon juice. Mix in beaten egg, then add cod bits. Transfer mixture to a small casserole, top with crumbs, and bake for 15 minutes.

CODFISH AND EGG ON TOAST

1½ cups cooked codfish
7 Tablespoons butter, melted
5 eggs, beaten

Salt and pepper to taste
¼ cup minced green onion
5 slices toast

Chop cooked codfish fine, melt 6 tablespoons of the butter and add them, then beaten eggs, and season with salt and pepper and green onion.

Heat a heavy skillet, add the remaining tablespoon butter, and tip the pan to grease the sides. Pour in egg-cod mixture and cook over medium-low heat, stirring one way, until eggs are cooked, but not hard. Spoon over toast and serve.

COD FRITTERS

1 cup cooked codfish, flaked
½ cup mashed potatoes
½ cup fine dry bread crumbs
¼ cup minced green onion
2 eggs, separated
½ cup cream

½ teaspoon salt
Pepper to taste
Cracker crumbs
Oil for frying
Minced parsley

Mix flaked cod, potatoes, crumbs, and onion. Beat egg yolks with cream and seasonings, then add to the fish mixture. Mix well and form into cakes. Beat egg whites until frothy, dip the cakes into the whites, then into cracker crumbs, and fry in oil until golden. Sprinkle with parsley and serve hot.

Butterfish

BUTTERFISH, OR DOLLARFISH as New
Englanders call them, are slender,
roundish, silvery blue fish found
from the Gulf of St. Lawrence to
Cape Hatteras. They appear when the
first mackerel come in to spawn, then dis-
appear and show up erratically, as do mackerel, until late summer. The
young are abundant inshore during August and September, and are commonly seen swimming about with the jellyfish.

Finger-size baby butterfish are a rare treat. You just rinse these tasty
morsels, dry, shake in flour, then deep fry in hot oil until crispy, and serve
with cold beer.

Only a small percentage of the butterfish catch brought in by trawlers
get to local markets—most are bought up by the smoked fish trade or are
sold to Japan.

Pumpkinseed, an almost identical looking and tasting relative of
dollarfish, are found in the southern range.

About Butterfish Meat

Butterfish is rich, delicate, and mild in flavor. The meat is off-white
and has a soft almost buttery texture. Most butterfish weigh less than
one-third pound.

These panfish are best butter sautéed, pan fried, or broiled. When
cleaned, cook them whole, with skin slashed, head and tail left on or
removed. Large fish may be split for broiling, leaving the skin intact.

BROILED BUTTERFISH
WITH BÉARNAISE SAUCE

6 large butterfish, pan dressed
Juice of ½ lemon
Salt and pepper to taste
1½ cups mushrooms

5 Tablespoons butter
Pinch of sugar
Béarnaise Sauce (p. 423)
Chopped chives

Have Béarnaise Sauce ready.

Rinse and pat fish dry. Slash skin diagonally across the sides with cuts 1 inch apart (or split fish). Rub butterfish with lemon juice and sprinkle with salt and pepper; set aside. Preheat the broiler and pan. Wash mushrooms, dry, and cut stems even with caps. Sauté caps in 2 tablespoons of the butter for 3 minutes. Sprinkle and mix with salt, pepper, and sugar, then set aside.

Oil the broiling pan and arrange fish on it. Brush them with the 3 remaining tablespoons of melted butter, and broil (see Oven Broiling Chart, page 14). Transfer broiled fish to warm plates, place several mushrooms on each fish, and spoon Béarnaise sauce over. Garnish with chopped chives and serve at once.

SAUTÉED BUTTERFISH
WITH ORANGE-ALMOND BUTTER SAUCE

6 large butterfish, or smaller fish
  pan dressed
Salt and pepper to taste
Flour
½ cup Clarified Butter (p. 430)
1 Tablespoon orange juice

½ teaspoon grated orange rind
1 teaspoon soy sauce
¼ cup sliced blanched almonds
1 large orange, peeled, sectioned, and
  sliced

Sprinkle butterfish with salt and pepper inside and out, dust lightly with flour, and shake off the excess. Heat clarified butter. Place butterfish in skillet and sauté about 4–5 minutes on each side, until crispy, brown, and done. Remove cooked fish to warm plates. Combine orange juice, rind, and soy sauce; add this, with almonds, to the pan. Raise the heat and cook for a minute or two, scraping the pan to loosen all the crumbs. Spoon orange-almond sauce over the fish, garnish with sliced oranges, and serve at once.

Monkfish

MONKFISH ARE INSHORE FISH, common from Newfoundland to North Carolina. They swim close to the tide line
in winter, moving into deeper water during warm
weather. Locally, monkfish are known as goosefish,
bellyfish, angler, and lotte. They are brought in by
trawlers as incidental catch.

Their bizarre appearance, odd method of attracting
food, and notorious gluttony are what make this fish
truly unique.

Monkfish is mostly all big, round, flattened head, with an enormous
toothy mouth. The pectoral fins are thick and fleshy handlike structures
sticking out of the side of the head. A thin body tapers to the small tail fin.
It is scaleless, thin-skinned, and mottled brown to resemble the sea floor.
The whole fish, even jaws and lips, is margined with a seaweed-looking
fringe that waves in the current.

Just behind the upper lip, a long spine with a baitlike tip becomes its
"fishing lure." The hungry monkfish flutters its "fishing lure" to attract
prey. When a curious fish investigates the bait, gluttonous monkfish opens
its vast toothy mouth and in the victim goes. It can swallow a fish almost
its own size. Monkfish can be two to four feet long and weigh more than
thirty pounds.

The insatiable monkfish eats flounder, cod, dogfish, skates, eel, sea
gulls, cormorants, ducks, and other birds, as well as crab and squid.

About Monkfish Meat

The tail meat of monkfish, which is the part eaten, is light, delicate, firm,
and without bones, similar in texture and taste to lobster. The dressed tail
is delicious baked with vegetables, poached, steamed, or braised, and
served with a creamy sauce. Grilling and broiling tend to toughen and dry
out the meat. Monkfish requires a little longer cooking than most fish. If
underdone, it has a gelatinous taste.

To dress monkfish: Cut the tail away from the head with a sharp knife. Paper towels will help to firm your grip on the fish. The head may be discarded (or used for soup). Rinse the tail section in cold water splashed with a little vinegar, then wipe with toweling and slit the skin down to the tail fin on the underside, cut and pull it off. Trim away all pinkish tan membrane between the skin and meat (which becomes tough), leaving only the white meat surrounding the backbone, which you may fillet.

MONKFISH IN CREAM SAUCE

2 pounds monkfish fillet
2 Tablespoons minced onion
2 Tablespoons minced green pepper
2 Tablespoons chopped mushrooms
1 Tablespoon butter
2 cups Cream Sauce (p. 419)

1 Tablespoon chopped pimiento
3 Tablespoons sherry
Dash of cayenne pepper
Salt and pepper to taste
¼ cup dry crumbs
¼ cup grated Parmesan cheese

Poach fish in barely simmering salted water for 25 minutes; remove from heat and drain. Cut fish into bite-size pieces and place them in a buttered casserole. Sauté onion, green pepper, and mushrooms slowly in butter until soft, then remove from heat. Preheat the oven to 350°F. Make cream sauce, then mix in sautéed vegetables, pimiento, sherry, and cayenne. Season sauce with salt and pepper, and pour it over fish in casserole. Mix crumbs with cheese and scatter them on top. Put the casserole in the oven and bake until sauce bubbles and crumbs are brown.

MONKFISH SALAD

2 pounds monkfish fillet
1 head lettuce
Tomatoes, cut in wedges
Pitted black olives

Sour Cream Cucumber Sauce (p. 429)
2 Tablespoons capers
4 rolled anchovy fillets

Trim off ragged edges and cut fillet into serving pieces. Poach fish in barely simmering salted water for 25 minutes; remove and let cool to room temperature.

Put a large crisp lettuce leaf on each salad plate and a bed of shredded lettuce on each leaf. Place a slice of fish in the center and surround it with tomato wedges and black olives. Spoon sour cream cucumber sauce over the fish, sprinkle with capers, and place a rolled anchovy fillet on top.

MONKFISH BOURRIDE (SOUP)

2 pounds monkfish fillets
1 pound sea robin fillets (or seabass)
1 lobster tail, thawed
Salt to taste
1 large onion, chopped
2 Tablespoons olive oil
1 teaspoon tomato paste
2 cloves garlic, crushed
1/2 teaspoon thyme
2 bay leaves
1/2 teaspoon fennel

Two 2-inch pieces orange rind
1/4 cup brandy
1 cup Chablis
1/2 cup white vermouth
1 1/2 cups water or stock
Pepper to taste
Croutons
Butter
2 egg yolks
Aioli Sauce (p. 424)

Rinse, pat dry, and cut fillets of both fish into 2-inch pieces. Cut lobster (in shell) into 4 pieces; sprinkle fish with salt and set aside. Sauté onion in oil until soft and yellow. Stir in tomato paste, garlic, thyme, bay leaves, fennel, and orange rind. Pour in brandy, wines, and water, bring to a boil, then simmer for several minutes. Arrange fish in the pan, thicker pieces on the bottom. Bring to a boil again, season with salt and pepper, cover, and reduce heat to simmer until fish is cooked. Remove fish to a warm platter, pour a ladle of broth over the fish, cover the platter with foil, and place it in the oven to keep warm. Strain the broth into a clean pan.

Fry croutons in butter, put them in a bowl and keep warm.

Reheat broth over low heat. Beat egg yolks, mix with a little of the hot broth, then stir them carefully into the pan. Stir constantly until soup is scalding, then remove from heat. Portion fish into soup bowls, ladle in hot broth, and serve. Pass warm croutons and the bowl of aioli sauce at the table.

MONKFISH STEW

2 pounds monkfish fillet
Salt and pepper to taste
Flour
4 Tablespoons olive oil
1 small onion, chopped
1 clove garlic, minced
1 carrot, sliced thin
1/2 cup chicken broth

3 Tablespoons tomato purée
1/2 cup Chablis
1/2 cup Madeira
12 small boiling onions cooked and
    drained, or 1 can whole boiled
    onions, drained
Dash of cayenne pepper
Soft bread crumbs

Cut monkfish into ¾-inch-thick small slices, sprinkle with salt and pepper, and dust lightly with flour. Heat oil in a large pan and stir-fry fish, onion, and garlic for a few minutes. Stir in carrots, then add chicken broth, tomato purée, wines, and boiled onions. Cover and simmer gently for about 20 minutes, until fish is cooked. Season with cayenne and salt and pepper. Thicken sauce, if you like, by adding bread crumbs and cooking for 3 minutes more.

Porgy

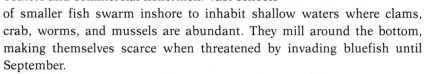

PORGIES (SCUPS) APPEAR off the Northeast
coast in late May. The larger two- to three-
pounders, nicknamed "dinner plates"
and "shad porgies," take up residence
in the mid-depths of the continental shelf
and are eagerly sought by New England party
boaters and commercial fishermen. Vast schools
of smaller fish swarm inshore to inhabit shallow waters where clams,
crab, worms, and mussels are abundant. They mill around the bottom,
making themselves scarce when threatened by invading bluefish until
September.

Silvery, oval-shaped scups are fished from docks, piers, and bridges,
and from anchored skiffs. Chumming, by dropping some crushed clams
into the water, usually brings the schooling fish to your spot. They are
plentiful, willing biters, fun to catch, and very good to eat.

The whitebone porgy is the most common species south of the Carolinas;
and the jolthead is abundant in the Bahamas.

About Porgy Meat

Porgy is delicious, delicate-flavored meat. The texture is fairly coarse, but
firm and moist. It does have small sharp bones. The problem of small
bones and tough skin can be solved in two ways: 1. For *larger fish*, careful
filleting and skinning can eliminate most bones; the rest can be felt for
and picked out with tweezers. 2. Clean and scale *small fish* soon after they
are caught, then score (by cutting) the skin of the whole dressed porgies.
Cook, then lift the meat free from the backbone after cooking.

Most recipes for grunts, spadefish, and porgy are interchangeable.

PORGY MIXED GRILL IN FOIL

4 porgy fillets, skinned	Butter
12 raw shrimp	Pepper to taste
Salt to taste	2 Tablespoons chopped green onion
2 chicken thighs	1½ Tablespoons lemon juice
8 large mushrooms	2 Tablespoons bottled tempura sauce

Wipe fillets with a damp cloth, sprinkle with salt, then set aside. Shell and clean shrimp. Parboil them in slightly salted boiling water for 1 or 2 minutes; drain and set aside. Bone and skin chicken, cut into 1¼-inch pieces and score each piece with deep cuts; set aside. Wash and slice mushrooms vertically in ¼-inch-thick slices.

Preheat the oven to 475°F. (or use a charcoal grill when coals are hottest). Tear off four 12 × 12–inch pieces of heavy-duty foil and butter them to within 1½ inches of the edges. Place a portion each of porgy, shrimp, chicken, and mushroom, and a pat of butter on each foil. Sprinkle lightly with salt and pepper. Combine green onion, lemon juice, and tempura sauce; spoon mixture over the portions. Fold foil in half, then double fold the edges to seal the packages tightly. Place them on a baking sheet in the oven and bake 15–20 minutes (or grill above the coals without turning, for 10 minutes). Serve the packages to be opened at the table.

Sole, perch, or grunt may substitute for porgy.

BARBECUED PORGY

4 porgies, pan dressed (heads and tails removed)	8-ounce can tomato sauce
	2 teaspoons Worcestershire sauce
¼ cup chopped onion	Pinch each thyme, basil, and oregano
1 clove garlic, minced	Salt and pepper to taste
8 Tablespoons (1 stick) butter	

Sauté onion and garlic in butter until tender, then stir in all ingredients, except fish, and let cool to room temperature.

Score sides of fish with several diagonal slashes. Place porgies in a baking dish and pour marinade over them. Marinate, turning several times, until coals have burned down to medium hot. Place fish on hot greased grill 6 inches from the coals and cook, turning once, until brown and done on both sides. Baste frequently with marinade during cooking. Transfer fish to warm plates and serve.

Good for other panfish too.

PAN-FRIED PORGY AND OTHER PANFISH

4 porgies, skinned and dressed (heads
    and tails removed)
½ cup flour
½ cup cornmeal
1 teaspoon salt
¼ teaspoon pepper

¼ cup milk
8 Tablespoons (1 stick) butter
½ cup vegetable oil
2 Tablespoons chopped olives
2 Tablespoons minced green onions
1 lemon, cut in wedges

Rinse and wipe porgies with a damp cloth. Combine flour, cornmeal, and salt and pepper. Dip fish in milk, then in cornmeal mixture, and lay them on waxed paper until ready to cook.

Heat butter and oil and in it fry porgies, over medium heat, until brown, about 5 minutes. Turn carefully and cook the other side until crispy and done. Remove fish to a warm platter, sprinkle with chopped olives and onion, and serve with lemon wedges.

PAN-FRIED PORGY
WITH BLACK BEAN SAUCE

4 porgies, about ¾ pound each
Salt and pepper to taste
2 Tablespoons fermented black beans*
1 clove garlic, minced
2 teaspoons soy sauce
2 teaspoons brandy

2 teaspoons cornstarch
1 cup cold water
½ cup salad oil
Flour
2 eggs, beaten
1 green onion, chopped

*See Glossary.

Rinse and pat fish dry, score skin with diagonal cuts, 1 inch apart, sprinkle with salt and pepper, and set aside. Scald black beans in boiling water, drain, crush, and mix them with garlic, soy sauce, and brandy, then set aside. Mix cornstarch with the 1 cup cold water.

Heat oil over high heat in a large skillet. Dust fish lightly with flour, then dip in beaten egg and fry porgies on each side for a minute. Reduce heat to medium and cook, turning fish over every 3 minutes, until they are brown and done.

Pour off all but 1 tablespoon of oil, then fry black bean mixture and green onion for a few seconds, stirring constantly. Stir in cornstarch-water mixture and cook, stirring, until sauce thickens. Spoon sauce onto fish and serve.

Grunt or other panfish of the same size may be used.

Idea for Leftover Porgy

PORGY LOAF

1 1/2 cups porgy, cooked
1 large onion, chopped
3 Tablespoons butter
1 Tablespoon flour
1 1/2 cups tomato juice
1 Tablespoon lemon juice

1 1/2 cups matzo meal (plus extra to
  dust pan)
2 eggs
1 teaspoon salt
Generous milling of pepper

Flake cooked porgy with a fork. Sauté onion slowly in butter until it yellows. Mix in flour, then tomato juice, and stir while cooking until smooth and thickened. Add lemon juice, simmer 2 more minutes, and remove from heat. Stir in flaked fish and matzo meal. Beat eggs and salt and pepper with a fork, then mix thoroughly with the other ingredients. Preheat the oven to 350°F.

Butter a 5 × 9-inch loaf pan, dust it with additional matzo meal, and pour in the fish mixture. Bake for 35–40 minutes. Allow fish loaf to set for 5 minutes before unmolding.

Any lean white fish listed on page 446 (III A1) may be used.

White Perch

WHITE PERCH, in spite of their name, are really bass—relatives of the striped bass. Their name could also confuse them with freshwater silver perch. These narrow, deep-bodied, greenish silver fish are found in fresh-water and also in the salty Atlantic Ocean from Nova Scotia to South Carolina. But their favored habitat is in brackish estuaries, bays, and sea-connected ponds. Schools of perch hibernate in protected bays and creeks during winter. In spring the schools migrate up tributary streams to spawn. When a school has been located, still-fishing at anchor can bring you lots of fun and a string of those delicious panfish.

About White Perch Meat

White perch are superb table fish, excelled by none in the New York, Washington, or Richmond markets. These popular game fish average about ten inches, and one to two and a half pounds. To prepare perch for pan frying, simply clean, scale, behead, rinse, and dry them. Larger fish may be filleted and deep fried, poached, and served with oysters and/or sautéed. Use them in chowder or try them smoked.

See Kelp, Rock, and Spotted Sand Bass chapter, pages 65–72, for additional recipes.

RYE-FRIED WHITE PERCH

4 white perch fillets, 6–8 ounces each; or 4 small whole white perch, cleaned and scaled
¼ cup cream
1 teaspoon salt
1 egg, beaten

1 cup rye flour
2 Tablespoons (¼ stick) butter
2 Tablespoons vegetable oil
Generous milling of pepper
Lime wedges

Rye flour adds a delicious nutty flavor to fish. Mix cream and salt with egg. Dip fish in egg mixture, then in rye flour. Heat butter and oil until foamy, add fish, and fry golden crisp on both sides. Remove to warm plates, sprinkle generously with pepper, garnish with lime wedges, and serve.

This recipe is good for any lean fillet or panfish listed on page 446 (III A1).

DEEP-FRIED WHITE PERCH

1 pound white perch fillets	1 teaspoon cornstarch
1 teaspoon salt	1 egg, beaten
1/4 teaspoon pepper	1/2 cup blanched almonds
1/4 teaspoon monosodium glutamate	Oil for deep frying
1 Tablespoon dry vermouth	

Cut fillets into 1/2-inch strips. Combine salt, pepper, monosodium glutamate, vermouth, and cornstarch in a bowl with beaten egg. Grind almonds to fine crumbs in blender. Dip fish in egg mixture, then in nut crumbs, and place on waxed paper. Deep fry a few strips at a time in hot (365°F.) oil, until golden straw color. Drain them briefly on toweling, spear with cocktail picks, and serve.

Any of the firm lean fillets listed on page 447 (III A2) may be used.

WHITE PERCH FILLETS
WITH SOUR CREAM SAUCE

4 white perch fillets, 6–8 ounces each; or 4 small whole perch, cleaned and scaled	1 Tablespoon minced fresh mint
	1 cup sour cream
	Salt and white pepper to taste
2 Tablespoons grated onion	Poaching Liquid (p. 23)

Make sour cream sauce several hours before serving to allow time for flavors to meld: Stir grated onion and mint into sour cream, season with salt and white pepper to taste, and chill until ready to use.

Rinse fish, pat dry, and sprinkle with salt and pepper. Poach fish using Basic Poaching methods on pages 23–5.

Drain perch, and remove skin from whole fish. If serving cold, let perch cool to room temperature, place them in lettuce cups, mask with chilled sauce, and garnish attractively. If serving perch hot, preheat the broiler. Place fish on sizzle platters, mask them with sour cream sauce, and slide them under the broiler to heat the sauce thoroughly. Serve at once.

Tilefish

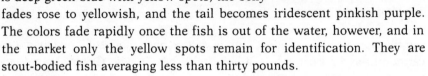

TILEFISH pulled from the water are
the most colorful fish outside the
tropics. The head is reddish on top
and white underneath, the upper body
is deep green blue with yellow spots, the belly
fades rose to yellowish, and the tail becomes iridescent pinkish purple.
The colors fade rapidly once the fish is out of the water, however, and in
the market only the yellow spots remain for identification. They are
stout-bodied fish averaging less than thirty pounds.

Tilefish roam the ocean floor in water temperatures 47°–53°F. and
along the outer continental shelf from Nova Scotia to Florida and the Gulf
of Mexico.

Charter and party boaters out of New York and New Jersey fish
tilefish on the slopes of the Hudson Canyon, particularly in late fall
and winter. Considerable quantities are commercially taken throughout
most of the year by long-line boats fishing the deep grounds of the
Baltimore Canyon.

About Tilefish Meat

Tilefish is exceptionally good eating fish. The meat is lean, moist, fine
textured, firm, and pink. Its mild flavor has been compared to striped bass
or codfish. Steaks or fillets are sold relatively inexpensively at most
Eastern fish markets.

You can broil, barbecue, bake it in foil, oven fry, deep fry, poach, steam,
or braise tilefish. It is delicious fish for salads, cocktails, chowder, or
served raw for sashimi, ceviche, or sushi. It is also good smoked.

The meat of the white seabass (see pages 77–83) is very similar to that
of the tilefish: mild-flavored, lean, and firm-textured. You may substitute
tilefish most successfully in any of the white seabass recipes.

TILEFISH SUSHI

Sushi is the "rice sandwich" of Japan. It is made of cold vinegared rice, pressed and shaped into small patties (and other forms). On top of each patty a delicacy is placed such as: sliced fish or shellfish, egg and/or vegetables, and a spicy condiment such as pickled ginger and Japanese horseradish. This sushi will be made of thin slices of raw tilefish, seasoned mushrooms, and pickled ginger on top of sushi vinegared rice.

1 pound tilefish	At least ¼ cup soy sauce
Juice of 1 lime	Wasabi (Japanese horseradish)*
4 dried black mushrooms	Pickled ginger*
3 Tablespoons sugar	1 lime, cut in wedges
2 Tablespoons sake (rice wine)	

*See Glossary.

Pour boiling water over raw tilefish, then quickly dunk it in ice water, and pat dry. Sprinkle lime juice over tilefish and refrigerate until used.*
   Salmon, tuna, white seabass, or yellowtail may be used.

*If you prefer tilefish cooked: Marinate thin tilefish slices for 10 minutes in ½ cup each water and rice vinegar, ½ teaspoon sugar, and 1 teaspoon soy sauce. Grill slices on skewers for 2 minutes, cool slightly, remove skewers, and place on prepared rice.

SUSHI VINEGARED RICE

¼ cup sugar	½ teaspoon monosodium glutamate
1 teaspoon salt	(optional)
¼ cup rice vinegar	4 cups cooked short-grain rice

Mix ¼ cup sugar and salt with vinegar (and monosodium glutamate, if you want it) and toss well with hot rice. Let it cool to room temperature, but don't refrigerate.

Cover mushrooms with hot water and soak for 20 minutes; add the 3 tablespoons sugar, the sake, and ¼ cup of the soy sauce and simmer until the liquid is completely absorbed. Let cool to room temperature.

To shape rice, scoop about 2 tablespoons of cool rice into your moistened hand, and press it into an oblong patty shape. Brush the tops of the shaped rice with soy sauce, and smear on a pinch of wasabi (horseradish). Cut raw tilefish into slices approximately the same size as the rice patties. Press the fish into rice. Slice mushrooms into strips and place them decoratively on top. Serve sushi with slices of pickled ginger and/or wedges of lime.

FOIL-BAKED TILEFISH WITH MUSHROOMS

2 pounds tilefish, cut into 4 thick fillets	6 Tablespoons (¾ stick) butter,
Juice of 1 lime	softened
Salt and pepper	Flour
8 large mushrooms	4 slices lime
¼ teaspoon each basil, thyme, fennel,	2 Tablespoons minced parsley
marjoram, and sage	

Wipe fillets with a damp cloth, sprinkle with lime juice and salt and pepper and set aside. Wash and slice mushrooms vertically into ¼-inch-thick slices and set aside. Tear off four 12 × 12-inch pieces of heavy-duty aluminum foil and butter the foil to within 1½ inches of the edges. Mash basil, thyme, fennel, marjoram, and sage into softened butter, and mix well.

Preheat the oven to 475°F. Dust fillets lightly with flour and shake off the excess. Spread them with half of the butter and let it settle for a few minutes. Place fish on foil pieces (butter side down) and butter the other side. Arrange mushrooms and a slice of lime on each portion, sprinkle lightly with salt and pepper, then scatter parsley on top. Fold foil in half, then double fold the edges to seal packages tightly. Place them on a baking sheet and bake for 15–20 minutes. Serve the packages to be opened at the table.

Any firm lean fillet listed on page 447 (III A2) may be used.

OVEN-FRIED TILEFISH WITH SKORDALIA SAUCE (GARLIC-ALMOND MAYONNAISE)

2 pounds tilefish fillet	1 cup dry bread crumbs
1 teaspoon salt	4 Tablespoons (½ stick) butter
Flour	4 Tablespoons salad oil
2 Tablespoons milk	1 lemon, cut in wedges
1 egg	

Cut tilefish into serving pieces, season with salt, dust with flour and shake off the excess. Beat milk with egg. Dip fish in egg, then press into crumbs. Set coated fish on waxed paper to dry for 30 minutes; turn pieces once after 15 minutes. Meanwhile, make Skordalia Sauce.

Skordalia Sauce

½ cup blanched almonds
1 egg
2 cloves garlic, sliced

3 Tablespoons wine vinegar
Salt to taste
⅔ cup salad oil

Preheat the oven to 350°F. Spread almonds in a baking dish and toast them until straw colored, about 10 minutes. Raise oven temperature to 500°F. and preheat the pan to cook tilefish. Grind almonds to fine crumbs in blender, remove, set them aside. In the same container, combine egg, garlic, vinegar, and salt, then blend for a few seconds. Blend in oil, a few drops at a time, until mixture thickens, then add remaining oil in a slow, thin stream. Add almonds and whirl until mixed. Spoon sauce into a serving bowl.

Remove the pan from the oven and put in butter and oil. Tilt the pan to spread butter and oil around. Place fillets in the pan, then turn them over so both sides are buttered. Return pan to oven and bake, uncovered, until crispy golden brown. Arrange fillets on a warm platter, sprinkle with a little more salt, garnish with lemon wedges, and serve with bowl of Skordalia Sauce.

Thick, lean, firm fillets listed on page 447 (III A2) may be substituted.

TILEFISH WITH GRAPEFRUIT AND ALMONDS

1½ pounds tilefish fillets
Salt and pepper to taste
Cornstarch
2 large grapefruit
2 Tablespoons honey

4 Tablespoons salad oil
½ cup sliced blanched almonds
3 cloves garlic, minced
1 teaspoon minced ginger
1 Tablespoon minced parsley

Cut fillets into ¾ × 2-inch strips, season with salt and pepper, and dust lightly with cornstarch, then set aside. Peel and section grapefruit and mix it with honey. Heat oil in a skillet and sauté almonds until they turn straw colored, then remove with a slotted spoon and set aside. Turn fire to high, add garlic and ginger to oil, stir-fry a few seconds, lower heat to medium, add fish and sauté for 4 minutes, then turn and cook the other side. Transfer fish to a warm platter. Add grapefruit and parsley to the skillet; heat through and pour over fish. Scatter almonds over the platter and serve at once.

Any lean white fillet listed on page 446 (III A1) may be used.

Atlantic Black Seabass

IN MAY, fishermen from Cape Cod to Cape Hatteras look forward to the return of the seabass—black will, blackfish or humpback, they call them. They are brownish black fish with chunky bodies and long, sharp, light-spotted dorsal fins. The elongated upper ray of their tail fin, which sticks out past the rest of the tail, identifies them. Their peculiarity is a bump on the head, which males develop during spawning season.

Black wills enter the bays, sounds, deep channels, and creeks, where clear water currents move briskly and the bottom is rocky hard. They remain inshore, feeding close to the bottom on barnacles, mussels, crab, and small fish throughout the summer.

Shore anglers fish black wills from piers and wharves. Small-boat fishermen drop anchor and still-fish for the one- to three-pounders. Party boaters and those who fish deep water catch the big four- and five-pounders farther out.

Late in October each year, black seabass travel into deep water off the coast of Virginia and North Carolina, where they are commercially fished all winter.

About Atlantic Black Seabass Meat

Black seabass is a long-standing favorite at Chinese restaurants on the East Coast. It is excellent table fish, with the same lean, mild, white flesh and texture as West Coast rockfish. Cooked whole or filleted, it is good fish to barbecue, fry, poach, or steam.

See Rockfish chapter, pages 110–18, for additional recipes.

BLACK SEABASS FILLET BAKED IN FOIL

2 pounds black seabass fillets	2 teaspoons minced parsley
¼ cup olive oil	Salt
¼ cup lemon juice	Freshly ground black pepper
¼ teaspoon rubbed oregano	4 thin slices lemon

Mix a marinade of olive oil, lemon juice, oregano, and parsley. Tear off four 12 × 12-inch pieces of heavy-duty foil and butter them to within 1½ inches of the edges. Preheat the oven to 450°F.

Rinse fillets, pat dry on toweling, and cut fish into serving pieces. Dip pieces in marinade and portion them on the squares of foil. Sprinkle lightly with salt and freshly ground pepper. Place a slice of lemon on each portion and pour remaining marinade onto the fish. Fold foil in half, then double fold and crimp the edges to seal the packages tightly. Place packages on a baking sheet and bake for about 20 minutes, until cooked.

Shad

AMERICAN SHAD inhabit the
entire Atlantic Coast. These two-
to eight-plus–pound fish are the
largest members of the herring family.
Their smaller cousins, hickory shad, are a more
southern species.

Shad are anadromous fish; i.e., they make their way up bays, rivers, and streams into freshwater to spawn. Newly hatched fish remain in freshwater until the weather cools, then migrate to the ocean where they spend the next two to five years.

Northern shad spawn at least twice, but those south of North Carolina reproduce only once. They have no particular migratory pattern, as do salmon, who always go back where they originated. Water temperature triggers shad migrations. Shad season (spawning runs) begins early in Florida, around late November, whereas the season peaks in the Gulf of St. Lawrence in May.

Shad was transplanted to the West Coast in the 1870s. They have become commercially important fish, though not profuse. The runs begin in January in Central California and continue through May in the Northwest.

Fresh from the sea, shad are game fighters. Early in the morning or evening, they can be caught on light tackle by trolling the mouth of bays and rivers or by still-fishing the deep holes or surf casting.

About Shad Meat

"Poor man's salmon," as some call this delicious fish, is meaty and has moderately oily white flesh. It is regrettable that shad has so many small bones, which makes it difficult to bone. During the season fresh whole shad is available in local markets. Then, too, the markets carry fresh shad roe (as well as canned).

Boning Shad

The old professionals who mastered the art of boning shad are becoming increasingly hard to find. It takes skill and practice to cope with shad's complex bone structure.

To bone your shad, fillet it soon after it is caught, as you would any round fish; leave on the skin. Wrap and ice-down the fillets for two to three days to firm the meat enough for deboning. Then place fillets on a solid surface, skin down, and feel out the three parallel rows of bones that run the length of each fillet. Start with the row nearest the thickest side and, cutting from head toward tail end, run your blade along both sides of the bones (but only to the depth where they branch out into upside-down Ys). Then change the angle of your knife and lay open the row of bones down to the skin. Carefully pull the whole row of bones away from the skin (use the knife tip to aid removal). Cut out the other outside row of bones the same way, then lastly tackle the center row of bones.

Having removed all three rows of bones, you are left with four strips of boneless meat, which are barely connected to the skin. You may want to wrap the boned fillet in foil to hold it together and retain shape. Or you can remove the boned strips from the skin and roll them "pinwheel-fashion" into steaks held together by thin wooden skewers.

Bone the other fillet the same way.

BROILED SHAD

3 pounds shad, dressed and split
6 Tablespoons (¾ stick) butter, melted

Juice of 1 lemon
Salt and pepper to taste

Split a cleaned, dressed shad along the back and remove the large bone, but don't bone it further. Preheat the broiler and pan. Combine butter and lemon juice. Rub fish with lemon-butter, sprinkle with salt and pepper, and place it skin side up on the oiled broiler pan. Broil shad, turning once, for 10 minutes per inch thickness of fish. Baste every 3 minutes while broiling. Serve with herbed butter.

SHAD MEUNIÈRE

Dip boned fillets (skin on or off) briefly in milk, then roll in flour, and sauté in butter and oil until crisp and brown.

BAKED SHAD

3-4-pound shad, cleaned
Salt and pepper
Garlic powder
8 Tablespoons (1 stick) butter

1 teaspoon freshly snipped rosemary
1 Tablespoon white wine vinegar
1 lemon, cut in wedges

Leave the head and tail on a cleaned, scaled shad, rinse and dry fish. Cut several shallow diagonal slashes on both sides and sprinkle salt, pepper, and garlic powder inside and out.

Preheat the oven to 425°F. Arrange shad in a buttered baking dish, dot generously with butter, and sprinkle rosemary over the fish. Bake for 10 minutes per inch thickness of fish, basting about every 3 minutes. When fish flakes easily, transfer it to a warm platter. Mix vinegar with pan juices, then pour them over the fish. Garnish with lemon wedges and serve with new potatoes.

FOIL-BAKED SHAD ORIENTAL

2 pounds or 1 shad, boned
1 Tablespoon fermented salted black
   beans*
¼ cup salad oil
3 Tablespoons soy sauce
2 Tablespoons dry sherry
1 teaspoon sugar

1 green onion, split lengthwise, then
   cut in ¾-inch pieces
1 Tablespoon minced ginger
1 cucumber, cut in chunks
1 Tablespoon cornstarch
¼ cup cold water

*See Glossary.

Rinse and dry boned fillets, cut them into serving pieces. Soften black beans in hot water for 5 minutes, then drain and mash them with oil. Mix in soy sauce, sherry, sugar, onion, and ginger, and marinate fillets in sauce for 15 minutes.

Preheat the oven to 450°F. Tear off a large strip of foil, enough to line a baking dish and envelop the fish. Butter the foil to within 1½ inches of the edges. Place it in the dish and arrange the shad on it. Pour marinade over the fish, then wrap, double folding the edges to seal. Bake for 10 minutes per inch thickness of fish, plus 5 minutes for heat to penetrate fish.

Open foil and pour sauce into a saucepan. Heat cucumber chunks in the sauce. Mix cornstarch with water, stir it into sauce and cook, stirring, until thickened. Remove shad to a platter, spoon cucumber around fish and pour sauce over it.

Red drum (redfish) may be used.

SHAD WITH CORN BREAD STUFFING

1 shad, dressed and split (or boned)
Juice of ½ lemon
Salt to taste
1 green onion, minced
¼ cup minced celery
1 Tablespoon minced green pepper
1 cup chopped mushrooms

4 Tablespoons (½ stick) butter
1 cup crumbled corn bread
¼ teaspoon dill
Pepper to taste
¼ cup water
Butter

Split a cleaned, dressed shad, and remove the backbone (or bone the shad, page 211). Sprinkle with lemon juice and salt. Preheat the oven to 425°F. Make stuffing: Sauté vegetables in butter for 5 minutes. Mix in corn bread crumbs, season with dill, salt, and pepper, then stuff fish and sew the sides together. Place shad in a buttered baking pan and pour in water. Dot fish generously with butter and bake for 10 minutes per inch thickness, measured after stuffing. Baste every 3 or 4 minutes.

Steelhead, salmon trout, whitefish, or whiting may be substituted for shad.

STEAMED SHAD WITH HAM

2 pounds whole shad, cleaned
5 Tablespoons soy sauce
2 Tablespoons dry sherry
4-5 slices fresh ginger
1 green onion, split, then cut in
  1½-inch pieces

⅔ cup cooked ham, cut in thinnest
  possible strips (julienne)
3 Tablespoons rice vinegar
2 teaspoons minced ginger

Scale and clean, rinse and dry shad and place on a deep platter (cut fish in half, if need be). Brush inside and out with a mixture of 2 tablespoons of the soy sauce and sherry. Place half of the ginger, green onion, and ham strips in the cavity and sprinkle remaining over the top. Wrap the platter and steam shad (see page 27). Serve steamed shad with a dipping sauce made by warming together the remaining 3 tablespoons of soy sauce, the vinegar, and minced ginger.

SMOKED SHAD (KIPPERED)

Shad is smoked the same way salmon is smoked and may be served the same. See Kippered Salmon, pages 174-5.

Shad Roe

The pair of roe taken from shad need careful handling. Remove them without breaking the membrane that encases the eggs. Rinse carefully, and cut the pair apart. Blanch roe to firm the egg mass, to shorten cooking time, and to make further cooking easier. Do so by covering roe with boiling water; add to it 2 teaspoons salt and 1 tablespoon lemon juice. Cook, barely simmering, until the roe just turn opaque. Drain, plunge into a bowl of ice water for half a minute, then drain again on toweling.

Cooking with too-high heat can cause eggs to explode; over-cooking toughens them. Roe poached in court bouillon (p. 26) for about 8-9 minutes and then drained and allowed to cool, can be used for salads. If you sauté roe after blanching (or even if you don't blanch), prick the membrane with tiny holes here and there, to keep the eggs from exploding, and sauté over very, very low heat.

SAUTÉED SHAD ROE

Quote the fisherman: "Just me and my shad — roe."

1½ pounds (2 pairs) shad roe
Flour
3 Tablespoons butter
2 Tablespoons oil
Salt and pepper to taste

Sprig parsley, minced
4 slices bacon, cooked crisp
  and crumbled
1 lemon, cut in wedges
Cucumber slices

Roll roe in flour and fry them slowly in butter and oil until nicely brown, about 6 minutes on each side. Season with salt and pepper and serve them on a warm platter, sprinkled with parsley and crumbled bacon. Garnish with lemon wedges and cucumber slices. New potatoes in Parsley White Sauce (p. 418) complement this dish.

Blackfish (Tautog)

BLACKFISH (TAUTOG) is favored
game for spear fishermen and
small-boat anglers, who find
them in shallow coastal water from
Cape Cod to Delaware Bay. They are
chunky, thick-bodied, brown-mottled, one- to five-plus-pound fish.

In spring, tautog move into rocky-bottom, sheltered seaweed-covered
areas, seeking mussel beds, crab, and barnacles. They are lightning-fast
bait stealers and, when hooked, pull all their line-tangling tricks. They
swim within their protected territory until fall, then move offshore into
very deep water to hibernate during winter.

About Blackfish Meat

Blackfish is thick-textured, lean meat, excellent for fish and chips, and
also for chowders, stews, and soups. The meat remains tender-firm and
does not fall apart when simmered. Creamy rich and flavorful sauces,
herbed and spicy marinades all go well on firm, thick blackfish fillets.
Fillets may be baked in buttered crumbs, fried, poached, or steamed, and
served hot or cold.

Tautog has a tough skin. Remove it before cooking by freezing the fish
only enough to stiffen the skin, then cut through and work it off.

Most recipes for tautog, hogfish, or cunner (relatives of the tautog)
may be used interchangeably.

Blackfish meat is similar to that of sheepshead. Refer to California
Sheepshead chapter, pages 54–9, for additional recipes.

GINGER-PEACHY BLACKFISH

2 pounds blackfish fillets	2 teaspoons grated fresh ginger
Salt and pepper to taste	1 Tablespoon cornstarch
4 Tablespoons (½ stick) butter	2 Tablespoons lemon juice
16-ounce can sliced peaches	2 Tablespoons water

Preheat the oven to 400° F. Wipe fillets with a damp cloth, cut into serving pieces, place them in a buttered baking dish, and sprinkle with salt and pepper. Melt butter over very low heat until hazelnut brown; remove from heat and mix with drained peaches (reserve the juice). Arrange peach slices on fish, pour butter over both and bake, uncovered, until fish flakes easily, about 20 minutes.

Meanwhile, simmer peach juice with ginger for 10 minutes. Dissolve cornstarch in lemon juice and water, add to peach juice and cook, stirring, until it thickens. Remove fish to warm plates. Mix peach sauce with pan juices and taste for seasoning. Pour sauce over the fish and serve.

Also good for ling cod, California sheepshead, and California halibut.

BLACKFISH STEW

1 ½ pounds blackfish fillet	10-ounce bottle clam juice
½ pound raw shrimp	1 bay leaf
1 cup fresh raw small oysters	1 cup milk
½ cup minced green onions	1 cup half-and-half
½ cup sliced mushrooms	Pinch of saffron
½ cup finely diced cooked ham	Salt and pepper to taste
3 Tablespoons butter	2 teaspoons brandy
2 Tablespoons flour	4 slices French bread toast, buttered

Wipe fillet with a damp cloth, slice into ¾-inch cubes, and set aside. Shell and clean shrimp and set aside. Heat oysters in their liquor for 3–4 minutes to plump, then chop them coarsely, and set aside.

Sauté onions, mushrooms, and ham in butter until lightly brown; mix in flour. Add clam juice and cook, stirring, until smooth. Add bay leaf, blackfish, and shrimp, bring to a boil, then lower heat and simmer for 3 minutes. Stir in milk, half-and-half, and saffron. Add oysters with their liquor and heat to scalding. Season with salt and pepper and stir in brandy. Remove bay leaf. Place a slice of buttered toast in each bowl, ladle stew on top, and serve.

Sheepshead, ling cod, or black drum may be used.

Skates and Rays

SKATES AND RAYS are primitive relatives of the shark. These weird-looking fishes are diamond shaped, flat, scaleless, and brown gray in color. Some are two- to six-pound shallow-water varieties; others can weigh over one hundred pounds. Their mouths are underslung, like sharks', and strong for crushing mollusks and crustacean shells. They have long ratlike tails (big Atlantic barndoor skates have spines, and sting rays have stingers) that they can whip around dangerously with great dexterity. They swim by undulating or flapping their winglike fins. A school of skates or rays could resemble flying bats.

On the Atlantic Coast barndoor skates and sting rays are frequently brought in by commercial trawlers. The fishes' large-size wings are cut off and then stamped with small, round cutters and used as a substitute for scallops. Small, shallow-water clear nose skates (about six pounds) that are so common between Long Island and the Carolinas, and also little skates (one- to three-pounders) that hug the New England shore in the winter, are fished by anglers using light tackle.

Pacific big skates and longnose skates (that are similar to barndoors) and bat rays (California skate) are found in great numbers up and down the entire West Coast. Skates and rays live on the ocean floor but come into shallows of bays and beaches to feed in mud flats at any time of the year. During April and May, their spawning season, they are found inshore in great profusion. There is a group of sport fishermen who fish for bat ray in San Francisco Bay mud flats, using a solid six-and-a-half-foot rod with light tackle and heavy mono leader with three-way swivel and barrel. A thirty- to eighty-pound ray usually takes bait hard and fast, and a lot of line plays out before the odd-shaped giant can be turned. A ray's fighting strength and relentlessness are a challenge to any fisherman's equipment and stamina. When the fight is over, the ray is pulled from the water by the leader; during landing it must be flipped onto its back, to partially immobilize its poisonous stinging tail.

About Skate Meat

The skate wing is the only part we eat; like grayfish, it must be very fresh and without a hint of ammonia odor. Skate meat is delicately flavored, lean, and somewhat gelatinous. To eat it, you scrape down the wing, taking the meat off the center bone in long strips.

Dressed skate wings are marketed year round. Large wings, always skinned and trimmed, should be cut into serving pieces before cooking. Small skates may be served whole. If the wings were not skinned before, skin may be scraped off wings after they are poached. Skate is best when butter sautéed, pan fried, deep fried, or poached.

SKATE SAUTÉ MEUNIÈRE

1½ pounds skate wings	½ teaspoon pepper
2 cups boiled milk, chilled	6 Tablespoons (¾ stick) butter
¾ cup flour	2 Tablespoons minced parsley
½ teaspoon paprika	Lemon wedges
1 teaspoon salt	

Soak skate wings in cold milk for 1 hour, drain and wipe dry. Dust in flour seasoned with paprika, salt, and pepper. Sauté wings slowly in 4 table-spoons of the butter, basting with more butter as they cook to golden brown. Serve on a warm platter, with hot butter poured over fish, garnished with a scattering of parsley and lemon wedges.

PAN-FRIED SKATE

Remove skin from a large ray wing. Cut meat off the center bone, then cut the meat in 1-inch-thick fillets. Soak fillets in milk for several hours in the refrigerator, then dry them. Dust with seasoned flour and fry fillets in garlic oil. Serve with lime wedges and a piquant chili sauce.

DEEP-FRIED SKATE

2 pounds very small skate wings, skinned	Salt and pepper to taste
	Oil for deep frying
2 cups boiled milk, chilled	Tomato Sauce (p. 433)
Flour	Melted butter

Soak skate wings in milk for 1 hour. Dry them on paper toweling and roll them in flour seasoned with salt and pepper. Deep fry a few wings at a time in hot (375°F.) oil until they are nicely brown. Drain briefly and keep warm until all are fried. Have ready a rich tomato sauce and melted butter to serve with fish.

SKATE WITH BLACK BUTTER

2 pounds skate wings
Basic Court Bouillon (p. 26)

Black Butter (p. 430)
1 Tablespoon capers

Make court bouillon, then poach skate until cooked. Drain fish and reserve poaching liquid for use some other time. Remove meat from the bone in as large pieces as possible and place them on a deep platter. Keep fish warm and covered until black butter is ready. Pour hot butter over the skate, sprinkle on a spoonful of capers, and serve at once.

SKATE WITH ONION AND CHEESE

2 pounds skate wings
Flour
1 bay leaf
1 clove garlic, minced
¼ teaspoon thyme
2 cloves
1 teaspoon salt

Pepper to taste
2 Tablespoons (¼ stick) butter
Milk
1 can, or fresh, small boiled onions, drained
1 cup grated Swiss cheese
3 slices buttered toast

Dust skate wings with flour and place them in a heavy saucepan. Add spices, butter, and enough milk to cover the fish. Bring to a boil, reduce heat, and simmer until skate is cooked. Remove cooked skate with a wide spatula, strain and reserve the stock. When cool enough to handle, take the meat off the bone.

Add drained onions to the reserved stock, season with salt and pepper, and heat slowly to a boil. Preheat the oven to 425°F., butter a deep casserole, and sprinkle the bottom with part of the cheese, then place fish on it. Cut buttered toast slices into pieces and arrange them and the onions around the skate, then pour in the boiling stock. Cover the top with the rest of the grated cheese and bake until casserole is bubbly and the cheese browns.

SKATE EN CASSEROLE WITH MORNAY

Poach skate wings in acidulated water (p. 25), then drain and remove meat from bone. Preheat the oven to 425°F. Line a buttered casserole with seasoned mashed potatoes and fill the center with skate meat. Pour Mornay Sauce (p. 420) over fish and sprinkle with grated cheese and crumbs on top. Bake for about 15 minutes.

Idea for Leftover Skate

SKATE SALAD

Arrange a bed of lettuce on a platter (or individual plates) and place on it chunks of cooked skate scraped from the bone, a few thin rings of fresh Bermuda onion, and ½ cup (4-ounce can) drained, sliced black olives. Mix Caper Sauce (p. 428) and ladle it over the salad.

Eels

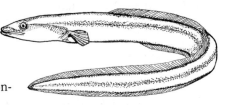

EELS are long-bodied fish which, except for their fins, are almost snakelike in appearance. They are born in deep ocean; become transparent, ribbonlike creatures; and gain color only gradually as they make their way toward shore. In spring, masses of three- to six-inch yearlings enter marshy tidelands and rivers, from the mouth of St. Lawrence River to the Gulf of Mexico. They settle in rocky areas and make narrow crevices their homes. Eels are often found in deep waters of brackish estuaries, around pilings and piers, and near tide pools where food is plentiful. They forage at night over the weed-covered bottom for small fish, crabs, and squid.

Eels grow slowly, taking five to twenty years to mature. Females are generally larger than males. When fully mature, eels cease feeding for a period of months, change their color to blackish, and, traveling at night, head out to their deep-sea spawning ground—which is located in the Sargasso Sea, one thousand miles east of Florida, near the Bermuda Triangle. There, evidently, they complete their life cycles.

There are large commercial eel fisheries on the St. Lawrence River and Chesapeake Bay. Eels are night-fished with nets, then transported in aerated tank trucks to metropolitan centers, where you can purchase them live from the fishmonger's tank.

And if you fish a lot from piers, it is almost unavoidable that you will wind up with one on your own line at some point. Don't throw it away; peculiar-looking as it might be, it is delicious food.

About Eel Meat

Fresh eel is available year round, especially in ethnic neighborhood fish markets. It is a traditional pre-Christmas dish and winter specialty for many Americans. Eels vary in size from one-quarter pound to ten or more pounds. Medium size weigh between one and two pounds. They are rich and fatty fish, which should be dressed and cooked or frozen within hours of being killed. Ask your fishmonger to skin, clean, and cut the eel into sections of fillet for you. The meat can be grilled, sautéed, baked, smoked, or simmered into a good herb-flavored stew or soup.

When you catch your own eel, a hard blow across the back will subdue the hard-to-kill eel. Even then, reflex action keeps it wriggling and its dangerous jaws snapping for quite a while. If you cook the eel unskinned, scald and scrape the skin to remove slime.

To Skin an Eel

Tie a strong string around the dead eel's head and secure the string to a nail. Cut the skin loose around the eel's neck, just below the head, and peel back enough skin to grip well with your pliers. Peel the skin down and off with a quick jerk. Cut off the head, gut, clear the cavity thoroughly, and trim off the fins. If you want fillets, cut the meat away from both sides of the backbone. Otherwise, slice the eel into sections for cooking.

DANISH EEL STEW

1½-2-pound eel skinned and cut into 1-inch long sections	6 peppercorns
	1 bay leaf
Salt	6 pitted prunes, halved and plumped ½ hour with water
1 smoked ham bone, or other meat bone	1 apple, peeled, cored, and thinly sliced
1 small carrot, chopped	White vinegar to taste
1 cup chopped celery	Sugar
3 leeks, washed and trimmed	

Sprinkle eel lightly with salt and set aside. Put ham bone, carrot, celery, and leeks in a soup kettle. Wrap peppercorns and bay leaf in cheesecloth; add them and water (enough to cover) to the pot. Bring to a boil, reduce heat, and cook partially covered, for 1 hour. Remove spices and bone, but cut off and reserve meat from the bone.

Purée the vegetables, then return them to the broth. Add eel sections, reserved meat, prunes, and apple, bring to a boil, and simmer gently for 20–25 minutes. Season stew with vinegar, sugar, and more salt, if necessary, and serve.

FRIED EEL

1½–2 pounds large eel, skinned,
   filleted, or sliced
Salt
¼ cup flour
Milk

1 cup crushed rusk or dried
   bread crumbs
2 Tablespoons (¼ stick) butter
Lemon wedges

Sprinkle eel with salt and set aside for 30 minutes. Dry fish, coat pieces
with flour, dip in milk, and roll them in crumbs. Fry eel in butter until
evenly brown and done. Serve with lemon wedges.

SMOKED EEL WITH OMELETTE

Sections of smoked eel
At least 2 Tablespoons (¼ stick)
   butter
4 eggs

½ teaspoon salt
4 Tablespoons water
1 green onion, minced
¼ teaspoon paprika

Preheat the oven to 275°F. Melt butter in a heavy skillet over low heat. Dip
smoked eel in melted butter and put pieces in a baking dish in the oven.
Keep remaining butter warm in skillet while you beat eggs well, mix in
salt, water, and onion, and cook omelette over low heat. Lift the edges with
a spatula and tilt the pan to let uncooked egg reach the bottom and cook.
When it is all an even consistency, sprinkle with paprika, and put the
skillet, uncovered, in the oven until the omelette is firm. Cut omelette into
slices and serve them warm with smoked eel and buttered dark bread.

EEL SOUP

1 1-pound eel, skinned
1 large onion, thinly sliced
1½ Tablespoons bacon fat

8 cups beef consommé
Salt and pepper to taste
Minced parsley

Cut eel into 1-inch slices and set them aside. In a large heavy skillet, sauté onion in bacon fat until golden. Add eel slices and fry for 3-4 minutes. Pour in consommé, bring to a boil, then reduce heat and simmer gently for 30 minutes. Degrease the soup. Season with salt and pepper, garnish with parsley, and serve.

Bluefish

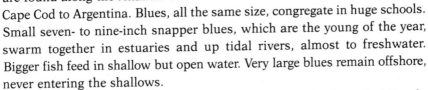

BLUEFISH ARE FAST, agile, deepwater game fish, blue green above, fading to silvery white underneath. Seasonally, they are found along the Atlantic Coast from Cape Cod to Argentina. Blues, all the same size, congregate in huge schools. Small seven- to nine-inch snapper blues, which are the young of the year, swarm together in estuaries and up tidal rivers, almost to freshwater. Bigger fish feed in shallow but open water. Very large blues remain offshore, never entering the shallows.

Bluefish appear off the tip of Florida in late winter. By the end of March, they are abundant along the entire Florida peninsula. During April, vast schools begin to migrate up the coast, past Georgia and the Carolinas, reaching New England in May. As the main body of blues moves north, masses leave the migration to remain in chosen areas of coast along the way. Sport angling begins in June off New England and gets steadily better until the peak of the season in September.

Bluefish on a feeding rampage are the most savage, gluttonous predators in the sea. They destroy everything in their path, including other bluefish, and chop up schools of fish, even ones their own size, leaving only the pieces. An oily slick on the water and faint odor of cucumbers in the air are signs of bluefish.

Night-fishing from party boats is popular summer sport. Blues are caught by trolling, still-fishing, and surf casting—there is no best way to catch them, and they are not choosy about bait.

About Bluefish Meat

Bluefish is mild-flavored, tender-textured meat. It is high in oil content and consequently is extremely perishable. Avoid getting fishy-tasting bluefish by looking for fish that are straight and firm, fish with smooth, tight skin, bright clear eyes, and red gills—and smell the fish before you buy. Before cooking, *large bluefish* should be skinned and trimmed of the strip of dark, oily meat that lies under the skin along the midsides. They are good barbecued, baked, broiled, poached, or smoked. *Medium-size blue-fish* (harbor blues), three- to five-pound fish, may be blanched in boiling water, then plunged into ice water for a few moments, to freshen. They are delicious grilled or poached in court bouillon, then, when they are cooked, herbed and spiced. They may be prepared in any way that suits mackerel. Refer to Mackerel chapter, pages 245–52, for additional recipes. *Tiny seven- to nine-inch snapper blues* are lean, delicate panfish; simply clean, scale, and pan fry.

When fishing, gut and degill bluefish at the time they are caught, and if possible, bring an ice chest aboard to stash your catch.

BARBECUED BLUEFISH

2 pounds bluefish fillet, cut into
  4 thick steaks
Salt and pepper to taste
1 small onion, grated

Juice of 1 lemon
1 bay leaf, crumbled
2 sprigs fresh dill, chopped
8 Tablespoons (1 stick) butter, melted

Remove skin, any overlooked bones, and trim off all dark meat. Place steaks in a baking dish and season with salt and pepper. Mix grated onion, lemon juice, bay leaf, and dill with melted butter, pour it over the fillets, and marinate until cooking time. Grill fish 6 inches above medium-hot coals. Brush frequently with marinade during cooking and turn fish when brown. You may serve bluefish with scalloped potatoes.

Mahi mahi, yellowtail, snook, or cobia may be used.

BROILED BLUEFISH
WITH YAKIMONO SAUCE

1 medium-size bluefish, about
  3 pounds, dressed and split into
  2 fillets
Juice of 1 lemon plus 1 teaspoon
Salt and pepper to taste
1 bag dashi-no-moto*

3 cups plus 2 teaspoons water
1 Tablespoon soy sauce
1/4 cup sake (rice wine)*
2 teaspoons cornstarch
Boiled rice
2 teaspoons grated orange rind

*See Glossary.

Cut fish in half crosswise, to make 4 fillets, and remove any bones with tweezers. Rinse and wipe dry. Rub fish with lemon juice, reserving 1 teaspoon of the juice, sprinkle with salt and pepper, then set aside for 25–30 minutes.

Meanwhile, make sauce: steep bag of dashi in 3 cups of the water for 10 minutes, as directed on package. Add soy sauce and sake to 2 cups of the broth. Dissolve cornstarch in the remaining 2 teaspoons of water, then stir it into the hot broth. Cook, stirring constantly, until sauce thickens. Season with the remaining teaspoon of lemon juice.

Preheat broiler. Arrange fillets, skin side up, on the lightly oiled broiler pan and place them 3 inches below the flame. When skin has browned, turn fish to broil the other side. Serve bluefish fillets on a mound of rice, garnish with a sprinkle of grated orange rind, and pass the sauceboat of hot dashi broth at the table.

Spanish mackerel or mullet may be used for this dish.

BLUEFISH FILLETS WITH NUT TOPPING

4 bluefish steaks, about ½ pound each
½ cup plus 1 Tablespoon lime juice
½ cup dry sherry
½ small onion, grated
Flour
5 Tablespoons butter
2 Tablespoons oil

Salt and pepper to taste
½ cup nuts (almonds and/or filberts)
2 teaspoons fine bread crumbs
2 teaspoons grated lime rind
White wine

Skin, bone, and trim bluefish steaks of dark oily meat. Rinse, pat dry, and lay pieces in a baking dish. Combine ½ cup of the lime juice, the sherry, and the onion, pour over the fish, and marinate, covered, for 4 hours (or overnight) in the refrigerator. Turn steaks occasionally to marinate evenly.

Remove steaks from marinade, dry them on paper toweling, and dust with flour. Heat 2 tablespoons of the butter and the oil in a skillet and sauté steaks until brown on both sides. Preheat the oven to 400°F. Then arrange bluefish in a lightly buttered baking dish and season with salt and pepper. Chop nuts in blender, then in a small bowl mix with the remaining 3 tablespoons of butter, the bread crumbs, lime juice, the rind, and enough wine to make a paste. Spread nut mixture over steaks and brown for about 5–8 minutes.

Mahi mahi, snook, or cobia may be used in this dish.

BAKED BLUEFISH

3-4-pound whole bluefish, cleaned
2 lemons
4 Tablespoons (½ stick) butter, melted
Salt and pepper to taste

Garlic powder
1 teaspoon marjoram
Flour
Cilantro Butter (p. 432), warmed

Preheat oven to 425°F. Leave head and tail on a cleaned, scaled bluefish; rinse and dry fish. Cut several shallow diagonal slashes on each side, and rub fish with lemon and butter. Sprinkle fish with salt, pepper, garlic powder, and marjoram, inside and out, then dust fish with flour. Arrange it in a buttered baking pan and bake, allowing 10 minutes baking time per inch thickness of fish. Transfer cooked fish to a warm platter, and serve with a sauceboat of warmed cilantro butter.

BAKED BLUEFISH WITH OYSTER STUFFING

3-4½-pound whole bluefish, cleaned,
  scaled, and degilled
Juice of 1 lemon
Salt and pepper to taste
Oyster Stuffing (p. 230)

Oil
Flour
Romaine lettuce leaves
Lemon wedges
Sprigs watercress

Rinse and pat fish dry with toweling; leave the head and tail intact. Slit belly cavity to the tail for more stuffing space, and cut 2 or 3 shallow diagonal slashes along the sides. Brush fish with lemon juice, sprinkle with salt and pepper, then set aside while making stuffing.

Preheat the oven to 425°F. Stuff bluefish, sew the sides or fasten with skewers. Brush with oil, dust lightly with flour, then place fish in an oiled baking dish. Bake, uncovered, for 10 minutes per inch thickness of fish. Serve bluefish on a bed of romaine lettuce, garnished with lemon wedges and sprigs of watercress.

Striped Bass

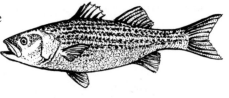

STRIPED BASS are, by far, the favorite game and food fish on the Atlantic Coast. They are silvery with olive stripes tinged with gold. The average size is six to ten pounds, but it is not unusual to catch a thirty- or forty-pounder. Stripers are abundant in coastal waters between Massachusetts and South Carolina and are taken from the Gulf of St. Lawrence to northern Florida, and in the Gulf from western Florida to Louisiana. In the South, striped bass are called "rockfish." Landlocked "rockfish" are found in southeastern inland lakes and are generally caught by trolling.

Striped bass populations from these widely different areas have different spawning patterns and migration habits. Many travel up into brackish estuaries and backwaters of bays to spawn; others run one hundred miles upriver to spawn in freshwater. The landlocked bass never leave their freshwater home, and those bass that hatch in Delaware or Chesapeake bays remain there until they are at least two years old. Bass from Delaware or Chesapeake bays make two migrations; one is for spawning, and the other (for two year olds and older) is a journey into cool water. Bass travel northward along the coast to southern Canadian waters, where in the summer they mingle with northern bass populations. The striped bass sport-fishing season, from the Carolinas to New England, takes place during this run.

Stripers were introduced to the Pacific Coast in the late 1800s, when several hundred fish arrived by train from the East Coast. They flourished and today are found from Oregon to Monterey. Pacific striped bass migrate into fresh-moving water in the fall and stay until spring when they are river- or stream-fished. After spawning, they travel down bays or rivers again into saltwater, where they are caught by trolling or angling from piers or banks. In the ocean they stay in shallow, usually turbulent water, right off the beach, feeding around rocky pockets.

About Striped Bass Meat

On the Atlantic Coast, striped bass are commercially fished. The average commercial catch includes nearly one-pound to five- or ten-pound bass. They are marketed whole dressed, in chunks, or filleted as steaks. Like other bass, they are mild flavored with firm, flaky white meat. Stripers bake well whole stuffed, or butterflied planked, and may be barbecued, grilled, fried, poached, or steamed.

GRILLED STRIPED BASS

2 pounds bass fillet
⅔ cup olive oil
3 cloves garlic, mashed
2 Tablespoons lemon juice

1 teaspoon salt
Generous milling of pepper
1 teaspoon paprika

Marinate serving portions of bass in this garlic-oil marinade for several hours before barbecuing.

OYSTER STUFFING FOR
5-6-POUND STRIPED BASS

1 ¼ cups freshly shucked oysters
½ cup each minced onion, green
    pepper, and celery
4 Tablespoons (½ stick) butter
1½-2 cups fine cracker crumbs
1 teaspoon salt
Pepper to taste

⅛ teaspoon dry mustard
1 Tablespoon paprika
1 teaspoon Worcestershire sauce
2 Tablespoons lemon juice
Dash of cayenne pepper
Sprig parsley, minced

Sauté minced vegetables in butter until soft. Remove from heat and mix with cracker crumbs, salt, pepper, mustard, and paprika.

Bring ½ cup oyster liquor (or water) to boil, add oysters, and simmer slowly for 5 minutes until oysters are plump. Drain them and reserve the liquor. Cut oysters into small pieces, stir in Worcestershire sauce, lemon juice, cayenne, and parsley, then mix with the crumbs. Use reserved oyster liquid to moisten stuffing and add water or white wine if more liquid is necessary. Taste for seasoning, then stuff into fish.

Bluefish or any whole lean fish for baking listed on page 447 (III A3) may be used.

STRIPED BASS
WITH CHEESE-FRENCH BREAD STUFFING

3-4-pound striper, pan dressed
Flour
Salt and pepper to taste
1/3 cup chopped green onion
2 cloves garlic, minced
1/4 cup minced parsley
1/3-1/2 cup olive oil
1 Tablespoon grated Parmesan cheese

2 cups soft sourdough French bread
   crumbs
2 green onions, split
Thinly sliced lemon
Thinly sliced tomato
Garlic powder
1/4 cup dry white wine or water

Wipe bass dry, dust lightly with flour, sprinkle with salt and pepper inside and out, then set aside while making stuffing.

Sauté onion, garlic, and parsley in olive oil until soft. Combine cheese and crumbs, then toss with sautéed vegetables. Season with salt and pepper and stuff the fish. Sew the sides or fasten with skewers.

Preheat the oven to 425°F. Lay split green onion on the bottom of a buttered baking dish, place bass on top and brush it with oil. Arrange alternating lemon and tomato slices on top of bass. Season with garlic powder and salt and pepper. Add wine (or water) to the dish and bake, uncovered, for 10 minutes per inch thickness of fish.

Use any whole lean fish for baking listed on page 447 (III A3).

STRIPED BASS-SHRIMP CASSEROLE

1 1/2 pounds bass fillet
1 pound raw shrimp (medium size,
   about 25)
Salt and pepper to taste
2 onions, chopped
2 green peppers, chopped
1 clove garlic, minced

1/2-1 small dried chili, or dash of
   cayenne pepper
3 Tablespoons oil
2 tomatoes, peeled and diced
1 Tablespoon minced cilantro
1/2 cup cream of coconut

Cut bass into 1-inch strips. Wash, shell, and devein shrimp. Salt and pepper both bass and shrimp and let stand while making sauce.

Sauté onions, green peppers, garlic, and chili in oil until vegetables are tender, then remove from heat. Mix in tomatoes and minced cilantro and season to taste with salt.

Preheat the oven to 350°F. Layer a greased casserole first with fish, then with vegetable mixture, alternating layers, until all is used. Pour coconut cream over all. Cover casserole and bake for 15-20 minutes.

STRIPER WITH GLEN COVE STUFFING

3-4-pound white striped bass
Flour
¼ cup plus 1 Tablespoon
   chopped onion
¼ cup chopped green pepper
¼ cup grated carrot
½ cup chopped celery
6 Tablespoons (¾ stick) butter
At least ½ teaspoon salt
¼ teaspoon each thyme and
   fennel seed

1 cup fine dry bread crumbs
1 tomato, peeled and diced
2 teaspoons capers with juice
2 Tablespoons bacon chips
Pepper to taste
¼ teaspoon garlic powder
1 bay leaf
1 cup red wine

SAUCE

½ cup each tomato sauce and
   red wine
1 ½ Tablespoons flour

Garlic powder to taste

Clean, degill, and dry bass, then dust with flour; set it aside while making stuffing.

Sauté ¼ cup of the onion, the green pepper, carrot, and celery in 4 tablespoons of the butter until tender. Season with salt, thyme, and fennel, then remove from heat. Mix in bread crumbs, add tomatoes, capers, and bacon chips. Toss to mix all ingredients, then stuff fish. Skewer or sew cavity closed.

Preheat the oven to 425°F. Brush fish with the remaining 2 table-spoons of butter, then sprinkle with salt, pepper, and garlic powder. Place bass in a buttered baking dish. Add a bay leaf and the remaining table-spoon of chopped onion to the dish, pour in 1 cup red wine, and bake for 10 minutes per inch thickness of fish.

Transfer cooked bass to a platter and keep warm while making sauce. Make a paste of tomato sauce, wine, and flour, then mix it with pan juices. Add garlic powder to taste. Cook, stirring constantly, until sauce thickens. Remove bay leaf. Serve sauce with fish.

If striped bass is not available, use any whole lean fish for baking listed on page 447 (III A3).

OVEN-FRIED STRIPED BASS
WITH CREOLE SAUCE

2 pounds striped bass fillet
1 teaspoon salt
Flour
2 Tablespoons milk
1 egg

1 cup crumbs
Creole Sauce (p. 434)
4 Tablespoons oil
4 Tablespoons (1/2 stick) butter

Cut fillet into serving pieces, season with salt, and dust with flour, shaking off the excess. Beat milk with egg, dip fish in the egg, then press into crumbs. Set coated pieces on waxed paper to dry for 30 minutes, turning them once.

Preheat pan and oven to 500°F. for 10 minutes. Have creole sauce ready.

Mix oil and butter in the hot pan, put in fillets and turn each over to coat both sides. Oven fry fillets until crispy golden brown. Spoon Creole sauce over cooked fish or serve sauce at the table.

BOILED STRIPED BASS TO SERVE COLD

2 pounds bass fillets
3 cups cold water
1/2 cup lemon juice
1 Tablespoon olive oil

3 bay leaves
1 1/2 teaspoons salt
4 peppercorns, cracked

Wipe fillets with damp toweling, trim off dark meat, and slice into 3/4-inch cubes.

Combine cold water, lemon juice, oil, and seasonings in a large enamel pot; heat and boil vigorously for 5 minutes. Add fish cubes and enough boiling water to cover. Bring to a boil, then lower heat and simmer, loosely covered, for 5-7 minutes. Drain and cool to room temperature, then cover and chill.

Serve chilled fish as salad, sprinkled with lemon juice and covered with Rémoulade Sauce (p. 426), or as an appetizer, with Fish Cocktail Mayonnaise (p. 425).

Ideas for Leftover Striped Bass

STRIPED BASS CASSEROLE

1 cup striped bass, cooked and flaked	2 Tablespoons cream
1/4 teaspoon salt	1 cup mashed potatoes
Pepper to taste	2 hard-boiled eggs, sliced
1 Tablespoon grated onion	Herbed butter

Preheat the oven to 350°F. Season flaked fish with salt, pepper, and grated onion; moisten with cream. Butter a small casserole and arrange in alternating layers the potato, fish, and egg slices. Cover and heat in oven for 15 minutes. Serve with a melted herbed butter.

STRIPED BASS CROQUETTES

1 cup striped bass, cooked and flaked	1/2 teaspoon salt
2 teaspoons grated onion	Dash each of pepper and garlic
1 Tablespoon minced parsley	powder
1 teaspoon lemon juice	2 eggs, beaten separately
1/8 teaspoon nutmeg	2 cups fine dry bread crumbs
1 1/2 Tablespoons butter	1 Tablespoon milk
2 1/2 Tablespoons flour	Oil for frying
2/3 cup hot milk	Mushroom Sauce (p. 421)

Combine onion, parsley, lemon juice, and nutmeg with flaked fish and mix well.

Stir butter and flour over medium heat until bubbly. Beat in 2/3 cup hot milk with a whisk, and cook until sauce thickens and boils. Season with salt, pepper, and garlic powder. Stir in fish and heat to a boil again. Lower heat, stir in 1 beaten egg, and cook for a few seconds, then pour into a buttered deep plate to cool thoroughly.

Wet your hands to prevent fish from sticking and form mixture into sausage shapes. Roll them in pulverized bread crumbs, then in the other egg beaten with the tablespoon of milk. Roll again in crumbs and set them aside to dry for about 2 hours.

Heat oil to 390°F. and deep fry croquettes in a wire basket, no more than 4 at a time, until delicately brown. Drain on toweling and serve with mushroom sauce.

Any lean fish listed on page 446 (III A1) may be used.

Blowfish (Sea Squab)

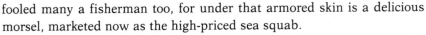

AN ALARMED PUFFER (blowfish)
inflates its belly like a balloon
and its sharp scales point out-
ward, thus becoming too large and
prickly a mouthful for predators.
Pulled from the water this way, it has
fooled many a fisherman too, for under that armored skin is a delicious
morsel, marketed now as the high-priced sea squab.

Northern puffer (blowfish) in their normal (uninflated) state are eight- to
ten-inch, moderately stout fish, olive green on top, with yellow green
blotched sides and white underneath. They inhabit shallow water no more
than a few fathoms deep, feeding on shrimp, worms, sea urchins, and
crab. Fishermen consider them a nuisance because they strip bait from
hooks. The next time one takes your hook, don't throw it back: it's edible
and quite delicious.

About Blowfish Meat

The solid piece of white meat surrounding the backbone of blowfish is the
only part of the fish that may be eaten. It is firm and moist, and has a
delicate flavor, similar to chicken leg. It is best sautéed, broiled, or deep
fried.

To get to the edible meat through the sandpapery skin, use a sharp
knife and grasp the fish with a thick cloth to protect your hands from the
spines. Make a cut to the spine in the back of the head. Separate the skin
from the flesh with the knife tip. Separate enough to be able to grab the
skin with fish pliers. Then pull the skin back toward the tail, exposing the
firm white meat. Yank hard and you will pull the meat-covered bone loose
from the rest of the body. Rinse the drumsticklike piece in salted water and
dry on paper toweling.

PAN-FRIED BLOWFISH
WITH SAVORY HOT BUTTER

12 blowfish, dressed	½ cup cornmeal
Milk	1 cup oil for frying
Salt and pepper to taste	Savory Hot Butter (p. 431)
½ cup flour	

Soak blowfish in cold milk for 30 minutes, then pat fish dry and sprinkle with salt and pepper. Combine flour with cornmeal; roll fish in the mixture, coating them well. Heat oil and fry several fish at a time, until brown and crispy, then turn and cook the other side. Remove fish to a plate lined with paper toweling and keep them warm in the oven until all are cooked. Serve blowfish attractively arranged on a warm platter, accompanied by a bowl of savory hot butter sauce.

Frog's legs may be substituted for blowfish.

SEA SQUAB SOUTHERN STYLE

12–16 blowfish, dressed (3 or 4 per serving)	1 Tablespoon cream
	Salt and pepper to taste
Milk	1 cup corn flour*
2 eggs	Oil for deep frying

*Obtainable at health food stores.

Cover blowfish with milk and refrigerate for 1 hour.

SAUCE

4 Tablespoons (½ stick) butter	Sprig parsley, minced
3 Tablespoons flour	2 cups bouillon, or 2 bouillon cubes dissolved in water
1 onion, minced	
4 cloves garlic, minced	2 cups canned tomatoes
½ cup minced celery	Dash of cayenne pepper
1 small green pepper, minced	Salt and pepper to taste

Melt butter in a heavy saucepan, mix in flour and cook slowly, stirring, until the roux is nicely brown. Add onion, garlic, celery, green pepper, and parsley and continue cooking until vegetables are soft. Stir in bouillon and tomatoes (break them up with a spoon). Season with cayenne and salt and pepper, then simmer sauce for 1 hour, stirring occasionally.

Drain blowfish and wipe them dry. Beat eggs with cream and salt and pepper. Dip fish in egg, then in corn flour, and deep fry in hot oil until golden brown. Drain briefly on toweling, then arrange blowfish on a deep platter. Pour hot sauce over the fish and serve at once.

Frog's legs may be substituted for blowfish.

Sea Robin

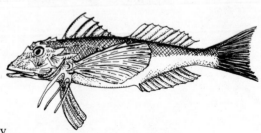

SEA ROBIN is a strange name for
a fish, but then this is an odd
fish that "walks" on the sea
floor with its modified pectoral
rays. The pectoral fins are long
and resemble wings, used not only
for darting about in short bursts, but for burrowing the creature into
the sand, where it can hide with only its eyes exposed.

The sea robin has a reddish body and a bony hard head. This little
one- to one-and-a-half-pound fish is found from the Bay of Fundy to South
Carolina. It is a notorious bait stealer and grunts or "barks," as fishermen
say, when taken from its shallow-water habitat.

About Sea Robin Meat

Sea robin is a delicately flavored, firm, lean, white-meat fish. It is sold in
Eastern markets, not by name usually, but simply as "fresh or frozen
fillets." It is known in France as *grondin*, a fish used in bouillabaisse. It is
excellent broiled, fried, sautéed, poached, or used in stews. If you catch
your own, skin and fillet sea robin before cooking.

See Greenling chapter, pages 134–9, for additional recipes.

SEA ROBIN TURBANS IN OYSTER SAUCE

1 1/2 pounds sea robin fillets
Salt and pepper to taste
1/3 cup toasted almonds
2 Tablespoons capers plus caper liquid
2 cups dry white wine
1 green onion, minced
1/2 cup chopped mushrooms

2 Tablespoons (1/4 stick) butter
1/2 pint freshly shucked oysters
1/2 teaspoon basil
1 teaspoon cornstarch
1 teaspoon water
1 egg, beaten
Celery leaves, minced

Slit thick fillets into thinner rollable strips and season with salt and pepper. Pulverize almonds in a blender, then mix with capers. Add enough caper liquid to make a paste. Spread fish strips with the caper-nut mixture, then roll and secure with wooden cocktail picks. Place rolls side by side in a saucepan, cover with wine, bring to a boil, then simmer for 4 minutes. Remove from heat and let poached fish stand, covered, while making sauce.

Sauté onion and mushrooms in butter until lightly brown. Add 1 cup of the poaching liquid, cover, and simmer slowly for 10 minutes. Meanwhile, heat oysters in their liquor until plump, then cut each into several pieces and set aside. Add ½ cup of oyster liquor and the basil to the simmering sauce. Stir cornstarch with water and combine with egg. Stir a spoonful of simmering sauce into the egg, then mix egg into the sauce, stirring constantly, until sauce becomes smooth and thickened (don't allow it to boil). Season with salt and pepper. Add oysters and heat through. Arrange turbans on warm plates, spoon oyster sauce over them, garnish with a sprinkle of minced celery leaves, and serve.

Sole or snapper are good for this dish.

SEA ROBIN WITH OLIVE MAYONNAISE

Serves 2

4 sea robin fillets	2–3 drops Angostura bitters
1 Tablespoon vegetable oil	1 teaspoon minced parsley
Juice of 1 lime	20 pitted black olives, halved
Salt and pepper to taste	¼ cup mayonnaise, at room
3 Tablespoons heavy cream	temperature

Preheat the oven to 425°F. Wipe fillets with a damp cloth. Dip fish in oil and arrange pieces in a buttered baking dish; sprinkle with lime juice and salt and pepper. Cover baking dish tightly with foil and bake for 10 minutes per inch thickness of fish. Remove from oven and let fish stand, covered, for several minutes.

Meanwhile, blend cream, Angostura bitters, parsley, and olives with mayonnaise. Arrange fillets on a warm platter, cover them with mayonnaise sauce, and serve at once.

Greenling, sole, or pompano may be used.

Weakfish

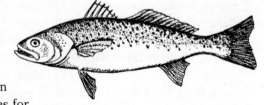

WEAKFISH: the name refers to the fish's delicate mouth, from which a hook can easily tear free. Grayfish and squeteague, an Indian word, are other nicknames for this croaker. These beautifully shaped one- to five-pound fish are identifiable by their dark multicolored, burnished, diagonally striped upper sides and silver white bellies.

Weakfish fishing begins around Chesapeake and Delaware bays in April. Great concentrations of weakfish spread from there along the coast to New England. They are essentially surf fish, and prefer shallow sandy-bottom areas, where they can feed on sea worms, shrimp, mollusks, and small fishes. They also school in sounds, channels, inlets, and bays, but never go into freshwater. "Weaks" are fished by trolling, drift-fishing deep holes, bottom-fishing at anchor (around dusk), and surf angling—an hour before and after high tide.

About Weakfish Meat

Bland-flavored weakfish is enhanced by herbs, spices, and flavorful sauces. The fine-textured lean flesh is soft and moist and has a tendency to break apart when cooked. It has been found that freezing fish for two or more days actually improves the quality, by firming up soft, moist flesh. Bake, broil, barbecue, or fry weakfish for best results.

Weakfish deteriorates rapidly. Special attention should be given to selecting only the freshest fish: those straight and firm that don't bend easily, with tight skin, clear eyes, red gills, and a fresh smell. Then refrigerate and cook or freeze them as soon as possible.

Weakfish should be cooked thoroughly and not used in raw fish recipes.

When fishing, gut and degill weakfish at the time they are caught, and if possible, bring an ice chest to stash your catch.

Weakfish meat is similar to that of speckled seatrout. Refer to Speckled Seatrout chapter, pages 264–6, for additional recipes.

CHARCOAL-BROILED WEAKFISH FILLETS

2½ pounds weakfish fillets	2 Tablespoons molasses
1 onion, grated	½ cup soy sauce
1 teaspoon grated ginger	½ cup dry white wine
Grated rind of ½ lemon	½ teaspoon garlic powder
Juice of 1 lemon	1 teaspoon sesame oil

Make basting sauce by mixing together all ingredients except fish. Let mixture stand 1–3 hours for flavors to meld. Place grill 6–7 inches from coals. When coals have burned down to medium-hot, grease the grill. Cut fillets into serving pieces, dip them in basting sauce, and put them on the grill. Barbecue fish until it is well done (allow extra time if you have partially frozen fish). Turn once during cooking and baste frequently with sauce.

BAKED WEAKFISH MOROCCAN

4-5-pound whole weakfish, cleaned, scaled, and degilled	1½ teaspoons salt
	Dash of cayenne pepper
½ cup each chopped cilantro and parsley leaves	1 cup sliced celery
	3 tomatoes
5 cloves garlic, sliced	3 bell peppers
½ cup plus 1 Tablespoon lemon juice	¼ cup salad oil
2 Tablespoons cider vinegar	1½ Tablespoons tomato paste
1 teaspoon paprika	¼ cup water
1 teaspoon cumin	

Trim fins, but leave head and tail intact; rinse and dry fish. Prick sides several times with a sharp-tined fork. Place cilantro, parsley, garlic, 6 tablespoons of the lemon juice, vinegar, paprika, cumin, salt, and cayenne in a blender container and purée. Rub fish, inside and out, with the mixture, and let stand (refrigerated) for 3–4 hours.

Preheat oven to 375°F. Oil a roasting pan and scatter celery around on the bottom. Place weakfish on the celery. Halve the tomatoes and the peppers, and seed them. Dip them in puréed sauce and arrange them in the pan. Mix salad oil, tomato paste, the rest of the lemon juice, and the water with remaining purée and pour it over the fish. Bake for 10 minutes per inch thickness of fish, plus a little longer for weakfish that has been frozen.

Flounder

WINTER, SUMMER, AND SOUTHERN

Unfortunately, there is no sole in American waters quite like the European Dover or English sole used so famously in French cooking. Small shipments of Dover are iced-down and flown to select U.S. markets. The closest families in U.S. waters are Atlantic winter flounder and Pacific petrale sole. They might cook a little faster and break up if sliced too thin, but if thin fillets are folded or rolled and care is taken with poaching, a fairly successful dish of "fillet of sole" can be turned out.

WINTER FLOUNDER range from Labrador to Georgia and are abundant off the New England coast. New Englanders call fish up to three pounds "blackbacks" and larger ones "lemon sole." Flounder come inshore to warmer waters during winter in their southern range; hence the name winter flounder.

This is the thickest, firmest, and meatiest flounder on the Atlantic seaboard. The fine-quality fillets may be treated like fillet of sole (see pages 122–8).

SUMMER FLOUNDER, or fluke, are flatfish weighing two to five-plus pounds, mottled brown on top with regularly placed dark and light spots. They are found in shallow to fairly deep water from Maine to South Carolina, although they prefer sandy mud bottoms of bays, harbors, and the mouths of estuaries. They come inshore during the summer and retreat to deeper and warmer water for the winter.

Fluke are a mainstay with sport anglers, who fish them from bridges, jetties, and small boats, using light tackle and killifish or squid bait. Commercially, they are the most important catches of the mid-Atlantic states. They are excellent fish to fry, grill, bake, or poach.

Winter, summer, and southern flounder are some of the best of the many Atlantic flatfish. Other important and delicious Eastern species are listed and described in the chapter Flatfish—Flounder, Sole, and Sand Dabs, pages 119-28. All methods of preparation, and recipes there, apply to both East and West Coast varieties of flounder.

SOUTHERN FLOUNDER range from the Carolinas to Texas. They occur in greatest number in areas where saltwater mixes with fresh. These twelve- to twenty-inch, green-backed flounder often enter freshwater en masse. They are taken from inshore Gulf waters all year.

A popular method of fishing on the Gulf Coast is called gigging or gig-fishing. It is flounder hunting on the flats at night by strong torch-light. The flounder, which is found when torchlight gleams on the fish's beady eyes, is stabbed with a spearlike instrument called a gig.

Suggested recipes for winter, summer, and southern flounder are also in the chapter Flatfish—Flounder, Sole, and Sand Dabs, pages 119-28.

FLOUNDER MARGUÉRY

4 flounder fillets	1 Tablespoon chopped shallot
12 raw shrimp, shelled and cleaned	1 clove
1 cup freshly shucked small oysters	1 bay leaf
1/2 pound mushrooms, quartered	Pinch of thyme and pepper
8 Tablespoons (1 stick) plus	Dash of cayenne pepper
2 Tablespoons butter	3 egg yolks
2 teaspoons lemon juice	1 Tablespoon white vermouth
Salt to taste	1/8 teaspoon arrowroot
1 cup water	2 Tablespoons heavy cream

Sauté mushrooms in 2 tablespoons butter until lightly brown, season with lemon juice and salt; remove with a slotted spoon, cover, and keep warm. Add the cup of water, the shallot, clove, bay leaf, thyme, pepper, and cayenne to the pan, boil for 2-3 minutes, then add shrimp. Reduce heat, cover, and simmer about 4 minutes until shrimp are cooked; remove shrimp, cover, and keep warm. Reserve the broth.

Preheat oven to 425°F. Arrange flounder and oysters in a buttered baking dish and season with salt and pepper. Add oyster liquor to the broth, bring to a boil, and pour over flounder. Cover baking dish tightly with foil, then place in the oven to poach. Use the ratio of 10 minutes per inch thickness of fish to estimate cooking time.

Remove poached oysters, cover, and keep warm. Transfer poached fillets to a broiler-to-table platter and keep warm. Strain poaching liquid into a saucepan and boil it down until reduced to 1 tablespoon, then remove from heat.

Over low heat, in the top of a double boiler, mix egg yolks with vermouth and arrowroot. Whisk in the remaining stick of butter, a piece at a time, beating until smooth with each addition. Beat for a minute or two after butter is absorbed and sauce is thickened. Stir in reduced poaching liquid.

Heat the broiler. Drain fish, discarding collected liquid. Spoon sauce on and around fillets. Whip cream until stiff and smear dabs on each fillet. Arrange shrimp, oysters, and mushrooms in the sauce, then slide the platter under the broiler to lightly brown the top. Serve at once.

Pompano may be used for this dish.

Mackerel

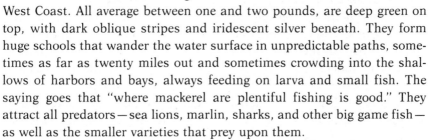

THREE SMALL MACKEREL
have important fisheries in
our waters, Atlantic and
chub mackerel on the East Coast,
and Pacific mackerel taken along the
West Coast. All average between one and two pounds, are deep green on
top, with dark oblique stripes and iridescent silver beneath. They form
huge schools that wander the water surface in unpredictable paths, sometimes as far as twenty miles out and sometimes crowding into the shallows of harbors and bays, always feeding on larva and small fish. The
saying goes that "where mackerel are plentiful fishing is good." They
attract all predators — sea lions, marlin, sharks, and other big game fish —
as well as the smaller varieties that prey upon them.

Often, where an area has been chummed for fishing, fishermen can't
get their bait through to their intended catch because greedy, schooling
mackerel grab it first. They literally can be scooped up from the water by
the netful.

SPANISH MACKEREL differ from
king mackerel and cero, having no stripes on their
sides; instead they are
marked with yellow orange
spots. They average two to three
pounds; ten pounds is large. They are present all year along the Gulf and
tropical Atlantic coasts. In summer they range as far north as Chesapeake
Bay. Small-boat fishermen catch them frequently close to shore and in
sheltered bays and sounds, using spinning tackle with strip or shrimp
bait.

CERO DIFFER FROM king and Spanish mackerel, having both spots and stripes on their sides; five to ten pounds is average. King mackerel (cavalla or kingfish) are the largest of the Spanish mackerel; some weigh a hundred pounds. They range north to Chesapeake Bay in the summer and are abundant along Florida's east coast, the West Indies, Texas, and Louisiana coasts in late fall and winter. It is a frequent and spectacular sight to see perhaps a hundred boats, big and small, of all different kinds, huddled together fishing over a school of mackerel.

The meat is interchangeable in recipes throughout.

About Mackerel Meat

Mackerel meat is rich, firm textured, and high in oil content. Both small and large fish are best broiled, barbecued, baked, or poached, and served with a tart or spicy sauce.

Because of its high oil content, mackerel deteriorates rapidly. Carefully selecting fresh fish can avoid that "fishy taste." Look for straight firm fish that don't bend easily, have tight skin, clear eyes, red gills, and smell fresh.

When fishing large mackerel, remove the head when the fish is caught, then hang it by the tail to bleed. Plan ahead so you can ice-down (see page 3) the fish while still aboard. Later it can be filleted and skinned, trimmed of dark meat, and cut into steaks. Cook, smoke, or freeze (see page 12) mackerel as soon as possible.

Fresh raw Spanish mackerel, unlike other fish, will become soggy and fall apart if soaked in a liquid marinade. Cook it first, then marinate.

Cero, king mackerel, and yellowtail meat have similar qualities and may be prepared in the same ways. Refer to California Yellowtail chapter, pages 42–5, for additional recipes.

SALT BARBECUED MACKEREL

4 mackerels, pan dressed	2 Bermuda onions, chopped
3 Tablespoons salt	4 limes
Salad oil	

Dress fish, remove heads, and sprinkle inside and out with salt. Let fish stand for 1 hour to allow salt to penetrate meat, and don't rinse or wipe salt off before cooking. Baste with oil while grilling. When cooked, place fish on a bed of chopped onions, sprinkle generously with lime, and serve at once with lime wedges.

SKEWERED MACKEREL FILLETS GRILLED

1 pound mackerel fillets
4 Tablespoons soy sauce
6 Tablespoons mirin (Japanese sweet
  liquor)

1 Tablespoon sake or dry sherry

Mix soy, mirin, and sake and marinate mackerel fillets in it for 15 minutes. Skewer each fillet on 2 wooden skewers (which have been soaked 10 minutes in cold water) and grill about 7 inches from the coals, until meat is golden brown and glazed. Brush with marinade while grilling.

Snapper blues or small mullet may be used.

OVEN-BROILED MACKEREL
IN BUTTERMILK

1½ pounds mackerel fillets
Salt and pepper to taste
1 cup buttermilk
2 Tablespoons minced parsley

2 Tablespoons minced fresh fennel or
  dill leaves
Pinch of thyme

Preheat the oven to 500°F. Salt and pepper fillets. Pour enough buttermilk into a baking pan to cover the bottom ⅛ inch deep. Arrange fillets in the pan without crowding and cover with remaining buttermilk. Sprinkle with parsley, fennel or dill, and thyme and bake, allowing 10 minutes per inch thickness of fish.

BAKED MACKEREL
WITH ONION AND TOMATO

Four 8-ounce mackerel fillets
2 Tablespoons olive oil
Juice of 1 lemon
Salt and pepper to taste

Garlic powder
Pinch of thyme
1 onion, chopped coarse
2 tomatoes, peeled and diced

Preheat the oven to 425°F. Arrange fillets in an oiled baking dish, skin side down, and brush them with olive oil and lemon juice. Sprinkle with salt, pepper, garlic powder, and thyme. Combine onion and tomatoes and spoon them over and around the fillets. Bake for 10 minutes per inch thickness of fish.

SAUTÉED MACKEREL

Split and bone mackerel, dust lightly with flour, and sauté in butter. Season cooked fish with salt and pepper, sprinkle generously with lime juice, and serve.

TWICE-COOKED MACKEREL FILLETS

1 1/2 pounds mackerel fillets
Salt and pepper to taste
1 egg white, slightly beaten
Cornstarch
5 Tablespoons oil
1 tomato, peeled and diced
1 medium onion, chopped

1/2 cup water
1 green pepper, minced
2 cloves garlic, pressed
1 Tablespoon minced ginger
1 teaspoon dried basil
1 Tablespoon white vinegar
Dash of cayenne pepper

Salt and pepper fillets, dip them in egg white, then in cornstarch. Sauté on both sides in oil until fish is cooked, then remove from pan and keep warm. Discard all but 2 tablespoons oil.

Purée tomato, onion, water, green pepper, garlic, ginger, and basil together in a blender. Add purée to oil in pan and cook for 2 or 3 minutes. Return fish to pan, cover with sauce, and cook another 2 minutes, or until fish is hot and sauce bubbles. Stir in vinegar, cayenne, and season with salt, then serve promptly.

Bluefish or mullet may be used.

DEEP-FRIED MACKEREL

1 1/2 pounds mackerel fillets
1/2 cup dry sherry
Salt and pepper to taste

Oil for frying
Catsup
Prepared hot mustard

SOY-SEASONED BATTER

1/2 cup flour
1/2 teaspoon baking powder
2 teaspoons soy sauce

1/2 cup water, or less
1 egg white

Beat all batter ingredients but egg white together to make a smooth, thin mixture. Set aside for 30 minutes. When ready to use, beat egg white stiffly and fold it in.

Fillet, skin, trim away dark meat, and cut mackerel into bite-size pieces. Dip them in sherry, season with salt and pepper, then dip in batter and deep fry in hot (375°F.) oil until golden. Serve with one small dish of catsup and one of hot mustard for dipping.

Good with snapper blues or small mullet.

POACHED WHOLE MACKEREL

Poach several mackerel in acidulated water (with vinegar), as per recipe on page 25. Remove fish from poaching liquid and drain. Skin and fillet fish when cold. Place fillets on a platter and pour Basic French Dressing (see page 427, adding 1 tablespoon chopped parsley for each 3 tablespoons French dressing), over the fish.

POACHED MACKEREL FILLETS

Poach fillets in enough salted water to cover to which 2 bay leaves, 5 peppercorns, and a slice of lemon have been added. Serve fish hot with Parsley White Sauce (p. 418) or Mustard White Sauce (p. 418). Or let mackerel cool and serve them cold with Rémoulade Sauce (p. 426) or Green Mayonnaise (page 426).

MACKEREL FILLETS IN MISO BROTH

1½ pounds mackerel fillets,
  cut in 2-inch pieces
1 bag dashi-no-moto*
3 cups boiling water
1 Tablespoon sugar

¼ cup sake or dry sherry
1 Tablespoon minced fresh ginger
1-2 Tablespoons white miso paste*
1 green onion, minced
Thinly sliced lemon

*See Glossary.

Steep dashi in boiling water for 10 minutes; remove bag and add sugar and sake, stirring until sugar is dissolved. Arrange fish in an electric fry pan or skillet without crowding, add ginger, and pour in hot broth. Cover and simmer until fish are cooked, about 5 minutes, then remove fish carefully, and keep warm. Stir miso into a small amount of broth until it is smooth, then pour this back into the rest of the broth, bring to a boil, and simmer for 2-3 minutes. Portion fish into soup bowls, ladle hot broth over the fish, sprinkle with green onion, garnish with a slice of lemon, and serve.

PICKLED MACKEREL

5 pounds mackerel fillets
Salt
1 quart distilled vinegar
3 cups water
¼ cup sugar
3 cloves garlic, sliced

1 cup coarsely chopped onion
1 teaspoon each whole allspice,
  peppercorns, crushed nutmeg, and
  cloves
Bay leaves
1 lemon, sliced

Clean, wash, and fillet mackerel, then cut fillets into 2-inch lengths. Dredge them with salt, put them in a crock or nonmetal bowl, and let them stand for 1 hour. Rinse fish well in cold water and drain.

Combine vinegar, the 3 cups of water, sugar, garlic, onion, and spices in a large enamel kettle, bring just to the boiling point (don't boil), and simmer for 10 minutes. Add fish, bring back to boiling point, then simmer for 10 minutes longer. Remove fish tidbits to drain, remembering to save the marinade. Pack mackerel into sterilized jars. Add a bay leaf and a slice of lemon to each jar.

Strain the spiced vinegar, bring it to a boil again, and fill the jars with the hot marinade, covering the fish completely. Seal jars immediately, cool, and store in the refrigerator.

SPANISH MACKEREL WITH RHUBARB SAUCE

3-pound Spanish mackerel, filleted
Salt and pepper to taste
1 onion, minced
6 Tablespoons (¾ stick) butter

Dash of nutmeg
Pinch of fennel seed
1 teaspoon grated orange rind

Cut fillets in half crosswise to make 4 fillets; put them in a buttered baking dish and sprinkle with salt and pepper. Preheat the oven to 425°F. In a saucepan, sauté onion in butter until soft, mix in a dash of nutmeg, fennel seed, and orange rind, then pour butter over the fillets. Cover the baking dish tightly with foil, and bake for about 20–25 minutes (allow longer cooking time if fillets are not completely thawed). Meanwhile, make rhubarb sauce.

RHUBARB SAUCE

2 cups rhubarb
¼ cup sugar

Pinch of baking soda
2 Tablespoons hot water

Cut rhubarb into ½-inch pieces, place them in the top of a double boiler, cover, and cook 15–20 minutes, until almost tender. Dissolve sugar and a pinch of soda in hot water, pour it into the rhubarb, and cook 2 more minutes. Pour chunky sauce into a serving bowl. (If you prefer a smooth sauce, purée it.) Serve with baked mackerel.

SMOKED MACKEREL

Remove heads, split mackerel down the backbone, and lay fish open in 1 piece. Clean cavity and remove the black skin. Soak fish in cold fresh water, with a few ice cubes added, for 30 minutes, then drain. Make brine in a nonmetal container.

BRINE

2 cups salt
½ cup brown sugar
1 gallon water

⅓ cup lemon juice
2 cloves garlic, pressed
1 teaspoon ground allspice

Dissolve salt and sugar in water, then mix in remaining ingredients. Brine should float a raw egg in its shell. Soak fish in brine for 15–30 minutes, then rinse in fresh water and drain. Sprinkle fish with black pepper and lay the pieces on racks to dry until they have a smooth glossy, dry surface. An electric fan blowing cold air on fish speeds drying.

Grease the smoker racks with lard or Pam. Place fish, skin side down, single layer and without touching, on the racks, then load the smoker. Use oak, alder, or hickory sawdust/chips and smoke until fish is brown or done to your liking.

KINGFISH STEAKS
WITH MUSTARD HOLLANDAISE

4 kingfish steaks, 1½ inches thick
½ cup Basic French Dressing (p. 427),
    made with lemon juice
1 cup Hollandaise Sauce (p. 422)

1 Tablespoon Dijon-type mustard
3 Tablespoons heavy cream
2 Tablespoons grated Gruyère cheese

Trim steaks, if needed. Marinate them in French dressing for 30 minutes, turning occasionally.

Preheat broiler and pan. Arrange steaks on pan and cook them 3 inches from heat, allowing about 7–8 minutes on each side. If steaks are not completely thawed at time of cooking, allow longer cooking time; baste during cooking.

Have hollandaise sauce ready. Blend mustard and cream until smooth; mix into hollandaise. Cover cooked steaks with tangy mustard hollandaise, sprinkle them with grated cheese, then slide them under the broiler until the tops brown.

Shark, Swordfish, and Marlin

THE SHARK POPULATION never seems to diminish, no matter how it is exploited. These supreme predators of the sea are not just able to survive, they flourish, when more intelligent whales and porpoises are dwindling. Sharks are now essentially the same as they were 200 million years ago. Their entire body skin is rough, covered with oblique rows of tiny toothlike denticles. The real teeth in their notorious jaws are arranged in rows four deep. If they lose a tooth, a new one flips into its place. Sharks' skeletons are of cartilage instead of bone and enable them to glide to the source of food a mile away in two minutes or dive to the bottom and rocket to the surface in a moment. Many sharks come into the shallows of bays during May to bear their live young.

The following sharks are exceptionally good-tasting species.

Mako sharks are the number-one game shark on the Atlantic Coast and are considered the best tasting of all sharks.

Atlantic porbeagle (mackerel shark) look very much like mako but are not sport fish. The meat of both fish is similar enough in taste and texture to readily pass as swordfish. Most are taken in gill nets, some by hook and line.

Smooth dogfish are small shark that school inshore along the Atlantic Coast from Cape Cod south. Large numbers are taken by fishermen throughout the summer. Their meat is fine-textured and more tender than large sharks.

Thresher sharks are also good food fish. These large surface dwellers are found on both coasts and around Hawaii.

Half of their body is upper tail, which they use to stun their prey or to thresh the water, frightening fish into a tighter school and thereby making them easier prey. Generally they stay offshore, but frequently they will chase a school close inshore.

Big soupfin sharks are found along the Pacific Coast. An odd thing about them is that from Northern California to British Columbia, most of the soupfins are males; in the Central California area the ratio is 50-50, but in the Southern areas females predominate.

Leopard sharks are small gray and black leopard-spotted fish, found in shallow water from Baja California to Oregon. Most taken by anglers are about two and a half to three and a half feet long.

Swordfish

Commercially valuable, swordfish are harpooned as they bask on the surface in the morning sunshine. This is the same method that has been used down the centuries to catch these creatures.

Veteran sportsmen, anxious for battle, have been frustrated by lack of response as they trolled every kind of enticement to a swordfish lying topwater, until they learned (recently) that swords are deepwater nocturnal feeders rising to the surface in the early hours only after feeding.

Deepwater moonlight fishing has become exciting summer sport during the full-moon cycle. A good skipper, elaborate equipment, and advance preparation, as well as a strong angler and good luck, can make the expedition a success. On the fishing ground a spotlight is essential. A hook, sewn into squid bait, is maintained at precise depths (between 600–1,200 feet) by using weights and marked cable. Light sticks attached to the swivel (lasting about three hours), produce a greenish yellow glow that helps to attract big fish, as well as enabling the angler to see movement of the line near the bait after the strike.

Almost all big fish surface within the first hour of fight to see what is going on. Some swim close to the boat and lie there, as if contemplating action. About one-third of the fish will be chargers. Outmaneuvering a 200–500-pound charging swordfish, capable of putting a hole through a three-inch plank, can offer a bit of excitement. Most sports anglers tag their catch, letting the big ones go.

Marlin

White marlin, popular Atlantic game fish, are forty- to fifty-plus–pounders, multicolored, with a white belly. These marlin migrate up the coast as far as Cape Cod in the spring, and south again in the fall. In summer, around the middle Atlantic states, they are angled offshore from power boats.

Blue marlin, largest of the species, are taken off North Carolina in the summertime. It is thought that they make regular north and south migrations, moving away from the equator in the warm months and south again as the temperatures cool.

Striped marlin are valuable West Coast game and food fish, found around the Santa Barbara islands and south. Sport fishermen take them by trolling. Commercially they are taken on long lines. There is a considerable demand for their excellent quality meat.

About Shark, Swordfish, and Marlin Meat

All three fish have rich, mild flavor and a firm, dense, meatlike texture. They are best when grilled, broiled, or fried. Swordfish is a comparatively rare catch on both coasts, so all that is available is imported and sold frozen.

Shark is marketed year round, often under the name of "grayfish." The meat must be very fresh and cooked as soon as possible. Raw shark varies in color from off-white to reddish, but turns white with cooking. The flavor of the meat varies with the species of shark. Generally, the larger fish have coarser texture and may tend to be tough. It sometimes has a slight flavor of ammonia, which can be dissipated by soaking in cold, slightly salted milk, or in lemon juice diluted with water (which also tenderizes it).

BARBECUED MARLIN CHUNKS

Cut a 2-pound, 2-inch-thick marlin steak into several pieces and marinate the chunks overnight in oil and sliced garlic. Barbecue them over medium-hot coals for about 15 minutes, turning and basting with marinade repeatedly while on the grill. They need no sauce.

BROILED OR GRILLED SWORDFISH

2 pounds swordfish (4 steaks)   Juice of 1 lemon
Salt and pepper to taste   8 Tablespoons (1 stick) butter, softened
Flour   Paprika

Preheat the broiler and pan. Wipe steaks, salt, pepper, and dust them with
flour, shaking off the excess. Mash lemon juice into softened butter, mix
and spread it generously over the steaks. Let it settle a few minutes, then
turn the steaks over and butter the other side. Sprinkle with paprika and
place steaks on a hot greased broiler pan under broiler, about 4 inches from
the heat, or on the greased grill to barbecue 4–6 inches above medium-
hot coals. Baste during cooking.

   Delicious complements for swordfish served hot are a Hollandaise
Sauce (p. 422), Anchovy Butter (p. 432), or Tomato Sour-Sweet Sauce
(p. 434). Cold broiled swordfish is excellent with Parsley Dressing (p. 427)
or Tartar Sauce (p. 426).

BROILED SHARK OR SWORDFISH
WITH SICILIAN DRESSING

2 pounds swordfish or shark steaks   1/2 teaspoon basil
1/2 cup olive oil   1/2 teaspoon oregano
1/2 cup lemon juice   1 teaspoon salt
2 cloves garlic, minced   1/4 teaspoon pepper
1/4 cup chopped parsley

Mix together all ingredients except fish and let dressing stand at room
temperature for 1 hour before using. Cook shark or swordfish steaks as for
Broiled or Grilled Swordfish (preceding recipe). When steaks are cooked,
transfer them to a warm serving plate, pour sauce over the sizzling fish,
and serve.

GRAYFISH IN TERIYAKI SAUCE

Soak shark (grayfish) steaks or fillets in Teriyaki Marinade (p. 439) for
an hour or so. Then bake, oven broil, or grill the drained steaks or fillets
10 minutes per inch thickness of fish.

SPICY MARINATED SHARK OR SWORDFISH

2 pounds shark (grayfish) or
   swordfish steak, 1 inch thick
1/2 cup oil
1/3 cup lemon juice
1 medium onion, chopped
1/2 cup chopped cilantro
6 cloves garlic, pressed

1-inch piece of ginger, sliced
1/2–1 small green chili, seeded
   and chopped, or dash of
   cayenne pepper
1 teaspoon salt
Lemon wedges

Combine all ingredients except fish and lemon wedges in a blender and purée to a smooth paste. Cut fish into 2-inch chunks and marinate them in the purée for 1 hour or more, turning occasionally to coat them evenly.

Broil marinated fish chunks either in the oven or over medium-hot coals and brush with marinade while broiling. Serve fish chunks with lemon wedges and rice.

Mullet, king mackerel, or cero may be used for this dish.

PAN-FRIED SHARK OR SWORDFISH

2 pounds shark or swordfish steaks
Juice of 1 lemon
Salt
1 Tablespoon butter
1 Tablespoon olive oil
1 large onion, chopped
1 clove garlic, minced
1 Tablespoon minced parsley

1 large (28-ounce) can tomatoes
1 teaspoon basil
1/4 teaspoon pepper
2 Tablespoons capers
10 black olives, pitted
Half butter/half olive oil for frying
Flour

Sprinkle shark or swordfish steaks with lemon juice and salt and let them stand for an hour.

Heat butter with olive oil and sauté onion, garlic, and parsley for 3 minutes. Stir in tomatoes (break them up with a spoon), basil, pepper, and capers, then cover and simmer for 10 minutes. Add olives in the last 5 minutes of cooking and season to taste.

Heat frying butter and olive oil very hot, dust fish with flour, then fry the steaks until brown and crisp. Serve sizzling hot accompanied by a bowl of sauce.

BAKED SWORDFISH STEAK

2 pounds swordfish, 1 inch thick	1 1/2 cups sour cream
Salt and pepper	1 teaspoon paprika
1/4 cup dry sherry	1 cup grated sharp Cheddar cheese
Dash of cayenne pepper	Parsley

Preheat the oven to 425°F. Wipe steaks, sprinkle with salt and pepper and arrange them in a buttered baking dish. Mix sherry, cayenne, sour cream, and paprika, then spoon it onto the steaks. Scatter grated cheese on top and bake for 10 minutes or until done. Serve steaks smothered in sauce, garnished with snips of parsley.

DEEP-FRIED SHARK 'N' CHIPS

Cut steaks into small pieces, dip them into Light Batter for Fish (p. 20), and deep fry them until golden brown. Serve them with malt vinegar or Tartar Sauce (p. 426), French fries or potato chips.

SHARK TACO

1 pound shark steak	Sour cream
1 teaspoon salt	Hot chili sauce, Mexican style
1 egg, beaten	2 tomatoes, chopped
Cornstarch	1/2 green pepper, chopped
1 cup oil	1/4 cup chopped onion
Shredded lettuce	Tortillas, warmed

Beat salt with egg. Cut steaks into 1-inch strips, dip them in egg, dust with cornstarch, and fry in hot (375°F.) oil, browning both sides. Have ready, in separate bowls, shredded lettuce, sour cream, chili sauce, and the vegetables, chopped and mixed together. Place a piece of fried fish on each warm tortilla and let everyone help themselves to the trimmings.

STRIPED MARLIN SASHIMI

Marlin may be prepared in the same manner as tuna (see Tuna Sashimi recipe, p. 33). As with tuna, dark meat should be removed.

Shark Fin

Shark fin is used extensively in Oriental cooking. There used to be a large industry in Southern California for curing the fins. Soupfin shark was principally used, but any shark with big enough fins—ideally twelve to fourteen inches—could do for drying. The fins were trimmed to the cartilaginous rays, washed and spread out on bamboo frames to dry in the sun. No salt was used, just a dusting of lime and an occasional turn; the fins were brought into dry shelter at night. After drying for two or three weeks, the fins were packed in sacks and sent to San Francisco Chinatown merchants.

Today, *yu-chee*, dried shark fin, can be bought for about $30.00 a pound, but luckily it does come in smaller packages. Shark fin soup, which uses the dried fins, is a popular Chinese dish. It is a subtly satisfying gelatinous soup, delicately flavored, and customarily served at Chinese New Year celebration feasts.

SHARK FIN SOUP

2 ounces dried shark fins
8 fresh raw prawns
6 cups water
3 slices fresh ginger
1 1/2 quarts chicken broth
1/2 teaspoon each salt and sugar

1/4 teaspoon pepper
1 Tablespoon sherry
1 chicken breast, boned
2 teaspoons soy sauce
1/4 teaspoon monosodium glutamate
2 teaspoons minced green onion

Pour hot water over shark fin and soak it until the water cools, then wash fin well and place it in cold water to soak overnight. After soaking, the 2 ounces should yield about 2 cups.

Bring water to a boil, add ginger and shark fin and simmer, covered, for 1 hour, then set aside to cool in the pan. When cold, drain and rinse the fin briefly under cold water.

Bring chicken broth to a boil, add shark fin, salt, sugar, and pepper and simmer slowly for 20 minutes. Meanwhile, shell and devein prawns, rinse them and sprinkle them with sherry and salt. Cut chicken breast into shreds, add them to the broth, and simmer for 8 minutes. Add soy sauce, monosodium glutamate, and prawns, bring to a boil and remove from the heat immediately. Let soup stand, covered, for 15 minutes. Serve shark fin soup hot, garnished with minced green onion.

Spot

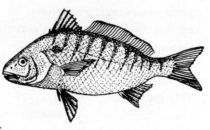

SPOT, A POPULAR SMALL CROAKER, takes its name from the spot on its shoulder. It is also identified by the fifteen oblique bars extending down the upper sides. This small gray and silver fish seldom weighs a pound.

Spot are found on the Gulf and Atlantic coasts from Texas to Cape Cod. Sometimes they appear in vast numbers along the Gulf Coast. Spawning takes place in deep water during winter, then they travel into the shallows in spring, frequenting sheltered bays and estuaries, congregating over sandy bottoms or oyster and shell reefs. They are one of the staple foods of striped bass. Angling is good during runs, using clam or worm bait.

About Spot Meat

Spot are panfish and may be butter sautéed, pan fried, oven fried, or broiled. Their flesh is soft and has fine flavor. They should be cooked thoroughly and should not be used in raw fish dishes.

Refer to Croaker chapter, pages 60–4, for additional recipes.

OVEN-FRIED SPOT WITH VEGETABLES

8 whole spot, 6–7 ounces each,
  cleaned, scaled, heads removed
3–4 cloves garlic
1 cup salad oil
Juice of 1 lemon
Salt and pepper to taste
3 medium potatoes
3 bell peppers

Butter
Fine dry bread crumbs
Paprika
1 cup chopped green onion
1/2 cup chopped cilantro
3 tomatoes, sliced
Flour

Slice garlic into oil and let it stand for several hours. Rinse and pat fish dry on toweling, cover with lemon juice, sprinkle with salt and pepper, and refrigerate until ready to cook.

Peel and slice potatoes 1/8 inch thick and blanch by immersing and swishing in scalding water for 1 minute; drain on toweling. Slice peppers in julienne strips, parboil strips in boiling salted water until brilliant in color, then plunge them immediately in cold water and drain.

Preheat the oven to 400°F. and butter a baking dish generously and sprinkle with crumbs. Dip potato slices in garlic oil and cover the bottom of the prepared dish with the slices. Sprinkle lightly with one-third of the salt, pepper, paprika, green onion, and cilantro. Repeat seasoning with the bell peppers and sliced tomatoes in alternating layers. Cover with aluminum foil and bake for approximately 40 minutes. When potatoes are cooked, remove dish from oven and keep covered and warm.

Raise oven heat to 500°F. and heat a flat pan large enough to hold the fish. Dust fish with flour and shake off the excess. Remove pan from oven and pour garlic oil 1/8 inch deep into the hot pan. Lay fish in pan, in a single layer, then turn them so both sides are covered with oil. Now, return pan to oven and bake, uncovered, until fish are brown and done. (Use the ratio of 10 minutes per inch thickness of fish to estimate the cooking time.) Put vegetable dish back into oven for last 5 minutes to reheat. Remove foil from the baking dish, arrange spot on top of the vegetables, and serve.

Trout, scrod, or other panfish may be used for this dish.

Atlantic Croaker

Atlantic croakers (hardheads) are
important one- to four-pound food
and game fish, found from Massachusetts to Cape Canaveral and in
the Gulf. They are silvery gray, fading

to white below, with a brownish wavy bar pattern on the sides. The whole
fish changes color to golden tones during spawning season and consequently is also known as golden croaker.

Hardheads move into bays and estuaries in the spring and remain
inshore until fall. In the winter they return to deep water by the continental
shelf. In the Gulf, especially on the Texas coast, they appear in their
golden spawning colors around late October. Apparently they spawn in the
open Gulf and die after their second year. The Gulf fish are seldom more
than two pounds.

About Atlantic Croaker Meat

Hardheads are good panfish. The meat is soft, similar to spot and speckled trout, but not quite such good quality. Methods of cooking most
croaker family fish are similar. See Speckled Seatrout chapter, pages
264–6; Spot chapter, pages 260–1; and Croaker chapter, pages 60–4,
for additional recipes.

Croakers should be thoroughly cooked and not used in raw fish dishes.

CROAKER BAKED IN CATSUP WINE SAUCE

2 pounds croaker fillets
Salt and pepper to taste
Juice of 1 lemon
1 small onion, grated

2 Tablespoons (1/4 stick) butter, melted
1 1/2 cups tomato catsup
1/2 cup dry white wine

Preheat the oven to 375°F. Wipe fillets with a damp cloth, sprinkle lightly with salt and pepper, and arrange them in a buttered baking dish. Squeeze lemon juice onto the fish and spread with grated onion. Combine butter, catsup, and wine, then pour the mixture over the fish. Bake until fish flakes easily.

FRIED GOLDEN CROAKER PIQUANT

2 whole croakers, 2 pounds each, pan dressed
Juice of 1 lemon
1 cup flour
1½ cups plain yogurt
2 teaspoons ground coriander

¼ teaspoon ground cloves
¼ teaspoon black pepper
Salt to taste
8 Tablespoons (1 stick) butter
½ cup vegetable oil
2 lemons, cut in wedges

Rinse fish, pat dry, and rub with lemon juice inside and out. Make 2 or 3 shallow diagonal cuts on each side and dust fish with flour, shaking off the excess. Mix yogurt with coriander, cloves, pepper, and salt. Heat butter with oil in a large skillet. Roll fish in yogurt-spice mixture and place them in the skillet. Fry over medium heat, turning once to cook the other side. Transfer cooked fish to warm plates, garnish with lemon wedges, and serve with rice pilaf.

Speckled Seatrout

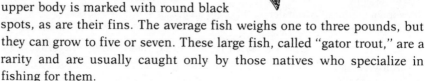

SEATROUT ARE DRUMS, related to croakers and weakfish. "Trout" as they are called, are dark gray on top, have iridescent blue sides and silver bellies. The upper body is marked with round black spots, as are their fins. The average fish weighs one to three pounds, but they can grow to five or seven. These large fish, called "gator trout," are a rarity and are usually caught only by those natives who specialize in fishing for them.

Speckled trout are fished from Chesapeake Bay to Texas and south, both in the coastal waters and inland. They are the most popular bay fish caught in the South. They are also common in bayous, grass flats, lagoons, and coastal canals. When they move out into the ocean or the Gulf during cold winter months, they usually school in deep holes along a shallow coastline.

Fishing season on the Atlantic seaboard as well as on the Gulf is from spring through fall, but winter catches are made along the coastal beaches. Schooling seatrout are often located by trolling. Anglers catch them by casting from boats or piers; some anglers wade up shallow water, casting into deep holes. Popular bait for seatrout are live shrimp, cut mullet, and small crab.

About Speckled Seatrout Meat

Speckled seatrout is excellent lean, mild-flavored meat, with flesh similar to that of weakfish, but firmer and of better quality. It should be cooked thoroughly, and it is not suitable for use in raw fish dishes.

See Croaker chapter, pages 60–4, for additional recipes.

STUFFED SEATROUT WITH OLIVE RICE

2 whole seatrout, 1 1/2–2 pounds each
Salt and pepper to taste
4 Tablespoons (1/2 stick) butter
1 cup chopped green onion
1 cup minced celery
1 pimiento, chopped
1 1/3 cups cooked rice

1/2 cup chopped olives
Pinch of thyme
Dash of garlic powder
Dash of cayenne pepper
Flour
2 slices bacon

Clean, scale, and degill trout and scrape blood from cavity. Rinse well, pat dry, and pierce the skin on sides with a sharp-tined fork. Sprinkle fish inside and out with salt and pepper.

To make dressing: Melt butter in a skillet, add onion and celery, and sauté until tender. Stir in pimiento, rice, olives, and spices, and season with salt and pepper. Stuff trout loosely with dressing and then close fish with small skewers. Preheat the oven to 400°F. Dust fish with flour. Place remaining dressing in a greased baking dish. Arrange fish on top and place a slice of bacon on each. Add 1/4 cup water to the dish, and bake until fish flake, about 25 minutes.

Good for other lean fish of the same size.

SPECKLED SEATROUT FILLETS WITH PECANS

4 fillets, from two 2-pound seatrout
12 Tablespoons (1 1/2 sticks) unsalted
   butter
1 cup milk
1/2 cup flour

Salt and pepper to taste
6 Tablespoons fresh lemon juice,
   strained
1/2 cup chopped pecans
2 Tablespoons minced parsley

To clarify the butter, see page 430. Dip fillets in salted milk, then in flour, shaking off the excess. Heat clarified butter, place fillets in the skillet, and sauté them, over medium heat, to a golden brown on both sides. Season with salt and pepper and remove cooked fish to warm plates. Add lemon juice, pecans, and parsley to the pan. Raise the heat and cook a minute or two, scraping the pan to loosen all the crumbs and fry the pecans. Spoon buttery pecan sauce over fillets and serve at once.

Flounder, walleye, or firm lean white fillets listed on page 447 (III A2) may be used.

SPECKLED SEATROUT BROILED

4 seatrout, 1 pound each	1/4 teaspoon pepper
2/3 cup olive oil	Dash of cayenne pepper
Juice of 1 lemon	1 Tablespoon water
1 teaspoon dry mustard	2 Tablespoons minced parsley
1 teaspoon salt	

Gut and scale fish, remove the head, but leave the tail intact. Extend the cut along the cavity to the tail and spread the sides open. Slip the knife tip under the ribs and cut the rib bones loose from the meat on both sides. Now, sever the backbone from the tail and pull it up gently, lifting out the bone structure in one piece. Pick out any stray bones and trim off the fins. Rinse the fish and pat it dry. Debone and butterfly the other trout the same way. Preheat the broiler and pan.

Mix a marinade of oil, lemon juice, mustard, spices, and water. Dip fish in marinade and arrange them on a hot broiler pan, skin side down, then broil (see Oven Broiling Chart, page 14). Brush fish with marinade while it is broiling and spoon the remainder over the cooked fish. Sprinkle with parsley and serve.

Trout and mullet may be used.

Atlantic Sheepshead

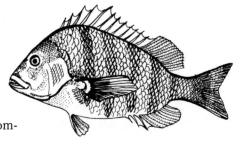

SHEEPSHEAD are coarse-scaled silvery fish, commonly called "convict fish" because of the dark vertical stripes on their sides. They average three to ten-plus pounds. Their bodies are compressed and high-backed with a long, stoutly spined dorsal fin.

Sheepshead are common and considered game fish south of the Carolinas. They can be fished around piers and pilings, rocks, old bridge abutments and wrecks, or in channels—anywhere there are crustaceans and mollusks for them to dine upon.

About Sheepshead Meat

Atlantic sheepshead (porgy family) is a different species from Pacific sheepshead (wrasse family), but equally prized as fine food. The Atlantic sheepshead's meat is white, firm textured, and mild flavored. The lining of the body cavity is black, which looks odd but makes absolutely no difference to the taste.

Small fish (¾ to 1½ pounds) can be scaled and gutted, leaving the fins on. These pan-size fish are delicious grilled, pan fried, baked, or poached.

Larger fish must be skinned and filleted: cut the skin along the fillets, then pull the skin off with pliers. Cut out the fillets without removing either head or innards. The fillets are suited to all methods of cooking. Sheepshead is particularly good fish for stews, chowders, soups, and poached fish dishes.

Atlantic sheepshead meat is similar to that of California sheepshead. Refer to California Sheepshead chapter, pages 54–9, for additional recipes.

COLD SHEEPSHEAD SLICES
WITH MARINATED MUSHROOMS

2 pounds sheepshead fillets
Salt and pepper to taste
⅔ cup dry white wine
⅓ cup plus ½ cup water
1 bay leaf
1 shallot, chopped
½ teaspoon thyme
⅔ cup olive oil
Juice of 2 lemons

3 cloves garlic
2 small bay leaves
6 black peppercorns
1 pound button mushrooms, washed
    and trimmed
Romaine lettuce leaves
2 tomatoes, cut in wedges
Black olives
1 Tablespoon minced parsley

Preheat the oven to 425°F. Cut fillets into serving pieces, arrange them side by side in a baking dish, and season with salt and pepper. Combine wine, ⅓ cup of the water, the bay leaf, shallot, and thyme in a saucepan, bring to a boil and pour over fish. Cover dish tightly with foil, and place in the oven to poach. (Use the ratio of 10 minutes per inch thickness of fish to estimate cooking time.)

Remove the dish from the oven and let fish cool to room temperature, then refrigerate in the covered baking dish overnight.

In a saucepan, combine olive oil, the remaining ½ cup of water, the lemon juice, garlic, bay leaves, peppercorns, and 1 teaspoon salt; simmer for 10 minutes. Add mushrooms and simmer until tender (5–10 minutes). Let mushrooms cool in marinade to room temperature, then refrigerate, covered, overnight.

When ready to serve, line a platter with romaine lettuce leaves. Drain and arrange fish slices on lettuce. Spoon mushrooms around fish, reserving their marinade, and garnish with tomatoes and olives. Mix parsley into mushroom marinade, pour marinade over fish and vegetables, then serve cold.

Blackfish, halibut, or ling cod may be used.

SHEEPSHEAD CASSEROLE

2 pounds sheepshead fillet
Salt and pepper to taste
2 onions, chopped
1 clove garlic, minced

4 Tablespoons olive oil
¼ cup minced parsley
2 cups tomatoes, peeled and chopped
¼ cup dry white wine

Preheat the oven to 425°F. Wipe fillets with a damp cloth. Cut fish into 1-inch cubes, arrange them in single layer in a buttered baking dish, and sprinkle with salt and pepper. Fry onions and garlic in olive oil until soft. Mix in parsley, tomatoes, and wine, then pour ingredients over fish chunks. Bake, uncovered, for about 20 minutes, or until fish flakes easily when tested. Baste during cooking with juices in dish.

Black Drum

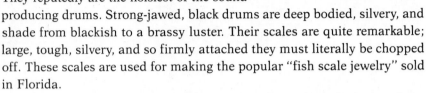

BLACK DRUMS (oyster cracker
or oyster drum) are frequently
big fish (twenty to forty-
plus pounds), and heavy to
haul in from off the bottom onto a boat.
They reputedly are the noisiest of the sound-
producing drums. Strong-jawed, black drums are deep bodied, silvery, and
shade from blackish to a brassy luster. Their scales are quite remarkable;
large, tough, silvery, and so firmly attached they must literally be chopped
off. These scales are used for making the popular "fish scale jewelry" sold
in Florida.

Black drums are common from New York southward. Some of the
largest fish are caught in the surf off the Carolinas, during the spring run.
Party-boat skippers use fish finders and fathometers to locate the popular
schooling fish. Small oyster crackers are fished from piers and skiffs, in
bays, lagoons, and in the surf.

About Black Drum Meat

Small pan-size drums are very good eating. Refer to Croaker chapter, pages
60–4, for recipes. Those up to fifteen pounds are lean and mild flavored,
with tender-firm meat. Large fish are poorly flavored and coarse. Steaks
may be butter sautéed, oven fried with coating, baked in foil, poached, or
used in stews and chowders. The meat should be cooked thoroughly and is
not suitable for raw fish dishes.

BAKED DRUM À LA GRECQUE

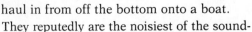

2 pounds black drum (4 fillets cut
  1 ½ inches thick)
Juice of 1 lemon
Salt and pepper to taste
Fine dry bread crumbs
4 Tablespoons olive oil

3 cloves garlic, pressed
Dash of cayenne pepper
1 cup chopped parsley
2 tomatoes
2 Tablespoons (¼ stick) butter, melted

Wipe fillets with a damp cloth, cover with lemon juice, season with salt and pepper, and let stand until ready to cook.

Preheat the oven to 350°F. Dip fillets in crumbs and arrange them side by side in a buttered baking dish. Mix together olive oil, garlic, ½ teaspoon salt, and ¼ teaspoon pepper, the cayenne, and the parsley; spoon onto fish. Slice tomatoes, dip them in crumbs, and place slices on the fillets. Mix ½ cup or so of crumbs with melted butter and scatter them on top. Place dish in the oven and bake, uncovered, until fish flakes easily when tested.

Any lean firm fillet listed on page 447 (III A2) may be used.

BLACK DRUM CHOWDER

2 pounds black drum steaks
Milk and water for poaching
1 stalk celery, minced
½ cup chopped green onion
1 clove garlic, minced
3 Tablespoons butter
3 Tablespoons flour

2 cups tomatoes, peeled and chopped
¼ teaspoon baking soda
2 cups milk
Salt and pepper to taste
2 Tablespoons minced cilantro leaves,
  or ½ teaspoon dried cilantro
1 cup shredded American cheese

Wipe steaks with a damp cloth and cut into 1½-inch pieces. Fill a sauté pan to the depth of 1 inch with half salted water/half milk and heat to a boil. Add fish, cover, reduce heat, and simmer until fish flakes easily. Remove from heat, drain (discarding poaching liquid), and keep fish warm.

Sauté celery, onion, and garlic in butter over medium heat until vegetables are soft. Mix in flour and cook 2 more minutes. Add tomatoes and simmer slowly a few minutes. Stir in soda and 2 cups milk, heat to scalding, and season with salt and pepper. Add poached fish, cilantro, and cheese, then heat, stirring, until cheese melts. Serve in wide soup bowls, accompanied by hot biscuits with butter.

Cod, monkfish, sea robin, halibut, sheepshead, ling cod, or pike may be used in this dish.

Mullet

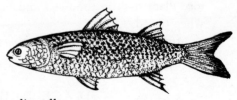

ONE OF THE HUNDRED VARIETIES
of mullet is common on every tropical or temperate stretch of coastline
in the world, but nowhere are they so
abundant as in the Gulf of Mexico. They literally
swarm in sheltered shoal water—especially in the Florida Keys. Mullet
schools wander from one food-rich spot to another, readily entering brackish and even freshwater in their search for food. Fishermen locate mullet
schools at night by listening for sounds of splashing water, caused by
jumping mullets. Only rarely will mullet take a hook, because what they
eat, or rather cull, are tiny food particles from off the bottom. They are
caught in seines, gill nets, or cast nets.

About Mullet Meat

Mild-flavored mullet is tender-firm, flaky white meat, which contains a
yellowish, milk-flavored (polyunsaturated) oil. It is the most generally
popular food fish on the Southern seaboard, where it is relatively inexpen-
sive because of its abundance. Mullets are sold whole or pan dressed, in
sizes of one-half to three-plus pounds. They are readily adaptable to
broiling, baking, deep frying or oven frying, poaching, or steaming. Mullet
roe is considered a delicacy.

Mullet can taste muddy when it feeds from muddy bottoms. If you take
mullet from muddy waters, marinate the meat before cooking.

BROILED MULLET

If mullet is taken from muddy waters, you may bone and butterfly small
fish (see Speckled Seatrout Broiled, page 266) or fillet large mullet. Trim
off all dark oily meat along the midsides. Cover fish in a thick layer of salt
for 1 hour, then rinse, wipe dry, and broil, basting with lemon-butter.

OVEN-BROILED MULLET

4 mullets, about 1 pound each, head
  removed, boned, and butterflied
Salt and pepper to taste
1 1/2 teaspoons Dijon-type mustard
1/2 teaspoon dried basil
Pinch of thyme

1 teaspoon minced chives
4 drops Tabasco
4 Tablespoons (1/2 stick) butter,
  softened and creamed
Lime wedges

Preheat the broiler and pan. Trim fins and feel for any remaining bones, then sprinkle with salt and pepper. Mash mustard, basil, thyme, chives, and Tabasco into creamed butter and spread the skin side of mullets with half of it. Arrange fish on the hot greased broiler pan skin side up and broil 2 inches from the heat. When brown, turn fish with a wide spatula, spread the remaining seasoned butter on top, and broil until fish flakes easily when tested. Serve with lime wedges.

BAKED MULLET FILLETS

2 pounds mullet fillets, skinned and
  trimmed
4 Tablespoons olive oil
1 teaspoon salt
1 1/2 teaspoons ground cumin

1/4 teaspoon white pepper
1 bay leaf, crushed
1 onion, sliced thin
1/4 lemon, sliced thin
1/4 cup chopped parsley

Wipe mullet with damp toweling and arrange fillets side by side in a deep flat dish. Make a marinade of olive oil, salt, cumin, pepper, and bay leaf. Pour it over the fish and marinate for an hour to two, turning fish occasionally.

Preheat the oven to 400°F. Butter a baking dish lightly, line it with onion and lemon slices, and sprinkle parsley over the bottom. Arrange fillets in baking dish, pour marinade over fish again, then cover the dish tightly with foil. Place dish in the oven and bake for about 20 minutes, until fish flakes easily.

DEEP-FRIED MULLET

Deep fry tiny mullet (dressed and boned) in batter. See Deep-fried Mackerel, page 248.

GRILLED MULLET

Mullets are delicious grilled over open flame or coals.

4 mullets, ¾–1 pound each
4 Tablespoons vegetable oil
Juice of 1 lemon
1 onion, grated

1 teaspoon basil
1 teaspoon salt
¼ teaspoon pepper

Clean and scale the mullets, but leave heads and tails on. Prick the skin all over with a sharp-tined fork, then place fish in a flat baking dish. Mix a marinade of oil, lemon juice, onion, basil, and salt and pepper. Pour mixture over fish and marinate for 1 hour or more, turning occasionally. Cook fish on a well-greased grill placed 4 inches above the coals. Baste at least twice with marinade during cooking.

SMOKED MULLET FILLETS

5-10 pounds mullet
Oil

Generous milling of pepper

Clean, scale, and fillet mullets (leave skin on, if you like) and remove black cavity lining with an old toothbrush. Cut fillets into 1½-inch strips and soak fish in cold water for 30 minutes. Make a brine in a glass or plastic container.

BRINE

1 cup salt
⅔ cup brown sugar
1 Tablespoon lemon juice

1 teaspoon garlic salt
1 gallon cold water

Stir all ingredients together until salt is dissolved. Soak mullet in brine for 1-2 hours, depending on how salty you like smoked fish. Rinse fish, pat dry on toweling, and place pieces on racks to dry for several hours. When shiny and dry, brush mullet with oil and sprinkle generously with pepper.

Chips (oak, hickory, or palmetto roots, etc.) should be soaked for several hours prior to smoking. Heat the smoker (or adjust vents on gas or charcoal barbecue). Arrange fish on greased racks skin side down and place them in the smoker. Smoke (cover down on barbecue) at about 90°F. for 30 minutes, then raise heat to 150°F. until fish flakes easily and is as brown as you like it. (For fast smoke, raise heat to 200°F.)

FRIED MULLET

1 mullet, about 3 pounds, cut into
  2 fillets
¼ cup vinegar
1 egg, beaten
¼ cup milk
1 teaspoon salt
Generous milling of pepper

Fine dry crumbs
Butter
Oil
1 Tablespoon chopped fresh tarragon
1 Tablespoon chopped parsley
½ cup dry white wine

Remove the cavity lining with an old toothbrush, and all fatty dark meat, and cut fillets into 3-inch pieces. Marinate fillets in vinegar for 15 minutes; rinse and wipe dry. Combine egg, milk, and salt and pepper. Dip fish in egg mixture, then in crumbs. Heat butter and oil until it foams, add mullet and fry to golden brown on both sides; remove to a warm platter. Add tarragon, parsley, and wine to the pan, simmer mixture for a few seconds and pour it over the mullet.

COLD JELLIED MULLET

2 pounds mullet fillets, skinned and
  trimmed
Salt and pepper to taste
1 large clove garlic

2 Tablespoons olive oil
Juice of 5 lemons
Water
1 teaspoon curry powder (optional)

Rinse, wipe fillets with a damp cloth, and season with salt and pepper. Sauté garlic in olive oil for a minute, until it turns color, add mullet, and pour on lemon juice. Add enough water barely to cover the fish. Add curry, if you like. Cover tightly and simmer slowly for 20 minutes. Allow fish to cool. Mullet is ready to eat when broth has jelled; serve cold.

Snappers

SEVERAL HUNDRED FEET BELOW the surface of warm Gulf waters, brilliant red snappers school over live coral ocean floor, seeking food brought by eddying currents. Some are caught by our commercial snapper fleet and landed in Florida, where the red snapper industry is centered.

Snappers have several recognizable family characteristics: sloping flattened snout and shovel head, prominent eyes, and big mouth. The average snapper weighs one to five pounds, but there are king-size snappers that can weigh fifteen to twenty-five pounds. Within the snapper family there are about 15 species taken inshore off the Atlantic and Gulf coasts. Some of the common snappers are:

Atlantic gray snapper (mangrove snapper) are gray with reddish fins and eyes. They are common from the Carolinas through Florida and the West Indies, in salt or freshwater, in bayous, tidal streams, around bridges and wharves.

Schoolmaster are yellow, vertically striped, with orangeish fins and red eyes; most weigh less than a pound and are abundant about Florida and the Keys.

Lane snapper are pink silver fish with yellow stripes and a black spot. They are fished from shore, bridges, and piers around Florida.

Mutton snapper are green and red, average two to five-plus pounds, and are common from Florida to Texas.

About Red Snapper Meat

Red snapper—and all of the snappers—are excellent table fish. The meat is pure white, lean, moist, and firm, with a mild but distinctive flavor. Snapper is marketed fresh, dressed, or filleted. It is iced-down and expressed to markets all over the country. It is also marketed frozen. Broiled, baked, steamed, or poached, snapper is a delicacy.

Refer to Rockfish chapter, pages 110–18, and Grouper chapter, pages 286–7, for additional recipes.

BROILED SNAPPER

Recipe for marinade and instructions for broiling or barbecuing snapper are in Rockfish chapter, pages 110–118.

BATTER-FRIED SNAPPER
WITH SOUR CREAM DIP

2 pounds snapper fillets   Salt and pepper to taste
Lemon juice

Wipe fillets with a damp cloth. Cut into ½ × 1½-inch strips. Sprinkle with lemon juice, salt and pepper, and set aside while making batter.

BATTER

½ cup all-purpose flour   1 teaspoon salt
½ cup cornstarch   1 egg
2 teaspoons baking powder   ⅔ cup milk

Sift together flour, cornstarch, baking powder, and salt. Beat egg lightly with milk, then combine with sifted ingredients, and whisk until batter is smooth.

DIPPING SAUCE

1 cup sour cream   1 teaspoon minced parsley
2 Tablespoons Dijon-type mustard Oil for deep frying
1 teaspoon horseradish

Mix together sour cream, mustard, horseradish, and parsley. Pour sauce into a serving bowl and refrigerate until ready to use.

Heat 2 inches of oil to 375°F. Coat snapper with batter and shake off the excess. Deep fry a few pieces at a time; turn fish once or twice, and when they are golden brown, remove them. Drain fish on toweling, spear with cocktail picks, and serve with sour cream dipping sauce.

RED SNAPPER CREOLE

2 pounds red snapper fillets
2 strips bacon
2 Tablespoons (¼ stick) butter
1 small onion, minced
1 green onion, chopped
1 clove garlic, minced
1 stalk celery, chopped
⅔ cup sliced mushrooms

2½ cups plum tomatoes
3 Tablespoons tomato paste
1 bay leaf
1 teaspoon Worcestershire sauce
1 Tablespoon lemon juice
2 Tablespoons brandy or sherry
Salt and pepper to taste

Fry bacon until crisp, drain, and set aside. Add butter, onion, green onion, garlic, celery, and mushrooms to the skillet and sauté vegetables in bacon fat and butter until soft. Stir in tomatoes, tomato paste, bay leaf, Worcestershire sauce, lemon juice, and crumbled bacon. Bring to a boil, then simmer, stirring occasionally, for 15 minutes. Mix in brandy, season with salt and pepper, and simmer 5 more minutes.

Wipe fillets with a damp towel, cut them into serving pieces, and either broil or bake. *To Broil the Snapper:* Preheat the oven (see Oven Broiling Chart, page 14). Coat fish with melted butter, season with salt and pepper, and broil on a greased pan. Spoon creole sauce over cooked snapper. *To Bake the Snapper:* Preheat the oven to 400°F. Place fish in an oiled baking dish, pour a cup of creole sauce over, and bake until fish flakes when tested. Serve with the rest of the sauce passed at the table.

Grouper, white seabass, whiting, or giant California black seabass may be used.

Pompano

POMPANO ARE handsomely slender fish, deep bodied, silver
blue, with gold flecks underneath. Weighing anywhere
from half a pound to more
than four pounds, pompano are among
the swiftest of all fish.

Atlantic pompano range north to Chesapeake Bay during the warm
months. Baby fish travel even farther north. They are present year round
in the Gulf and Caribbean, schooling in the surf along sandy beaches,
moving in and out with the tide. They also travel into bays and inlets
where mollusks and crustaceans are abundant food.

Some of the best pompano fishing takes place in early winter around
the offshore oil rigs of Louisiana. Anglers cast shrimp-baited hooks from
piers along the Texas coast and from bridges in southern Florida, all with
good results. But pompano are not easy fish to catch; they nibble bait and
take it off the hook but don't bite readily. Once hooked, the skittish
creatures will use all their tricks: amazing speed, quick changes of direction,
dives and jumps. They even slip across the water surface on their sides like
skipping pebbles.

About Pompano Meat

Pompano is served as an expensive delicacy in our country's finest restaurants and is considered (by some) the most delicious of all fish. The meat
is white and firm, with a mild but rich, distinctive flavor. Pompano are
sold whole, drawn, on the Gulf Coast. Most are commercially taken,
immediately iced, and air freighted to metropolitan centers, where they
bring premium prices in select markets. Pompano fillets and sole have
similar qualities and may be prepared in the same ways.

See Flounder chapter, pages 242–4, for additional recipes.

BARBECUED WHOLE POMPANO

3 pompano, 1–1½ pounds each
8 tablespoons (1 stick) butter, melted
Juice of 1 lemon

Salt and white pepper to taste
Dash of cayenne pepper

Clean pompano, rinse, and pat dry. Leave heads and tails intact. Cut 2 or 3 shallow slashes with a sharp knife on each of the sides. Combine melted butter and lemon juice, brush it on fish inside and out and season with salt, pepper, and cayenne. Place fish on a well-greased grill to cook 6 inches above medium-hot coals. Baste often while grilling. When light brown and cooked on one side, turn with a wide spatula to cook the other side.

Also good for flounder.

BROILED POMPANO FILLETS

4 large or 8 small pompano fillets
Juice of 1 lemon
8 Tablespoons (1 stick) butter, melted

Salt and white pepper to taste
Dash of cayenne pepper

Wipe fillets with a damp towel and lay them in a baking dish. Combine lemon juice with melted butter, pour mixture over the fillets to marinate for 15 minutes or so; turn once or twice. Preheat the broiler.

Arrange fish on an oiled broiler pan, season with salt, pepper, and cayenne, and broil (see Oven Broiling Chart, page 14, for cooking time).

POMPANO À LA MEUNIÈRE

4 large pompano fillets, about
    ½ pound each
16 Tablespoons (2 sticks) unsalted
    butter
Milk

Corn flour* (or use supermarket corn
    meal whirled in a blender)
Salt and white pepper to taste
6 Tablespoons lemon juice, strained
Sprig parsley, minced

*Obtainable at health food stores.

To clarify the butter, see page 430. Dip fillets in milk, dust them with corn flour, and shake off the excess. Heat clarified butter and sauté fillets to a golden brown on both sides. Season with salt and pepper, then remove fish to warm plates. Add lemon juice to the butter and scrape the crumbs loose from the pan. Raise the heat and cook until butter is light brown. Pour sauce over the fish, sprinkle a little parsley on each, and serve immediately.

Fillet of sole may be used.

POMPANO EN PAPILLOTTE

2 pompano, 2½ pounds each	1 Tablespoon minced parsley
1 cup cooked shrimp	4 Tablespoons (½ stick) butter
1 cup lump crab meat	Dash of cayenne pepper
Basic Court Bouillon (p. 26)	2 Tablespoons flour
Salt and pepper	1 egg, beaten
2 green onions	¼ cup cream
1 clove garlic, minced	¼ cup dry white wine

Clean pompano, cut fish into fillets, then set fillets aside while making stock. Place bones, head, and tail trimmings in a saucepan with ingredients for court bouillon; cook for 30 minutes. Strain the bouillon, then bring it to boil again.

Preheat the oven to 425°F. Place fillets in a buttered baking dish, sprinkle with salt and pepper, and pour in enough boiling bouillon almost to cover fish. Cover the dish tightly with foil and slide it into the hot oven for 6–7 minutes, then remove dish, and let fish rest in the poaching liquid.

Turn down the oven to 400°F. Meanwhile, sauté green onions, garlic, and parsley in 2 tablespoons of the butter until they are tender. Season with salt, pepper, and cayenne. Stir in shrimp, then remove pan from heat and set it aside.

To make sauce, melt the remaining 2 tablespoons of butter in a saucepan, stir in flour, add 1 cup of poaching liquid and cook, beating constantly with a whisk, until smooth and thickened. Boil sauce gently for 2–3 minutes, then reduce heat. Mix together beaten egg, cream, and wine, then whisk them into the sauce. Stir in onion-shrimp and lump crab meat and warm for 4–5 minutes over low heat. Correct seasoning with salt and pepper.

Cut four 12 × 12-inch hearts out of parchment paper (or use heavy-duty foil). Butter the top side well, crease hearts down the center, and place a pompano fillet on one side of each heart. Cover each fillet with one-quarter of the sauce. Roll the parchment edges to make tight packages. Place them on a baking sheet and slide them into the 400°F. oven for about 15 minutes, until the parchment is brown. Place papillottes on warmed plates to be opened at the table.

Winter flounder, fluke, or petrale (brill) may be substituted for pompano.

POMPANO IN ROCK SALT

Pompano in rock salt is elegant and simply delicious. To make this dish a tin loaf pan is needed, one about 4 inches deep and large enough to hold the fish, and plenty of salt — rock salt, ice cream salt, or kosher salt.

Preheat the oven to 400° F. Pour 1 inch of salt in the bottom of the pan. Wash a fresh-caught pompano and wipe it with 1/3 cup vinegar mixed with 2 cups cold water. Then without cleaning the fish, lay it on top of the salt. If it is too long for the pan, cut off the tail. Pour in more salt to surround the fish completely, then cover with another inch of salt. Moisten the salt with water. The water will make the salt solidify. Place the pan in the oven and bake until the water is completely evaporated, leaving the salt a hard block.

Serve pompano encased in the salt block, with a hammer, for each diner to crack open. The cooked white meat turns out perfectly flavored, not at all salty tasting.

Mullet may be used.

Red Drum

RED DRUM are hard-fighting game and food fish, favorites of surf casters along the southern Atlantic seaboard. They are recognizable by their iridescent coppery red color and by the black spot on the upper body just ahead of the tail.

Atlantic red drum migrate as far north as the Barrier Islands off the coast of Virginia during the summer; the largest red drum (fifteen to fifty-plus pounds) are caught in this range. Farther south, in the Gulf of Mexico, they average five to six pounds. These fish, from Florida to Texas, are popularly called redfish, channel bass, or puppy drums. Southern Florida puppy drums can be fished all year, using a fly and spinning tackle.

Though redfish are present year round in the Gulf, there are seasons and places of greater activity. Louisiana's coast is one of those active places where tremendous runs of redfish appear during October through November.

About Redfish Meat

Redfish is tender-firm, lean, white meat, with a mild flavor—similar to striped bass. It is marketed seasonally, October through February, in the Southeast and Gulf states.

Redfish over fifteen pounds have coarse flesh and are only fair food. Those under ten pounds are of better eating quality. Whole fish may be baked plain or stuffed, planked whole or butterflied. Steaks are fine for barbecuing, grilling, frying, poaching, or steaming. Small fish should be cut into fillets.

See Striped Bass chapter, pages 229–34, for additional recipes.

BAKED REDFISH STUFFED

5–6-pound redfish, pan dressed
1 cup chopped shrimp
Salt and pepper to taste
8 Tablespoons (1 stick) butter
1/2 medium onion, minced
1 stalk celery, minced
1/4 cup chopped green pepper
2 cloves garlic, minced
2 Tablespoons chopped green onion
1 cup boiling water

1/4 cup claret
2 teaspoons Worcestershire sauce
Dash of Tabasco
1 1/2 cups dry corn bread crumbs
2 Tablespoons parsley
2 Tablespoons pimiento
Oil
1/2 cup each wine and water
Creole Sauce (p. 434) (optional)

Rub fish with salt, let stand 10 minutes, then rinse and pat dry on toweling. Sprinkle fish with salt and pepper inside and out, and set aside while making stuffing. Heat butter in a heavy skillet and sauté onion, celery, and green pepper over medium heat for 5 minutes, then add garlic and green onion and sauté 2 minutes longer. Add the cup of boiling water and the claret, then shrimp, Worcestershire sauce, and Tabasco; simmer for 10 minutes. Mix in crumbs, parsley, and pimiento until all liquid is absorbed.

Preheat the oven to 425°F. Stuff the fish and truss with skewers or sew sides closed. Cut 3 diagonal shallow slashes on the sides of the fish, brush the skin with oil, and place fish in an oiled roasting pan. Add 1/2 cup each of wine and water to the pan and bake for 10 minutes per inch thickness of fish. Baste often while cooking. Serve with creole sauce, if desired.

If redfish is not available, use any whole lean fish for baking listed on page 447 (III A3).

REDFISH IN COURT BOUILLON

5–6-pound redfish, pan dressed
Salt to taste
6 Tablespoons salad oil
4 Tablespoons flour
1 large onion, chopped
1 stalk celery, minced
2 cups tomatoes (1-pound can)
4 green peppers, chopped
4 green onions, chopped
2 cloves garlic

2 bay leaves
1 whole allspice, or 1/4 teaspoon
   ground allspice
2 slices lemon
Sprig parsley, minced
1 cup water
1/2 cup dry red wine
Pepper to taste
1 Tablespoon port wine

Rub fish with salt, let stand 10 minutes, then rinse, drain, and pat dry on toweling. Slice redfish crosswise into 5 or 6 large pieces, sprinkle with salt, and set aside while making bouillon.

Heat oil in a Dutch oven, mix in flour and cook slowly, stirring, until roux is golden brown. Add onion and brown lightly. Mix in all other ingredients, except fish and port, and simmer, stirring occasionally, for 30 minutes. Season bouillon with salt and pepper.

Place redfish in the court bouillon, spoon sauce over the pieces, and simmer slowly until the fish flakes easily when tested. Remove fish slices to a warm deep platter. Stir port into the bouillon, bring to a boil, pour it over the redfish, and serve.

Grouper

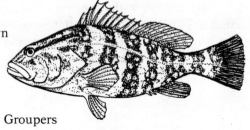

OF THE FOUR HUNDRED known
species of grouper, more than
fifty are found around Florida. They are predatory fish
with broad heads, big mouths,
and powerful "basslike" bodies. Groupers
are generally brown, gray, or black patterned fish, while their cousins
the rock hinds (also considered groupers) are speckled with every color.

Many groupers are large, solitary bottom dwellers that establish individual territories over coral reefs or rocky areas. Most spend their lives
sitting on the bottom waiting for prey; a few are wanderers.

Head boat captains regularly fish the known "grouper beds" on the
Atlantic seaboard, from the Carolinas to the Florida Keys. (Head boats are
so called because anglers pay by the head for a day's fishing.) Groupers
are commercially important food fish wherever they range. Scuba divers
often find them friendly to the point of being pesty, and therefore an easy
catch. The more common groupers are:

Gag Grouper are plain gray, fifty pounds, common from the Carolinas
to Louisiana. *Red Grouper* are common around southern Florida and the
Caribbean. Small fish are angled inshore from small boats, large sizes
commercially taken offshore. *Scamp Grouper* are common in the southern
Atlantic and Gulf, taken by trolling. *Nassau Grouper* are common around
southern Florida, the Bahamas, and the West Indies.

About Grouper Meat

Grouper (mero) is lean, moist, firm meat, so similar in taste to seabass
one could be mistaken for the other.

Small fish may be cooked whole or filleted. They bake, broil, fry, poach,
or steam beautifully.

Large fish are cut into steaks or chunks, which are superb broiled.
They bake well in foil or sauce and may be pan or oven fried, deep fried, or

poached. This versatile meat combines well with highly seasoned or mild sauces and is a good choice for soups and stews.

Refer to Kelp, Rock, and Spotted Sand Bass chapter, pages 65–72; California Black Seabass chapter, pages 73–6; and White Seabass chapter, pages 77–83, for additional recipes.

GROUPER ON A SKEWER

2 pounds grouper fillet	1 teaspoon curry powder
6 Tablespoons vegetable oil	1/2 teaspoon salt
2 Tablespoons lemon juice	1/4 teaspoon pepper or to taste
1 Tablespoon onion, scraped	Bay leaves
1/4 teaspoon dry mustard	Mango or papaya slices

Wipe fillet with a damp cloth, cut fish into walnut-size pieces, and place them in a nonmetal bowl. Combine oil, lemon juice, onion, mustard, curry, and salt and pepper; mix well and pour marinade over the fish. Marinate grouper for 30 minutes, or longer, turning pieces now and then.

When coals are almost ready, spear 5–6 pieces of fish on each skewer, with a bay leaf between each piece. Grill over medium-hot coals, turning the skewers only once. Baste with marinade while cooking. Serve grilled grouper with mango or papaya slices.

Giant black seabass, shark, swordfish, cobia, or snook may be used.

GROUPER TURBANS STUFFED WITH CRAB

1 1/2 pounds grouper fillets,	2 Tablespoons milk
cut into 8 thin slices,	1/2 teaspoon salt
about 4 inches square	1 egg
1/2 pound crab meat, or 8 king crab	Flour
legs, thawed	2 Tablespoons each butter and oil
Salt and pepper to taste	Rémoulade Sauce (p. 426)
Juice of 1 lime	

Season fillets with salt and pepper. Place equal amounts of crab meat or a crab leg on each slice and sprinkle with a few drops of lime juice. Roll and secure turbans with wooden cocktail picks. Beat milk and 1/2 teaspoon salt with egg. Dip fish in egg mixture, then roll in flour.

Sauté turbans in hot butter and oil over medium heat, turning and moving fish around carefully, until golden and cooked. Remove fish to a warm platter and serve with rémoulade sauce.

Snapper, tilefish, halibut, or bass may be used.

Cobia

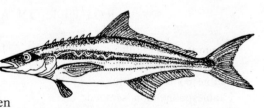

THE FAST, TOUGH, FIGHTING
COBIA is identified by three
black stripes running the length
of its long brown body. Fishermen
refer to this inshore game fish as sergeant fish (because of the stripes),
crabeater, lemonfish, and coalfish. It has no relatives—it is a class
species all by itself—but is found all over the world in warm or tropical
waters. Those caught around Chesapeake Bay average twenty-five to thirty
pounds. In the Gulf of Mexico big thirty- to eighty-pounders are taken.
They are solitary wanderers and stay out in open ocean, usually close
to shore.

Young fish are found swimming in bays and inlets, often lazing around
buoys, pilings, and places where crab, shrimp, and small fish are plentiful.
They are caught from piers, boats, or from casting in the surf, using live
crab as bait.

Cobia have a funny habit of swimming along under anything that
floats—logs, crates, boxes, paper, and other debris. They have been known
to swim directly to a boat.

About Cobia Meat

Cobia is delicious gourmet-quality fish. The meat is firm, moist, and lean,
similar to lobster in flavor. During the season, it is often found in Southeastern and Southern markets. This fine game fish may be grilled, baked
in foil, pan or oven fried, deep fried, poached, or smoked.

When fishing large cobia remove the head at the time the fish is
caught, then hang the body by the tail to bleed. Once bled, it can then
be filleted, skinned, trimmed, and cut into steaks. The meat should be
iced or refrigerated immediately, and then cooked, frozen, or smoked as
soon as possible.

GRILLED COBIA STEAKS

2 pounds cobia, cut into four 1-inch-
thick steaks
Salt and pepper to taste
2 Tablespoons light rum

Juice of 1 lime
2 cloves garlic, minced
2 Tablespoons olive oil
3 Tablespoons butter, melted

Rinse and pat fillets dry, lay them in a baking dish, and sprinkle with salt and pepper. Mix a marinade of rum, lime juice, garlic, olive oil, and melted butter, then pour it over the fish. Marinate for at least 1 hour, turning occasionally.

Grill steaks over open flame or in a preheated broiler. Baste frequently with marinade during cooking.

FRIED COBIA WITH MUSHROOM WINE SAUCE

2 pounds cobia, cut into 1-inch cubes
Salt and pepper to taste
Flour for dusting
3 Tablespoons butter
2 Tablespoons oil
1 egg, separated
½ pound mushrooms, quartered

2 cloves garlic
½ cup sliced green onion
2 Tablespoons minced parsley
3 Tablespoons flour
2 cups hot milk
4 Tablespoons dry white wine
Grated cheese

Season cobia cubes with salt and pepper, dust with flour, and shake off the excess. Heat butter and oil together in a large skillet. Toss fish cubes in slightly beaten egg white and fry them in butter and oil until brown, turning to cook the other side. Transfer fish to a baking dish, cover, and keep warm.

Add mushrooms, garlic, onion, and parsley to the pan and sauté to brown them lightly. Season with salt and pepper, then remove them with a slotted spoon and keep warm. Stir the 3 tablespoons flour into the pan, then add hot milk and beat with a whisk until sauce thickens and boils. Stir in wine and cook 2 or 3 minutes. Mix a small amount of hot sauce into beaten egg yolk, then return the mixture to the sauce and cook over low heat, stirring constantly, for 1 minute. Stir in reserved mushroom mixture and taste sauce carefully for seasoning. Pour sauce over fish cubes, sprinkle generously with grated cheese, and put under the broiler for several minutes to brown cheese.

IV

FRESHWATER FISH

The Black Basses

SMALLMOUTH BASS and largemouth bass rank among the most popular of North American freshwater game fish. They are the largest members of the sunfish family, averaging 1½ to 3-plus pounds, look alike, and often share the same waters. The largemouth is distinguished by its black to greenish color and its long jaw that extends behind the eye. The smallmouth bass is bronze, fading to silver underneath.

Both fish are native to limited sections of North America, but have been transplanted and thrive in almost every state now. They do best in cool, clear, shallow, weedy lakes or in river backwaters that furnish them protection and an abundant diet of fish, frogs, crayfish, and insects. Their habit is to hole up during the day, then move into the shallows to forage from dusk to dawn.

Sunfish, from the angler's standpoint, are divided by size into two groups: the larger fish are collectively called black bass, and smaller, panfish size are collectively called bream. The following are common and delicious panfish (see also Panfish, page 445).

Crappies. They are short, deep-bodied, roundish fish that average 1–1½ pounds or less. They are found throughout the country in lakes, ponds, or streams. Black crappies (calicos) prefer cool northern waters with some current. White crappies (speckled bass), on the other hand, will tolerate the sluggish warm waters of the South.

Bluegills (dollardee or bream). They are the most widely distributed of all sunfish and are stocked in thousands of farm ponds. They are fine-quality panfish. Bluegills are delicious filleted and skinned, cut into strips, dipped in cornmeal, and deep fried in hot (425°F.) oil.

About Black Bass Meat

Black bass is excellent firm, lean meat. The quality of the meat is very similar to that of other basses. The fish may be cooked whole or filleted and skinned. See Kelp, Rock, and Spotted Sand Bass chapter, pages 65–72, for additional recipes.

BAKED LARGEMOUTH BASS

1 largemouth bass, about 3 pounds, dressed, head on
Flour
8 Tablespoons (1 stick) butter, melted

Salt and pepper to taste
Garlic powder
1/4 cup dry white wine or water
2 limes, cut in wedges

Preheat the oven to 450°F. Rinse and pat fish dry. Make 2 or 3 diagonal shallow cuts on the sides and dust lightly with flour. Brush bass with melted butter, inside and out, then sprinkle with salt, pepper, and garlic powder.

Place fish in a buttered baking dish. Pour wine into the dish and bake for 10 minutes per inch thickness of fish, basting several times during cooking. Serve with lime wedges.

BLACK BASS STEW

1 bass, 2 1/2–3 pounds, filleted
Salt and pepper to taste
4 Tablespoons olive oil
1 large onion, chopped
2 stalks celery, chopped
1 green pepper, chopped

1 pimiento, chopped
1 clove garlic
1/2 cup wine vinegar
1/2 cup tomato sauce
About 1 cup water

Wipe fillets dry on toweling, cut into portions, and sprinkle with salt and pepper. Put all ingredients, except fish and water, in a large, heavy pan or Dutch oven, mix well, and simmer for 15 minutes.

Arrange fish pieces side by side in the pan in the sauce, and add enough water so the fish is barely covered. Bring sauce to a boil, then lower the heat until the liquid no longer bubbles, and cook until fish is done. Remove fish to a warm platter. Reduce sauce over medium heat until it is thick, pour it over the fish, and serve.

PAN-FRIED BASS (AND OTHER PANFISH)

2 pounds bass
Salt and pepper to taste
½ cup flour
½ cup cornmeal

2 Tablespoons (¼ stick) butter
2 Tablespoons bacon fat
Sprig parsley, minced
1 lemon, cut in wedges

Dress the fish (bass, crappie, bluegill, pumpkinseed, or other), rinse and wipe dry on toweling. Make a shallow S-shaped cut on each side and sprinkle with salt and pepper. Roll fish in a mixture of flour and cornmeal. Heat butter and bacon fat to sizzling and fry fish over medium heat until golden brown, then turn and brown the other side. Remove fish to warm plates, sprinkle with parsley, garnish with lemon wedges, and serve at once.

PAN-FRIED BASS IN TOMATO SAUCE

8 bluegills (or other bream)
Salt and pepper to taste
½ cup plus 1 Tablespoon flour
½ cup cornmeal
Oil for frying
2 cloves garlic

2 cups fresh or canned tomatoes, puréed
1 teaspoon rosemary
4 bay leaves
4 Tablespoons vinegar

Dress fish, rinse and dry on toweling, and make a shallow S-shaped slash on each side. Sprinkle with salt and pepper and roll fish in a mixture of ½ cup of the flour and ½ cup cornmeal. Fry 2 or 3 fish at a time in hot oil to a golden brown on both sides. Remove cooked fish to a paper towel–lined platter and keep warm while cooking the rest. When all fish are fried, pour out all but 3 tablespoons of oil. Add garlic to the remaining oil, and cook until yellow. Add tomatoes, rosemary, and bay leaves; cover and simmer for 10–15 minutes. Mix remaining tablespoon of flour with vinegar, then stir it into the tomato sauce and cook for 2 minutes. Turn fire to low. Place fish in the sauce (2 or 3 at a time) for a minute or two, then return them to the platter (discard the towel lining). Pour remaining sauce over the fish and serve.

Good for other panfish.

Pike and Pickerel

PIKE FAMILY FISH are distinguished
by their long, slender bodies,
dorsal fins close to the tail,
and large duckbill-like mouths
crammed with sharp teeth. They are
the carnivorous villains of freshwater, who lurk
in shallow water among the weeds, waiting to dart out for their next meal.

Smallest of these game fish are one- to three-plus-pound pickerel, which range over the Eastern and Southern regions of the United States. They don't lose their appetites in cold weather and are taken by ice fishermen all winter.

Northern pike are solitary marauders. Their range is more extensive than any other freshwater game fish: from Maine to Nebraska, and north. These two- to ten-plus-pound fish are most at home in large rivers and middle-size lakes, or bays and straits of the Great Lakes.

Muskellunge are prize game fish, the largest of the "look-alike" pikes, five- to thirty-plus pounders. They are common in the Great Lakes, St. Lawrence River, and large lakes of New York, Wisconsin, Minnesota, Michigan, Ohio, and Tennessee.

About Pike Meat

Pike is excellent delicately flavored, lean, flaky meat. The flesh has a tendency to break up, and because of this quality, it is frequently used for quenelles, mousse, stuffings, and creamed dishes. Pike have a complex bone structure (like shad), which makes filleting more difficult than with most fish. Take care in cooking to keep meat from becoming too dry. Grill fish wrapped in foil or in bacon or bake fish covered or sauté fillets, or poach, steam, or braise. Pike under five or six pounds are most tender. Large pike and muskellunge are inclined to be tough, but make fine-flavored stews and chowders. Pike roe is poisonous at spawning time and is not generally eaten, but the liver is considered a delicacy and is used in stuffing or added to sauce.

Scald pike with boiling water to remove some of the slime and loosen scales. Scale fish, remove head and tail, and trim the fins. Leave small fish whole for baking, etc., or fillet them. Larger (longer) fish may be cut into steaks or into sections (center section is good stuffed and baked), or fillets.

GRILLED PIKE WITH MINT

3-4-pound pike, pan dressed and split	1 Tablespoon minced fresh mint
Juice of 1 lemon	4 Tablespoons (1/2 stick) butter,
Salt and pepper	softened
Rind of 1 lemon	1/2 cup sour cream

Rinse and pat fish dry. Brush fish halves, on both sides, with lemon juice and sprinkle with salt and pepper. Mash lemon rind and mint into softened butter, then spread mixture all over the fish. Tear off enough heavy-duty foil to wrap the fish. Butter the foil. Place pike halves together and lay fish on foil; wrap, double fold edges, and crimp to seal securely.

Place wrapped pike on an oiled grill over medium-hot coals and grill for 6–8 minutes on each side. Test fish to see that it is cooked (it is if flesh flakes) before removing from foil.

Transfer pike to a warm platter, cut into portions, put a dollop of sour cream on each, and serve.

Walleye or sauger may also be used.

PIKE PIE

2 pounds pike fillets, frozen	Juice of 1 lemon
Salt and pepper to taste	1 1/4 cups sharp Cheddar cheese
2 green onions, chopped	2 cups biscuit mix
4 Tablespoons (1/2 stick) butter, melted	1 cup milk

Place partially defrosted fillets, side by side, in a lightly buttered casserole and sprinkle with salt and pepper. Preheat the oven to 400°F. Mix onion with melted butter, add lemon juice, and pour mixture over the fish. (If fillets are more than 1/2 inch thick, put them in the oven to bake for 5 minutes.)

Shred cheese, combine it with biscuit mix, and stir in milk. Spread batter evenly, covering the fish, then slide the casserole into the oven to bake, uncovered, for 15–20 minutes. Serve hot.

Cod, ocean perch, snapper, or rockfish may be used.

MOUSSE OF PICKEREL

2-pound pike or pickerel, cleaned and
  scaled
Salt
3 cups water
1 small onion, cut in half
1 stalk celery, sliced
2 sprigs parsley
1 slice lemon
1 cup Chablis
6 peppercorns

1 cup Medium-Thick Béchamel Sauce,
  cold (p. 418)
1 teaspoon unflavored gelatin
1 cup heavy cream, whipped
Romaine lettuce
Fresh dill and/or chives, minced
Stuffed olives
Cucumber, sliced thin
Radishes

Remove head and tail and split the fish. Sprinkle sides with salt and arrange in a buttered baking dish, then set aside while making stock. Put fish head and tail in a saucepan with water, onion, celery, parsley, lemon, wine, and peppercorns; bring to a boil and simmer for 25–30 minutes.

Meanwhile, make béchamel and set aside to cool. Preheat oven to 425°F.

Strain boiling stock onto pike, cover the baking dish tightly with foil, and oven poach fish until cooked. Then remove cooked pike from stock and set fish aside to cool.

Strain stock into a clean pan. Measure 1/4 cup stock into a bowl, and when cool dissolve gelatin in it. Reduce the rest of the stock to 1/2 cup, mix with dissolved gelatin, and set aside until cold.

Skin, bone, and flake pike, then combine fish with cold béchamel. Put through the meat grinder twice, using the fine blade; or add the cold stock now and purée mixture in blender until smooth. Taste for seasoning, then fold in whipped cream.

Rinse mold in cold water, pour mousse into it, and chill until firm. Unmold onto a bed of romaine lettuce, sprinkle with dill and/or chives, and garnish attractively with stuffed olives, cucumber slices, and radishes.

Any lean fish listed on page 446 (III A1) may be used.

Carp

CARP ARE HEAVY-BODIED, large-scaled fish, darkly silver to yellowish in color, with two fleshy barbels hanging from their jaws. They can be found in ponds, lakes, and rivers, preferably warmer water. They are wandering bottom feeders that eat any organic matter they can grub off the bottom. Because they muddy the water, destroying aquatic plants and the habitat of native game fish, they are not highly esteemed by sport fishermen. Carp were introduced to both Canada and the United States from Germany in the 1870s, by the United States Fish Commission, and the adaptable carp then literally took over. Today, the problem is how to curb their number.

About Carp Meat

Israeli, French, and Bohemian strains of carp are selectively bred, fast-growing pond fish. Carp taken from fresh clear water (breeding ponds, clear lakes, or live from the fish market tank) are mild-flavored, coarse-grained, firm-flesh fish. The roe is considered a delicacy.

Fresh carp are available around the Great Lakes and other inland lakes and rivers; sold whole, dressed, steaked, and filleted. Small carp may be fried, grilled, or cooked *au bleu* (see Trout *Au Bleu*, page 311). Steaks and fillets are grilled, pan or oven fried, poached or braised. Whole 3–5-pound carp are usually poached, baked plain, or stuffed.

It is important to trim out the dark flesh, which is tough and unappetizing.

Carp's flavor can be improved by coating the dressed fish thickly (inside and out, if whole) with the following mixture: 1 cup salt, 1 cup grated onion, 2 tablespoons vinegar. Leave fish covered with this mixture for 1 hour, then rinse thoroughly under cold running water for a full minute, to remove all of the salt. Pat fish dry. It is now ready for cooking.

If you catch your own fish, remember that carp taken from muddy warm waters taste muddy. They have less of a muddy flavor in the cooler seasons. Those dressed and skinned immediately after killing have the best flavor. If you don't wish to skin the fish, clean it carefully and soak it in several changes of salted water, then in vinegar and water. Scale fish; if scales are difficult to remove, scald the fish with boiling water to loosen them. If carp is to be poached, scales can be removed with the skin after cooking.

BAKED CARP SLICES

2 pounds carp, cut into 4 thick slices	About 1 Tablespoon oil
1 teaspoon salt	2 onions, chopped
1/4 teaspoon pepper	2 cloves garlic, minced
2 teaspoons garlic powder	1 cup boiling water
2 teaspoons paprika	

Combine salt, pepper, garlic powder, and paprika with enough oil to make a paste. Rub carp flesh well with the spicy mixture, then put the slices in a bowl, cover, and refrigerate for 24 hours.

Preheat the oven to 350°F. Butter a baking dish lightly. Mix onions and garlic; scatter half of them over the bottom of the dish. Arrange carp in the dish and scatter the remaining onions around the fish. Pour boiling water into the dish and slide it into the oven to bake until fish flakes easily when tested.

BAKED CARP STUFFED WITH PRUNES

3-3 1/2-pound carp, scaled, butterflied, backbone removed, head and tail left on	5 Tablespoons butter
	2 teaspoons sugar
	Powdered ginger
1 cup salt	1/4 teaspoon pepper
1 cup grated onion	1/2 cup blanched almonds, ground
2 Tablespoons vinegar	1 1/2 cups pitted prunes
1 cup water	2 Tablespoons minced onion
2 Tablespoons cream of rice cereal	1/2 teaspoon cinnamon

Prepare carp for cooking, coat with mixture of salt, grated onion, and vinegar (see About Carp Meat section, page 299) for 1 hour, then rinse thoroughly, pat dry, and set aside while making stuffing.

Bring 1/2 cup of the water to boil, add a pinch of salt, and stir in cream of rice. Cook, stirring, for 30 seconds, then remove from heat. When cream of rice is cool, mix in 1 tablespoon of the butter, the sugar, 1/4 teaspoon ginger, pepper, and all but 3 tablespoons ground almonds. Open the prunes and stuff each with a small spoonful of the creamy almond mixture. Stuff the carp with prunes, and sew or skewer the fish closed.

Preheat the oven to 350°F. Melt the remaining 4 tablespoons of butter. Place stuffed carp in a buttered baking pan, brush with melted butter, and sprinkle with a dash or two of ginger. Add minced onion and the remaining 1/2 cup water to the pan, and put it in the oven. Bake carp for 35–40 minutes, basting frequently, then remove from oven.

Raise heat to 500°F. Remove skewers and carefully lay fish open in the pan. Arrange prunes around the carp. Scatter reserved almonds over the fish and sprinkle cinnamon over both fish and prunes. Slide the dish back into the oven until the almonds are straw colored and crunchy. Serve at once.

GEFILTE FISH

Gefilte fish is traditionally made with carp, pike, and whitefish. Substitute these, instead of using the saltwater fish, when referring to recipe for Gefilte Fish on page 75.

FRIED CARP FILLET
WITH WINE VINEGAR SAUCE

2 pounds carp fillets, skinned	3 cloves garlic, minced
Salt and pepper to taste	1 teaspoon rosemary
Flour	1/4 cup white wine vinegar
2 Tablespoons each butter and oil	1/4 cup dry white wine

Cut fillets into serving pieces, sprinkle with salt and pepper, and dust with flour. Heat butter and oil, and when it foams add carp. Fry fillets over medium heat to golden brown on both sides. Remove fish to a serving platter and keep warm.

Pour out all but 1 tablespoon fat from the pan. Add garlic, rosemary, and 1 tablespoon flour, and cook, stirring, until flour is nut brown. Remove pan from heat, blend in vinegar, then wine. Bring to a boil, cook for 1 minute, then pour sauce over the carp and serve at once.

Buffalo may be used.

CARP STEW

3-4-pound carp, pan dressed, skinned,
  and trimmed
1 cup salt
1 cup grated onion
2 Tablespoons vinegar
2 large onions, minced

6 Tablespoons (¾ stick) butter
3 cloves garlic
6 peppercorns
1 cup water or stock
3 cups claret or Pinot Noir
1 cup croutons

Skin and pan dress carp, coat it with mixture of salt, grated onion, and vinegar for 1 hour (see About Carp Meat section, page 299), then rinse well and pat dry. Cut fish into large chunks. Brown minced onions in 4 table-spoons of the butter, then put them in a stew pot. Add a little more butter to the pan, brown the carp chunks for 2 minutes, then remove and arrange them in the stew pot. Add garlic, peppercorns, water, and wine. Cover the pot, bring slowly to a boil, then barely simmer for 20 minutes.

Fry croutons in the remaining butter, place them in a bowl, and keep warm. Taste broth for seasoning, then serve carp chunks in wide bowls, ladle broth over fish, and pass the croutons at the table.

Buffalo may be used.

CARP ROES

Soak roes in cold water for 1 hour, then pat dry. Heat 3 tablespoons butter in a small, heavy pan, add ¼ cup minced onion, 1 tablespoon white port, and the carp roe; cover, and cook very, very slowly and gently. Season with salt and pepper. Serve on buttered toast points.

Catfish

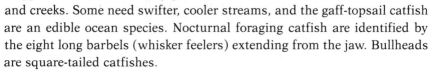

CATFISH ARE essentially warm-water fish. They are found in every state except Alaska. Most species inhabit mud-bottomed, sluggish rivers, lakes, weedy ponds, and creeks. Some need swifter, cooler streams, and the gaff-topsail catfish are an edible ocean species. Nocturnal foraging catfish are identified by the eight long barbels (whisker feelers) extending from the jaw. Bullheads are square-tailed catfishes.

Blue, white, and channel catfish are farmed in ponds throughout the country, and the demand is great for these increasingly popular fish. Big channel cats, blues, and flatheads are commercially fished with gill nets and trotlines (a series of baited hooks strung out on a long line). You can catch most species using a variety of natural bait, from dough balls to whole small sucker fish.

About Catfish Meat

Catfish is excellent mild-flavored, lean, moist, white-to-pink meat. One- to forty-plus-pounders are taken commercially, and there are a number of very edible species marketed. Whole pan-dressed small fish, as well as fillets and steaks from large fish (fresh or frozen), are generally available throughout the country. The white-meat catfish is commercially more popular than pink-meat bullhead or "red cat."

Skinned and filleted catfish are delightful served as fish and chips, broiled, pan or oven fried. Small fish or steaks are delicious baked in sauce or in foil, poached, in casserole dishes, and in stews.

When you catch your own, handle catfish with caution to avoid getting stung on their poisonous sharp dorsal and pectoral spines. Catfish and bullheads are best skinned and dressed just out of the water. They are the hardiest of fish and can be kept alive in a submerged wire basket or even a bucket of water for hours, until ready to skin and clean. Catfish have tough, slick, scaleless skin. Some fishermen find it easier to skin them with the fish's head nailed to a board. The alternative is to hold the head with your hand. Remove the fins, and cut through the skin in back of the head and around the fish in back of the pectoral fins. Then hold the head (if not nailed down), grab the skin in back of the head with pliers, and pull the skin back over the tail. Cut off the head and remove the innards at the same time. Finish cleaning, wash the fish well, and pat it dry. Large fish may be cut into steaks or sections. Meat that is not to be cooked immediately should be dipped in salted water, tightly wrapped, and stored in your freezer at 0°F. or lower. See page 12 for freezing instructions.

BAYOU CATFISH BARBECUE

4 catfish, about 1 pound each, skinned
   and pan dressed
Salt and pepper to taste
2 onions, minced
1 green onion, minced

1 bell pepper, minced
8 Tablespoons (1 stick) butter
1/2 teaspoon garlic powder
1 Tablespoon Worcestershire sauce
Juice of 1 lime

Rinse fish, pat dry, and sprinkle with salt and pepper. Tear off 4 squares of heavy-duty foil, 18 inches each, and butter them. Place a fish on one-half of each square.

Sauté both onions and pepper in butter until soft. Stir in garlic powder, Worcestershire sauce, lime juice, and salt and pepper. Spoon sauce equally over fish. Fold other half of foil over fish and seal the edges with double folds. Place packages of fish on an oiled grill, 6 inches from medium-hot coals. Cook 12 minutes on each side. Open one package and test for doneness. To serve, cut a big crisscross on the top of the packages and fold back the foil.

OVEN–FRIED CATFISH WITH SESAME SEEDS

2 pounds catfish fillets, cut 1 inch
   thick
Salt and pepper
2 Tablespoons milk
Dash of cayenne pepper
1 egg, beaten

1/2 cup cornmeal
1/2 cup sesame seeds
Flour
4 Tablespoons each butter
   and oil

Wipe fillets with a damp cloth, sprinkle with salt and pepper. In a wide dish beat milk and cayenne with egg. Mix cornmeal and sesame seeds in a pie plate. Dust fish lightly with flour, dip in egg mixture, then turn in sesame mixture until evenly coated.

Set pieces on waxed paper to dry for 30 minutes; turn once after 15 minutes.

Preheat the oven and pan at 500°F. for 10 minutes. Then, melt butter and oil in hot pan and lay fish in the hot fat, turning so both sides are coated, and return pan to oven. Oven fry fish, uncovered, about 10 minutes, until cooked.

Any lean white fillet listed on page 446 (III A1) may be used.

DEEP-FRIED CATFISH WITH HUSH PUPPIES

2 pounds catfish fillet
Milk
Salt and pepper

Cayenne pepper
Cornmeal
Lard for frying

HUSH PUPPIES

1 cup cornmeal
2 Tablespoons baking powder
1/2 teaspoon salt
1/4 teaspoon pepper

1/3 cup minced onion
1 egg, beaten
1/4 cup milk

Rinse and pat catfish dry. Cut fillet into 1/2-inch-thick pieces. Dip pieces of fish in milk, sprinkle with salt, pepper, and a dash of cayenne. Roll fish in cornmeal and set pieces on waxed paper to dry. Heat 1 1/2 inches of lard to 375°F.

Meanwhile, make hush puppy batter: Mix together 1 cup cornmeal, baking powder, and salt and pepper. Add minced onion, then beaten egg, and stir vigorously. Mix in milk to make a stiff batter. Form into small patties, 2 inches round, then poke a hole through the center of each (doughnutlike).

Deep fry fish, turning once, until nicely browned. Drain briefly and keep warm on a towel-lined plate until all fish are cooked. Fry hush puppies in the same lard until they are crusty and golden brown. Drain and serve at once with fish.

Bullhead or any lean white fillet listed on page 446 (III A1) may be used.

CATFISH COURT BOUILLON

2 pounds catfish, cut in 2-inch-thick
  pieces
6 Tablespoons vegetable oil
1/2 cup flour
2 onions, chopped
1 cup chopped celery
3 cloves garlic, minced
1/2 cup minced parsley
2 cups fresh or canned tomatoes,
  chopped
1/2 can tomato paste

1/2 cup Burgundy
4 cups stock or water
1/2 lemon, sliced
2 bay leaves
1/4 teaspoon each thyme and basil
1/8 teaspoon each allspice and
  cayenne pepper
Salt and pepper
Cooked rice
Parsley

Heat oil in a Dutch oven, add flour, and stir until creamy and free of lumps. Turn fire low and cook the roux, stirring, until nut brown. Add onions, celery, garlic, parsley, and cook until onions are soft. Mix in tomatoes, tomato paste, wine, stock or water, lemon, and spices. Let the mixture simmer slowly for 1 hour, stirring and scraping the bottom of the pot occasionally. Season with salt and pepper.

Wipe catfish with a damp cloth and arrange pieces in the pan. Raise the heat, return to a boil, then simmer slowly until fish is cooked, about 20 minutes. Serve over cooked rice, garnished with parsley.

Freshwater drum (thunder pumper) may be used.

Trout

THE FAMILY OF TROUT dominates
the freshwater fishing scene,
because of their general dis-
tribution throughout the country
and their fine sporting and table
qualities. Some of the more common
trout are: golden trout, which are found in high mountain streams; brook
trout (speckled), which are native to the Northeast, from New York State
to the Arctic; brown trout, which were introduced to the United States
from Germany in the 1880s. Cutthroat trout, found in rivers and lakes
from Wyoming to Oregon, are anadromous (which means that they migrate from the sea into freshwater to spawn). Rainbow trout that are taken
from streams are small, from lakes, large. Steelheads are also anadromous.
Lake trout (togue or mackinaw) are chars. Many species of trouts have
crossbred naturally, others have been selectively crossbred to create stur-
dier hybrids. They all have a delicately rich flavor that is universally
appealing.

About Trout Meat

Trout is firm-textured meat, high in fat content. It should be cooked or
frozen as soon as possible to retain its quality. Trout have very small scales
and need not be skinned or scaled. All sizes of trout are easily boned
before cooking; and after cooking bones may be lifted out.

Methods of cooking trout depend on size.

Small trout, ⅓ to 1 pound, are delicious broiled, butter sautéed, pan
fried, or poached. Refer to Speckled Seatrout chapter, pages 264–6, for
additional recipes.

Medium trout, 1 to 3 pounds whole or filleted, grill, bake, poach, and
braise beautifully.

Large trout, 3 to 10-plus pounds, such as steelhead, lake trout, salmon, brown trout, etc., may be cooked whole, cut into fillets or steaks, then grilled, poached, or baked plain or stuffed. Refer to Salmon chapter, pages 164–77, for additional recipes.

Recipes for trout may also be prepared using grayling and chars of the size of the trout indicated.

Small Trout

PAN-FRIED SMALL TROUT
(AND OTHER PANFISH)

Small trout ⅓ to ½ pound (cleaned and dressed) may be sprinkled inside and out with lemon juice and salt, then rolled in cornmeal (flour or bread crumbs). Melt enough butter to cover the bottom of the skillet, add trout, and sauté to a golden brown on both sides. Add a little lemon juice to the butter left in the pan, stir in a few drops of Worcestershire sauce, salt and pepper, and pour it over the trout.

PAN-FRIED SMALL TROUT
WITH MUSHROOM SAUCE

⅓–½-pound trout, cleaned and dressed	8 Tablespoons (1 stick) butter
Lemon juice	½ cup fresh or canned sliced mushrooms
Salt	1 Tablespoon minced parsley
Milk	½ teaspoon salt
1 egg, beaten	Pepper
Fine dry crumbs	

Sprinkle trout with lemon juice and salt. Mix the milk with the egg, dip fish in the mixture, then coat with fine crumbs. Sauté trout in 4 table-spoons of the butter until they are brown on both sides and flesh flakes easily, then remove to warm plates. Raise heat to high, add the remaining 4 tablespoons of butter to the hot pan, stir in drained mushrooms, parsley, 1 tablespoon lemon juice, ½ teaspoon salt, and pepper. Serve hot sauce with trout.

Spot or other panfish may be used.

DEEP-FRIED SMALL TROUT
WITH GREEN PEPPERS

4 trout, 7–8 ounces each, cleaned and
  cut into fillets with skin on
Salt
1 Tablespoon sake
Sesame-Vinegar Sauce (p. 81)
Oil for deep frying

3 bell peppers
Flour
1 ½ cups dashi or chicken broth
  (optional)*
Cooked rice

*See Mackerel Fillets in Miso Broth, page 249, for directions on making dashi broth.

Rinse trout and pat dry. Score the inside of the fillets with shallow parallel cuts placed ¼ inch apart (to allow heat to penetrate quickly and also to keep fish from curling in the hot oil). Sprinkle fish with salt and sake, and set aside. Make sesame-vinegar sauce. Heat 2 inches of oil to 350°F. While oil is heating, cut peppers in vertical slices and dust them lightly with flour. Blot trout on paper toweling. Heat dashi or chicken broth in a small saucepan.

Fry pepper strips briefly in hot oil, a few at a time, then drain on toweling, and keep warm. Dust fillets in flour and fry 2 or 3 at a time in the hot oil for about 2 minutes, until the skin is crisp. Drain them briefly. Serve trout and peppers in hot broth, with rice, and a bowl of sesame-vinegar sauce.

Other panfish may be used.

BAKED WHOLE TROUT WITH SOUR CREAM

4 trout, 9–12 ounces each, cleaned and
  pan dressed
Salt and pepper
5½ Tablespoons butter
½ small onion, grated
1 Tablespoon parsley

1 teaspoon dried chervil
¼ teaspoon dried tarragon
¼ cup dry white wine or lemon juice
4 Tablespoons sour cream
½ cup buttered crumbs

Remove heads and tails, trim fins, and wipe trout with a damp cloth inside and out. Salt and pepper fish and arrange them in a buttered baking dish. Preheat the oven to 425°F. Melt butter with onion, parsley, chervil, tarragon, and wine or lemon juice, then pour mixture over the fish. Cover dish tightly with foil and bake for 12–15 minutes. Remove foil, spoon sour cream over fish, sprinkle with buttered crumbs, and slide under the broiler until crumbs are browned.

BAKED STUFFED TROUT

4 whole trout, about 8-9 ounces each
Salt and pepper
6 green onions
Butter for sautéing
1 clove garlic, minced
½ cup chopped mushrooms
¼ cup grated carrot
1 teaspoon minced parsley
1 teaspoon lemon juice

⅓ cup plus 2 Tablespoons cream
¼ cup plus 2 Tablespoons port wine
4 Tablespoons bread crumbs
1 bay leaf
¼ cup water
4 Tablespoons (½ stick) butter, melted
Pinch of thyme
Beurre Manié (p. 430) (optional)
1 egg yolk, beaten

Leave heads and tails on trout, and gut through the gill openings. To gut trout without slitting the belly: Cut the throat loose, reach in the opening, and pull out the innards and gills together. Rinse and pat fish dry (inside and out), sprinkle with salt and pepper, then set aside while making stuffing.

Chop 1 green onion and sauté with garlic and mushrooms until the edges brown lightly. Add carrot, parsley, and lemon juice; cook another minute or two. Stir in 2 tablespoons each of cream and port, season with salt and pepper, and remove from heat. Stir in crumbs, then set aside until cool.

Preheat the oven to 400°F. Butter a baking dish and place the remaining 5 green onions, whole, across the bottom. Stuff trout through the gill openings and place fish on the bed of onions. Add to the dish a bay leaf, the remaining ¼ cup of port, and the water. Spoon melted butter onto trout and sprinkle with thyme. Cover the baking dish with foil and slide it into the oven for 15 minutes. Remove the foil and cook 10 more minutes. Transfer cooked trout to a warm platter. Strain pan juices into a saucepan, bring to a boil, then lower heat. Sauce may be thickened with beurre manié. Mix beaten egg yolk with the remaining ⅓ cup of cream and blend it into the hot sauce; cook, stirring, for a minute. Taste for seasoning, pour sauce over trout, and serve.

POACHED TROUT

Serves 2

Two 12-inch trout, boned and
  butterflied
Salt and pepper
Garlic powder
2 cups water
1 small whole onion

½ stalk celery, sliced
6 peppercorns
3-inch strip tangerine
  rind
¼ cup Chablis

Gut trout, remove the head, but leave the tail intact. Extend the cut along the cavity to the tail and spread the sides of the fish open. Slip the knife tip under the ribs and cut the rib bones loose from the meat, on both sides. Sever the backbone from the tail and pull up the bone gently, lifting out the bone structure in one piece. Pick out any remaining bones, and trim off the fins. Rinse and pat fish dry. Debone and butterfly the other trout the same way. Sprinkle trout with salt, pepper, and garlic powder, and set aside.

Make poaching stock by combining heads and bones of trout with water, onion, celery, peppercorns, tangerine rind, and wine. Simmer stock slowly, covered, for 30 minutes. Strain stock into a clean saucepan, discarding solids. Bring strained stock back to a boil.

Preheat the oven to 425°F.

Place trout in a buttered baking dish. Pour boiling stock over the trout. Cover baking dish tightly with foil and oven poach for 10 minutes. Serve trout warm, with the delicious broth and rice, or let fish cool in poaching liquid and serve cold.

TROUT AU BLEU

A few restaurants around the country serve this unusual dish, and this is how they cook any small trout to a vivid blue. The chef pulls a 9–10-inch live wiggling trout from the water, breaks the neck, quickly removes the innards, and without washing the fish, sprinkles it well with warm vinegar. (The film that covers the trout skin reacts with the vinegar to turn it blue.) Next, he places the fish in simmering Fish Stock–Wine Poaching Liquid (p. 27) and poaches it for 8–9 minutes. The now blue trout is served hot, with Chivry Butter (p. 432) or Hollandaise Sauce (p. 422), or left to cool in the poaching liquid, then served with mayonnaise.

Medium-Size and Large Trout

GRILLED TROUT WRAPPED IN BACON

1½–3-pound trout, filleted	Bacon strips
Salt and pepper	Lemon wedges
Garlic powder	Baked potatoes

Wipe trout fillets with a damp cloth, trim, and cut in half to make 4 fillets. Sprinkle fish lightly with salt, generously with pepper and garlic powder. Wrap fillets with strips of bacon and place in an oiled hinged wire grill. Barbecue over medium-hot coals. Bacon will baste and keep trout moist. When bacon is crisp, trout should be cooked, but test by flaking meat before removing fish from grill. Serve trout on warm plates, with lemon wedges and baked potatoes.

BAKED WHOLE SALMON TROUT
WITH BREAD STUFFING

5–7-pound salmon trout	1 teaspoon poultry seasoning
Salt	¼ teaspoon garlic powder
3 Tablespoons minced onion	Pepper
½ cup minced celery	3 cups soft bread crumbs
8 Tablespoons (1 stick) butter	Bacon strips
1 apple, peeled and minced	½ cup dry white wine
½ teaspoon monosodium glutamate	

Scale, clean, rinse, and dry salmon trout. Sprinkle with salt inside and out and let stand for 30 minutes. Preheat the oven to 425°F. To make stuffing, sauté onion and celery in butter until tender, add apple, and cook another minute or two. Combine seasonings with bread crumbs, add sautéed mixture, stir well, and stuff fish. Sew the sides together, cut 3 diagonal gashes across each side, and place fish in a greased roasting pan. Cover with strips of bacon, pour wine in the pan, and bake, basting every 4–5 minutes.

Whitefish, bluefish, or any whole fish for baking listed on page 447 (III A3) may be used.

BAKED LAKE TROUT FILLETS

1 1/2–2 pounds lake trout fillets
Salt and pepper
Flour
1 small onion, chopped
2 Tablespoons (1/4 stick) butter
1/2 cup chopped dill pickle

1 cup sour cream
2 Tablespoons lemon juice
1/4 cup chili sauce
1/2 teaspoon dry mustard
1/2 teaspoon basil
Sprig parsley, minced

Wipe trout with a damp cloth and cut into serving pieces. Sprinkle with salt and pepper, dust with flour, and arrange pieces in a buttered baking dish, skin side down. Preheat the oven to 400°F. Sauté onion in butter until soft, then stir in all other ingredients. Spread evenly over the fish, and slide baking dish into the oven to bake until fish flakes—about 15–25 minutes.

BAKED SALMON TROUT FILLETS

2 pounds steelhead fillets
Salt and pepper
Garlic powder (optional)

4 Tablespoons (1/2 stick) butter, melted
Juice of 1/2 lemon

Preheat the oven to 425°F. Cut fillets into serving pieces, sprinkle with salt, pepper, and garlic powder. Line a baking dish with enough foil to wrap the fillets. Mix melted butter with lemon juice. Dip the fillets in lemon-butter, then arrange them on foil. Wrap them, double folding the ends to seal. Bake in the oven, allowing 5 minutes for heat to penetrate foil and 10 minutes per inch thickness of fish.

The baked fillets may be served hot or cold, with spicy Parsley Dressing (p. 427). Another choice is to serve baked fillets with:

Horseradish-Walnut Sauce

1/2 cup walnut halves
6 Tablespoons sour cream
2 Tablespoons heavy cream
1 Tablespoon fresh horseradish, grated

1 teaspoon powdered sugar
1/4 teaspoon salt
Lemon

Preheat the oven to 450°F. and bake walnuts for 4–5 minutes, then rub off skins. Slice them, then whirl them in the processor until pulverized. Mix creams, stir in walnut crumbs, horseradish, sugar, and salt. Add lemon to taste. Serve with hot or cold salmon or salmon trout.

Idea for Leftover Steelhead

STEELHEAD CAKES

4 cups cooked steelhead
1 small onion, chopped
1/2 green pepper, chopped
1/2 cup chopped celery
3 Tablespoons butter
1 cup dry bread crumbs

2 eggs, beaten
2 teaspoons Worcestershire sauce
Salt and pepper to taste
Butter for frying
Parsley

Flake cold cooked steelhead coarsely. Sauté vegetables in butter until they are tender, but not brown. Stir in bread crumbs, then mix with fish. Add beaten eggs and seasonings, mix well, moistening mixture with a little water. Form into patties and chill for 1 hour. Fry patties in butter, browning them nicely on both sides, then serve garnished with parsley.

Good for shad, salmon, whitefish, carp, buffalo, sucker, or catfish.

Walleye, Sauger, and Other Perch

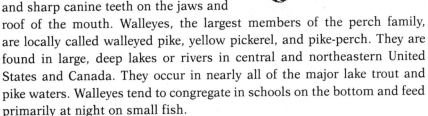

WALLEYE, A GAME FISH, and
sauger are closely related and
almost identical fish. Both are
round and long bodied, have big
glassy eyes that shine in the dark
and sharp canine teeth on the jaws and
roof of the mouth. Walleyes, the largest members of the perch family,
are locally called walleyed pike, yellow pickerel, and pike-perch. They are
found in large, deep lakes or rivers in central and northeastern United
States and Canada. They occur in nearly all of the major lake trout and
pike waters. Walleyes tend to congregate in schools on the bottom and feed
primarily at night on small fish.

Sauger are slightly smaller (one- to five-plus-pound-) fish, found in
deep lakes, rivers, and dam reservoirs, especially on the Tennessee, Missouri,
Mississippi, and Ohio tributaries and rivers. Sauger like to travel from one
body of water to another. They, too, are caught during dusk and dark hours.

Yellow perch are found in clear small and large lakes of central and
northeastern United States and southern Canada. These quarter-pound to
two-plus-pound panfish are popularly fished all year, for the fun of angling,
as well as delicious eating. They are considered superior to bluegills. Perch
over half a pound are commercially marketed.

About Walleye and Sauger Meat

Walleye and sauger meat are identical, and are both unexcelled for eating.
It is lean, firm, flaky white flesh. Sauger, averaging around two pounds,
are marketed commercially. Whole fish are delicious baked (covered),
poached, or steamed. Fillets, skinned or not, may be cooked the same way
as sea perch or flounder.

See Flounder chapter, pages 242–4; and Perch chapter, pages 96–103,
for additional recipes.

PERCH FILLETS WITH HERBS

4 perch	1 green onion, minced
Salt and pepper	2 Tablespoons (1/4 stick) butter
1/3 cup minced parsley	2 Tablespoons flour
1/3 cup minced fresh dill leaves	Baked potatoes

Clean and fillet perch. Wipe fillets with a damp cloth, sprinkle with salt and pepper, and set aside. Simmer the trimmings in 1 cup water for 10 minutes.

Mix together minced parsley, dill, and onion. Butter a baking dish and cover the bottom with half of the green herbs. Lay fillets side by side on the bed of herbs and dot with butter. Scatter the remaining herbs over the fish. Preheat the oven to 300°F.

Strain the fish broth and mix it gradually with flour until smooth and thickened. Pour the sauce over the perch. Cover the dish tightly with foil and bake for 30–40 minutes. Serve with baked potatoes.

WALLEYE FILLETS
WITH VEGETABLES AND CREAM

2 pounds walleye fillets	2 Tablespoons minced shallot or green
Salt and pepper	onion
1 stalk celery	1 bay leaf
1 small carrot	1/3 cup heavy cream
1/2 zucchini	Dash of cayenne pepper
1/2 cup dry vermouth	Paprika

Wipe fillets with a damp cloth, cut into serving portions, sprinkle with salt and pepper, and set aside. Slice celery diagonally in 1/8-inch-thick slices. Cut equally thin slices of carrot and zucchini. Heat wine in a heavy skillet, add celery and carrot and simmer, covered, for 6 minutes. Add zucchini and cook another 4 minutes. Remove cooked vegetables with a slotted spoon and keep warm.

Raise heat and boil wine down until reduced to 2 tablespoons. Cool. Mix shallots, bay leaf, and cream with wine, bring to a boil and add fillets. Cover tightly and barely simmer until walleye flakes easily when tested, about 10 minutes.

Transfer cooked fish to a warm platter and surround with vegetables. Boil down pan liquid to a creamy consistency, season with cayenne and salt to taste. Remove bay leaf. Spoon sauce over the fish, garnish with a sprinkle of paprika, then serve at once.

BAKED PERCH WITH STUFFING

4 perch, about 8–10 ounces each,
  cleaned and dressed
2 onions, chopped
2 Tablespoons oil
4 tomatoes, peeled and chopped
¼ teaspoon thyme
Salt and pepper

¼ pound mushrooms, chopped
4 Tablespoons (½ stick) butter
2 ounces soft bread crumbs
1 Tablespoon minced parsley
4 anchovy fillets, chopped
1½ cups dry white wine
Minced parsley

Wipe perch with a damp cloth and set aside. Brown onions lightly in oil. Add tomatoes and season with thyme and salt and pepper; cover and simmer slowly for 15 minutes.

Meanwhile, sauté mushrooms in butter. Mix bread crumbs with parsley and anchovies, then mix well with mushrooms. Add a spoonful or two of onion-tomato mixture and season to taste. Stuff fish with mushroom mixture and close with small skewers.

Preheat the oven to 350°F.

Pour tomato sauce into a baking dish, arrange the perch in the dish, and add wine. Bake for 30 minutes. Serve garnished with parsley.

PICKLED PERCH

2 pounds perch, cleaned and scaled
Salt
1 carrot, sliced
1 onion, sliced
6 peppercorns

4 cloves
1 bay leaf
4 Tablespoons (½ stick) butter
1 Tablespoon flour
⅔ cup vinegar

Wipe fish with a damp cloth, make a shallow S-shape cut through the skin on each side. Sprinkle with salt and set aside while making poaching liquid.

Combine carrot, onion, peppercorns, cloves, and bay leaf with 3 cups water, and simmer for 20 minutes. Then add perch, and if necessary, enough additional boiling water almost to cover fish. Bring to a boil, reduce heat, cover tightly, and barely simmer until fish are cooked.

Remove fish carefully to a deep platter. Melt butter, mix with flour, and whisk in the stock. Heat the sauce, stirring constantly with a whisk, until it boils. Allow to boil for 2 minutes, then remove from heat. Stir in vinegar, then pour hot sauce over the perch.

Whitefish and Cisco

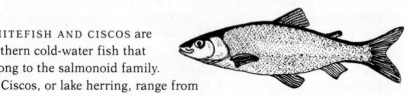

WHITEFISH AND CISCOS are
northern cold-water fish that
belong to the salmonoid family.

Ciscos, or lake herring, range from
New England through the Great Lakes and
northward. They are delicately flavored fish, delicious broiled or butter
sautéed, and exceptional when smoked. Cook them as you would herring
or smelt.

Lake whitefish are a dominant Arctic species, as are ciscos, lake trout,
and grayling. Whitefish are found in the lakes of Maine, through the Great
Lakes, and throughout Canada. They are slow-growing, satiny white fish
that average one to six pounds. Those caught in summer have soft and
fatty meat, but in winter their meat is lean, firm, and delicious. Winter
whitefish are an important Canadian fishery; most are marketed smoked.

A four- to five-pound whitefish is a beautiful fish to plank or bake
stuffed. See Basic Baking, pages 15-17.

Rocky Mountain whitefish are different species, found in lakes and
streams west of the Rockies. They are comparable to Eastern chub.

BAKED WHITEFISH

2 whitefish, about 1 1/2 pounds each,   1 medium onion, chopped
  pan dressed   3/4 cup sherry
Salt and pepper   1 cup sour cream
2 stalks celery, chopped

Preheat the oven to 300°F. Wipe fish inside and out with a damp cloth and
pat dry. Salt and pepper fish and arrange them in a buttered baking dish.
Scatter chopped celery around fish. Mix onion with sherry and sour
cream. Pour mixture over the fish and bake slowly for 1-1 1/2 hours.

V
SHELLFISH

Abalone

ABALONES WERE HUNTED, harvested, and dried by Indians on the West Coast as far north as Canada long before the white man came. In the late 19th century Oriental settlers made fortunes from the quantities of dried abalone they shipped to Hawaii, the Philippines, and China. As the popularity and demand for these delicious mollusks have grown, they have been recklessly overfished. Restrictions on size, limit, and season have been imposed, but still abalone that once could be pried off the rocks in the middle tide zone are now rarely found in less than fifteen feet of water.

These mobile mollusks travel slowly over the rock surface on their enormous suction foot, grazing in dense growth of brown algae. Divers hunt abalone down to about twelve fathoms, in rocky channels where the tide sweeps through. They pry them off rocks with an abalone iron, which resembles a tire iron. If the iron is slipped quickly under the animal, the abalone comes away easily, but with any hesitation it contracts its powerful foot and can hardly be pried loose. A four-inch abalone can exert about 350 pounds of force.

An undersized abalone may not be thrown back in the water. Law requires that it be replaced on the rock it came from because, being a single-shell animal like the turtle, if it lands on its back it will lie helpless and unable to turn over; easy prey waiting to be devoured.

There are four varieties of abalone along the West Coast, named for the color of the shells. In Southern California small green abalones are the most common; small pink abalones are also found; and red abalones, a deep-water species, are the largest. Black abalones are common on the central and northern coasts, being able to withstand the strong ocean waves.

About Abalone Meat

Abalone is lean, white, very tough muscle meat with distinctive flavor. Unless sliced extremely thin, it needs tenderizing; even then, it could take a few taps with a mallet. Instructions for cleaning and tenderizing are on page 7. Cleaned raw abalone can be kept up to a week if immersed, covered, in fresh water and refrigerated. Water should be changed daily.

Abalones are primarily sport fish, but occasionally they are sold in coastal markets already cleaned, sliced, and tenderized. Canned abalone (from Mexico), however, is obtainable in many supermarkets. Tenderized crosscut steaks may be grilled, baked, sautéed, or deep fried. Abalone may also be sliced vertically in thin pieces, which can be used in enchilada fillings, hors d'oeuvres, salads, stews, and soups.

Heat toughens abalone. It needs only to be warmed through. One pound of abalone makes four servings.

ABALONE STEAK SAUTÉ

1 pound abalone steaks, pounded
2 eggs, lightly beaten
Salt and pepper
1/4 teaspoon garlic powder
1/4 cup flour

1/2 cup fine dry bread crumbs
3 Tablespoons vegetable oil
3 Tablespoons butter
Lemon wedges

Season eggs with salt, pepper, and garlic powder. Roll tenderized abalone steaks in flour, dip them in egg, then press into crumbs. Place them on waxed paper and refrigerate for 1 hour.

Heat oil and butter very hot in a large skillet. Add the steaks and sizzle about 20–30 seconds on each side. Garnish with lemon wedges.

Abalone may be dipped in egg, then in cracker crumbs, and quickly sautéed in Clarified Butter (p. 430).

Abalone steaks may be marinated in 1 cup dry white wine and the juice of a lime for 10 minutes, dried, then dipped in egg, lightly floured, and sautéed in butter and oil.

BAKED ABALONE LU WETZEL

12 large abalone slices
1/4 cup chopped green onion
2 Tablespoons (1/4 stick) butter
1 cup fresh or canned mushrooms,
   drained and chopped fine

1/4 cup slivered almonds
Salt and pepper
1 cup dry white wine
12 slices Monterey Jack cheese,
   4 × 4 × 1/8 inches

Sauté onion in butter until soft but not brown. Add chopped mushrooms and almonds, cook for a minute, and season to taste with salt and pepper. Add 1/2 cup of the wine and reduce mixture over high heat until moist, but not watery.

Preheat the oven to 325°F. Place 6 tenderized abalone slices in a buttered baking dish. Spread with mushroom mixture, cover each piece with 1 slice of cheese, then top with another slice of abalone. Drizzle the remaining 1/2 cup of wine over all and bake for 12–15 minutes.

Remove dish from the oven, cover cooked abalone with the remaining 6 slices of cheese, and slide the dish under a hot broiler to quickly melt and brown the cheese.

CAMPFIRE ABALONE IN THE SHELL

Line an abalone shell with wet seaweed and place a whole tenderized abalone in it. Cover the meat well with more seaweed. When the fire has burned down to glowing embers, not hot enough to burn the shell, place it on the embers to cook (steam) until the meat is warmed through.

Serve abalone sliced, with a lemon-soy sauce made by mixing together:

1 1/2 Tablespoons lemon juice
2 teaspoons bottled tempura sauce

1/4 teaspoon pepper
Several drops of sesame oil

ABALONE HANGTOWN

4 abalone steaks, tenderized
4 slices bacon
5 eggs
Salt and pepper

1/2 cup flour
1/2 cup fine cracker crumbs
2 Tablespoons oil
2 Tablespoons (1/4 stick) butter

Sprinkle abalone lightly with salt, cut steaks in half, and set aside. Fry bacon crisp, drain, and crumble. Beat eggs well and season with salt and pepper. Roll abalone in flour, dip in beaten eggs, and then press in crumbs. Heat oil and butter in a heavy skillet until very hot. Add abalone and sizzle about 20 seconds. Turn steaks over and immediately add eggs and bacon. Lift pan from heat when necessary to cool it off a bit. With a spatula, nudge and lift cooked egg, allowing uncooked egg to set. Transfer to a warm platter and serve at once.

DEEP-FRIED ABALONE

Canned abalone strips may be dipped in Light Batter for Fish (p. 20) and fried in hot (390°F.) oil.

A combination fry of abalone, sole, and shrimp makes a pleasing meal. Serve with Tartar Sauce (p. 426) or mayonnaise mixed with minced green onion and thinned with dry white wine.

ABALONE IN OYSTER SAUCE
WITH VEGETABLES

1 pound abalone, tenderized (or canned)	2 Tablespoons oil or lard
2 Tablespoons soy sauce	1 clove garlic, minced
1 Tablespoon sherry	1/2 teaspoon salt
2 teaspoons cornstarch	2 Tablespoons bottled oyster sauce
4 dried black mushrooms	1 Tablespoon sugar
1 pound Chinese chard cabbage (bok choy)	

Cut abalone into very thin slices, 1/2 inch wide, and marinate them in soy sauce, sherry, and cornstarch. Soak dried mushrooms in hot water for 20 minutes; then drain and slice them. Cut bok choy head into 11/2-inch lengths.

Heat oil or lard in a large skillet or wok. Add garlic and mushrooms and stir-fry until garlic yellows. Add bok choy, stir-fry for 2 minutes, add salt, and cook another minute. Add abalone mixture and stir-toss until the abalone is hot. Add oyster sauce and sugar, cook and toss until the liquid simmers and thickens. Serve.

ABALONE SOUP

1/2 of 1-pound can abalone	Two 10-ounce cans concentrated chicken broth
2 teaspoons cornstarch	2 cups water
2 teaspoons soy sauce	Salt to taste
2 teaspoons sherry	1 green onion, sliced thin
1 small cucumber	

Cut abalone into strips ¼ inch thick and ½ inch wide, and mix them with cornstarch, soy sauce, and sherry. Peel cucumber and slice it very thin.

Bring chicken broth and water to a boil, add green onion and cucumber. Reduce heat and simmer for 1 minute, covered. Add abalone mixture and continue simmering for 2 minutes more, then serve.

CREAMED ABALONE AND MUSHROOMS

1½ cups raw abalone, tenderized
  and diced
2 cloves garlic, pressed
2 green onions, minced
6 Tablespoons (¾ stick) butter
¾ pound mushrooms, sliced
Salt and pepper
1 cup dry white wine

½ cup heavy cream
2 Tablespoons flour
1½ cups hot milk
1 teaspoon lemon juice
Pinch of powdered bay leaf
Pinch of thyme
2 Tablespoons parsley

In a large skillet, sauté garlic and onions in 4 tablespoons of the butter until they begin to brown. Add mushrooms, cover and cook, stirring occasionally, for 8 minutes. Season with salt and pepper, then remove them from the pan and keep warm. Pour wine into pan juices and, over high heat, reduce to about 2 tablespoons. Add cream and continue reducing until the liquid is thick.

Meanwhile, melt the remaining 2 tablespoons of butter in a saucepan. Stir in flour and cook for a minute. Add hot milk and beat with a whisk until sauce thickens and begins to boil; reduce heat. Season the sauce with lemon juice, powdered bay leaf, thyme, and salt and pepper. Cook 2 or 3 minutes, then mix in the reduced wine-cream. Add mushrooms and abalone, simmer for 2 minutes, and serve on toast, garnished with parsley.

ABALONE CUCUMBER SALAD

1-pound can abalone
Curry Sour Cream Sauce (p. 428)
Lettuce

2 small cucumbers, peeled
1 large tomato, cut in wedges

Make sauce several hours before using and let it chill. Place lettuce on individual salad plates. Cut cucumbers into irregularly shaped bite-size pieces. Drain abalone and cut them into ¼-inch-thick slices. Alternate bits of abalone and cucumber on the lettuce and arrange tomato wedges on each. Spoon on curry sour cream sauce just before serving.

HORS D'OEUVRES

MARINATED ABALONE SLICES

Cut canned abalone into thin slices and marinate in Sesame Sauce (p. 61) at room temperature for 1 hour. Drain and skewer the slices on wooden cocktail picks. Place a leaf or two of lettuce on a flat platter, arrange the abalone on them with a small bowl of the marinade for dipping.

YACHTSMAN'S COCKTAIL

Combine very thin slices of raw abalone with bits of uncooked Pismo clam meat and three large cooked shrimp per serving. Marinate the shellfish combination in lemon or lime juice for 2–4 hours, then serve chilled in sherbet glasses, with Cocktail Sauce III (p. 436).

Clams

CLAMS ARE BIVALVE MOLLUSKS that live in the mid- to low-tide zone. Some live in the fine sand of wave-pounded beaches. Some grow in gravel-hard, rock-studded tide pool flats, and others bury themselves in muddy bays and inlets, using their siphons as snorkels to suck in air and food.

Clamming is a year-round activity. Low tides, especially minus tides, expose the clam beds—that's the time to gather them. Among the many varieties of clams the following are choicest.

EXPOSED SAND BEACH CLAMS

Eastern surf clams (skinner clam, sea clam, or "chowder clam"), heavily fished off New Jersey and Virginia, have become the most important commercial species in the United States. About five million pounds of shucked surf clams are landed in New Jersey and Virginia each year, where canners process and sell them as "chopped clams." The clams are taken from the sandy bottom, in turbulent waters off outer beaches, just beyond the breaker zone. Huge hydraulic dredges wash clams off the bottom, then lift them into dredge boats.

Skinner shells are tan, smooth, elliptical, and large—often seven inches in length. Shuck skinners the same as other hard-shell clams (see page 8). When the clam has been removed from the shell, set aside the tender adductor muscles, and prepare them as you would small scallops. The tough clam body meat can be sliced into thin strips, breaded, and deep fried, or ground to use in minced clam dishes.

Razors grow about six to ten inches long on the Atlantic Coast; Pacific varieties average five inches. The shells are thin, sharp, and fragile, with a brown varnished appearance. They are found on fine-grained sand beaches that are free of gravel or clay on the East Coast, and on broad, level, sandy beaches of the Pacific Northwest. At low tide, follow the receding waves and, scanning the surf as the water runs out, watch for a dimple or squirt or tip of clam neck sticking out of the sand. Dig your narrow-blade shovel eight inches to the seaward side of the dimple. Reach down (follow the blade with your free hand) and grab the clam before it gets away. Be quick, because in seven seconds it will have burrowed away.

Razors are excellent served raw in cocktails. They are ideal for deep or pan frying, and delicious for pies, patties, stews, and soups. Cleaned fresh razor clams are sold locally in the Northwest; frozen are generally more obtainable. Washington and Alaska razors are canned. Cleaning instructions are on page 8.

Pismos are large triangular-shaped clams with heavy, smooth-polished white shells, some marked with radiating brown lines. From Half Moon Bay, California, to mid–Baja California, they live just below the low-tide line of wave-pounded beaches. At low tide, wade out onto the sandbars and probe the bottom with a potato fork. When you strike a shell, reach down and lift the clam from the sand.

Pismos are excellent for cocktails, ceviche, minced dishes, or frying. Cleaning instructions are on page 9.

Donax clams. Tiny donax clams (pompano clams) with pink, blue, yellow, or white shells that are found in profusion on sandy beaches from Long Island to the Gulf of Mexico are commonly used for broth. The broth can be enjoyed, or used as a soup base, a basting liquid when baking fish, or a flavor booster for other sauces.

TIDE-FLAT CLAMS

American quahogs are the most popular food clams of the Atlantic Coast and are always in season. The heart-shaped (Venus family) shells are thick, chalky white, and have single ridges circling the clam. Quahogs lie one to three inches under the surface in sandy or muddy bottoms. Northern varieties are harvested in subtidal zones of bays and estuaries from Massachusetts to Chesapeake Bay. Wade out in the water with sneakers on your feet and a bucket tied to an inner tube (or boat) to a likely clam area. Good clam beds are often muddy and weedy spots. As you wade in the water, feel around with your toes. Dig them into the sandy mud. When they strike the first hard shell, others will be close by for you to gather.

Southern varieties occur in the intertidal zone from Chesapeake Bay to the West Indies and Texas. Walk across the tide flats to where you see small bubbly holes. Dig your clammer's rake into the sand or mud, pull it along for several feet, then lift it and gather your clams.

Small quahogs, one-inch thick to one-and-seven-sixteenths-inches thick (about one and a half inches in diameter), are called littlenecks. Half-grown quahogs, one-and-seven-sixteenths- to one-and-five-eighths-inches thick (two to two and a half inches in diameter), are known as cherrystones. Both of these tender young clams are popularly served raw on the half shell. They are also good baked or broiled in the shell, or fried: breaded, egg-dipped, floured, or battered. Large quahogs, three inches or more in diameter, and thicker than one and five-eighths inches, tend to be tough, and are best minced for chowders, fritters, and other cooked dishes. Cleaning and opening instructions are on page 8.

Butter clams (Washingtons) are West Coast delicacies. They have rather smooth shells, etched with circular growth lines, and grow, on an average, to three and a half inches. The smaller clams are more tender. Butter clams occur in rocky beach areas from the tidal zone out to five fathoms. At low tide, dig down about twelve inches in gravel-mud areas, where white shell fragments are most concentrated.

All the meat of versatile butter clams can be eaten. They are delicious served raw in the half shell or in cocktails, or broiled, baked, steamed, or any way — in or out of the shell. Clean and shuck them the same way as other hard-shells (see page 8).

Cockles are recognized by the deep, even ridges that radiate fanlike to a scalloped rim on their shells. Find them in sandy or muddy soil, one to three inches below the surface in tide flats. They have a short neck and a foot to move about, which they can retract into a tightly closed shell when disturbed. At low tide they can be harvested, using a rake, at many points along the California and Oregon shores. They are abundant in Puget Sound. The varieties in Cape Cod and Long Island waters, however, are nonedible.

Small cockles may be served raw and are good cooked in court bouillon until the shells open. Larger cockles make excellent fritters, chowder, minced clam dishes, and sauce.

It is important to soak cockles in seawater for a few hours, so they can rid themselves of sand. Clean and shuck them the same way as other hard-shell clams (see page 8).

Rock clams are also called littlenecks by Westerners. Their shells have ridges running both around and across the shell, giving a cross-hatched appearance. They are found like cockles, just under the surface, one to three inches deep, often in the same beds as cockles, and in the same tide flats as butter clams. They may be eaten raw on the half shell, steamed, stuffed, or in rice and other dishes, in or out of the shell.

MUD CLAMS

Soft-shell clams (longnecks or steamer clams) are found on most coasts in the Northern Hemisphere but are of greatest importance on the Atlantic Coast. They live six to fourteen inches down in sandy mud of bays, coves, estuaries, and protected areas from Labrador to Cape Hatteras. The fragile, elliptical shells are thin, grayish, and grow to about three and a half inches in length. There is a tubular sheath around their long siphon.

Soft-shell clam beds in Chesapeake Bay are harvested by dredge, because the clams are always underwater. In New England, vast soft-shell beds are exposed at low tide. A tiny hole in the mud reveals a clam's location. If you stamp the ground near the hole, a live clam will squirt a jet of water in the air. Dig your short-handled clam fork into the mud right there—or use your hands. About six to eight inches down, feel carefully around in the mud until you find the soft-shell in its burrow.

The delicate soft-shell clams are an ideal size for serving raw on the half shell or for deep frying. Their plump meat is tender enough to roll in cracker crumbs and broil in butter. Pan fried or in chowder, they are delicious. But the most popular method of cooking them is steaming (see page 334). Cleaning and shucking instructions are on page 8.

Gapors (horse clams, blue clams, Empires, or summer clams) are six- to eight-inch clams, among the largest of the Pacific Coast—up to four pounds. The shells are fragile and too small to house the long siphon, so they always remain open. Gapors lie two to three feet under the surface in mud-sand of flats and outer beaches from San Diego to Alaska. At low tide, walk out onto the mud flats where you can see little jets of water squirting a foot or so in the air periodically. Locate the brown tip of a siphon sticking out of the mud and dig wide to one side of the dimple. When down a foot and a half, slice carefully toward the clam and expose the tunnel that, feeling with your hand, will lead you to the clam. Ease it out gently without breaking the shell.

The tender body meat is good for frying. Necks are tougher, so unless pounded and prepared like abalone, they should be minced. Cleaning instructions are on page 9.

Geoducks, the largest burrowing clams on our shores, average three pounds, but can weigh six or seven. Their shells are white and marked with growth lines. Their siphon is huge, and ample meat bulges their sides, preventing the shells from closing. Geoducks live two to four feet below the surface. They may be dug from muddy bay flats from San Diego to the Columbia River, and from North Carolina to the Gulf of Mexico. But they thrive abundantly in Washington; most of the commercially sold meat comes from there.

A three-pound geoduck will yield about one pound of meat in minced form or steaks. Fresh tenderized steaks, cut a quarter-inch thick, are usually available in fish markets or supermarkets in the Northwest; frozen are sometimes found in markets elsewhere. Clean geoducks the same as gapors (see page 9).

BARBECUED STEAMER CLAMS AND OYSTERS

Allow 6 clams and 3 oysters per serving. Scrub shells well and place them, deep cup side down, on the grill over medium-hot coals until the shells pop open. Remove the top shell, sprinkle with lemon juice, and serve them with melted butter for dunking.

CAMPFIRE FOIL-WRAPPED CLAMS

Roll freshly cleaned clams in melted butter. Tear off squares of heavy-duty foil and arrange a portion of clams on each. Sprinkle them with lemon juice and salt and pepper, then drizzle with melted butter. Double fold the foil edges, enveloping clams tightly. Place clam packages on the embers for 3–4 minutes and serve.

CHARCOAL-BROILED CLAMS

2 dozen raw clams
1/2 cup soy sauce
1/2 cup sake* or dry sherry

2 Tablespoons white miso paste*
3 Tablespoons sugar
1/4 teaspoon monosodium glutamate

*See Glossary.

Combine and bring to a boil all ingredients except clams; let sauce cool to room temperature. Clean clams and marinate them for 1 hour in sauce. Soak wooden skewers in water for 10 minutes, then skewer the clams. Broil them 7 inches from the hot coals for 2–3 minutes on each side; baste during cooking.

DEEP-FRIED CLAMS

Use razor, butter, gapor, soft-shell, or Pismo clams.

2 cups raw clams	½ teaspoon pepper
About 25–30 Saltine crackers	¼ teaspoon garlic powder
1 egg	2 cups oil for frying
1 teaspoon salt	

Pulverize crackers in a blender (you should have about 1 cup crumbs), then transfer them to a wide bowl. Beat egg with salt, pepper, and garlic powder. Dip clams in egg and press each into crumbs (open and spread so clams lie flat and are well coated). Place them in single layer on waxed paper to dry for 1 hour on each side.

Heat oil to smoking point, fry several clams at a time until they brown—about 30–45 seconds on each side. Drain on several layers of toweling. Serve hot, plain or with Tartar Sauce (p. 426).

FRIED GEODUCK STEAK

Cut trimmed clam body into ¼-inch-thick steaks and tenderize them. Dip slices in egg and then flour or crumb them. Sauté steaks in half butter/half oil for about 20 seconds on each side.

CLAM PATTIES

2 cups raw clams, ground	6 Tablespoons (¾ stick) butter
1 small onion, minced	2 cups mashed potatoes
2 Tablespoons minced green pepper	Salt and pepper to taste
2 Tablespoons minced parsley	Pinch of thyme

Put clams through the food chopper, using the coarsest blade. Sauté onion, green pepper, and parsley in 2 tablespoons of the butter until tender. Combine mashed potatoes with sautéed vegetables, season with salt, pepper, and thyme, and mix in clams. Form into patties and fry them slowly in the remaining 4 tablespoons of butter until crispy brown on both sides.

FRIED CLAM CAKES

2 cups minced clams, plus
  enough clam liquor to moisten
  the batter
1 cup biscuit mix
1/4 cup cornmeal
2 Tablespoons minced parsley

1 egg, lightly beaten
1 Tablespoon oil
1/2 teaspoon salt
Pepper to taste
Half butter/half oil for frying

Mix together all ingredients except butter and oil. Heat butter and oil and drop the soft mixture by spoonfuls into it and fry until nicely brown. Serve with catsup.

CLAM CHEESE CORN FRITTERS

1 cup ground clams, drained
2 eggs, separated
2 Tablespoons flour
Salt and pepper to taste

1 cup whole-kernel corn, drained
1 cup grated Cheddar cheese
Oil for frying

Beat egg yolks until they are frothy. Beat in flour and salt and pepper and mix well with clams, corn, and cheese. Beat egg whites until stiff and fold carefully into mixture. Drop by spoonfuls onto a hot oiled griddle and fry like pancakes.

CLAM CORN CASSEROLE

2 cups raw clams, drained and
  chopped
3 slices bacon
1 green onion, chopped
1/2 green pepper, chopped
1 can cream-style corn

4 eggs
1 cup clam liquor (or enough milk
  added to liquor to make 1 cup)
1/4 teaspoon garlic powder
Dash of cayenne pepper
Salt and pepper to taste

Fry bacon crisp, drain on toweling, crumble, and reserve. Sauté onion and pepper in bacon fat until tender; stir in corn. Preheat the oven to 375°F. Beat eggs well with clam liquor and seasonings. Mix together eggs, vegetables, chopped clams, and crumbled bacon. Pour into a buttered casserole and bake for 40 minutes, or until custard is set.

STEAMED CLAMS

Allow 10–12 clams per portion, depending on size (about a quart). Fill a large kettle with ½ inch boiling slightly salted water (the juice of a lemon may be added, or use half water and half white wine), and put in clams. Cover tightly and steam over moderate heat only until the shells open, about 6–10 minutes. Discard any that do not open. Serve clams in soup bowls. Strain the broth through several thicknesses of cheesecloth, and season to taste. Serve broth in cups with clams and individual dishes of melted butter.

GARLIC CLAMS

4 dozen steamer clams
4 Tablespoons olive oil
3 cloves garlic, pressed
¼ cup chopped parsley

Pinch of thyme
¼ teaspoon dried basil
4 drops of Tabasco

Heat oil in a large, heavy pan and add garlic, spices, Tabasco, and clams; cover and cook until shells open. Lift the shells and pour their juice into the pan and simmer, uncovered, for another 2 minutes. Ladle clams into soup plates and pour the broth over them. Serve with hot crusty French bread.

CLAMS WITH RICE

3 pounds steamers or small cockles
5 cups clam liquor, water, and bottled
  clam juice
1 medium onion, chopped
6 Tablespoons (¾ stick) butter

2 cloves garlic, minced
2 cups uncooked long-grain rice
1 teaspoon paprika
Salt and pepper to taste
¼ cup minced parsley

Scrub clams and steam them in ½ cup water until the shells open. Shell and reserve clams; strain the clam liquor through several layers of cheesecloth. Add an equal amount of water to the strained liquor, then add enough bottled clam juice to make 5 cups liquid. Heat it to a boil and keep simmering.

Sauté onion slowly in butter until it browns. Add garlic and rice; cook, stirring constantly, until it becomes evenly brown. Stir in paprika and boiling clam liquid, season with salt and pepper, cover, and cook over very low heat for 30 minutes. Liquid should be absorbed and rice almost cooked. Stir in parsley and clams for the last 5 minutes of cooking.

CLAMS IN SAUCE BORDELAISE

2 cups raw clams, chopped or sliced
1 onion, minced
2 Tablespoons (¼ stick) butter
2 Tablespoons flour
10-ounce can concentrated chicken broth
1 Tablespoon tomato paste
½ cup dry white wine
1 green onion, minced

1 clove garlic, pressed
1 small bay leaf
½ teaspoon dried chervil
¼ teaspoon dried tarragon
Pinch of thyme
2 sprigs parsley, minced
Lemon juice
Salt and pepper to taste

Sauté onion slowly in butter until golden. Add flour and cook, stirring, until the roux is brown. Measure out chicken broth and add enough water to make 2 cups. Add this and tomato paste to the roux; stir and cook until thickened.

Meanwhile, pour wine with green onion and garlic into a saucepan and over medium-high heat reduce it down to about 1 tablespoon. Pour sauce into the reduced wine mixture, add bay leaf, chervil, tarragon, and thyme and cook over low heat for 10 minutes. Add parsley, then lemon juice and salt and pepper to taste. Stir in clams and cook just under a boil for 2-3 minutes. Serve on rice or noodles or in an omelette, or on pork, with hot French bread.

CLAM SAUCE WITH SPAGHETTI

White Clam Sauce (p. 437)
½ pound hot cooked spaghetti or linguini

Sprigs parsley
Salt and pepper to taste

Put clams in the sauce to heat when pasta is done and drained. Cook sauce, stirring, for about 2 minutes, or until clams are heated through. Add parsley, and toss clam sauce with the pasta, season with salt and pepper, and serve at once.

PAELLA

2 dozen steamer clams
1/2 pound lean pork, diced
1 medium onion, chopped
2 cloves garlic, minced
4 Tablespoons olive oil
1 teaspoon paprika
1 1/2 cups uncooked long-grain rice
1/2 teaspoon salt
Pinch of saffron
8-ounce bottle clam juice

1/2 cup dry white wine
1/2 cup water
10-ounce can concentrated chicken
    broth, diluted with equal amounts
    of water
10-ounce can water
12 large shrimp, shelled and deveined
2 Tablespoons minced parsley
1 pimiento, chopped
Lemon wedges

In a Dutch oven or large casserole that can be placed over direct heat, sauté pork, onion, and garlic in olive oil. Sprinkle with paprika and cook until nicely browned. Add rice, salt, and saffron, stirring well to glaze with oil.

Preheat the oven to 350°F. Meanwhile, mix and heat to a boil clam juice, wine, water, and chicken broth. Slowly stir 3 cups of the hot broth into the rice and let it boil 2–3 minutes. Cover and bake for 25 minutes, stirring twice to mix ingredients. Stir in the remaining 1 1/2 cups of broth, cover, and bake 10 more minutes.

Have ready scrubbed clams and shelled, deveined shrimp. Uncover paella, stir in parsley and pimiento, then push clams in shells and shrimp into the rice. Cover and continue baking for 15 minutes, or until clams open. Serve with lemon wedges.

TOMATO CLAM SAUCE

2 cups chopped clams
2 large onions, chopped
4 Tablespoons olive oil
4 large tomatoes, peeled and diced
2 cloves garlic, pressed

1 Tablespoon flour
1/2 teaspoon salt
Generous milling of pepper
Sprig parsley, minced

Fry onions slowly in oil until golden. Mix in tomatoes, garlic, flour, salt, and pepper; simmer until tomatoes are cooked. Add clams and parsley and simmer for 2–3 more minutes. Serve with noodles or as the filling for an omelette.

CLAM CHOWDER WITH BACON

2 cups chopped or ground clams
4 slices bacon
2 medium onions, chopped
3 Tablespoons chopped green pepper
3 stalks celery, diced fine
2 carrots, grated
1 clove garlic, minced
5 medium potatoes, peeled and diced

2 cups water
1 teaspoon salt
1 teaspoon Worcestershire sauce
6 drops of Tabasco
1/2 teaspoon pepper
2 cups half-and-half
1 Tablespoon minced parsley

Fry bacon until crisp, drain, crumble, and reserve. Slowly fry onions, green pepper, celery, carrots, and garlic in bacon fat until tender. Boil potatoes in salted water until cooked. Combine vegetables, add seasonings, and beat in a mixer until creamy (if you beat longer it will be smooth and thick).

In a separate pan, cook clams at just under a boil for 3 minutes. Add them and crumbled bacon to the mixture. Stir in half-and-half, heat, and serve garnished with a sprinkle of parsley.

CLAM CHOWDER WITH SALT PORK

2 cups minced clams
1/2 pound lean salt pork
3 medium onions, chopped
2 cups finely diced celery
4 medium potatoes, peeled and diced
2 cups clam broth
1 cup water

1 small bay leaf
1/4 teaspoon each marjoram, basil, thyme, and rosemary
1/8 teaspoon each freshly ground nutmeg and pepper
2 cups whole milk

Cut salt pork into small dice, rinse bits in a colander under cold water, and dry them on toweling. Fry pork slowly in a heavy skillet until crisp, then remove bits with a slotted spoon and reserve.

Sauté onions slowly until golden; add celery, potatoes, clam broth, water, and spices. Cover and simmer slowly until potatoes are cooked. Stir in pork bits, minced clams, and milk. Bring chowder to boiling point and cook just under a boil for 3 minutes.

If possible, let chowder stand for at least 1 hour before serving to allow flavors to mingle.

MANHATTAN CLAM CHOWDER

2 cups chopped or ground clams

3 slices bacon

1 large onion, chopped

3 Tablespoons flour

3 cups hot clam liquor or broth

2 1/2 cups potatoes, peeled and diced

2 stalks celery, diced fine

1 clove garlic, minced

3 cups tomato juice

1 bay leaf

1/2 teaspoon thyme

6 drops of Tabasco

Salt and pepper to taste

2 Tablespoons (1/4 stick) butter

Several parsley tips

In a large skillet, fry bacon until crisp; drain, crumble, and reserve. Brown onion slowly in bacon fat, blend in flour, add hot clam liquor and cook, stirring, while mixture thickens and boils for several minutes.

In a saucepan place potatoes, celery, garlic, tomato juice, bay leaf, and thyme. Cover and cook until potatoes are soft, then add the clam broth. Stir in clams, crumbled bacon, and Tabasco. Season with salt and pepper and cook at just under a boil for 3 minutes. Swirl in butter and serve garnished with a few parsley tips.

CLAM SOUP

2 cans minced clams

1 quart milk

Salt and pepper to taste

Butter

Parsley

Combine minced clams and milk, heat to scalding, season with salt and pepper, and swirl in a lump of butter. Garnish with parsley and serve soup with crackers.

HORS D'OEUVRES

CLAMS ON THE HALF SHELL

Open shells and remove the tops, leaving clams in the deep-cup half of shells. Place a small lettuce cup filled with Cocktail Sauce I (p. 436) on a bed of crushed ice in a soup plate. Arrange clams on the ice around the sauce and garnish with lemon wedges and parsley.

PISMO CLAM CEVICHE

Allow one raw Pismo clam with its liquor per serving and to each add:

2 Tablespoons tomato, peeled and
  chopped
1 Tablespoon mild white onion
1 teaspoon chopped cilantro

Dash of salt
Juice of 1 small lime
1 teaspoon Mexican hot chili sauce,
  or to taste

Open the shell and clean clam on a plate to save the liquor. Cut raw clam meat into small pieces and put them in a sherbet glass. Add tomato, onion, and cilantro; sprinkle with salt; and mix ingredients. Squeeze lime juice and strained clam liquor into the glass. Sprinkle on a little hot chili sauce and serve chilled.

Razor, littleneck, cherrystone, small cockle, rock, and butter clams may be used.

PICKLED STEAMER CLAMS

2 dozen steamer clams
1/4 cup soy sauce
1/4 cup vinegar

1/2 cup sake or dry sherry
4 Tablespoons sugar

In a nonmetal bowl, mix a marinade of soy sauce, vinegar, wine, and sugar. Steam clams until shells open, remove meat and marinate it, refrigerated, for 24 hours. Drain and serve clams on wooden cocktail picks.

CLAM AVOCADO DIP

1 cup fresh or canned minced clams
2 ripe avocados
4 Tablespoons California green chilis
2 Tablespoons mayonnaise

1/4 cup taco sauce
Several drops of lemon juice
Salt to taste

Mash avocados. Seed and chop chilis, then combine with mayonnaise and taco sauce. Season with a little lemon juice and salt. Drain and mix in clams and serve with chips.

MINCED CLAM TEMPURA

1¼ cups fresh clams minced, or a   ¼ teaspoon salt
  10-ounce can minced clams   2 cups oil for deep frying
1 egg, separated   Cocktail Sauce II (p. 436), or
1 teaspoon oil   dipping sauce (see below)
½ cup flour

Drain clams, reserving ¼ cup liquor (if necessary, add enough milk to make ¼ cup). Beat egg yolk until frothy, mix in oil, flour, salt, and clam liquor. Beat egg white until stiff and fold into batter, then add clams, stirring only enough to mix them with the batter. Let batter rest at room temperature for at least 1 hour.

Drop batter by spoonfuls into hot (375°F.) oil and deep fry until golden brown, approximately 4 minutes. Drain them on toweling and serve hot on wooden cocktail picks, with the cocktail sauce or dipping sauce made by mixing together 2 tablespoons soy sauce and 4 tablespoons each of sake and mirin.

Mussels

MUSSELS, much like clams, are bivalve mollusks. Marine blue mussels are found from Alaska to Mexico, and also along the Atlantic Coast, particularly around Maine, Massachusetts, Connecticut, and Rhode Island. The shells are blue black on the outside, pearly inside. Adult edible blues are oval to pear shaped, and usually two to five inches long on the West Coast. Atlantic mussels grow to three inches. California bay mussels, also edible, are brown with purple and are wider and more wedge shaped. Both are found in the intertidal zone from high tide to several fathoms, but most cluster in masses near the low-tide mark along rocky shores and harbor structures. They anchor themselves to rocks, pilings, etc., with strong brownish threads called byssal threads, secreted by their foot.

Horse mussels (edible) are usually solitary and found partly buried in gravel or mud, attached by their byssus (beard) to some solid object.

Young mussels, up to one-sixth-inch long, move around freely on their long extended foot or pull themselves along by throwing out new byssal threads and cutting off the old. Adult mussels usually remain in one location.

Mussels have been a popular and cultivated food in coastal regions of Europe for centuries. Although there is no West Coast commercial fishery, mussels are often found in San Francisco markets. Increasing amounts are being harvested from Northern Atlantic shores for knowing seafood lovers all over the country.

About Mussel Meat

Cleaning instructions are found on page 9.

Mussel meat is soft, orange in color, black fringed like oyster flesh, and mild in flavor. Mussels may be shelled raw, or steamed open in a small amount of liquid. Steam them only until the shells open, about six to ten minutes. Add no salt to the cooking liquid because liquor from the shells is apt to be salty. Shaking the tightly covered pot several times during cooking facilitates their opening. If some shells remain closed, cook those an extra minute or two to open. Discard any that remain closed. Avoid overcooking; they could become dry and shriveled. Remove meat from the shells and pull off the beard from steamed mussels. I also trim out the soft dark food sac behind the beard. Strain the cooking liquid through a fine strainer or triple layer of cheesecloth to remove tiny sand particles, then use the broth in any accompanying sauce.

Mussels may be placed under the broiler to cook open and may be served on the half shell. They may be sautéed, fried, or steamed to use in casseroles, soups, salads, stews, or for garnish, etc. In fact, mussels may be substituted in most clam recipes.

Freshly shucked mussels can be frozen for future use.

STEAMED MUSSELS

Scrape, scrub, and soak mussels. Place in a large, heavy pot and add ¼ cup water for each quart of mussels. Cover tightly and cook over high heat, shaking the pot frequently, until shells open.

To serve, ladle mussels, in their shells, into soup bowls. Accompany each serving with a small dish of melted butter, garlic or parsley butter, for dunking, and lemon wedges. Provide extra bowls for the empty shells and a large napkin for each diner.

FRIED LARGE PACIFIC MUSSEL STRIPS

3 dozen very large mussels   Half butter/half oil for frying
3 eggs, beaten   Salt and pepper to taste
Flour   Garlic powder to taste
1 cup fine cracker crumbs

Scrape and clean mussels. Open shells by cutting through the muscle binding the 2 shells and cut the halves apart. Loosen meat around the rim of the shell with a knife blade and pull meat away from the white muscle. Trim out soft dark area (food sac) from meat. Rinse mussel strips under running water and blot them on toweling.

Dip meat in beaten eggs, then in flour. Dip again in egg and press each piece into crumbs. Set coated strips aside for 30 minutes or so to dry. Heat butter and oil and sauté mussels until brown on both sides. Drain on toweling, season with salt, pepper, and garlic powder and serve at once.

DEEP-FRIED LARGE MUSSELS

Prepare mussels for deep frying as in preceding recipe. Fry them, a few at a time, in deep hot (375°F.) fat until nicely brown. Drain them on toweling and heap them on a hot serving platter. Garnish with parsley and lemon wedges and serve with a tomato or tartar sauce on the side.

MUSSELS FOR GARNISHING

2 dozen mussels	6 peppercorns
1 cup dry white wine	Pinch of thyme
½ cup chopped onion	Several parsley stems
1 bay leaf	

Clean and soak mussels, then place them with other ingredients in a pot, cover, and boil until the shells open. Pour mussels and juice into a colander placed over a bowl so the mussels drain and the liquid is collected. Strain the broth through a fine sieve to use in sauce. Pick meat from the shell, pull off beards, and trim out soft dark meat. Keep the mussels moist in broth until ready to use them.

MUSSELS MARINIÈRE

4 dozen mussels	2 Tablespoons flour
1 cup dry white wine	Generous milling of pepper
2 shallots, chopped	Juice of ½ lemon
4 Tablespoons (½ stick) butter, softened	2 sprigs parsley, minced

Place clean soaked mussels in a heavy pot with wine and shallots and steam them, over high heat, until the shells open. Remove the top shell from each mussel, pull off the beard, and place mussels in a covered bowl to keep warm. Strain the cooking liquid through a fine sieve into a saucepan. Cream butter and flour together, then whisk it into the broth while heating to a boil. Simmer broth for 5 minutes, then season with pepper, a few drops of lemon juice, and minced parsley.

Divide mussels into portions and place them, on their half shells, in soup bowls. Pour hot broth over and serve at once. Pass around a plate of hot garlic sourdough French bread.

TWICE-COOKED MUSSELS

3 dozen mussels, steamed   3 Tablespoons minced parsley
1/3 cup fine dry bread crumbs   Salt and pepper
4 Tablespoons olive oil   Lemon wedges
2 cloves garlic, minced
3 Tablespoons finely chopped green
  pepper

Cook cleaned mussels as in preceding recipe. Remove meat from shells, pull off beards, and trim out dark section. Mussels may be cooked the day before and kept in strained broth until ready to use.

Drain mussels on toweling and roll in dry bread crumbs. Heat oil with garlic in a heavy skillet. When garlic turns golden, add mussels, green pepper, and parsley. Sauté mussels until nicely browned on both sides. Season with salt and pepper and serve at once on a hot platter garnished with lemon wedges:

MUSSEL SEAFOOD CASSEROLE

2 dozen mussels, steamed   2 Tablespoons flour
1 cup fresh (or a 6-ounce can) crab   1 cup hot mussel liquor
  meat, picked over   1/2 cup cream
1 can artichoke hearts, drained and   1/2 cup grated Gruyère cheese
  sliced   1 teaspoon lemon juice
1 clove garlic, minced   Dash of cayenne pepper
1 green onion, sliced   2 Tablespoons minced parsley
1 1/2 cups fresh mushrooms, quartered   1/4 cup buttered crumbs
5 Tablespoons butter

Steam and prepare mussels as in recipe for Mussels for Garnishing (p. 343). Mussels may be cooked earlier and kept in strained broth until ready to use. Reserve mussel liquor.

Place mussels in a buttered casserole and arrange artichoke slices among them.

Sauté garlic, onion, and mushrooms in 2 tablespoons butter for 2 minutes, stir in crab meat and cook another minute, then remove from heat.

Melt the remaining 3 tablespoons of butter in a saucepan, stir in flour and let it bubble. Whisk in hot mussel liquor, then cream, and cook until sauce is smooth and thickened. Stir in cheese and season with lemon juice, cayenne, and parsley. Preheat the oven to 350°F.

Combine sauce with mushroom-crab, then pour the mixture over the mussels in casserole. Sprinkle crumbs on top and bake for 15 minutes, or until the crumbs are browned.

MUSSELS WITH VERMICELLI

3 dozen mussels
1 cup dry white wine
2 cloves garlic, minced
1 green onion, chopped
3 Tablespoons chopped green pepper
3 Tablespoons olive oil

4 large tomatoes, peeled and chopped
1/4 cup minced parsley
1/4 teaspoon dried rubbed oregano
Generous milling of pepper
1 pound vermicelli, cooked

Clean and soak mussels and steam them in wine until the shells open. Remove meat from shells, pull off beards, and trim out dark section. Strain the broth through a triple layer of cheesecloth and reserve it. Mussels may be steamed the day before and kept in strained broth until ready to use.

Sauté garlic, onion, and green pepper in hot oil until garlic turns yellow. Add tomatoes, parsley, oregano, and reserved mussel broth. Cook over medium heat for 10 minutes. Season to taste with pepper. Mix half of the sauce with cooked vermicelli and portion it into soup bowls. Add cooked mussels to the remaining sauce, heat to a boil, and ladle over the vermicelli.

FISHERMAN'S MUSSEL SOUP

4 dozen mussels, cleaned and soaked
2 Tablespoons olive oil
4–5 cloves garlic, sliced
2 cups light Rhine wine

1/2 cup water
6 peppercorns, cracked
1/4 cup chopped parsley

In a large, heavy pot heat oil and sauté sliced garlic until it turns straw colored. Add wine, water, peppercorns, and mussels. Cover and steam, shaking the pot frequently, until the shells open. Pour mussels and juice into a colander placed over a bowl to drain and collect the liquid. Remove the top shell and beard from mussels and put them in a covered bowl to keep warm. Strain the broth through triple thickness of cheesecloth into a clean pot, add chopped parsley, and heat to a boil. Portion mussels into soup bowls, pour hot broth over them, and serve. Pass around crispy hot buttered sourdough French bread.

HORS D'OEUVRES

MARINATED MUSSELS

2 dozen mussels, cleaned and soaked   2 Tablespoons brown sugar
1 Tablespoon soy sauce   2 Tablespoons dry sherry
2 Tablespoons rice vinegar

Steam mussels in water, shaking the pot frequently, until the shells open.
Drain them, remove meat from shells, pull off beards, and cut out dark
soft section. Leave them to cool to room temperature.

Meanwhile, combine soy sauce, vinegar, sugar, and sherry in a saucepan,
bring to a boil, then cool the mixture. Mix cool sauce with mussels and
marinate them, refrigerated, for 6–8 hours before serving. Stir occasionally
while marinating to coat them uniformly with marinade. Serve chilled.

CHILLED COATED MUSSELS

Steam and prepare mussels as in recipe for Mussels for Garnishing
(p. 343), then chill them thoroughly. Dry chilled mussels on toweling,
cover them with Tartar Sauce (p. 426), and serve them on wooden cocktail
picks; garnish the tray decoratively with parsley.

Oysters

OYSTERS NORMALLY GROW in shallow brackish warm bays, but most varieties are too small to be considered food. These mollusks, native or cultivated, spawn spontaneously when water temperature exceeds 60°F. A first oyster spawns, carrying a hormonelike substance that sets off a chain reaction, causing a whole oyster population to spawn on the same day.

Young larvae ejected from shells swim about freely for a week or two, then they select a rock, shell, or root to settle on. When settled, they attach themselves permanently with a cementlike substance excreted by their glands. They subsist by filtering small particles from the water.

Because cold coast water deters spawning, most coast farmers buy cultivated seedlings that have been grown in laboratories or in spawning grounds.

Seed growers use thousands of old shucked shells, some strung like beads, which they place in established spawning areas, ready and waiting for newly spawned seedlings to settle on them. When seedlings are permanently attached, the shells, covered with seed, are retrieved, broken up into smaller pieces and shipped to coastal farmers, who scatter them over their silty-mud beds to grow.

Cultivated oysters need not grow only on mud bottoms. Some farmers grow oysters to maturity on the strings of seeded old shucked shells. They hang hundreds of these strings of seeded shells from platforms or booms moored in shallow fertile growing areas—a hanging garden of oysters. Farmers can inspect and work on their crops at low tides when the beds are exposed.

It takes one and a half to five years for oysters to grow to maturity. They vary in size, texture, and flavor according to species and where they are harvested. Eastern oysters, such as Bluepoints and Rockaways, are taken from the vast oyster beds around Long Island and in Chesapeake Bay. Massachusetts, Delaware, and Virginia are also oyster-growing areas. Fine oysters come from the Gulf Coast of Louisiana. Pacific oysters, developed from Japanese seed, grow to be ten-inch giants. Pacific varieties are harvested primarily from Puget Sound and the Northwest Coast.

About Oyster Meat

Oysters purchased live in the shell should be tightly closed or close quickly when handled. If they don't, they are dead and unfit to eat. Refrigerated, they will stay alive for three days maximum. Oysters should remain refrigerated at 32–4°F. until cooking or serving time. Open unshucked oysters immediately before eating for better flavor. Instructions for cleaning and opening are on page 10.

On the West Coast, shucked small- and medium-size oysters are commonly marketed in eight-, ten-, and twelve-ounce and quart jars. Small-size oysters weigh about one ounce each, medium-size about one and a half ounces each. Allow four large or six small oysters per serving.

Eastern shucked oysters are marketed in pint or quart metal or waxed containers. Extra selects are the largest oysters; select are medium-size and good for frying; and small are cocktail size. Shucked oysters will remain fresh for about ten days, if properly refrigerated. Once thawed, never refreeze oysters.

Oysters are eaten raw, barbecued, baked, fried, simmered, smoked, etc. They should be cooked at low temperature and only until they are plump and the edges begin to curl. Overcooking makes them tough and rubbery.

All of the following recipes are for fresh raw oysters.

PACIFIC OYSTER COCKTAIL

12 small oysters (12-ounce jar)   Lemon wedges
Cocktail Sauce II (p. 436)   Oyster crackers

Pacific oysters are too large to be served raw on the half shell. Allow 3 or 4 oysters per serving. Cut them into bite-size pieces and put them in chilled cocktail cups. Pour cocktail sauce over each, garnish with lemon wedges, and pass a bowl of oyster crackers.

BARBECUED OYSTERS

Scrub shells clean under cold water. When fire is medium hot, place oysters, cup side down, on the grate and barbecue until the shells open. Remove from the grill and take off the top shell. Sprinkle oysters with pepper, a little salt, a dab of butter, and serve hot in the shell with lemon wedges and Worcestershire sauce to taste.

BROILED OYSTERS IN THE SHELL

Preheat the oven to 450°F. Cover the bottom of a baking sheet with rock salt to make a level bed for oysters. Arrange them cup side down and bake until the shells open, about 15 minutes. Remove top shells and sprinkle oysters with celery salt, pepper, a drop or two of Tabasco, and some lemon juice; or accompany them with dipping sauce.

Oyster Dipping Sauce

1 green onion, minced	1/2 teaspoon Worcestershire sauce
1 teaspoon minced parsley	6 drops of Tabasco sauce
1 teaspoon salt	1/2 teaspoon olive oil
1/2 teaspoon pepper	5 Tablespoons wine vinegar

Combine all ingredients and mix well. Serve dipping sauce in individual small dishes with chilled raw oysters or roasted oysters.

OYSTERS ROCKEFELLER

12 large-shell oysters*	1 teaspoon anchovy paste
10-ounce package frozen chopped spinach	Pepper
	2 cups Thick Béchamel Sauce (p. 417)
Salt	1 egg yolk
Pinch of fennel seed	2 Tablespoons heavy cream
1 Tablespoon each minced green onion and parsley	Lemon juice
	Paprika
1 Tablespoon butter	

*Jar or canned raw oysters may be cooked in shallow ramekins.

Shuck oysters. Reserve the cup half of shells. Rinse meat and set aside. Cook spinach with salt and fennel for 5 minutes, then drain. Combine spinach, green onion, parsley, butter, and anchovy paste in a blender and purée. Add pepper to taste.

Make thick béchamel sauce. Beat egg yolk with cream and mix it into the sauce. Stir in 2 teaspoons lemon juice.

Preheat the oven to 400°F. Arrange and level the 12 clean half shells on a rock salt bed. Mix 1/4 cup béchamel sauce into spinach and divide among the shells. Place an oyster on each spinach bed, then spoon the remaining béchamel sauce over the oysters. Sprinkle each oyster with a few drops of lemon juice and a dash of paprika. Bake them for about 10 minutes.

OYSTERS BAKED IN THE HALF SHELL

12 large-shell oysters*   Salt and pepper to taste
½ cup minced green onion   ¼ cup lemon juice
½ cup minced bell pepper   Cayenne pepper
4 Tablespoons (½ stick) butter   ½ cup fine dry bread crumbs

*Jar or canned raw oysters may be cooked in shallow ramekins.

Shuck oysters and reserve them, their liquor, and the cup half of shells.
Sauté onion and pepper in butter until tender. Season with salt and pepper.
    Preheat the oven to 400°F. Arrange the 12 clean half shells on a rock
salt bed. Place a spoonful of sautéed vegetables in each shell and an oyster
on top. Pour a teaspoon of lemon juice on each, then fill the shells with
reserved oyster liquor. Sprinkle each with a few grains of cayenne, then
with crumbs. Bake shells for 8–10 minutes, until the crumbs brown, then
serve at once.

OYSTERS ON THE HALF SHELL WITH MORNAY

12 large-shell oysters*   4 Tablespoons (½ stick) butter
⅔ cup minced celery   Salt and pepper to taste
⅓ cup minced parsley   Cayenne pepper
⅓ cup minced green onion   2 cups Mornay Sauce (p. 420)
2 cloves garlic, pressed   Fine dry bread crumbs

*Jar or canned raw oysters may be cooked in shallow ramekins.

Shuck oysters and retain the cup half of shells. Sauté vegetables slowly in
butter until celery is tender, then season with salt and pepper.
    Preheat the oven to 400°F. Cover the bottom of a baking sheet with
rock salt and arrange the shells in it. Divide vegetable mixture equally
among shells, place an oyster on each, and sprinkle with a few grains
of cayenne. Cover oysters with Mornay sauce, then sprinkle on fine bread
crumbs. Place oysters in oven to bake 8–10 minutes.

BAKED OYSTERS WITH CHEESE

1 quart oysters   ¼ cup crisp cooked bacon, crumbled
Juice of 1 lemon   1 cup Thick Béchamel Sauce (p. 417)
Salt and pepper   4 thin slices Cheddar cheese
4 Tablespoons minced green onion   ⅓ cup dry bread crumbs

Preheat the oven to 400°F. Divide oysters with their liquor among individual buttered ramekins. Sprinkle with lemon juice, salt, pepper, onion, and crumbled bacon. Spoon béchamel sauce over each and place a slice of cheese on top. Cover the cheese with crumbs and put the ramekins in oven for about 10 minutes. Serve at once.

SCALLOPED OYSTERS

1 pint oysters	Pinch of cayenne pepper
1 1/2 cups cracker crumbs	1 cup milk
1/4 teaspoon each celery salt	3 Tablespoons cream
and pepper	Butter

Preheat the oven to 425°F. Cover the bottom of a shallow buttered baking dish with some of the cracker crumbs. Drain oysters, reserving liquor, and place a layer of them on top of crumbs. Sprinkle with celery salt, pepper, and cayenne. Scatter on more of the crumbs and the remaining oysters. Don't make more than 2 layers of oysters because the middle layer would not cook. Top with crumbs, pour in milk, cream, and oyster liquor and dot thickly with butter. Bake for 20–25 minutes. Serve hot.

OYSTERS GARIBALDI

1 pint oysters	2 green onions, sliced
2 eggs, beaten	4 Tablespoons (1/2 stick) butter
1 teaspoon milk	Worcestershire sauce
1/2 teaspoon salt	4 English muffin halves, toasted and
At least 1/4 teaspoon pepper	buttered
1/2 cup fine dry bread crumbs	Lemon wedges

Pour oysters with their liquor into a saucepan and simmer them slowly until they plump, about 5 minutes. Drain, but reserve the liquor. Beat eggs with milk, salt, and 1/4 teaspoon pepper, roll oysters in it, then in crumbs.

In a heavy skillet, sauté onions in butter until tender. Add oysters and brown them quickly on both sides. Pour in any remaining egg and when it sets pour in reserved oyster liquor. Let it bubble and cook a few seconds, then remove from heat. Put a drop or two of Worcestershire sauce on each oyster and sprinkle with pepper. Divide oysters with egg onto each buttered toasted muffin and serve hot with lemon wedges.

DEEP-FRIED OYSTERS

1 quart large oysters	¼ teaspoon pepper
1 Tablespoon flour	2 eggs, beaten
5 Tablespoons milk	Lard or oil for frying
1½ cups fine dry bread crumbs	Lemon wedges
1 teaspoon salt	Tartar Sauce (p. 426)

Drain oysters and dry them on toweling. Mix a paste of flour and milk.
Spread crumbs mixed with salt and pepper on waxed paper. Roll oysters
in paste, then in crumbs, and set them aside to dry for at least 15 minutes.
Dip each in egg and roll again in crumbs, then set aside to dry for 30
minutes.

Deep fry a few at a time in hot (385°F.) fat for about 4 minutes. Drain
on toweling and serve them with lemon wedges and tartar sauce.

PAN ROAST OYSTERS

1 quart oysters	1 teaspoon lemon juice
3 Tablespoons butter	1 teaspoon Worcestershire sauce
1 teaspoon paprika	3-6 drops of Tabasco sauce
¼ teaspoon celery salt	2 Tablespoons heavy cream
¼ teaspoon pepper	Salt to taste
½ cup chili sauce	

Simmer oysters in their liquor for 5 minutes, then drain. Cut large oysters
into bite-size pieces. Heat butter over low heat with paprika, celery salt,
and pepper. Stir in oysters, making sure they are well coated. Mix together
chili sauce, lemon juice, Worcestershire sauce, and Tabasco and add to
oysters. Stir and heat to a simmer, add cream and salt to taste. Serve on
buttered toast.

HANGTOWN FRY

12 medium oysters (1 pint)	¼ cup milk
8 strips bacon	½ cup fine dry crumbs
8 eggs, beaten	3 Tablespoons butter
¼ teaspoon salt	Sprig parsley, chopped
Pepper to taste	Lemon wedges
¼ cup flour	

Fry bacon crisp, drain on toweling, and crush it into small pieces. Heat oysters in their liquor until plump, then drain and dry them. Beat eggs until mixed and season them with salt and pepper. Roll oysters in flour, dip in milk, and press in crumbs. Fry in butter until brown on one side, then turn. Scatter in bacon and pour eggs over the oysters; cook over low heat like an omelette. As eggs set, gently prod and lift with a spatula; tilt the pan, allowing liquid egg through to cook. Fold and turn eggs onto a warm platter, sprinkle with parsley, and serve with lemon wedges.

OYSTER LOAF

1 pint oysters	Flour
1 loaf white bread	2 Tablespoons minced green onion
6 Tablespoons (¾ stick) butter	2 Tablespoons minced parsley
1 egg white	Guacamole Sauce or Cheese Sauce
Salt and pepper	(p. 437)
Cayenne pepper	

Preheat the oven to 350°F. Cut off the top crust of a loaf of white bread, scoop out the soft center, leaving ½–¾-inch shell. Brush the outside of the shell with about 3 tablespoons of the melted butter, the inside with egg white. Put loaf in oven to toast until crisp.

Drain and dry oysters in toweling. Season with salt, pepper, and a few grains of cayenne and roll each in flour. Sauté in the remaining 3 tablespoons of butter until brown on both sides. Sprinkle with green onion and parsley. Place in the warm crust, replace the top. Serve hot slices smothered with guacamole or hot cheese sauce.

OYSTER STEW

1 pint small oysters	½ teaspoon salt
4 cups milk	⅛ teaspoon white pepper
3 Tablespoons butter	Savor salt

Heat milk in the top of a double boiler until scalding. Stir in 2 tablespoons of the butter and season with salt and pepper. Add oysters with their liquor and cook, just under a simmer, until oysters plump and rise to the top, about 30 minutes. Ladle oysters, then milk, into individual bowls. Place a dab of butter (using up the remaining tablespoon of butter) and a sprinkle of savor salt in each and serve.

OYSTER STUFFING FOR TURKEY

1 pint oysters
About 1 loaf day-old sourdough French
    or white bread
1 cup chopped celery
½ onion, grated

1 teaspoon salt
¼ teaspoon pepper
¼ teaspoon garlic powder
1 Tablespoon poultry seasoning
4 Tablespoons (½ stick) butter, melted

Simmer oysters in their liquor for about 5 minutes, until the edges curl. Drain and chop them, but reserve the liquor. Remove crust and cut semidry bread into ½-inch cubes. Add celery, onion, oysters, and seasoning; toss gently to mix. Combine cool oyster liquor with melted butter (add milk for more moisture) and toss stuffing lightly while slowly pouring it over the bread. Stuff turkey.

JAPANESE OYSTER STEW

1 pint small oysters
1 block tofu*
6 green onions
1½ cups celery cabbage
¼ pound fresh mushrooms
½ sliced water chestnuts

1–2 Tablespoons miso shiro bean
    paste*
¼ cup soy sauce
1 Tablespoon grated ginger
1 Tablespoon mirin*
2 cups dashi broth*

*All items may be purchased at Oriental food stores. See Mackerel Fillets in Miso Broth, page 249, for directions on making dashi broth.

Broil tofu on one side until brown, then slice it into 1-inch cubes. Slice green onions in 1-inch lengths, cabbage into 1½-inch lengths, mushrooms vertically; set water chestnuts with other vegetables. Combine bean paste, soy sauce, ginger, and mirin and place mixture in a large, heavy skillet. Arrange oysters, tofu, and vegetables around it.

   Pour over hot dashi broth and bring to simmer over high heat. Gently prod, mixing bean paste with oysters, tofu, and vegetables. Cook just under a simmer until oysters plump and their edges curl.

Olympia Oysters

Olympia oysters are tiny and very choice oysters, native to the lower Puget Sound area around Shelton and Olympia. They grow no other place in the world. They were favored food of the Indians and featured gourmet delights among the wealthy "lumber barons" of the Northwest in the late 1800s.

Today they are farmed in dyke beds by Indians and other independent oystermen of the area. With five years' growth the shell matures to the size of a silver dollar, the oyster itself to the size of a quarter. It takes two hundred or so oysters to make a pint, and they are all shucked by hand. They are rare, expensive, and very fine food.

OLYMPIA OYSTER SAUTÉ FOR TWO

½ pint Olympia oysters
1 Tablespoon minced green onion
2 Tablespoons (¼ stick) butter
½ cup half-and-half

Salt and pepper
Dash of Tabasco
Hot buttered toast

Sauté onion in butter until tender, add oysters, and cook until the edges curl. Stir in half-and-half, season with salt, pepper, and Tabasco. Bring to simmer and spoon the oysters and sauce onto hot buttered toast.

HORS D'OEUVRES

PICKLED OYSTERS

1 quart oysters
Oyster liquor
Salt
½ cup vinegar
½ cup dry white wine
2 teaspoons scraped onion

1 small clove garlic
¼ teaspoon allspice
6 whole black peppercorns
½-inch piece cinnamon stick
1 clove
Small sprig fresh fennel leaves

Strain oysters and to the liquor add enough water to make 1½ cups. Pour into a saucepan, add a little salt, bring to a simmer, then add oysters. Cook just under a simmer until oysters plump and the edges curl. Remove them to a nonmetal bowl to cool.

To the oyster liquor add vinegar, wine, onion, garlic, allspice, peppercorns, cinnamon, and clove. Simmer, in an enameled pot, for 10 minutes and let cool. Add a few fennel leaves to the oysters, pour in cool sauce, cover, and refrigerate. In 48 hours they will be ready to eat.

ANGELS ON HORSEBACK

1 pint oysters   Thin slices bacon
Salt and pepper to taste   Sprigs parsley
Paprika

Sprinkle oysters with salt, pepper, and paprika. Wrap a slice of bacon around each oyster and secure it with a wooden cocktail pick. Preheat the oven to 450°F. Place wrapped oysters on a rack in a shallow baking pan and bake, turning once, until bacon is crisp on all sides, about 10 minutes. Remove picks and serve on a platter garnished with parsley sprigs.

Scallops

SCALLOPS are also called coquilles Saint Jacques (Saint James' shell) or Pilgrim's Badges. Pilgrims traveling in search of the Holy Grail followed the route of St. James, to Santiago de Compostelo, the shrine of St. James, patron saint of pilgrims, in Spain. There they gathered scallop shells to use as cup, dish, and spoon, and wore them tied around their necks. Thus, the shell became the badge of the pilgrim and emblem of Saint James. The beautiful shell has been the inspiration of designs in all the arts and — today — the well-known emblem of Shell oil company.

Scallops, the only bivalves that swim, move around the seabed between the low-tide mark and 300 feet. Normally, they lie resting free, shells partly agape, curtained by their tentacles and mantle, around the edge of which are 100 tiny bright and shiny blue eyes. Should even a shadow pass over those eyes, the scallop will snap its shells closed with a click. When predators come near, of course, they swim away, in their typical jerky fashion, clapping their round shells together.

Large (five- to seven-inch) sea scallops are taken along the northern West Coast — southern varieties are smaller. Not all scallops are mobile. Rock scallops found along the entire coast anchor themselves to rocks, etc., like mussels. Other varieties cement themselves permanently, as do oysters. Their number one enemies are starfish and octopuses.

About Scallop Meat

There are two kinds of scallops: 1. Sea scallops (deepwater mollusks) have a large muscle, some big enough to slice crosswise or cut into halves and are taken all year round. 2. Bay scallops are taken from the shallow water of bays and estuaries during cool months of the year — oyster season. They are smaller, the muscle hardly more than half an inch wide, and are prized for their tender meat and sweet flavor. Both are prepared in the same ways.

If you should get fresh scallops in the shell, heat the oven to 250°F., put shells on a tray on the lowest rack of the oven until they open. Cut meat from the shells, trim off the beard and black parts, and discard all but the white (or cream-colored) adductor muscle, which is the only part of scallops we eat. Rinse well under running water and drain.

Scallops are sold shelled and cleaned, fresh or frozen in most fish markets. If frozen, they should be thawed before preparing further. They may be baked, sautéed, deep fried, or poached for main dishes, or used in soups, salads, and appetizers.

Cook scallops until just heated through; overcooking makes them tough.

BROILED SCALLOPS

1½ pounds scallops
½ cup vermouth
½ cup olive oil
1 clove garlic, crushed
½ teaspoon salt

Pepper to taste
4 slices buttered toast
8 strips bacon, cooked crisp
Tartar Sauce (p. 426)

Mix together wine, oil, garlic, salt, and pepper. Add scallops and marinate them for several hours in the refrigerator. Preheat the broiler. Place scallops in rows in a shallow baking pan, pour all the marinade over them and broil, 2 inches from the heat, for 5–6 minutes, turning them only once. Serve them with toast, bacon, and tartar sauce.

BAKED SCALLOPS

1½ pounds scallops
6 Tablespoons (¾ stick) butter
¼ teaspoon each salt and pepper
1 clove garlic, pressed
1 teaspoon scraped onion

2 Tablespoons minced parsley
2 teaspoons lemon juice
⅔ cup soft bread crumbs
Paprika

Butter individual shells or ramekins. Cut scallops into ½-inch slices. Melt 3 tablespoons of the butter and mix in salt, pepper, garlic, onion, parsley, and lemon juice. Stir in scallops, coating them well, then divide the mixture among buttered scallop shells. Preheat the oven to 400°F. Melt the remaining 3 tablespoons of butter, toss bread crumbs in it, and scatter them on the scallops. Bake shells for 10–12 minutes. Sprinkle lightly with paprika and serve.

SCALLOPS SAUTÉED IN GARLIC BUTTER

1 pound scallops
1 cup milk
Flour
4 Tablespoons (½ stick) butter

2 cloves garlic, minced
Salt and pepper
¼ cup minced parsley
Lemon wedges

Cut scallops in half, soak them in milk for 10 minutes, drain and dry on toweling, then dust them lightly with flour. Heat butter in a skillet, add garlic to the pan, and mix it around. Put in scallops and sauté until they are lightly brown and just heated through. Season with salt and pepper, stir in parsley, and serve at once with lemon wedges.

SAUTÉED SCALLOPS WITH TOMATOES

1½ pounds scallops
¼ cup flour
3 Tablespoons oil
1 clove garlic, minced
1 ounce brandy
¼ cup dry white wine

¼ teaspoon each thyme, marjoram,
  and rosemary
1 cup tomato, peeled and diced
Salt and pepper to taste
Sprig parsley, minced

Rinse and dry scallops, then shake them in a bag with flour. Heat oil very hot, add scallops and garlic and quickly brown them. Pour in brandy and wine, stirring scallops in the pan, then add herbs and tomato. Reduce heat and simmer until scallops are heated through. Season with salt and pepper. Transfer them to a warm platter, sprinkle with parsley, and serve.

BAY SCALLOPS WITH DILL

1 pound bay scallops
2 Tablespoons flour
3 Tablespoons butter
1 green onion, sliced thin
1 Tablespoon chopped fresh dill

Dash of Tabasco
2 Tablespoons dry white wine
Salt and pepper to taste
Toast

Dust scallops with flour. In a frying pan, heat butter with onion, dill, and Tabasco. When butter bubbles, add scallops and cook over high heat, stirring, for a minute. Add wine, lower heat, and simmer only until scallops are warmed through. Season with salt and pepper and serve with toast.

SCALLOP TEMPURA

Coat scallops with Tempura Batter (p. 397) and deep fry in hot (370°F.) oil. Try a tempura combination of scallops and shrimp with bits of tempura-fried carrots, green beans, and asparagus.

DEEP-FRIED SCALLOPS

Prepare a beer batter according to recipe on page 20. Dip scallops in batter and deep fry a few at a time in hot (370°F.) oil or lard until golden brown. Drain them briefly on toweling, then serve with Tartar Sauce (p. 426).

SCALLOPS COOKED IN WINE

1½ pounds scallops	Pinch of thyme
2 Tablespoons (¼ stick) butter	¼ teaspoon salt
2 Tablespoons chopped green onion	1 cup dry white wine, heated
½ bay leaf	Hot water, as needed

Thaw scallops if frozen, rinse and drain. Put butter, green onion, and spices in a saucepan, stir and cook until onion is soft. Add scallops, stir them around the pan, then barely cover them with hot wine and water as needed. Bring to the boiling point (but don't boil, or scallops will toughen immediately), lower heat and simmer (poach), covered, until tender, or slightly raw in the center—usually 3-4 minutes. Allow longer for large scallops. Remove and slice them if they are large; reserve the broth. Use them in any recipe calling for scallops cooked in wine.

COQUILLES CLASSIC

1½ pounds scallops, cooked in wine	2 egg yolks
7 Tablespoons butter	¼ cup cream
1 cup minced green onions	Salt and pepper to taste
½ pound mushrooms, chopped	½ cup bread crumbs
2 Tablespoons minced parsley	Sprinkle of paprika
1 teaspoon lemon juice	Snips of parsley
4 Tablespoons flour	

Cook scallops for 3 minutes, as in recipe for Scallops Cooked in Wine (p. 360). Drain and slice them; reserve the broth.

Combine 2 tablespoons of the butter, 2 tablespoons water, chopped vegetables, and lemon juice in a saucepan. Cover and cook slowly for 10 minutes, stirring frequently. Drain all the juice from vegetables into the reserved wine broth (there should be 2 cups, if not, add water to make up the amount) and warm it almost to boiling.

Heat 4 of the remaining tablespoons of butter in a saucepan, stir in flour, and cook the roux until it bubbles. Add hot broth all at once and beat with a whisk until the sauce thickens and boils. Beat egg yolks with cream, mix a little of the hot sauce with them, then beat them into the sauce. Season to taste with salt and pepper. Stir mushroom mixture and scallops into the sauce.

Preheat the oven to 450°F. Butter scallop shells or ramekins and fill them with scallop mixture. Scatter bread crumbs on top, dot with the remaining tablespoon of butter, and put in the oven until the crumbs brown. Sprinkle with a little paprika, a snip of parsley, and serve.

POACHED SCALLOPS FOR VARIOUS DISHES

Thaw if frozen and cut large scallops in half. Put them in a saucepan, cover with boiling salted water or Basic Court Bouillon (p. 26), and simmer them gently for 3 minutes. (Don't boil, or they will become tough immediately.) Drain well and chill, covered, until ready to use.

SCALLOPS IN MORNAY

1½ pounds scallops, cooked in wine
1½ cups Mornay Sauce (p. 420)
Sprig parsley, minced

Grated cheese (Swiss, Parmesan, or
  combination of both)
2½ cups seasoned mashed potatoes

Cook scallops for 3 minutes, as in recipe for Scallops Cooked in Wine (p. 360). Drain and slice them; reduce the wine broth, over high heat, to ½ cup. Preheat the oven to 450°F. Make Mornay sauce and mix the reduced broth into it. Stir parsley and scallop slices into the sauce, then spoon the mixture into individual buttered shells or a shallow buttered casserole. Sprinkle grated cheese on top. Using a pastry bag, pipe mashed potatoes around the rim of the shells or casserole, and place them in the oven until the potatoes are lightly brown.

CURRIED SCALLOPS

1½ pounds scallops, cooked in wine
1 onion, chopped
1 clove garlic, minced
4 Tablespoons (½ stick) butter
2 Tablespoons flour

1 teaspoon curry powder
½ cup cream
Salt and pepper to taste
Sprig parsley, minced

Cook scallops in wine for 3 minutes, as in preceding recipe. Drain and keep them warm; reserve the broth.

In a large saucepan, slowly sauté onion and garlic in butter for 8–10 minutes. Stir in flour and curry powder and continue cooking for a minute. Add hot scallop broth all at once and beat with a whisk while sauce heats to a boil and thickens. Mix in cream, simmer for 5 minutes, and season with salt and pepper. Stir scallops into sauce, pour all into a serving dish, sprinkle with minced parsley, and serve.

HORS D'OEUVRES

SCALLOP COCKTAIL

1 cup bay scallops
1 heart of celery, chopped fine
2 Tablespoons chopped chives

1 tomato, peeled and chopped
Fish Cocktail Mayonnaise (p. 425)

Pour just enough boiling salted water over the scallops barely to cover them and let them stand covered with water for 2 minutes, then drain. This will poach them. When scallops have returned to room temperature, chill them for 1 hour.

Mix chopped celery, chives, and tomatoes with chilled scallops. Combine scallop mixture with fish cocktail mayonnaise and serve chilled in sherbet glasses.

SCALLOPS IN SOY SAUCE

1 pound scallops
1 cup soy sauce
3 Tablespoons sugar

½ teaspoon monosodium glutamate
2 teaspoons grated ginger

Cut large scallops in half, leave small ones whole. Combine soy sauce, sugar, monosodium glutamate, and ginger and bring to a boil. Add scallops, lower heat, and cook just under a simmer, covered, for 2–3 minutes, until barely cooked, then drain. Serve scallops hot on wooden cocktail picks.

SCALLOPS AND BACON

Thaw scallops if frozen, rinse and dry them and, if large, cut them in half. Preheat the oven to 475°F. Wrap each in a thin slice of bacon, overlapping it a little, and secure it with a wooden cocktail pick. Place scallops in rows on a rack to bake or broil until bacon is crisp; turn once only. Serve with a dunking sauce of melted butter seasoned with lemon juice and Worcestershire sauce.

Crab

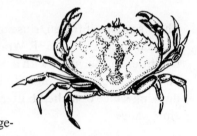

THERE ARE THREE commercially important species of crabs on the West Coast: 1. King crab lives along the continental shelf in the Gulf of Alaska and north into the Bering Strait. Typically, gigantic male king crabs have legs two feet long. 2. Dungeness, the common crab, is found from Lower California to Alaska on sandy, grassy bottoms, from shallow-tide zones to 300-foot ocean depths. The big fisheries are all north of Monterey Bay. Near San Francisco they are caught on the bar beyond the Golden Gate. Eureka has a similar area, and the entire northern coast is productively fished. 3. Rock crab resembles Dungeness, but is smaller. Though found from Alaska to the Gulf of California, they are taken commercially only in California.

Crabs are caught in crab rings (cages, commercially) or hoop nets that are baited with fish and dropped overboard to sink to the bottom. A line attached to the ring connects to a surface float marking the position of the ring and allows return to the ring spot. Crabs have a phenomenal sense of smell and are attracted to the bait from a considerable distance. They walk into the ring on the tips of their pointed claws to consume the bait. Returning to the marker float after a time, the line is hauled up quickly and the ring retrieved—if the person is lucky, loaded with crabs.

Crabs may be caught around harbors from piers, as well as midstream from boats. They require saltwater, so the lower areas of bays are more productive. Best fishing for sportsmen is in the deeper bay channels, at or near slack tide, on either incoming or outgoing tide.

BLUE CRABS are the common crab of the Atlantic Coast and Gulf of Mexico. These crabs are small, weighing up to a pound, more or less. Their shells are blue green, wide, sharp tipped, and white underneath. Their rear two pairs of legs are flattened swimming paddles. They come inshore to spawn from May to October, on the mid–Atlantic Coast, crowding into sandy mud-bottom bays and estuaries.

About three-fourths of all crab meat marketed in the United States is blue crab. They are harvested commercially by dredges, trawls, nets, seines, and pots. Hard-shell crab is cooked immediately after harvest, shelled, graded, packed in iced containers, and marketed as:

Lump meat: large solid lumps of pure white body meat, to be used for salads and cocktails, etc., where size and whiteness are important.

Backfin: smaller lumps of body meat.

Flake meat: small pieces from the rest of the body, shreds and flakes.

Claw meat: the brownish-tinged meat picked from the claws, to be used where appearance is not important. Claw meat is less expensive.

Boiling is the basic method of cooking crab. Boiled hard-shell meat may be used for recipes specifying cooked crab meat.

Cleaning and shelling instructions are on page 10. Crab fat (crab butter) is the creamy substance crabs store in the corners of their top shells. It is very edible, and can add greatly to the flavor of many crab dishes.

AT DIFFERENT seasons the "hard-shell crab" becomes the "soft-shell crab." Soft-shell crabbing is a large enterprise in the Gulf of Mexico as well as around Chesapeake Bay. When crabs are harvested, they are inspected by crabbers who separate them into big submergeable tanks. An expert crabber can tell the females from the males by their red-tipped claws, as well as by the shape of the apron. And he can see if one is a "buster" or "peeler," which is a crab about to molt (by splitting and backing out of its shell). These crabs are watched closely, and when the "buster" completely sheds the shell it becomes a vulnerable "soft-shell crab" for twenty-four hours, until the new shell hardens. The soft-shells are immediately lifted from the tank, carefully packed, and within hours are air-expressed to markets, where the still-alive crabs are sold.

Some of the harvest is flash frozen for off-season consumption, but they are best bought live; frozen soft-shells tend to be wrinkled and soggy.

To clean soft-shell crab: You may place crabs in the freezer for a few minutes to numb them, then stick a sharp blade into the body behind the eyes. Remove the apron from the lower underside. Lift and fold back the tapering points on either side of the back and remove the gray gills. Cut off the head, in back of the eyes, with scissors, then squeeze the body, in back of the head, to pop out the sand sac. Everything else about a soft-shell crab is good to eat, including the small legs and fins. Rinse them well under cold water and pat them dry.

STONE CRAB is a highly prized Southern delicacy — expensive and served in famous clubs and restaurants in the South and North. These comparatively rare crabs are harvested in certain areas from the Carolinas to Texas, such as Beaufort, North Carolina, and Charleston, South Carolina, but southern Florida is where they are most abundant and grow to the largest size.

They are burrowing crabs that live in deep sandy-mud holes near creeks, among mangrove roots, and under rocks in estuaries. They are caught in baited crab pots or with iron hooks. The fishermen remove one claw from each crab caught, then toss the animal back into the water, where it will regenerate a new claw in two seasons.

The black-tipped, thick-shelled crab claws are cooked by boiling in salted water for twenty to twenty-five minutes. With cooking, they turn yellow white, colorfully tinged with red. They are served either hot or cold. Crack the bulbous shells with a mallet before bringing them to the table. Served hot, the delicately rich morsels may be picked out with an oyster fork and dipped in melted lemon-butter, garlic butter, or mustard sauce. They are delicious served cold with tart mayonnaise.

About Dungeness
and Rock Crab Meat

As crabs grow they molt, discarding their old shell, replacing it with a larger one. Adult crabs also molt once a year, generally in late summer or fall. New shells are soft; the crabs are lightweight and should not be kept, because their flesh is sparse and of poor quality.

Pick up live crabs with tongs or from the center rear to avoid being pinched. Drop them one at a time into boiling salted water to cover. Simmer 15–20 minutes from the time the water resumes boiling, then drain and rinse. Cleaning and shelling instructions are on page 10.

One 2–2½-pound medium-size crab will yield about 2 cups of meat, approximately ½ pound.

Fresh-cooked Dungeness crab, in or out of the shell, is seasonally available in local markets. Frozen or canned crab is sold in most supermarkets. Both should be warmed through only; further cooking is unnecessary.

One pound of crab meat will feed four.

CRACKED DUNGENESS OR ROCK CRAB

Arrange fresh-cooked warm or chilled crab in cracked shells on a platter. Serve a bowl of mayonnaise, melted butter, tomato sauce, or catsup and plenty of hot French bread and a tossed green salad.

BOILED HARD-SHELL BLUE CRAB

Serves 6

24 hard-shell blue crabs $1/3$ cup salt
6 quarts boiling water

Plunge crabs into boiling salted water. Cover and return to boiling point. Simmer for 15 minutes. Drain. Serve hot or cold.

BROILED KING CRAB LEGS

Marinate split crab legs in half lemon juice/half melted butter, season with 1 teaspoon soy sauce and a pinch of cayenne pepper. Broil shell side down, over slow coals, basting as they heat and shells become brown.

CRAB MEAT SAUCE

1 cup crab meat $1/8$ teaspoon white pepper
3 Tablespoons butter   1 teaspoon lemon juice
2 Tablespoons flour   2 Tablespoons dry sherry or Cognac
$1\frac{1}{2}$ cups hot milk   1 egg yolk
$1/4$ teaspoon salt or to taste

Flake crab meat and set it aside. Make a cream sauce by cooking a roux of butter and flour, beating in hot milk, and stirring until thickened. Cook sauce for 3–4 minutes, then season with salt, pepper, and lemon juice. Lower heat and add crab meat. Mix sherry with egg yolk, then stir it into the sauce, heat to the boiling point, and serve.

CRAB TEMPURA

2-pound cooked crab (1¾ cups lump   1 cup ice water
   crab meat or two 6½-ounce cans)   1 cup all-purpose flour
2 Tablespoons fine cracker crumbs   ¼ teaspoon salt
2 eggs   2 cups oil for deep frying

Remove crab meat from shell, leaving claw meat whole and body meat in chunks. Flake remaining small bits in a wide bowl and mix them with cracker crumbs and 1 beaten egg. Dip crab chunks in egg mixture, then with floured hands shape into balls. Refrigerate balls for at least 1 hour.

Make a batter by beating the remaining egg lightly with ice water, then adding sifted flour and salt all at once. Give it 3–4 quick stirs and leave it lumpy.

Heat oil to 350°F., dip crab balls into batter one at a time. Let excess batter drip off, then carefully place into hot oil and fry until golden brown, about 2–3 minutes. Drain on several layers of toweling and serve with dipping sauce.

Tempura Dipping Sauce

1 cup chicken or clam broth   1 teaspoon lemon juice
¼ cup soy sauce   3 Tablespoons minced green onion
2 Tablespoons sake

Combine all ingredients in a saucepan, bring to a boil, then remove from heat. Serve cool sauce in individual small cups.

DEEP-FRIED SOFT-SHELL CRAB
WITH TARTAR SAUCE

8–10 medium-size soft-shell crabs   1 cup flour
3 eggs, beaten   1 cup commercial fish fry*
¼ cup milk   Vegetable oil for deep frying
2 teaspoons salt   Tartar Sauce (p. 426)

*Commercial fish fry is a combination of seasoned flour and meal especially prepared for frying or baking fish. Available in fish markets and grocery stores.

Combine eggs, milk, and salt. Shake crabs in flour, dip them in egg mixture, and roll them in fish fry, then put them in the refrigerator for 30 minutes to firm the coating.

Deep fry crabs, 2–3 at a time, in hot (375°F.) oil for 3–4 minutes, or until golden brown. Drain briefly on absorbent paper and transfer to a towel-lined platter in a warm oven while deep frying the rest. Have ready a bowl of tartar sauce to accompany the crispy crabs.

BUTTER-FRIED SOFT-SHELL CRABS

8 small or 4 large soft-shell crabs
1 egg, beaten
1 cup milk
1 teaspoon salt
1 cup corn flour (not cornmeal)*

8 Tablespoons (1 stick) butter
3 Tablespoons lemon juice
1/4 cup minced parsley
Toast points

*Corn flour can be purchased in health food stores, or use supermarket fine-ground cornmeal whirled in a blender.

Combine beaten egg, milk, and salt. Dip crabs in egg-milk mixture, drain on toweling, dust them in corn flour, and shake off the excess. Melt butter in a large skillet until the foam subsides. Fry several crabs at a time slowly, allowing 5–7 minutes on each side. As crabs turn golden on both sides, transfer to a towel-lined plate and keep them warm until all are done.

Just before serving, raise the heat and add lemon juice and parsley to the butter in the pan. Stir and scrape the skillet to release all the delicious brown bits. Place crabs on warmed dinner plates, arrange toast points on each, spoon butter sauce over the crab, and serve at once.

CRAB WITH VERA CRUZ SAUCE

1 pound lump crab meat
1 small onion, chopped
3 cloves garlic, minced
2 Tablespoons oil
2 cups tomatoes, peeled and chopped
   (or canned)
1/4 cup minced parsley
Pinch each of cinnamon and clove

4 drops of Tabasco
1 teaspoon Dijon-type mustard
3 Tablespoons ground almonds
1 heaping teaspoon capers and juice
1 canned pimiento, chopped
1/4 cup chopped green olives
3 Tablespoons butter
2 cups cooked rice

Make Vera Cruz Sauce: Sauté onion and garlic in oil until tender, add tomatoes, parsley, spices, Tabasco, mustard, and ground almonds. Simmer, stirring frequently, for 5 minutes, then add capers, pimiento, and green olives. Reduce heat so the sauce just stays hot.

Sauté crab in butter, tossing as needed until thoroughly hot. Serve crab on or with rice and spoon hot Vera Cruz Sauce over both.

CRAB SAUTÉ AMANDINE

1 pound lump crab meat
½ cup slivered almonds
2 Tablespoons oil
1 teaspoon minced fresh dill
2 Tablespoons minced parsley
Salt to taste

1 green onion, chopped
4 Tablespoons (½ stick) butter
¼ cup Cognac
¼ cup heavy cream
Pepper to taste
Steamed rice

Preheat the oven to 350°F. Mix almonds in oil, spread them on the bottom of a frying pan, and bake them, shaking the pan frequently, until they become golden. Remove from the oven, stir in dill, parsley, and a sprinkle of salt, then set aside.

Sauté onion in butter over medium heat until it starts to brown. Add crab and cook until hot, turning meat as necessary. Sprinkle with Cognac and set aflame. When flames subside, gently stir in cream, simmer for 2 minutes, and season with salt and pepper. Transfer crab to a warm platter, spoon almond and herbs over, and serve with steamed rice.

CURRIED CRACKED CRAB

2 large Dungeness crabs, cooked
1 Tablespoon salted fermented black
  beans*
2 cloves garlic, minced
½ teaspoon minced ginger
½ teaspoon salt
1 teaspoon sugar
1 teaspoon lemon rind
4 teaspoons curry powder

3 Tablespoons oil
½ cup minced lean pork
2 green onions, chopped
1 green pepper, seeded and cut in bite-
  size pieces
2 Tablespoons dry white wine
1 cup chicken broth
2 teaspoons cornstarch
2 Tablespoons water

*See Glossary.

Clean crab, disjoint and crack claws, chop bodies in half, and reserve the crab butter. Wash and drain black beans and mash them with garlic, ginger, salt, sugar, lemon rind, and curry powder.

Heat oil in a large skillet, add pork, and stir-fry over high heat until meat is firm and beginning to brown. Mix in black bean-curry, then add onions and green pepper and cook, stirring, for 2 minutes. Add crab, crab butter, wine, and chicken broth, cover, and cook 3 minutes. Mix cornstarch with water and blend into the broth, stirring constantly until sauce is thickened and smooth. Serve at once.

CRAB AND MUSHROOM STEW

1 pound crab meat
1 pound mushrooms, halved or
  quartered if large
2 green onions, chopped
2 cloves garlic, pressed
5 Tablespoons butter

Salt and pepper
1 Tablespoon whiskey (optional)
1 cup half-and-half
3 cups cooked rice
¼ cup chopped parsley

Sauté mushrooms, onions, and garlic in butter over high heat, stirring often until liquid has evaporated and mushrooms are golden brown. Season with salt and pepper, then remove them from the pan with a slotted spoon and keep warm. Add whiskey, if you like, swirl it around the pan, then add crab and mix while heating over moderate flame for a minute. Return mushrooms to the pan, stir in half-and-half, and heat until thoroughly hot. Correct seasoning if necessary.

Mix hot rice with parsley and pack it into an unbuttered 5-cup ring mold, then turn it out on a warm platter. Spoon hot crab-mushroom stew into the center and serve.

CRAB CIOPPINO

2 live large Dungeness crabs
18 steamer clams
12 large shrimp, raw in shells
1 large onion, chopped
6 cloves garlic, minced
6 Tablespoons olive oil
1 green pepper, cut in ¾-inch dice
2 stalks celery, chopped fine
⅓ cup minced parsley

2 cups tomatoes, peeled and chopped
6-ounce can tomato paste
2 cups water
1 bottle red wine
1½ teaspoons salt
1 teaspoon oregano
½ teaspoon each thyme and pepper
1 small bay leaf

In a large kettle, sauté onion and garlic in oil until tender. Add green pepper, celery, parsley, tomatoes, tomato paste, water, wine, and spices. Simmer, covered, until celery is soft, about 45 minutes.

Scrub clams, slit shells of shrimp and remove the black veins, then clean and crack crab as per instructions on page 10. Bring sauce to a boil, add crab and clams to the kettle and cover; when sauce returns to boil, simmer for 10 minutes. Add shrimp and simmer 10 more minutes or until clam shells open and shrimp are pink. Add salt and pepper if needed. Ladle into large soup plates and serve with hot sourdough French bread.

CRAB PANCAKE

½ pound crab meat
2 Tablespoons oil
1 cup cooked green peas, drained
1 cup chopped mushrooms
2 Tablespoons minced green onion
1 Tablespoon minced green pepper

1 teaspoon minced fresh cilantro
4 eggs
½ teaspoon salt
¼ teaspoon pepper
1 Tablespoon dry sherry

Pick over crab meat to remove any cartilage remaining. Heat oil in a large skillet and stir-fry vegetables with crab meat for 3 minutes. Beat eggs lightly with salt, pepper, and sherry, then pour into the crab mixture. Cook over medium heat like a pancake, turning to brown both sides. Cut into wedges and serve hot.

CRAB COQUILLES

1 pound fresh crab meat
2 eggs
1 teaspoon salt
¼ teaspoon pepper
½ teaspoon dry mustard
1 green onion, minced

2 Tablespoons minced green pepper
2 Tablespoons minced parsley
⅓ cup mayonnaise
1 teaspoon horseradish
Paprika

Preheat the oven to 350°F. Beat eggs with salt, pepper, and mustard, add green onion, green pepper, parsley, mayonnaise, and horseradish. Gently mix in crab meat, then divide mixture into buttered ramekins or shells. Sprinkle each with a dash of paprika and bake for 15–20 minutes.

CRAB IN PORT SAUCE EN CASSEROLE

1 pound lump crab meat
2 medium onions, minced
4 Tablespoons (½ stick) butter
6 tomatoes, peeled and diced
2 cloves garlic, pressed
½ cup minced parsley
½ cup dry white wine
1 teaspoon each salt, paprika, and dry
   mustard

¼ teaspoon each pepper and freshly
   ground nutmeg
Dash of cayenne pepper
Pinch of sugar
¼ cup tawny Port
¼ cup brandy

Sauté onions in 3 tablespoons of the butter until lightly brown. Add tomatoes, garlic, parsley, wine, and spices; simmer slowly, stirring frequently, until sauce becomes quite thick, about 30 minutes. Stir in Port, then brandy, and swirl in the remaining tablespoon of butter.

Preheat the oven to 350°F. Pick over crab meat to remove any remaining cartilage. Spoon half of the sauce into a casserole, spreading it evenly over the bottom. Arrange crab meat on top. Cover crab with the remaining sauce, cover, and bake for 15 minutes.

CRAB AND MUSHROOMS IN MORNAY

2 cups crab meat
1 green onion, minced
1/4 pound mushrooms, diced
5 Tablespoons butter
2 Tablespoons minced parsley
Salt and pepper to taste

1 teaspoon lemon juice
1 1/2 cups Mornay Sauce (p. 420)
2 Tablespoons grated Parmesan cheese
4 Tablespoons grated Gruyère cheese
3/4 cup soft bread crumbs

Preheat the oven to 350°F. Sauté onion and mushrooms in 2 tablespoons of the butter until tender, add parsley, and season with salt and pepper. Mix lemon juice with Mornay sauce, combine with mushrooms and crab, then taste for seasoning. Spoon mixture into a buttered au gratin dish, ramekins, or shells. Mix grated cheeses and sprinkle on top. Melt the remaining 3 tablespoons of butter, mix in crumbs, and scatter them on top of cheese. Bake until crumbs brown.

CRAB AND SWISS CHEESE QUICHE

1 1/2 cups crab meat
9-inch uncooked pastry shell
1 egg white
1 cup grated Swiss cheese
2 green onions, chopped
2 Tablespoons minced parsley
3 eggs

1 cup half-and-half
2 Tablespoons dry sherry
1/2 teaspoon grated lemon rind
Pinch of cayenne pepper
1/2 teaspoon salt
1/4 teaspoon pepper
Paprika

Brush the pastry with egg white. Sprinkle in grated cheese, then crab meat, then green onions and parsley. Preheat oven to 325°F. Beat eggs lightly with half-and-half, mix in sherry, lemon rind, cayenne, salt, and pepper, then pour over crab. Sprinkle with paprika. Bake for about 45 minutes, or until a knife inserted near the center comes out clean. Serve warm.

CRAB SOUFFLÉ

1 pound fresh crab meat	4 eggs
1 teaspoon grated lemon rind	3 cups milk
1 cup mayonnaise	1 teaspoon salt
1 small onion, chopped	¼ teaspoon each pepper and
1 cup chopped celery	dry mustard
¼ cup chopped green pepper	1 can condensed mushroom soup
1 canned pimiento, chopped	1 teaspoon paprika
10 slices soft white bread	½ cup grated Cheddar cheese

Mix lemon rind with mayonnaise and stir in chopped onion, celery, green pepper, and pimiento. Pick over crab meat and gently mix with vegetables. Remove crusts and dice bread. Layer bread and crab in a large shallow buttered casserole, making bottom and top layer bread. Beat eggs with milk, salt, pepper, and mustard, then pour into casserole. Cover and refrigerate for at least 4 hours, preferably overnight.

Preheat the oven to 325°F. and bake, covered, for 1 hour. Mix soup with paprika and bring to a boil. Uncover casserole, pour soup over top, sprinkle with cheese, and bake, uncovered, 15 minutes longer.

CRAB EGG FOO YUNG

SAUCE

½ cup chicken broth	1 teaspoon tawny port or dry sherry
1 teaspoon soy sauce	1 teaspoon cornstarch mixed with
¼ teaspoon sugar	1 Tablespoon water

Make sauce by combining ingredients in a small saucepan and stirring over low heat until thickened; set aside.

1 cup crab meat	4 eggs
2 green onions, cut lengthwise,	½ teaspoon salt
then sliced	⅛ teaspoon pepper
1¼ cups fresh bean sprouts	⅛ teaspoon garlic powder
½ cup thinly sliced mushrooms	2 Tablespoons oil for frying

Flake crab meat into a large bowl, add onions, bean sprouts, and mushrooms. Beat eggs with salt (omit salt if using canned crab meat), pepper, and garlic powder, then mix all ingredients together.

Heat a large frying pan over moderate heat, add enough oil to cover the bottom, and ladle in one-fourth of the egg mixture. Cook the omelette until set and golden brown, about 1 minute, then turn to cook the other side the same. Remove to a plate and keep warm while cooking the other 3 omelettes. Add oil to the pan as needed. When all are cooked, pour a little hot sauce on each and serve at once.

CRAB TOFU SOUP

3/4 pound crab meat	1 teaspoon grated ginger
1/2 package (2 cakes) tofu	2 cans concentrated chicken broth
2 Tablespoons oil	2 mushrooms, sliced
1/2 cup chopped green onion	2 Tablespoons dry sherry
1 clove garlic, minced	Salt and pepper to taste

Flake crab meat and set aside. Rinse, drain, and cut tofu into 1/2-inch cubes. Heat oil in a large skillet, add onion, garlic, ginger, and tofu and sauté for a minute or two. Pour in chicken broth diluted with 1 can of water, add mushrooms, and bring to a boil. Stir in sherry and crab meat, salt and pepper if needed, simmer for 2–3 minutes, and serve.

CRAB BISQUE

1 live Dungeness crab	2 medium carrots, grated
2 quarts water	1 onion, chopped
2 teaspoons salt	3 Tablespoons butter
3 sprigs plus 1/4 cup minced parsley	1 cup dry white wine
4 peppercorns	1 cup Thick Béchamel Sauce (p. 417)
1/2 bay leaf	1 cup half-and-half
1/2 teaspoon thyme	1/4 cup brandy

Clean live crab as instructed on page 10 and crack the shells. Boil 2 quarts salted water in a large pot, add the 3 sprigs of parsley, the peppercorns, bay leaf, thyme, and crab. Simmer 15 minutes from the time the water returns to a boil, then remove crab. Cool, pick meat from shells, and reserve.

Sauté carrots and onion in butter until tender, then add them, the wine, and picked empty shells to the broth and boil slowly for 30 minutes. Strain broth into a clean saucepan, discarding solids, and reserve.

Make béchamel sauce, beat it into the broth, then add half-and-half and brandy. Stir in reserved crab meat and the 1/4 cup of minced parsley. Add salt and pepper as necessary, heat to simmer for a minute, and serve.

SHE-CRAB SOUP (BLUE CRAB)

12 heavy she-crabs with roe*	1 ½ teaspoons grated onion
4 quarts boiling water	1 teaspoon grated lemon rind
4 Tablespoons salt	½ teaspoon white pepper
1 Tablespoon butter	¼ teaspoon mace
1 Tablespoon flour	1 teaspoon Worcestershire sauce
3 cups milk	Dry sherry
1 cup half-and-half	1 Tablespoon minced parsley

*About 1 cup of flaked canned or frozen crab meat may be used, and 2 hard-boiled egg yolks may be substituted for the roe.

Plunge crabs into boiling salted water, cover, and return to the boiling point. Simmer for 15 minutes. Drain, clean, and shell the crabs. Set the meat, roe, and crab butter aside and keep them cool.

Melt butter in a large, heavy saucepan. Stir in flour and cook for a few seconds. Gradually add milk and half-and-half, stirring constantly with a whisk until smooth. Add onion and lemon rind. When soup is scalding, add crab meat, roe, and crab butter; mix it around with a wooden spoon. Season with salt, white pepper, mace, and Worcestershire sauce. Remove soup from the heat and let it set for 15–20 minutes for the flavors to meld.

Reheat soup briefly. Place a tablespoon of sherry in the bottom of each warmed bowl, ladle in the soup, and garnish with a sprinkle of parsley.

CRAB-STUFFED CUCUMBERS

This low-calorie dish can be made with tomatoes or other vegetables.

1 cup crab meat	1 teaspoon Worcestershire sauce
2 small cucumbers	1 teaspoon grated onion
Salt	1 teaspoon minced parsley
Lemon juice	Hard-boiled egg yolks, sieved
2 heaping Tablespoons mayonnaise	

Pare the cucumbers, slice them in half lengthwise, then scoop out and discard the seeds. Sprinkle lightly with salt and lemon juice and chill.

Mix mayonnaise with Worcestershire sauce, onion, and parsley. Chop crab meat coarsely, toss it with mayonnaise, and mound it into the cucumbers. Serve chilled, sprinkled with egg yolk.

CRAB LOUIS

1 pound lump crab meat	4 hard-boiled eggs, cut in wedges
4 large lettuce leaves	Louis Dressing (p. 426)
4 cups shredded iceberg lettuce	12 black olives
4 tomatoes, cut in wedges	

Place a large crisp lettuce cup on each plate and in it a bed of finely shredded lettuce. Mound one-fourth of the crab on each lettuce bed and arrange tomato and hard-boiled egg wedges around it. Top with dressing and garnish with a few olives.

CRAB SALAD

Place half an avocado, peeled, on a romaine lettuce bed and stuff it with crab meat mixed with Thousand Island Dressing (p. 426).

HORS D'OEUVRES

CRAB SPREAD

2 cups crab meat	1/4 teaspoon salt
Half an 8-ounce package cream cheese	1/2 teaspoon lemon juice
1/3 cup sour cream	1 Tablespoon chopped chives
1/2 teaspoon curry powder	1 Tablespoon capers

Soften cream cheese with sour cream, then blend in curry powder, salt, lemon juice, chives, and capers. Chop crab meat fine and mix with cheese. Serve crab spread on toast rounds, crackers, or sandwiches.

CRAB-STUFFED MUSHROOMS

Remove mushroom stems, chop them fine, and sauté them with minced onion in butter until tender. Remove from heat and mix them with twice the quantity of chopped crab meat. Season with salt and pepper, a little lemon juice, Worcestershire sauce, and mayonnaise. Preheat the oven to 350°F. Heap filling high in the mushroom caps. Bake them on a greased baking sheet for 15–20 minutes.

CRAB COCKTAIL

½ pound fresh crab meat   1 lemon, cut in wedges
Cocktail Sauce I (p. 436)   Snipped parsley

Pick out any cartilage left in fresh chilled crab meat, then portion it into sherbet glasses. Spoon on cocktail sauce, garnish with lemon wedges and a snip of parsley. Serve chilled.

CRAB MEAT BOUCHÉES

2 cups crab meat   ½ teaspoon salt
½ cup chicken broth   ⅛ teaspoon white pepper
½ cup heavy cream   ½ teaspoon tarragon
¼ cup minced mushrooms   2 Tablespoons minced parsley
2½ Tablespoons butter   2 cups oil for deep frying
3 Tablespoons flour

Combine chicken broth and cream, heat to scalding and keep hot. In a saucepan, sauté mushrooms in butter until tender, then mix in flour. Add scalding broth all at once and beat constantly with a whisk until sauce thickens. Cook for 3-4 minutes, then remove from heat and stir in salt, pepper, tarragon, parsley, and crab meat. Spread mixture out onto a platter to cool to room temperature, then cover and refrigerate for 1 hour or more.

Form crab mixture into small balls and deep fry them, a few at a time, in hot (380°F.) oil until golden brown. Drain on toweling and serve the bouchées hot, on wooden cocktail picks.

PARTY-TIME CRAB CHEESEBURGERS

1 pound crab meat   ½ cup minced celery
1 pound sharp Cheddar cheese   1 small can chopped black olives
1½ cups minced onion   ½ cup oil
1 green pepper, minced

Pick over and flake crab meat, grate the cheese, and mince onion, green pepper, and celery. Mix all together, including olives and oil. Refrigerate overnight or for 24 hours.

Preheat the oven to 300°F. Spoon mixture onto hamburger buns, wrap each in foil, and bake for 45-60 minutes.

Lobster

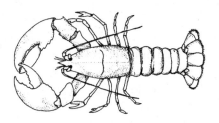

AMERICAN, OR MAINE, LOBSTERS are unequivocally the best in the world. They are found only on the Atlantic Coast, from the Maritime Provinces to North Carolina, and abundantly along the coasts of Maine, Nova Scotia, and Newfoundland. Those taken close to shore weigh between one and five pounds, but deepwater lobsters can weigh as much as forty-five pounds. In the sea they are speckled deep green or brown. These true lobsters have two big claws, one heavier and larger for crushing, the other lighter for snapping.

Adult lobsters live on the sea floor. In very cold weather they semi-hibernate, but as the water warms they become active. They move about using their various pairs of legs, swimmerets, fantail, and feelers, but essentially remain in a certain location along the shore. Lobsters shun the light. They spend their days hiding in rock crevices and other shady places and nights foraging for small fish and any slow-moving small sea creatures — including each other. In warm waters, half-pound-size females (three to four years old) carry eggs. Near the Bay of Fundy, where the waters are cold, females are eight to nine years old (weighing two and a half to three pounds) before they carry eggs.

Claw lobsters are commercially harvested year round. Throughout the nation there are markets selling live lobsters in holding tanks where you can choose your own.

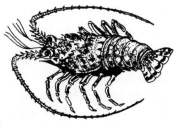

SPINY LOBSTERS are crustaceans related to shrimp and crab. They have no claws; instead they have two long whiplike antennae over the eyes. The color and markings of their segmented bodies differ with species. They are abundant in the Gulf of Mexico, southern Atlantic, and Caribbean. Related species are common in most temperate and tropical seas and are commercially important in areas such as Southern California, Australia, and South Africa.

About Lobster Meat

Lobster meat is lean, white, and firm textured and is at its tender best from lobsters weighing one to three pounds. Fresh lobster, available in local markets, should be actively alive when purchased and cooked. Lobsters may be kept alive for about twelve to fourteen hours if placed in a thick moist sack. (Don't refrigerate spiny lobsters.) Cook lobsters alive or within fifteen minutes of killing. Otherwise, remove the head section immediately and keep the tails (and claws) chilled. Freezing slows deteriorative changes.

Raw lobsters are green, brown, or tan, mottled or spotted; cooking turns the shell pigments bright red. When buying cooked lobster, the tail should be curled tightly under and spring back to that position.

Boiling is the basic method of cooking lobster. Instructions for boiling and opening or killing and cleaning fresh lobsters are on page 11. Boiled lobster meat is used in recipes specifying cooked lobster meat.

Two 1-pound lobsters yield about half a pound of cooked lobster meat.

HOW TO EAT A WHOLE LOBSTER

A whole boiled lobster should be served with the claws already off and cracked and drained of water. If they are not, simply twist them off and crack the shells with a nutcracker. Lay the solid chunk meat of the big claws aside for later consumption and proceed to disjoint and suck out the meat of the tiny claws first. Put the empty shells on a side plate. Pick up the lobster body, arch it backward until the body is separated from the tail section, or cut it apart. Break off the tail fins by bending them backward and use an oyster fork to push the tail meat out of the shell in one whole piece. Separate the front from the back shell, pull it apart, and search out the tasty tidbits in the shell. Place the empty shells on a side plate and then proceed to eat the delectable tail and claw meat, dipping each forkful into melted butter or other sauce.

Frozen Spiny Lobster Tails

Frozen spiny lobster tails are found in the frozen food section of super-markets. When buying them, check the cellophane package to see that it is not damaged, that there are no drips or discolorations — both indications of having been thawed and refrozen. Take only solidly frozen packages that are stacked well below the freezer's frost line.

Several species are marketed, weighing from four ounces to more than a pound each. Lobster tails from Florida and the Bahamas have smooth, brownish green shells, with large yellowish white spots on the first seg- ment of the tail. Southern and Baja California shells are smooth orange red to red brown in color. Australian tails are fairly smooth, reddish brown, with small white dots all over. South African and New Zealand shells are rough, but of a plain deep brownish maroon color. And those from the Mediterranean and southwestern Europe are rough shelled, reddish tan with white streaks and spots.

Lobster tail meat, boiled in the shell, may be used for recipes requiring cooked lobster meat.

One and a half pounds of frozen spiny lobster tails yield about three- fourths of a pound of cooked lobster meat.

BOILED SPINY LOBSTER TAILS

4–6 frozen spiny lobster tails (5–8 ounces each)	1 teaspoon Cognac (optional)
2 quarts boiling water	4 Tablespoons (½ stick) butter, melted (optional)
⅓ cup salt	Juice of 1 lemon (optional)

Put lobster tails in boiling salted water, cover, and return to the boiling point. Simmer them for 10–15 minutes, depending on the size of the tails. Drain and cool them; remove meat from the shells. If, however, the lobsters are to be eaten hot, drain them, then cut the shells in half lengthwise. Pour Cognac over each and serve with lemon-butter sauce, made by mixing the melted butter with the lemon juice.

BROILED SPINY LOBSTER TAILS

4 frozen spiny lobster tails (5–8 ounces each)	⅛ teaspoon dry mustard
4 Tablespoons (½ stick) butter, melted	Salt and white pepper to taste
⅛ teaspoon thyme	8 teaspoons Cognac

Thaw the lobster tails. Cut them in half lengthwise (shell and all), and lay the halves on a hot broiler pan. Brush meat generously with melted butter mixed with thyme and dry mustard, then season with salt and pepper. Broil them 4 inches from the heat, allowing about 10 minutes for smaller size lobsters and 15 for the larger. Pour 1 teaspoon Cognac on the cooked meat of each half and serve the lobsters at once.

LOBSTER OLIVE KABOBS

1½ pounds frozen lobster tails   Salt to taste
Basic French Dressing (p. 427)   1 Tablespoon minced fresh cilantro
½ cup chili sauce   1 jar stuffed olives
¼ teaspoon garlic powder

Thaw frozen lobster tails. Remove meat from shells and cut into 1-inch slices.

Mix a marinade by combining Basic French Dressing and chili sauce, seasoning with garlic powder and salt, and mixing in cilantro. Marinate lobster in the sauce for 15 minutes. Turn the pieces once or twice to marinate evenly.

Alternate lobster and olives on skewers, then grill them 6–8 inches from medium-hot coals. Baste often with marinade and turn skewers for even cooking.

COURT BOUILLON FOR LOBSTER

1 cup white wine   ¼ teaspoon thyme
1 carrot, cut in rings   2 cloves garlic, crushed
1 onion, quartered   2-inch strip orange rind
1 bay leaf   1 teaspoon salt
3 sprigs parsley   3 cups water

Combine all ingredients, bring to a boil, and simmer for 30 minutes. Use as stock for boiling lobsters.

BROILED LOBSTER

For the tenderest broiled lobster, boil them until three-fourths cooked (see page 11 for instructions), then split them lengthwise, remove the intestine and stomach, and place them on a hot broiler pan. Brush meat generously with melted butter, season with salt, pepper, and paprika, and put lobsters under a preheated broiler, 4 inches from the flame, for 5 minutes or until lightly browned. Serve with melted lemon-butter or a sauce.

LOBSTER NEWBURG

1½ cups raw lobster meat, cut in large pieces	2 egg yolks
3 Tablespoons butter	Salt and pepper
¼ cup brandy	Cayenne pepper
⅔ cup Madeira	Paprika
1 cup cream	Rice

Sauté lobster chunks slowly in butter for 5 minutes, then pour in brandy and light it. Spoon pan juices over lobster while it flames, then remove pieces from the pan and keep them warm. Add wine to the pan and boil it down over medium heat until almost entirely reduced. Place cream beaten with egg yolks in the top of a double boiler, whisk in reduced wine and stir constantly, until sauce thickens. Add lobster to the sauce, season with salt, pepper, cayenne, and paprika, and when thoroughly heated, serve it over rice.

LOBSTER THERMIDOR

2 live lobsters, 2 pounds each	2 teaspoons minced fresh tarragon, or 1 teaspoon dried
Olive oil	1 Tablespoon minced parsley
Salt and pepper	2 cups Mornay Sauce (p. 420)
⅔ cup dry white wine	1 teaspoon dry mustard
⅔ cup stock or bouillon	¼ cup grated Parmesan cheese
1 small green onion, minced	

Boil lobsters until three-fourths cooked, cool them enough so you can handle them, then split them lengthwise, clean and place them on a baking sheet, flesh side up. Brush meat (and shells) with oil, season, and put them under a preheated broiler for 5 minutes to finish cooking. When cool enough, remove meat from shells and slice it.

Combine wine, stock, onion, tarragon, and parsley in a saucepan and boil it down until only a tablespoon or two is left. Make Mornay sauce, then beat the reduced wine-herb mixture and mustard into the sauce and season with salt and pepper, if needed.

Preheat the oven to 400°F. Spread half of the sauce equally into the 4 half shells. Mix the rest with sliced lobster meat, then portion meat into the shells. Sprinkle each with Parmesan cheese and put them in the oven until the tops are brown, about 10 minutes.

BAKED LOBSTER STUFFED WITH CRAB

4 live lobsters
1 pound crab meat
16 Saltine crackers, crushed fine
2 Tablespoons (¼ stick) butter, melted
1 Tablespoon dry sherry

Milk
Dash of garlic powder
Salt and white pepper to taste
4 thin slices Cheddar cheese

Place lobster on its back; cut down with a sharp knife between body shell and tail segment to sever the spinal cord. Split lobster in half lengthwise. Remove the stomach, just back of the head, and the intestine that runs from stomach to tail, but leave in all else. Crack the claws.

Preheat the oven to 400°F. Pick over crab meat. Add crumbs and mix with butter, sherry, enough milk to moisten, and season with garlic powder and salt and pepper. Stuff high, with as much dressing as possible in the body cavities and spread over the surface of tail meat. Place a half-slice of cheese over each. Bake for 20–25 minutes until lightly browned.

LOBSTER AMÉRICAINE

2 live lobsters, 1½ pounds each
1 medium onion, chopped
⅓ cup grated carrot
3 Tablespoons butter
Salt and pepper to taste
4 Tablespoons olive oil
2 cloves garlic, minced
1 green onion, minced
¼ cup brandy, heated

½ cup fish or chicken stock
2 cups tomatoes, peeled and chopped
1 cup dry white wine
¼ cup minced parsley
1½ Tablespoons tomato paste
½ teaspoon thyme
1 teaspoon dried tarragon
½ bay leaf

Kill lobsters as directed on page 11. Remove and crack claws (antennae), cut the tail crosswise through the shell into slices, and split the body lengthwise. Discard stomach, but save the coral and tomalley (liver) and reserve in refrigerator.

Sauté onion and carrot slowly in butter until they begin to brown, salt and pepper them, then remove from heat.

Heat oil in a large, heavy skillet and sauté lobsters (legs and body included) until shells are red and meat is firm. Pour out half of the oil, add garlic and green onion, and sauté for a minute more. Add warm brandy and light it. When the flame dies, stir in sautéed vegetables, stock, tomatoes, wine, parsley, tomato paste, thyme, tarragon, and bay leaf.

Bring to the boiling point, then cover and simmer slowly for 15 minutes. Add the coral and tomalley in the last minute of cooking.

Remove lobster from the sauce, take meat from the shells and keep it warm; discard the shells. Put sauce through a food mill, then return it to the pan and correct seasoning with salt and pepper. You may thicken the sauce with Beurre Manié (p. 430). Add lobster meat to the sauce and warm it through. Serve with rice, in a pastry shell, or soufflé.

Variation: You may add to this recipe ½ cup thick cream in the sauce and ¼ pound cooked mushrooms to the lobster meat, and use the sauce and filling for lobster crepes.

LOBSTER WITH FRESH HERBS

2 cups cooked lobster meat
6 Tablespoons (¾ stick) butter
1 Tablespoon each fresh minced
   dillweed (or tarragon), parsley,
   and chives

2 Tablespoons dry white wine
Salt and white pepper to taste

Cut lobster into ½-inch slices. Melt butter in a skillet and when foam subsides, add lobster. Stir to coat well with butter and cook to a delicate brown. Mix in herbs, then wine, and simmer 2 minutes longer. Season with salt and pepper and serve on hot toast points.

DEEP-FRIED LOBSTER

2 frozen spiny lobster tails
2 Tablespoons cornstarch
1 egg, beaten
1 Tablespoon water
Oil for deep frying

Salt and white pepper to taste
Hot mustard
Chili sauce
Soy sauce

Thaw lobster tails. Remove meat from the shells and cut it into ½-inch slices. Mix cornstarch, egg, and water in a bowl, add lobster, and stir the pieces around.

Heat oil to 350°F. and drop the pieces one by one into the hot oil. Nudge and turn lobster to cook evenly, and remove pieces as they turn golden. Drain on toweling and sprinkle with salt and pepper. Serve with small dishes of hot mustard, chili sauce, and soy sauce to dip the lobster in.

LOBSTER WITH PORK IN CHICKEN BROTH

2 live lobsters, 1½ pounds each
4 Tablespoons vegetable oil
2 cloves garlic, crushed
¾ pound lean raw pork, minced fine
3 Tablespoons soy sauce
1 teaspoon salt
1 teaspoon sugar

½ teaspoon pepper
1¾ cups chicken broth
1½ teaspoons cornstarch
3 Tablespoons cold water
1 egg, beaten
3 green onions, minced

Kill lobsters as directed on page 11. Remove and crack claws and legs. Cut the tail crosswise (through the shell) into 1-inch slices and split the body lengthwise. Discard stomach, but save the coral and tomalley (liver); set them aside and keep them cool.

Heat oil in a large, heavy skillet or wok and sauté lobsters (legs and body included) until shells are red and meat is firm. Remove lobster from pan and keep warm.

Pour out all but 1 tablespoon of oil. Heat remaining oil with garlic, add pork and fry quickly until brown. Add soy sauce, salt, sugar, pepper, and stir in chicken broth. Add lobster pieces. Bring to the boiling point, then cover and simmer slowly for 10 minutes. (At this point, you may remove lobster meat from shells, or keep lobster as is, and eat it from the shell when served.)

Mix cornstarch with cold water and stir it into the broth until the sauce becomes thickened and smooth. Add coral and tomalley in the last minute. Remove from heat, add beaten egg and onions, stir again, and serve.

LOBSTER WITH TOFU IN MISO SAUCE

2 live lobsters, 1½ pounds each
1-pound package tofu
1 (heaping) Tablespoon white miso*
3 cloves garlic, minced
1 Tablespoon minced ginger
1 Tablespoon dry sherry and soy sauce

½ teaspoon sugar
1 Tablespoon cornstarch
1¼ cups chicken broth
3 Tablespoons vegetable oil
¼ cup minced green onion

*See Glossary.

Boil lobsters as instructed on page 11. Cut tofu in ¾-inch cubes, rinse briefly under cold water, then drain in a colander until ready to use. When lobsters are cool enough, shell them and cut meat into bite-size pieces. Mix white miso and garlic in a small dish. Combine ginger, sherry, soy sauce, and sugar in another dish and set aside. In a third dish, mix cornstarch with cold chicken broth.

Heat oil very hot in a heavy skillet or wok, add miso-garlic and stir over medium heat for about 30 seconds. Add lobster meat, mix and coat it thoroughly with the bean paste. Stir in soy-sherry mixture, then add chicken broth mixed with cornstarch. Heat and stir sauce until it thickens, then add tofu. Reduce heat and simmer slowly for 5 minutes, until tofu is heated through. Serve sprinkled with minced onion.

LOBSTER STEW

3/4 pound cooked lobster meat
2 Tablespoons (1/4 stick) butter
1 teaspoon flour
2 cups milk
2 cups half-and-half

Salt and pepper to taste
Dash of nutmeg
Dash of paprika
2 Tablespoons minced parsley

Cut lobster in small pieces. Melt butter in the top of a double boiler, add flour, and blend to a smooth paste. Gradually add milk and half-and-half, stirring constantly. Add lobster, season with salt, pepper, and a dash of nutmeg; heat almost to the boiling point. Serve in bowls, garnished with a dash of paprika and a sprinkle of parsley.

LOBSTER-ARTICHOKE SALAD

1 cup cooked lobster meat, chopped
1 head lettuce
Basic French Dressing (p. 427)
1/2 teaspoon dry mustard
1 jar marinated artichoke hearts

Tomato slices
Mayonnaise
Stuffed olives
Anchovy fillets

Take 3 large outside lettuce leaves and chop them fine with lobster. Moisten the chopped mixture with French dressing flavored with dry mustard, then refrigerate until ready to serve.

Place lettuce cups on 4 individual salad plates; shred more lettuce into them to make shallow beds. Mound lobster mixture on artichoke hearts and set them in the center of lettuce beds.

Arrange half-slices of tomato on the sides, dab them with mayonnaise, and place a stuffed olive, wrapped in an anchovy fillet, on the mayonnaise. Mix the marinade from artichoke hearts with remaining French dressing and spoon it on the salads.

LOBSTER ORANGE COCKTAIL

2 cups cooked lobster meat   Lettuce
1 cup orange segments, sliced
½ cup Fish Cocktail Mayonnaise
   (p. 425)

Chop lobster coarsely and fold with orange into fish cocktail mayonnaise; refrigerate for at least 1 hour to let the flavors blend. Serve in sherbet dishes lined with lettuce leaves.

HORS D'OEUVRES

LOBSTER BALLS

1 cup cooked lobster meat   1 teaspoon grated onion
1 cup potato (from freshly baked   ⅛ teaspoon anchovy paste
   potatoes)   1 egg, beaten
1 Tablespoon butter   Salt and pepper

Put lobster through the meat grinder, using the finest blade. Mash potato well. Mash in butter, onion, anchovy paste, and beaten egg; season with salt and pepper. When thoroughly mixed, form the mixture into 1-inch balls, then chill for about 1 hour. Deep fry lobster balls in hot (390°F.) oil until golden brown. Drain briefly on toweling and serve hot.

LOBSTER SPREAD

1 cup cooked lobster meat, minced   Dollop of mayonnaise
1 teaspoon lime or lemon juice
1 Tablespoon each minced parsley,
   onion, and capers

Mix all ingredients in a bowl and chill until ready to use. Serve on small toast rounds.

Shrimp

EDIBLE SHRIMP, both large and small species, are commercially fished from the Pacific, Atlantic, and Gulf coasts. However, the preponderance of shrimp comes from the Gulf of Mexico. In the Gulf, shrimp spawn in deep water and the young come inshore to live in mangrove creeks, canals, and bays until half grown. By day, they bury themselves in sand or mud, covering themselves completely by sweeping up sand with their antennae. After dark, the shrimp climb out, walking on two pairs of their hind legs, feeling their way with the front two pairs. They swim along the bottom using their tail swimmerets as paddles and can dart backward by suddenly bending their tails forward. When shrimp leave the coast on their migrations to deep water, the males are the first to leave. The females then follow to the breeding grounds.

The difference between shrimp and prawns is that in many areas the big ones are called prawns. Academically, the difference is in the upper half or heads of the animals.

Prawns such as the Northern prawn, found from Greenland to Martha's Vineyard, are a deepwater species. Few people see these prawns in their whole raw state, because they are usually cooked at sea aboard the otter trawlers that capture them. Large prawns, five inches or so, are commonly taken from Alaskan waters, too.

About Shrimp Meat

Whole fresh shrimp with the heads on are available in areas where shrimp boats come in. Buy only those that have a milk-fresh smell and shiny shells that tightly hug meat and that feel firm and springy when squeezed. Most of the catch is immediately processed to remove the inedible head section, leaving the edible tails. The raw tails are size graded; some are flash frozen with fantails on, some without. Others are peeled, cleaned, breaded, and packaged frozen. Read the label to know what quality shrimp you are buying and the amount of breading on them. When buying frozen shrimp, also check carefully to see that the container is intact and the cellophane packages are not discolored—a sign of freezer burn. Avoid those with "drip" or ice on the package, an indication that the contents may have been thawed and refrozen, and avoid packages that are stacked above the frost line of the store's freezer. Take only solidly frozen packages.

Shrimp are sold according to size:

Jumbo.	15 or fewer shrimp to the pound.
Large.	15 to 23 shrimp to the pound.
Medium.	23 to 30-plus shrimp to the pound.
Tiny.	60 or more shrimp to the pound.

All shrimp have the same distinctive flavor and food value, but the price varies considerably: the smaller the size of shrimp, the less expensive per pound.

Boiling is the basic method of cooking raw shrimp. They may be boiled and then peeled or peeled and then boiled. Note that the amount of salt used in the boiling water is different for peeled or unpeeled.

BOILING SHRIMP BEFORE PEELING

1 ½ pounds raw shrimp   ¼ cup salt
1 quart boiling water

Wash shrimp, then drop them into rapidly boiling salted water. Cover, return to the boiling point, and cook at a high simmer for 4–6 minutes. Sample one; if it is undercooked, the taste will tell you. Cooked shrimp will be opaque in the center, juicy and almost crunchy, and easy to peel. Drain, then peel and remove black sand veins. Rinse shrimp again and refrigerate until ready to use.

BOILING SHRIMP AFTER PEELING

1 ½ pounds raw shrimp   2 Tablespoons salt
1 quart boiling water

Peel shrimp. Make a shallow cut lengthwise down the back of each shrimp and remove the black vein. Wash shrimp, then drop them into boiling salted water. Cover, return to the boiling point, and cook at high simmer for 4–6 minutes. Drain, remove any particles of black vein remaining, and refrigerate until ready to use.

BUTTERFLYING SHRIMP

Wash shrimp and dry on toweling. Remove shells carefully, but leave the fantails attached. Cut shrimp halfway through around the inner curve and spread shrimp out flat. Remove black vein.

TO SAUTÉ SHRIMP

Raw shrimp in the shell may be sautéed in clarified garlic butter (or tossed in butter and oil, peanut oil, lard, etc., with garlic) until the shells turn red and meat is cooked.

SHRIMP TERIYAKI

16-20 raw jumbo shrimp
2/3 cup soy sauce
2/3 cup mirin*
1/3 cup sugar

2 Tablespoons peanut oil
2 Tablespoons sesame oil
1 clove garlic, crushed

*See Glossary.

Peel and devein shrimp and put them in a bowl. Combine soy sauce, mirin, sugar, oils, and garlic; pour the mixture over the shrimp and marinate for several hours.

Skewer each shrimp on a wooden skewer that has been soaked in water for 10 minutes. Broil in the oven or grill over hot coals for 3-4 minutes on each side. Serve on the skewers with warmed marinade and rice.

SHRIMP KABOBS
WITH BACON AND PINEAPPLE

1 1/2 pounds raw shrimp
4 slices bacon
1 (28-ounce) can sliced pineapple
1 Tablespoon Dijon-type mustard
Juice of 1 lime

1 teaspoon sugar
1 teaspoon salt
Pepper to taste
Dash of cayenne pepper
8 Tablespoons (1 stick) butter, melted

Peel and devein shrimp, rinse and drain them on toweling. Cut bacon in squares and pineapple slices in quarters. Spear alternating pieces of each on skewers. Combine remaining ingredients and brush sauce over the kabobs. Grill 6-8 inches over medium-hot coals. Turn the skewers as needed and baste frequently while cooking.

TANDOORI SHRIMP

24 raw large shrimp
¼ cup peanut oil
¼ cup lemon juice
1 Tablespoon grated onion
1 clove garlic, crushed
1 teaspoon minced fresh ginger
½ teaspoon ground coriander seed
¼ teaspoon ground cumin seed

¼ teaspoon sugar
¼ teaspoon curry powder
Pinch each of ground clove and
    cinnamon
Dash of pepper
1 hot red pepper, seeded and
    crushed

Peel shrimp, remove veins, and put shrimp in a nonmetal bowl. Place all other ingredients in a blender and whirl for a few seconds to blend, then pour the marinating sauce over shrimp and mix well. Cover and refrigerate overnight.

When ready to grill, drain shrimp briefly, then thread 6 shrimp on each of 2 skewers, to hold them steady. Grill them 6–8 inches from medium-hot coals, turning and basting often with marinade, until pink and cooked, about 10 minutes.

BAKED SHRIMP WITH FETA CHEESE

1½ pounds raw shrimp
4 Tablespoons olive oil
1 clove garlic, minced
3 cups canned plum tomatoes
1 green onion, chopped
½ teaspoon basil

½ teaspoon oregano
Dash of cayenne pepper
Salt and pepper to taste
¼ pound feta cheese
Juice of 1 lemon
Sprig parsley, minced

Peel and devein shrimp. Heat olive oil in a skillet, add garlic and shrimp, and sauté them for 30 seconds or so, just until shrimp turn pink, then remove them immediately from the pan and set aside. Add tomatoes to the skillet; break them up with a wooden spoon. Stir in onion, basil, oregano, and cayenne. Cook over low heat for 10 minutes, stirring occasionally. Season with salt and pepper.

Preheat the oven to 350°F.

Cut large shrimp in half and divide them among 4 ramekins or scallop shells. Spoon equal amounts of sauce over the shrimp, sprinkle crumbled cheese over the tops, and bake until bubbly. Squeeze lemon juice on tops, garnish with parsley, and serve at once.

FOIL-BAKED SHRIMP

1 1/2 pounds raw shrimp
1/2 pound mushrooms, quartered
1/3 cup minced parsley
1/4 cup chopped green onion
8 Tablespoons (1 stick) butter
Juice of 1/2 lemon

1 Tablespoon chili sauce
1/2 teaspoon garlic powder
1 teaspoon salt
1 teaspoon Worcestershire sauce
Dash of Tabasco

Peel and devein shrimp. Sauté mushrooms, parsley, and green onion in butter until tender, then add lemon juice, chili sauce, and seasonings. Mix well and remove from heat.

Preheat the oven to 425°F. if oven is to be used to cook shrimp. Cut 4 pieces of heavy-duty foil in 12-inch squares. Portion shrimp on 1 side of each piece of foil. Put equal amounts of mushrooms and sauce over them. Fold the foil over the shrimp and double fold the edges, making tight packages. Place packages about 4–5 inches from medium-hot coals, or in the oven for 10–12 minutes.

CURRIED SHRIMP

2 pounds raw shrimp
Flour
4 Tablespoons (1/2 stick) butter
2 cloves garlic, pressed
1/4 cup brandy
Salt and pepper

1/2 pound mushrooms, sliced
2 cups Mornay Sauce (p. 420)
2 teaspoons curry powder
1/4 cup grated Cheddar or Parmesan
   cheese
Rice

Peel and devein shrimp. Dust them lightly with flour and sauté quickly in butter until almost cooked. Add garlic, stir in brandy, and spoon juices over the shrimp for a minute; season with salt and pepper. Remove shrimp with a slotted spoon, arrange them in a shallow baking dish, and set them aside.

Cook mushrooms in the shrimp pan juices, then remove them with a slotted spoon and spread them among the shrimp. Boil down the pan juices until they are almost entirely reduced.

Preheat the oven to 450°F. Make Mornay Sauce, stir in curry powder and reduced pan juices. Pour sauce over shrimp and mushrooms, sprinkle with grated cheese, and put in the oven until the top browns. Serve with rice.

SHRIMP DE JONGHE

1 ½ pounds raw shrimp
4 Tablespoons (½ stick) butter,
  softened
1 teaspoon each fresh minced parsley,
  chives, shallot, tarragon, and
  chervil; or ¼ teaspoon dried
Pinch of thyme

2 cloves garlic, pressed
½ teaspoon salt
Pepper to taste
1 cup fine bread crumbs
Several drops of Tabasco
⅓ cup dry sherry

Cream butter until very soft, blend in herbs, garlic, salt, and pepper, and let mixture mellow for several hours. Then mix in crumbs, Tabasco, and sherry, and refrigerate until ready to use.

Parboil shrimp in salted water for 2 minutes, and when cool enough shell and clean them.

Preheat the oven to 400°F. Butter 4 individual ramekins or scallop shells and place alternating layers of shrimp and crumbs in each, topping with the crumb mixture. Bake for about 15 minutes, then serve.

SHRIMP STUFFED WITH CRAB

12 raw jumbo shrimp
½ pound crab meat
1 Tablespoon sherry or sake
2 egg whites

¼ teaspoon salt
Dash of monosodium glutamate
Oil or lard for frying
12 parsley snips

SAUCE

⅓ cup chicken broth
1 teaspoon sherry or sake
½ teaspoon cornstarch
1 green onion, minced

1 Tablespoon butter
Dash each of salt and monosodium
  glutamate

Shell shrimp, carefully leaving on the fantail. Slit the back (almost through) lengthwise to the tail. Remove the veins and spread the shrimp flat; set aside and keep cool.

Now make sauce: Combine chicken broth, sherry, and cornstarch in a small bowl. Sauté onion in butter until limp, add chicken mixture, and stir while heating, until sauce thickens slightly. Add a dash of salt and monosodium glutamate if you like, then set aside.

Flake crab meat and mix sherry with it. Beat egg whites until stiff, add salt (if using canned crab, salt is not needed) and monosodium glutamate, then mix crab into egg whites. Pile crab mixture on the shrimp. Heat oil or lard in a wide skillet and fry shrimp until done. Lift shrimp covered with crab very carefully from pan and arrange them on a warmed platter. Spoon a bit of sauce over each shrimp, garnish with a parsley snip, and serve.

SHRIMP ETOUFFÉE

2 cups fresh small shrimp, cleaned
1½ Tablespoons butter
1 green pepper, chopped
1 stalk celery, chopped
¼ cup minced onion

1 Tablespoon minced garlic
½ cup chopped green onion
Salt and pepper to taste
Parsley-buttered rice

Melt butter in a skillet and sauté green pepper, celery, and onion until tender. Add shrimp, garlic, green onion, and salt and pepper. Cover and cook slowly for about 10 minutes. Serve over parsley-buttered rice.

SHRIMP AND MUSHROOM IN CREAM SAUCE

1½ pounds raw large shrimp, peeled
  and deveined
¼ cup minced onion
½ cup minced leek (white part only)
4 Tablespoons (½ stick) butter
½ pound button mushrooms
¼ cup brandy, warm

1½ cups Rhine wine
⅔ cup sour cream
⅔ cup heavy cream
Salt and pepper
Cayenne pepper
Rice

Sauté onion and leek slowly in butter until tender, add mushrooms, and cook another 5 minutes. Add shrimp, stir them around in the pan, then add brandy. Stir shrimp to cook evenly. When they are pink on the outside and opaque in the center, remove them and mushrooms with a slotted spoon to a bowl and keep them warm.

Add wine and sour and heavy creams to the pan and cook over high heat, stirring constantly, until the sauce is reduced to half the original amount. Return shrimp and mushrooms to the pan to reheat briefly, season sauce with salt and pepper and cayenne, and serve with rice.

SHRIMP MARINIÈRE

1½ pounds raw shrimp	2 egg yolks
2 shallots	½ cup light cream
2 cups dry white wine	Juice of ½ lemon
1 cup chicken, fish, or oyster stock	Toast points
2 Tablespoons (¼ stick) butter	Snipped parsley
2 Tablespoons flour	

Peel and devein shrimp; mince shallots. Put both in a saucepan with wine and stock, bring to a boil, and simmer 4–6 minutes. Remove cooked shrimp from broth and set them aside. Keep broth hot. Melt butter in another saucepan, blend in flour, and cook for a minute or two. Add hot broth, stirring vigorously with a wire whisk until sauce becomes smooth and thickened. Return shrimp to the sauce and heat to the boiling point. Beat egg yolks with cream and lemon juice, then stir it into the sauce. Remove from heat immediately, serve on toast points, and garnish with parsley.

DEEP-FRIED SHRIMP STUFFED WITH WALNUTS AND HAM

Peel, clean, and slit 24 shrimp as in Deep-fried Shrimp Stuffed with Almond and Bacon (p. 398). Replace almonds and bacon with shelled and skinned walnuts (don't fry or salt them), and prosciutto ham. Dip shrimp in egg mixture, then in flour, and deep fry as in that recipe.

SHRIMP TEMPURA

Tempura is deep-fried food—fish or vegetable—dipped in a batter that becomes lacy light and golden crisp, served with a dipping sauce and grated white radish or ginger.

Tempura-fried fish may be served with any sauce for fried fish such as a mixture of half soy and half tomato sauce, or tartar sauce, etc.

16 raw jumbo shrimp	1 small green pepper
1 large carrot	1 quart vegetable oil
4 large white mushrooms	¼ cup sesame oil
1 zucchini	1 white radish (daikon), grated

Butterfly and devein shrimp (p. 11), leaving the fantail on, then dry them carefully and chill until ready to use. Cut vegetables into ¼-inch-thick pieces, about as large as prawns; slice carrot diagonally, mushrooms vertically, zucchini and green pepper in strips. Arrange them on a tray and chill until you are ready to cook them.

Tempura Sauce

Dipping sauce may be made in advance and poured into individual small condiment bowls. Serve grated radish in a separate dish.

1 cup dashi, cold*
¼ cup soy sauce
¼ cup sake or dry sherry

1 Tablespoon grated ginger
1 teaspoon sugar

*See Mackerel Fillets in Miso Broth, page 249, for directions on making dashi broth.

Tempura Batter

The secret of good tempura is the batter. Batter should be kept cold and put together with the least possible mixing. It can be made while frying oil is heating.

1 cup ice water
1 egg
½ teaspoon salt

½ teaspoon baking soda
1 cup plus 2 Tablespoons all-purpose
(or cake) flour, unsifted

Beat water, egg, salt, and soda together slightly. Add 1 cup of the flour all at once and stir only until flour is moistened. Add 2 more tablespoons of the flour and let it remain on top without mixing it in. Batter should be lumpy. Keep batter chilled by putting the batter bowl in a bowl of cracked ice.

Combine oils and heat to 350°–70°F. Test by dropping a small bit of batter in the oil. If it rises immediately to the surface, the oil is at the correct temperature.

Holding shrimp by the tail (or using tongs), dip shrimp, then a vegetable or two, into the batter and let the excess drip back into the bowl. Lower them into hot oil and fry for 2–3 minutes, turning as needed. Lift food out with a slotted spoon and remove any excess batter that remains in the oil. Drain pieces on a wire rack or toweling and serve at once with tempura sauce.

Variation: Tempura-fried shrimp may also be served with Sweet-and-Sour Pineapple Sauce (p. 38).

DEEP-FRIED SHRIMP WITH SESAME SEED

1½ pounds raw shrimp   1 cup toasted sesame seeds
Beer Batter (p. 20)   Oil for deep frying

Make beer batter and let it rest while cleaning shrimp. Peel shrimp, leaving on the fantail, slit to remove the black vein, rinse, and drain.

Hold shrimp by the fantail, dip in batter, then in sesame seeds, picking up as many seeds as will cling. Place several shrimp at a time in a wire basket and deep fry in hot (375°F.) oil until golden, but not brown.

DEEP-FRIED SHRIMP STUFFED
WITH ALMOND AND BACON

24 large raw shrimp   ¼ cup milk
4 strips bacon   1½ teaspoons salt
⅓ cup blanched almonds   Flour
2 eggs, beaten   Oil for deep frying

Fry bacon until soft, drain and shred. Heat almonds in a little oil until they turn light golden. Drain and salt them, then when they are cool chop them coarsely and combine them with the bacon.

Peel shrimp, leaving on the fantail, and slit and devein them without opening them out. Stuff half a teaspoon or so of the almond-bacon in the slit of each shrimp, then push the edges of the slit together gently.

Mix eggs, milk, and salt. Dip shrimp in mixture, then roll in flour. Deep fry in hot (375°F.) oil until golden. Drain on toweling and serve.

SHRIMP WON TON

½ pound raw shrimp   ¼ teaspoon sugar
1 raw pork chop   ¼ teaspoon salt
2 green onions, minced   Dash of pepper
2 large mushrooms, minced   1 teaspoon cornstarch
4 water chestnuts, minced   1 egg white
1 teaspoon minced cilantro   1 package won ton skins
1 Tablespoon soy sauce   Chili sauce and hot mustard for
1 Tablespoon dry sherry   dipping

Cut pork into strips and put both pork and shrimp through a food grinder, using a medium blade, or purée in a food processor. Mix vegetables with ground meat. Add soy sauce, sherry, seasonings, cornstarch, and egg white, and mix ingredients thoroughly.

Place a scant teaspoon of filling in the center of each won ton skin. Slightly moisten the edges of the skin with water so the edges will stick together. Fold each skin in half, making a triangle, pinch the seams together, then fold the points inward, bringing them almost together.

Arrange won ton on a platter lined with plastic or aluminum foil. Place them so they don't touch. Cover with plastic and refrigerate until cooking time.

Deep fry 5–6 won ton at a time in hot (360°F.) oil, nudging and turning until they become evenly golden brown, about a minute or two.

Serve them hot or at room temperature, with chili sauce and hot mustard for dipping.

To make won ton soup: Cook won tons in a large amount of boiling salted water for 5 minutes. Drain them in a colander and rinse briefly with hot water. Drop them into 1½ quarts of hot chicken broth. Bring to a boil and serve.

JAMBALAYA

1½ pounds raw medium shrimp, peeled and deveined	1 clove garlic, minced
1 Tablespoon bacon (or other) fat	¼ teaspoon ground bay leaf
1 Tablespoon flour	¼ teaspoon thyme
1 onion, minced	1 Tablespoon Worcestershire sauce
⅓ cup chopped green pepper	1¼ teaspoons salt
1 cup diced cooked ham	Pepper to taste
3 cups tomatoes, peeled and chopped	¼ teaspoon cayenne pepper
3 cups stock or water	1 cup uncooked rice

Melt fat in a Dutch oven, add flour, and stir constantly until brown. Add onion, green pepper, and ham and cook, stirring, for 5 minutes. Mix in tomatoes, stock, garlic, spices, Worcestershire sauce, salt, pepper, and cayenne. Cook for 2–3 minutes, then add rice and shrimp. Cover, bring to a boil, stir, then simmer slowly until rice is cooked.

Serve from Dutch oven.

SHRIMP GUMBO

2½ pounds raw shrimp
2 cups water
2 cups fresh or frozen okra, sliced
1 teaspoon oil
4 Tablespoons (½ stick) butter
2 Tablespoons flour
1 large onion, chopped
1 small green pepper, chopped coarse
1 stalk celery, sliced
1 cup (8-ounce bottle) clam juice

6 tomatoes, peeled and quartered (or
   a large can Italian plum tomatoes)
10-ounce can concentrated chicken
   broth
1 can water
1 bay leaf
¼ teaspoon thyme
½ red pepper, seeded and crushed
Salt and pepper
Minced parsley

Wash, peel, and devein shrimp and set them aside. Put shrimp shells in a saucepan with 2 cups water, simmer for 15 minutes, then strain shells out and reserve the water.

In a small pan, sauté okra in oil for 7–8 minutes and set aside.

In a Dutch oven over low heat, melt butter, blend in flour, and stir the roux until it is a rich golden color. Add onion, green pepper, and celery; sauté until soft. Mix in clam juice and reserved shrimp water, beating with a whisk until smooth and thickened. Add tomatoes, chicken broth, the can of water, cooked okra, spices, and salt and pepper to taste. Cover and let simmer, stirring frequently, for about 30 minutes. Add shrimp and simmer for 10 minutes longer. Serve in soup plates garnished with parsley.

SHRIMP IN GRAPEFRUIT CUPS

24 cooked shrimp
2 large grapefruit
A mayonnaise, vinaigrette dressing,
   or sour cream or yogurt sauce
   (pp. 428–9)

4 small sprigs mint

Halve the grapefruits and carefully cut loose the segments with a sharp knife. Remove the sections, being careful to keep them as whole as possible, and place the fruit in a bowl. Cut out the white divider pulp to make cups of the grapefruit halves. Arrange 6 shrimp in each cup, then spoon grapefruit sections back into the cups. Serve chilled, with choice of dressing, and garnish with mint sprigs.

SHRIMP AND AVOCADO MOUSSE

¾ pound cooked shrimp	½ Tablespoon minced pimiento
1 Tablespoon gelatin	½ cup chopped celery
¼ cup cold water	1 Tablespoon grated onion
½ cup boiling water	¼ teaspoon salt
2 Tablespoons lemon juice	Dash of Tabasco
1 Tablespoon Worcestershire sauce	½ cup mashed avocado
2 Tablespoons chili sauce	¼ cup mayonnaise

Devein large shrimp and cut in half. Soften gelatin in cold water for 5 minutes. Add boiling water and stir until dissolved. Stir in shrimp and all ingredients except avocado and mayonnaise. Chill until almost congealed. Mix mayonnaise with avocado and fold into the gelatin. Rinse a mold in cold water, then pour in mousse and chill until firm. Unmold onto a bed of lettuce.

SHRIMP WALDORF SALAD

¾ pound cooked shrimp	Salt and pepper to taste
1 cup diced apples	1 Tablespoon lemon juice
1 cup diced celery	¾ cup mayonnaise
½ cup walnut meats	Lettuce leaves

Devein and cut large shrimp in half. Combine shrimp, apples, celery, and walnuts in a bowl, season with salt and pepper, sprinkle with lemon juice, and mix in mayonnaise. Arrange lettuce cups on salad plates and mound shrimp mixture in the center. Serve chilled.

HORS D'OEUVRES

SHRIMP COCKTAIL

24 boiled shrimp, peeled and deveined	Cocktail Sauce II (p. 436)
Lettuce leaves	Lemon or lime wedges

Place 6 shrimp in each lettuce-lined cocktail or sherbet dish and spoon cocktail sauce over them equally. Serve with lemon or lime wedges.

SPICED SHRIMP

1½ pounds raw shrimp
Bunch of celery tops
1 large onion, coarsely chopped
Bunch of parsley
6 cloves garlic, chopped
1½ teaspoons black peppercorns
1½ teaspoons whole allspice
1½ teaspoons crushed bay leaf

1 small red pepper
¾ teaspoon whole cloves
2 Tablespoons Worcestershire sauce
6 Tablespoons lemon juice
¼ cup salt
1 quart water or beer (beer gives a
  more distinct taste)

Wash shrimp, but don't remove shells. Tie vegetables and whole spices in a piece of cheesecloth. Combine all ingredients, except shrimp, and simmer, covered, for 30 minutes. Add shrimp, cover, return to the boiling point, and simmer 5 minutes or until shrimp are cooked. Serve cold or at room temperature unshelled or shelled, and serve on wooden cocktail picks.

SHRIMP CANAPÉS

⅔ cup chopped boiled shrimp
2 Tablespoons (¼ stick) butter, melted
1 teaspoon lemon juice
Salt
Mustard
Bread rounds fried in olive oil

½ Tablespoon gelatin
1½ Tablespoons cold water
⅔ cup mayonnaise
Tiny shrimp for garnish
Minced parsley

Put shrimp meat through the food grinder, or purée in a food mill; then mix in melted butter, lemon juice, salt, and mustard to taste. Spread rounds of fried bread with mounds of shrimp spread. Place these on a cake rack set over a plate.

Soften gelatin in cold water, set the dish in hot water, and stir until it dissolves. When gelatin has a thick syrupy consistency, stir it gently into the mayonnaise, so no bubbles form in the aspic. Pour this over the shrimp mounds, letting the excess run off. Chill until the glaze is firm.

More coats may be added for thicker glaze, but each coat must be congealed before the next is added. Garnish the shiny, smooth mounds with tiny shrimp and parsley tips.

MARINATED SHRIMP

1 pound boiled shrimp
1/3 cup salad oil
1/4 cup tarragon-flavored vinegar
1 teaspoon sugar
1 Tablespoon grated onion
2 Tablespoons minced pimiento

2 Tablespoons minced green pepper
1 teaspoon celery salt
Salt and white pepper
Dash of cayenne pepper
Sprigs watercress

Shell and devein shrimp. Make a marinade by mixing together all other ingredients in a glass bowl. Toss shrimp gently in the marinade and refrigerate for 2–4 hours before serving. Stir shrimp occasionally. Drain marinated shrimp and serve them on crushed ice with sprigs of watercress.

CHILLED SHRIMP WITH DIPPING SAUCE

24 large shrimp, boiled

Peel, devein, and chill shrimp until ready to use. Then arrange them attractively on a serving tray garnished with parsley, lettuce, watercress, or cilantro. Accompany shrimp with a bowl of dipping sauce. Some suggestions for sauce are:

Homemade Mayonnaise (p. 424).

Louis Dressing (p. 426).

Cream cheese, softened with milk, seasoned with 1 tablespoon grated onion and 1/4 teaspoon dillweed.

3 ounces softened cream cheese, mixed with 1 ounce Roquefort cheese, 1 teaspoon chopped chives, and 1/2 teaspoon prepared mustard.

Curried mayonnaise, made with 1 cup mayonnaise, 1 teaspoon curry powder, 1 teaspoon lemon juice, 1 clove garlic (pressed), and 1/2 teaspoon salt.

4-ounce package Alouette cheese, softened with 2 teaspoons olive oil, 1 teaspoon lemon juice, and mixed with 1 tablespoon each chopped parsley and pimiento.

Guacamole Sauce (p. 437).

Octopus

THE HONG KONG OCTOPUSES inhabiting
the West Coast can grow to an enormous
sixteen-foot spread in northern Washington
waters. Commercial fishermen occasionally
haul in a big one. But the commonly fished
octopuses (Polypus bimaculatus, distinguished
by purplish round spots on their heads) seldom exceed twenty inches.
Both species are completely harmless. They live in the low intertidal zone
to eighteen fathoms, often moving to deeper, cooler water in the summertime.
They build their dens in caves or crevices and sleep in them all day. At
night they come out to forage, crawling about on the ocean floor on their
eight arms, searching for clams, oysters, and crabs, which they bring back
to the privacy of their den to consume. The entrance hole to their den is
betrayed by the clutter of shells they leave surrounding it.

Timid but curious octopuses have no ears—they neither hear nor
speak, but have large intelligent eyes. Their sight and sense of touch are
highly developed. They show emotions by changing colors. When angered
they turn red; when frightened they become white with fear, throw a black
ink screen and jet backwards, arms curled to their bodies. As masters of
camouflage, they become all but invisible by taking on the color and
texture of their surroundings; the change is almost instantaneous. Strong
suckers on their elastic tentacles can plaster them to anything.

Sportsmen hunt octopuses on minus tides in bays, lagoons, or sloughs.
Dressed in bathing suit and sneakers and equipped with a quart jar, can
of salt, a large battery syringe, and a collecting bag, they trudge along,
knee-deep in water, looking under the water for smooth worn holes surrounded by fresh shells. Finding one, they mix a heavy salt solution in
the jar, fill the syringe with it, and squeeze it into the hole. The disturbed
octopus spews out a cloud of bubbles, reaches out to feel if the exit is clear,
and emerges. The trick is to grab it quickly, before it gets away.

Most octopuses are caught by their curiosity, their readiness to grab
onto moving objects. Commercial fishermen catch them on hook-covered
lures when they rise to the surface at night.

About Octopus Meat

Octopus meat is lean, white, and mild flavored. However, the texture is tough and rubbery, almost like abalone, and it should be pounded before cooking. Instructions for how to clean and tenderize octopus are on page 9.

Most octopus meat marketed fresh or frozen has been dressed and possibly tenderized. Octopus should be boiled or steamed until fork-tender, which takes 1–2½ hours, depending on the size. The usual market size is 2½ pounds or under; small (½–1 pound) are the most tender. The meat of large octopuses may be sliced and pounded into steaks or ground to use in minced dishes.

Allow ½ pound of octopus meat per serving.

BOILED OCTOPUS

Two 1-pound octopuses	Lemon wedges
Boiling water	Pepper
Salt	Seasoned melted butter or olive oil

Clean and trim octopuses, put them in a large, heavy saucepan, and cover them with boiling water. For each pint of water add 1 teaspoon salt. Cover tightly and simmer slowly for about 2 hours, or until the flesh is tender. Remove octopuses to a warm platter and cut into serving pieces. The cooked meat may be used in other recipes, or served as is with lemon wedges, freshly ground pepper, and a bowl of seasoned melted butter or olive oil.

STEAMED OCTOPUS

Three ½–1-pound octopuses

Clean and trim octopuses, cut the tentacles from the heads, and place meat in a heavy pot. Add nothing—no oil or liquid. Cover tightly and simmer very slowly, to cook in its own juices until pink and tender, 1–2 hours. Drain and let meat cool.

Trim suckers from the tentacles and cut meat into bite-size pieces or thin slices. These may be served with Aioli Sauce (p. 424) or other sauce, or used in other recipes.

SAUTÉED OCTOPUS

Boil or steam octopus until tender. Sprinkle meat with salt, pepper, and marjoram and dust it with flour. Sauté it in hot oil until nicely browned and crisp and serve at once.

PAN-FRIED OCTOPUS STEAKS

1½-pound piece of large octopus
1 cup dry white wine
Juice of ½ lemon plus 1 Tablespoon
　lemon juice
2 eggs, beaten
½ teaspoon salt

Pepper to taste
½ cup fine dry bread crumbs
⅓ cup olive oil
8 Tablespoons (1 stick) unsalted butter
2 sprigs parsley, minced
Lemon wedges

Cut octopus into ½-inch-thick slices and pound each until the meat is soft with muscle broken. Marinate steaks in wine and 1 tablespoon of the lemon juice for 10 minutes. Dry them on toweling.

　Beat eggs with salt and pepper; dip steaks in egg, then roll each in crumbs. Heat oil and 4 tablespoons of the butter in a heavy skillet and brown the steaks less than a minute on each side. Remove them to a warm platter and keep warm. Pour fat from skillet and add the remaining 4 tablespoons of butter, let it get brown but not burned; add the remaining lemon juice and parsley. Pour the gravy over octopus and serve with lemon wedges.

OCTOPUS STEWED IN RED WINE

Two 1-pound octopuses
½ cup olive oil
1½ cups minced onion
¼ cup chopped celery
2 cups dry red wine

4 peppercorns, cracked
1 bay leaf
Salt to taste
2 Tablespoons chopped parsley

Cut dressed octopus into 2-inch pieces. Heat oil in a heavy skillet, sauté onion and celery slowly until lightly brown. Add octopus meat, wine, peppercorns, and bay leaf. Cover and simmer slowly, stirring occasionally, until it is tender and the sauce has thickened, about 1½–2 hours. Add salt, sprinkle with parsley, and serve hot.

OCTOPUS CAKES

1 1/2 pounds fresh octopus, or 2 cups
  ground octopus
2 cups potato, peeled and sliced
1 medium onion, sliced
2 eggs, beaten
1 teaspoon salt
1 teaspoon paprika

1/8 teaspoon garlic powder
Pinch each of thyme, basil, cayenne
  pepper, and pepper
2 Tablespoons flour (more
  if necessary)
5 Tablespoons olive oil or butter
Lemon wedges

Clean and trim octopus, cut tentacles from head, cover with boiling water, and simmer for 5 minutes. Drain, remove the skin, and cut into pieces. Put fish, potato, and onion through a food chopper, using the coarse blade. Add beaten eggs and seasonings, mixing well. Stir in enough flour to form mixture into 8 cakes.

Melt oil in a heavy skillet, add cakes and cook, covered, over medium-low heat until they are brown on both sides and cooked through. Serve hot with lemon wedges.

NORTH BEACH POLPO

Three 1-pound octopuses
Boiling water
6 dried black mushrooms
3 Tablespoons olive oil
1 large onion, chopped
2 cloves garlic, minced
1/3 cup plus 1 Tablespoon
  minced parsley

1 can tomato sauce
1 cup water
1/2 teaspoon rosemary
1/2 teaspoon salt
1/4 teaspoon pepper
Croutons

Place dressed and trimmed octopuses in a large pot. Cover with boiling water, cover the pot, and simmer for 15 minutes. Drain in a colander and cut the meat into 2-inch pieces. Soak mushrooms in warm water for 20 minutes, then drain and slice them.

Heat oil in a heavy skillet and sauté onion, garlic, and octopus pieces until lightly brown. Stir in mushrooms, 1/3 cup of the parsley, tomato sauce, and the cup of water, season with rosemary, salt, and pepper. Cover tightly and simmer slowly for about 1 1/2 hours, stirring occasionally until the octopus meat is tender. Spoon octopus and sauce onto a warm deep platter, sprinkle with the remaining tablespoon of parsley, and garnish with croutons.

OCTOPUS STEWED WITH TOMATO

Two 1-pound octopuses, steamed
3 cloves garlic
2 Tablespoons olive oil
Salt and pepper

6 tomatoes, peeled and diced
2 Tablespoons minced green pepper
1 teaspoon lemon juice
2 Tablespoons minced parsley

Preheat the oven to 325°F. Cook octopus as in recipe for Steamed Octopus (p. 405). When tender, cool meat and cut into 2-inch pieces. Sauté garlic in oil for a few seconds, add octopus chunks, season with salt and pepper, and cook, stirring frequently, for 5 minutes. Mix in tomatoes, green pepper, lemon juice, and parsley, and season generously with pepper. Pour all into a casserole and bake, covered, for 45 minutes. Stir and cook, uncovered, until sauce is thick.

OCTOPUS RICE

1½ pounds octopus, boiled
Salt and pepper
¼ teaspoon garlic powder
Flour
4 Tablespoons olive oil
3 onions, chopped
1 cup uncooked rice

3 Tablespoons chopped fresh dill, or
  2 teaspoons dried dill
⅓ cup chopped parsley
2 Tablespoons sliced filberts
3 cups broth (from cooking octopus)
2 Tablespoons tomato paste
1 teaspoon lemon juice

Cook octopus as in recipe for Boiled Octopus (p. 405). Drain, reserving broth, and cut into bite-size pieces. Sprinkle lightly with salt, pepper, garlic powder, and flour; sauté in hot oil. When nicely brown, remove them from the pan and keep warm. Add onions to the pan and cook slowly until they turn yellow. Stir in rice, dill, parsley, filberts, and reserved broth mixed with tomato paste and lemon juice. Bring to a boil, cover, and cook over low heat, stirring occasionally. When rice starts to swell, stir in octopus pieces. Continue to cook, covered, for about 25 minutes, stirring occasionally and adding more broth if rice sticks to the bottom.

HORS D'OEUVRES

All of the following hors d'oeuvres are made by first boiling or steaming octopus according to recipes on page 405.

OCTOPUS DUNKING BOWL

Arrange little chunks of warm octopus on wooden cocktail picks side by side around the rim of a bowl of hot garlic butter or Aioli Sauce (p. 424), or sauce of melted butter seasoned with lemon juice and Worcestershire sauce.

OCTOPUS TAPAS

Dip bite-size cubes of cooked octopus in garlic-flavored olive oil and grill them until golden brown. Serve the tasty morsels on wooden cocktail picks with equal amounts of large green olives.

OCTOPUS VINAIGRETTE

2 pounds cooked octopus
1/2 cup olive oil
1/2 cup wine vinegar
1 clove garlic

Salt and pepper to taste
Black olives, green and red bell
  pepper slices, lemon wedges

Mix together oil and vinegar with seasonings and pour the vinaigrette over cooked octopus chunks. Cover and marinate in the refrigerator for 12 hours, stirring occasionally. Drain and skewer them on wooden cocktail picks. Mound them in a dish garnished with black olives, green and red bell pepper slices, and lemon wedges.

Squid

COMMON OPALESCENT SQUID are odd-looking mollusks whose long (ten-inch) bodies are joined to their head, which has ten arms sticking out of it. Eight of the arms are short, with suckers on the undersurface, and two are long, with suction cups on the tips. At the tail end of their bodies are two triangular fins. Squid, as we see them, are whitish with tiny purple spots, but in the water they are opalescent. They generally inhabit both the Atlantic and Pacific oceans, at 350- to 1,000-foot depths.

Squid are important food for many large fish—whales, swordfish, and salmon, to name just a few. These small creatures protect themselves by changing their color and ejecting sepia, a black inklike substance, to cloud the water and confuse their predators in a fast getaway. They are among the swiftest swimmers of the sea, swimming backward by jet propulsion.

Squid are caught throughout the year, but the big fishing season is April to June, when tremendously large congregations gather at certain areas to spawn. The waters of Monterey Bay to Moss Landing are some of the most important squid-catching grounds off California. Squid fishing takes place at night when they rise to the surface. The schools are located during the dark of the moon, by the phosphorescent wriggling glow they make in the water. Nets are used to scoop up the catch.

About Squid Meat

Squid, called calamari by the Latins, is snowy white meat, similar in taste and texture to cuttlefish. There are two approaches to cooking squid. When flipped over in the pan for a few seconds on each side, small squid will be cooked enough without becoming tough. If squid are large or thick, however, they must be simmered until tender, which may take 30 minutes to 1 hour, before further preparation.

Squid are marketed whole, either fresh or frozen, year round. Instructions for cleaning whole squid are on page 10. Large tenderized squid steaks are now marketed as "abalone-squid." They may be sautéed or deep fried; for further suggestions see the Abalone chapter, pages 321–6.

One pound (2 cups) of raw sliced squid makes 1¼ cups when cooked. Allow ½ pound per serving.

DEEP-FRIED CALAMARI

2 pounds squid
At least ½ teaspoon salt
Dry sherry
½ cup flour

⅛ teaspoon pepper
1½ cups oil (part olive oil)
Cocktail Sauce I (p. 436)
Lemon wedges

Cut cleaned squid into rings or bite-size pieces, sprinkle with salt, and marinate them in sherry for 1 hour. Drain and dry them on toweling. Shake pieces in a bag of flour seasoned with ½ teaspoon salt and the pepper, then deep fry them, a few at a time, in hot (385°F.) oil until crisp. Serve at once with cocktail sauce and lemon wedges.

CHINESE STIR-FRIED SQUID

2 pounds squid
1 Tablespoon sherry
1 Tablespoon soy sauce
4 dried black mushrooms
2 teaspoons cornstarch
1 cup chicken broth
2 Tablespoons oil
1 clove garlic, minced

1 teaspoon grated ginger
1 pork chop, minced
¼ cup sliced green onion
1 small can (½ cup) sliced bamboo
  shoots
½ teaspoon salt
¼ teaspoon pepper
1 teaspoon white vinegar

Slit cleaned squid bodies and open to lay flat. Cut them into bite-size squares or strips and slice the tentacle portion. Place in a bowl, pour boiling water over, and let it stand for 1 minute, then drain. Mix sherry and soy sauce with the squid and set aside. Soak mushrooms in warm water for 20 minutes. then drain and quarter them. Mix cornstarch with chicken broth.

Heat oil in a heavy skillet or wok, add garlic, ginger, and pork. Stir-fry until meat is white and garlic starts to brown. Mix in vegetables, salt, and pepper, pour in chicken broth, and stir constantly while sauce thickens and heats to a boil. Lower heat, cover, and cook for 2–3 minutes. Add squid-soy mixture and stir while heating to a simmer; add vinegar and serve.

STUFFED SQUID

2 pounds squid (small)
½ cup coarsely grated carrot
½ cup coarsely grated onion
2 cloves garlic, pressed
¼ cup minced parsley
3 Tablespoons butter

1 cup fine dry bread crumbs
Salt and pepper to taste
¼ teaspoon thyme
1 Tablespoon sherry
½ cup olive oil for frying

Clean and drain squid. Cut tentacle portions into several pieces, dry the bodies on absorbent paper, and set aside.

Sauté carrot, onion, garlic, and parsley in butter until soft. Add crumbs, salt, pepper, and thyme, moisten slightly with sherry, and mix well. Stuff squid loosely with the mixture. Squid bodies may be slit for stuffing, then sewn together after. Heat oil very hot in a heavy skillet, add all of the squid, and fry until crisp.

STEWED CALAMARI

2 pounds squid
3 Tablespoons olive oil
2 cups tomatoes, peeled and diced
1 cup dry white wine
2 cloves garlic, pressed
3 teaspoons anchovy paste

¼ teaspoon each rubbed oregano
   and basil
½ small hot chili, seeded and crushed
Salt and pepper to taste
2 sprigs parsley, minced

Slice cleaned squid into ¼-inch rings, cut tentacles into strips, and drain them on toweling. Heat oil in a heavy skillet and stir-fry squid until it firms. Add tomatoes, wine, and seasonings, cover and cook very slowly, stirring frequently, for 1 hour, or until squid is tender. Correct seasoning with salt and pepper, transfer to a warm serving dish, sprinkle with parsley, and serve hot.

SQUID SALAD

2 pounds squid
2 Tablespoons vegetable oil
2 Tablespoons lemon juice
1 cup mayonnaise
2 Tablespoons wine vinegar
½ onion, chopped

¾ teaspoon Italian seasoning
1 teaspoon sugar
¼ teaspoon garlic powder
Salt and pepper to taste
2 Tablespoons minced parsley

Slit cleaned squid bodies lengthwise to open flat and cut them into 2 × 1½-inch strips; slice the tentacles. Heat oil and lemon juice in a heavy skillet, add squid, and sauté until firm but still tender, about 5 minutes. Drain them in a colander, transfer to a bowl, cover, and let cool to room temperature.

Combine mayonnaise, vinegar, onion, and seasonings in a blender and purée until smooth. Mix dressing with cool squid, season with salt and pepper to taste, sprinkle with parsley, and chill for 2 hours before serving.

SQUID VINAIGRETTE MONTEREY

2 pounds squid
2 cups boiling water
Rind of 1 lemon
¼ cup olive oil
2 Tablespoons white wine vinegar

1½ teaspoons lemon juice
½ teaspoon salt
1 clove garlic, pressed
1 Tablespoon minced parsley

Slice cleaned squid into ¼-inch rings and cut the tentacles into several pieces. Drop squid into boiling salted water, simmer for 3 minutes, add lemon rind, and continue simmering until squid is tender. Rinse cooked squid well in cold water and drain.

Mix together oil, vinegar, lemon juice, salt, garlic, and parsley. Pour the vinaigrette sauce over the squid, cover, and refrigerate for several hours before serving.

VI

SAUCES
AND MARINADES

SAUCES

There are several basic sauces such as Béchamel, Velouté, Hollandaise, Mayonnaise, and Vinaigrette, from which other classic sauces are derived. Each of these recipes will make 2 cups of sauce unless otherwise specified.

Béchamel Sauces

Béchamel, or basic white cream sauce, can be made in varying degrees of thickness.

Thin béchamel sauce, made with 2 tablespoons butter and flour, will thicken 2 cups milk enough for soup base. The more butter and flour used, the thicker the base.

THICK BÉCHAMEL SAUCE

is used as a base for creating other sauces. If used as a plain sauce, it must be diluted with more milk, or other liquid.

4 Tablespoons (1/2 stick) butter
4 Tablespoons flour
2 cups hot milk
1/2 teaspoon salt
1/8 teaspoon white pepper

Melt butter, stir in flour, and cook, stirring, for 3 minutes without browning. This cooks the flour so sauce will not taste starchy. Add hot milk all at once and beat sauce with a wire whisk, cooking over moderate heat until sauce is smooth and thickened. Simmer it slowly for 5 minutes, then season with salt and pepper.

MEDIUM-THICK BÉCHAMEL SAUCE

is used in creamed and scalloped dishes.

3 Tablespoons butter   1/2 teaspoon salt
3 Tablespoons flour   1/8 teaspoon white pepper
2 cups hot milk

Make a roux of butter and flour as in the preceding recipe, add milk, and cook, stirring with a whisk until the sauce is smooth and thickened. Simmer for 5 minutes, and season with salt and pepper. Two cups of béchamel sauce may be flavored with the following:

1 Tablespoon fresh herbs, or   2 teaspoons onion juice,
  1/2 teaspoon dried herbs or spices   or 2 teaspoons dry sherry,
2 teaspoons lemon juice   or 1 teaspoon Worcestershire sauce

WHITE SAUCE

2 cups Medium-Thick Béchamel   1 egg yolk (optional)
  Sauce, hot (above)   1 teaspoon vinegar
1 Tablespoon cream   1/2–1 Tablespoon butter (optional)

Make béchamel sauce. Combine cream with egg yolk and beat it into béchamel, then heat under a boil for 1 minute. Remove from heat, stir in vinegar, then swirl in butter.

Caper White Sauce

2 cups White Sauce, hot
2 Tablespoons each chopped capers
  and caper juice

Mustard White Sauce

2 cups White Sauce, hot   1 Tablespoon minced parsley
2 teaspoons prepared mustard

Parsley White Sauce

2 cups White Sauce, hot   1/2 cup minced parsley

CREAM SAUCE

2 cups Medium-Thick Béchamel Sauce   ½ cup heavy cream
  (p. 418)

Cook béchamel sauce over low heat, stirring until it is reduced to 1½ cups.
Stir in cream.

Anchovy Cream Sauce

1 cup Cream Sauce   1 teaspoon anchovy paste

Oyster Sauce

1 cup Cream Sauce   1 cup finely chopped oysters
1 teaspoon Worcestershire sauce   Sprig parsley, minced
Dash of paprika

Mix Worcestershire sauce and paprika into cream sauce, then, just before
serving, bring sauce to a boil and add oysters and parsley.

CURRY WHITE SAUCE

2 cups Medium-Thick Béchamel Sauce,   3 teaspoons each curry powder, lemon
  hot (p. 418)   juice, and minced onion

EGG SAUCE

2 cups Medium-Thick Béchamel   1 Tablespoon parsley, minced
  Sauce, hot (p. 418)   ½ teaspoon grated lemon rind
3–4 hard-boiled eggs, chopped   (optional)

HORSERADISH WHITE SAUCE

1½ cups Medium-Thick Béchamel   Pinch each of sugar and salt
  Sauce, hot (p. 418)
3–4 Tablespoons prepared (or fresh)
  grated horseradish

MORNAY SAUCE

2 cups Medium-Thick Béchamel
  Sauce, hot (p. 418)
2 egg yolks
4 Tablespoons cream

½ cup grated cheese (Parmesan,
  Swiss, Gruyère, or a combination
  of them)

Mix egg yolks with cream, stir in a spoonful or two of hot béchamel, then beat it into the rest of the sauce. Mix in grated cheese, heat to boiling point (but don't let it boil after adding eggs), and remove from heat.

SHRIMP SAUCE

2 cups Medium-Thick Béchamel
  Sauce, hot (p. 418)
½ cup chopped cooked mushrooms
½ cup chopped small cooked shrimp

2 Tablespoons tomato paste
1 teaspoon lemon juice
2 Tablespoons (¼ stick) butter
Dash of cayenne pepper

Combine béchamel with mushrooms, shrimp, tomato paste, and lemon juice. Swirl in butter mixed with cayenne.

Velouté Sauces

VELOUTÉ SAUCE

4 Tablespoons (½ stick) butter
4 Tablespoons flour
2 cups hot fish stock (see Salmon or
  Salmon Trout in Court Bouillon,
  p. 169, or Simple Fish Stock, p. 26)

Salt and pepper to taste
2 egg yolks (optional)
½ cup cream (optional)

Melt butter in a saucepan, stir in flour, cooking until it bubbles. Add hot stock all at once and beat with a wire whisk, cooking over moderate heat, until sauce is thick and creamy. Simmer for 5 minutes and season with salt and pepper. For richer sauce, beat egg yolks into cream, stir in a spoonful of the hot velouté, then beat this back into the rest of the sauce. Heat to boiling point (but don't let it boil after adding egg) and remove from heat.

BERCY SAUCE

2 shallots, minced
4 Tablespoons (½ stick) butter
½ cup fish stock
½ cup dry white wine

1 cup Velouté Sauce (preceding recipe)
Salt and pepper
1 Tablespoon minced parsley

Cook shallots in 1 tablespoon of the butter until tender. Add stock and wine, then boil until reduced to ½ cup. Add velouté sauce and stir while heating to the boiling point. Remove from heat, season to taste, add parsley, and swirl in the remaining 3 tablespoons of butter.

DILL SAUCE

2 cups rich Velouté Sauce (p. 420),
   using egg yolks and cream
1½ teaspoons sugar

1 Tablespoon cider vinegar
¼ cup chopped fresh dill

Heat velouté sauce and add remaining ingredients.

MUSHROOM SAUCE

½ pound mushrooms, chopped
2 Tablespoons (¼ stick) butter
2 cups Velouté Sauce (p. 420)
1 teaspoon lemon juice
1 clove garlic, pressed

Dash of nutmeg
1 egg yolk
½ cup cream
Salt and pepper

Sauté mushrooms in butter until they begin to brown. Mix in velouté sauce, lemon juice, garlic, and a dash of nutmeg. Cover and cook over low heat for 8 minutes, stirring often. Beat egg yolk with ¼ cup of the cream, stir in a little of the hot sauce, then blend into mushroom sauce. Heat to the boiling point, then remove. Correct seasoning and stir in the remaining ¼ cup of cream.

MUSTARD SAUCE

2 cups Velouté Sauce (p. 420)

2 teaspoons Dijon-type mustard

WHITE WINE SAUCE

1 cup chopped mushroom pieces and
  stems
½ cup dry white wine
1 ½ cups reduced fish stock (see
  Salmon or Salmon Trout in Court
  Bouillon, p. 169)

3 Tablespoons butter
1 Tablespoon flour
2 egg yolks
¼ cup heavy cream
1 teaspoon lemon juice
Salt and pepper

Cook mushrooms, wine, and ½ cup of the fish stock over moderate heat until liquid is reduced to ½ cup. Strain and set aside. Melt 1 tablespoon of the butter, stir in flour, then beat in wine-stock and the remaining cup of fish stock. Cook over low heat, stirring constantly, until sauce will coat a spoon thickly. Beat egg yolks with half the cream, stir in a little of the hot sauce, then mix back into the rest of the sauce. Bring just to the boil, then remove from heat. Stir in lemon juice, remaining cream, and salt and pepper to taste, then swirl in the remaining 2 tablespoons of butter.

Hollandaise Sauces

HOLLANDAISE SAUCE

Makes 1 cup

3 egg yolks
2 Tablespoons hot water
8 Tablespoons (1 stick) butter, melted

2 Tablespoons lemon juice
¼ teaspoon salt
Dash of cayenne pepper

Pour ½ inch water in the bottom of a double boiler, bring to a boil, then reduce heat to barely a simmer. Put egg yolks and water in the top of the double boiler; place it over the simmering bottom pan of water. Cook and beat yolks continuously until they thicken to a custard consistency. Don't let mixture cook too fast. Add butter, a drop at a time at first, then in a fine stream. Season with lemon juice, salt, and cayenne. Pour hollandaise into a serving bowl and keep it lukewarm by placing it in water at the same temperature as the sauce.

  Don't try to reheat hollandaise. If sauce should curdle, beat another egg yolk and gradually whisk the curdled mixture into the fresh egg yolk.

MOUSSELINE SAUCE

3 Tablespoons stiffly whipped cream

¾ cup Hollandaise Sauce (see above)

Just before serving, fold cream into hollandaise. Use over poached fish or soufflés.

BLENDER HOLLANDAISE SAUCE

Makes 1 cup

3 egg yolks
2 Tablespoons lemon juice
¼ teaspoon salt

Dash of cayenne pepper
⅛ teaspoon paprika
8 Tablespoons (1 stick) butter

Put egg yolks, lemon juice, salt, cayenne, and paprika in a blender. Cover and turn blender on and off immediately. In a saucepan heat butter until it starts to bubble. Turn blender on high, remove the lid, and pour the hot butter slowly into the egg mixture. Turn off blender. Keep the sauce warm over a pan of warm water until ready to use. Serve with baked or broiled fish or with shellfish.

BÉARNAISE SAUCE

1 cup Hollandaise Sauce (p. 422)
1 Tablespoon tarragon vinegar
1 teaspoon each chopped fresh
  tarragon, parsley, and chervil;
  or ¼ teaspoon dried herbs

CHORON SAUCE

1 cup Hollandaise Sauce (p. 422)
1 Tablespoon each tomato paste and
  chopped parsley

Worcestershire sauce to taste (optional)

HORSERADISH HOLLANDAISE

1 cup Hollandaise Sauce (p. 422)
2 Tablespoons grated horseradish

¼ cup stiffly whipped cream

Combine hollandaise with horseradish. Just before serving, fold in cream.

Mayonnaises

MAYONNAISE

Makes 1 cup

2 egg yolks
¾ teaspoon salt
¼ teaspoon white pepper
1 teaspoon dry mustard

2 Tablespoons lemon juice
1 cup olive or salad oil (or a
   combination of both)
1 Tablespoon water (optional)

Chill a blender container and all ingredients. Put egg yolks in blender and beat on low speed for 1 minute. Add salt, pepper, mustard, and 1 teaspoon of the lemon juice; beat 1 minute more. Add oil, ½ teaspoon at a time at first. Be sure that oil is well incorporated before each addition. When half the oil has been added and the mayonnaise is thick, add the remaining lemon juice and oil gradually—very slowly. Add water if mayonnaise is too thick.

Should mayonnaise separate because oil was added too fast, put another yolk into a clean bowl and gradually beat the curdled mixture into it.

AIOLI SAUCE (GARLIC MAYONNAISE)

1 slice white bread
3 Tablespoons milk
4–6 cloves garlic, mashed
2 egg yolks

½ teaspoon salt
¼ teaspoon white pepper
1 cup olive oil
1 Tablespoon lemon juice

Cut the crusts from a thick slice of bread and crumble it into a bowl. Stir in milk and let the bread soak for 10 minutes, then squeeze out the milk. Mash garlic in a garlic press and combine it with the squeezed bread in a mixing bowl. Add egg yolks, salt, and pepper, beat with an electric mixer until smooth and thick. Add oil, ½ teaspoon at a time at first. Be sure oil is well integrated after each addition. When half the oil has been added and the mayonnaise is thick add lemon juice and remaining oil very gradually.

Aioli should be thick. Serve with poached fish, squid, or octopus, or broiled fish.

FISH COCKTAIL MAYONNAISE

1 cup Mayonnaise (p. 424)
2–3 Tablespoons chili sauce
1 Tablespoon each Cognac and
dry sherry

3 Tablespoons whipped cream

Combine mayonnaise with chili sauce. Mix Cognac and sherry with whipped cream, then fold into mayonnaise mixture.

GREEN GODDESS DRESSING

2 Tablespoons tarragon vinegar
1 egg
3 anchovy fillets

4 green onions, chopped
1 Tablespoon minced parsley
¼ cup olive or salad oil

Put all ingredients except the oil in a blender and purée. Add oil, very slowly at first, more rapidly as mixture thickens, until all the oil has been added. Serve with cold fish.

IBERIA SAUCE

1 cup Mayonnaise (p. 424)
1 Tablespoon anchovy paste
½ teaspoon dry mustard
¼ teaspoon garlic powder
2 Tablespoons tarragon vinegar
Dash of cayenne pepper

3 hard-boiled eggs
¼ cup pimiento-stuffed olives
3 Tablespoons gherkins
1 teaspoon onion juice
Sprig parsley, minced

Blend mayonnaise with anchovy paste, mustard, garlic powder, vinegar, and cayenne. Chop eggs, olives, and gherkins and add them, onion juice, and parsley to sauce.

LEMON MAYONNAISE

1 cup Mayonnaise (p. 424)
½ teaspoon dry mustard

Juice of ½ lemon, strained

LOUIS DRESSING

1 cup Mayonnaise (p. 424)
2 green onions, chopped
2 Tablespoons chopped bell peppers
3 Tablespoons chili sauce

2 teaspoons lemon juice
1 teaspoon Worcestershire sauce
1/4 teaspoon salt
Dash of cayenne pepper

GREEN MAYONNAISE

1 cup Mayonnaise (p. 424)
1/2 cup spinach leaves, blanched in hot
   water, squeezed, and minced
1 Tablespoon parsley

1 Tablespoon green onion
1 teaspoon fresh dill
1/4 teaspoon dried tarragon

Make a purée of green vegetables and herbs, then mix them with mayonnaise.
Let stand for 2–3 hours before using.

RÉMOULADE SAUCE

1 cup Mayonnaise (p. 424)
1/2 teaspoon Dijon-type mustard
1 teaspoon lemon juice
1/2 teaspoon anchovy paste

1 teaspoon grated onion
1/4 teaspoon dried tarragon
2 Tablespoons capers, drained

TARTAR SAUCE

2 hard-boiled eggs
2 cups Mayonnaise (p. 424)
1/4 cup minced mild white onion
1/4 cup minced green pepper
2 garlic dill pickles, chopped

1 clove garlic, minced
1/4 cup chili sauce
2 Tablespoons prepared horseradish
1/4 cup sour cream

Mash egg yolks and chop whites. Mix with remaining ingredients. This is
also good as masking for cold fish, garnished with shrimp or crab.

THOUSAND ISLAND DRESSING

1 cup Mayonnaise (p. 424)
2 Tablespoons chili sauce
1 Tablespoon minced green pepper
1 Tablespoon chopped pimiento

1 teaspoon chopped chives
1 hard-boiled egg, chopped
1 teaspoon vinegar
Salt and pepper

Vinaigrette Dressings

BASIC FRENCH DRESSING

2 Tablespoons vinegar, or 1 Tablespoon
   each wine vinegar and lemon juice
6 Tablespoons olive or salad oil
1/4 teaspoon salt

1/8 teaspoon pepper
1/4 teaspoon dry mustard
1 Tablespoon minced parsley

Combine and mix all ingredients well. One tablespoon fresh herbs may be added, such as thyme, chives, chervil, tarragon, basil, marjoram, or cilantro; or use 1 teaspoon dried herbs.

ANCHOVY DRESSING

4 Tablespoons salad oil
2 Tablespoons vinegar
1/2 teaspoon salt

1/4 teaspoon paprika
6 drops of Worcestershire sauce
2 teaspoons anchovy paste

PARSLEY DRESSING

2 cups minced parsley
1/4 cup minced fresh basil
3 cloves garlic, minced
1/4 cup chopped anchovies (1 small
   can and oil)

1/4 cup chopped pimiento
3 Tablespoons capers
3 Tablespoons olive oil
2 Tablespoons wine vinegar
Pepper to taste

Mix all ingredients thoroughly and let stand for at least 4 hours. Serve as a garnish with hot or cold fish. Will keep refrigerated for about 2 weeks.

PICKLED ONION DRESSING

3/4 cup salad oil
3 Tablespoons vinegar
1/2 teaspoon dry mustard

1/4 cup chopped pickled onions
1/4 teaspoon each sugar and pepper
1 teaspoon salt

Combine all ingredients. Shake to dissolve dry ingredients, then shake again before serving. Serve on cold fish.

RAVIGOTE SAUCE

½ cup Basic French Dressing (p. 427)
1 teaspoon capers, drained
1 teaspoon chopped onion
1 egg yolk

½ teaspoon each fresh chopped parsley, chervil, tarragon (or savory or marjoram); or ¼ teaspoon dried herbs

Combine all ingredients. Ravigote sauce may be thickened with mayonnaise. Serve on fish salad.

ROQUEFORT CHEESE DRESSING

⅛ pound Roquefort cheese
4 Tablespoons salad oil
2 Tablespoons vinegar

¼ teaspoon salt
¼ teaspoon paprika
6 drops of hot pepper sauce

Mash cheese and oil together until smooth, then add remaining ingredients and mix well.

CAPER SAUCE

½ cup olive oil
Juice of 1 lemon

½ cup capers, drained
Salt and pepper to taste

Combine ingredients, mix well, and shake before using.

Sour Cream and Yogurt Sauces

CURRY SOUR CREAM SAUCE

1 cup sour cream
1 teaspoon curry powder
1 Tablespoon instant onion

¼ teaspoon salt
3 drops of hot pepper sauce
1 Tablespoon lemon juice

Combine all ingredients; chill for several hours before using.

COLD MUSTARD SAUCE

1 cup sour cream
2 Tablespoons prepared mustard

1 teaspoon prepared horseradish
1 teaspoon minced parsley

Mix ingredients and chill.

YOGURT-GREEN ONION CURRY SAUCE

1 cup yogurt
2 teaspoons curry powder

2 Tablespoons minced green onion
Salt and pepper to taste

Mix all ingredients and chill for 1 hour before using.

SOUR CREAM CUCUMBER SAUCE

1 cup chopped cucumber
1 cup sour cream
2 Tablespoons white wine vinegar

1/2 teaspoon garlic powder
1/2 teaspoon salt
1/4 teaspoon white pepper

Mix ingredients and chill before serving.

Butters

MAKING BUTTER

One cup heavy cream yields 1/4 cup butter. Pour a cup of cream in a blender and beat at high speed for 15 seconds. When cream has thickened around the blades, pour in 1/2 cup ice water and an ice cube; blend at high speed for 2–3 minutes. Turn off the blender and push the whipped cream down to the blades with a rubber spatula. If butter doesn't start to form, add another ice cube. Butter will separate from the liquid suddenly. Drain off liquid and remove butter to a bowl. Knead butter with a wooden spoon to remove all remaining liquid, then chill it. This creamy fresh butter can be blended with herbs or spices, pulverized nuts, grated cheese, or minced vegetables such as watercress, stuffed olives, etc., to top-broiled, grilled, or planked fish.

Of course for all these recipes you can also use bought butter.

BEURRE MANIÉ (FLOUR BUTTER)

Flour butter is used for thickening sauce. For example, to thicken 2 cups of sauce quickly, knead 3 tablespoons flour with 2 tablespoons softened butter and form into several small balls. Mix them into sauce, one at a time, until sauce is sufficiently thickened. Sauce must not be allowed to boil after flour butter has been added.

HOT BUTTER SAUCES

BLACK BUTTER

Makes ½ cup

Melt 8 tablespoons (1 stick) butter and cook over moderately low heat until dark brown, being careful not to burn the butter, then remove from heat. Add 2 tablespoons chopped parsley and lemon juice to taste.

BROWN BUTTER

Melt butter over very low heat until it is hazelnut brown. Very low heat is important for best flavor. Allow 2 teaspoons brown butter per serving. Add a few capers to the sauce and serve over grilled fish.

CLARIFIED BUTTER

This is used for frying and sauces (such as curry or basic brown sauce, etc.) because it doesn't burn, even at 400°F. Melt ½ pound (2 sticks) *unsalted* butter in the top of a double boiler or over very low heat. As foam accumulates on top, skim it off. Sediment will fall to the bottom of the pan. What is left is clarified butter. Strain into a jar, leaving behind the sediment. Refrigerated, it will keep for several weeks.

GARLIC BUTTER

16 Tablespoons (2 sticks) butter,   2-4 cloves garlic, slivered
    melted   2 teaspoons minced parsley

Melt butter, add garlic, and let it stand for an hour or so. Just before serving, remove garlic slivers, heat, and mix in parsley.

SAVORY HOT BUTTER

½ pound (2 sticks) butter
2 teaspoons Worcestershire sauce
4 teaspoons lemon juice
2 teaspoons prepared mustard

2 Tablespoons chili sauce
Tabasco to taste
Sprig parsley, minced

Combine all ingredients and heat. Serve hot with fish or shellfish.

WHITE BUTTER

8 Tablespoons (1 stick) very cold
   butter, cut into ¼-inch slices
½ cup white wine vinegar
2 Tablespoons dry white wine

2 Tablespoons minced shallot
Juice of ½ lemon
Pepper and salt

Cook vinegar, wine, shallot, and lemon juice in an enameled pan, over moderately high heat, until reduced to almost a glaze. Remove from heat and let the pan cool. Whisk in the butter, a piece at a time, adding another before the previous one is completely melted. Don't let the sauce get warm enough for the butter to liquify. Sauce should be the consistency of hollandaise: thick enough to coat a spoon thickly. Season with pepper, and salt if using unsalted butter.

COLD BUTTERS

Cold butters are easy to make. Prepared ahead of time, they may be stored in the refrigerator until needed. Use on sizzling broiled fillets, melt one into hot soups, soften to spread on canapés, or heat at the last minute and pour onto fish as a sauce.

To make cold butters: Cream butter until very soft, then mix in other ingredients. This is easy and quick to do in a food processor.

ALMOND BUTTER

4 Tablespoons (½ stick)
   creamed butter

3 Tablespoons pulverized almonds

ANCHOVY BUTTER

4 Tablespoons (½ stick)
  creamed butter
1 teaspoon anchovy paste

6 drops of onion juice
3 drops of hot pepper sauce
¼ teaspoon lemon juice

CILANTRO BUTTER

4 Tablespoons (½ stick)
  creamed butter
1 Tablespoon minced cilantro

1 teaspoon lime juice
2 Tablespoons minced green onion
Dash of cayenne pepper

CHIVRY BUTTER

4 Tablespoons (½ stick)
  creamed butter
1 teaspoon each minced fresh parsley,
  chives, shallot, tarragon, and chervil;
  or ¼ teaspoon dried herbs

DEVILED BUTTER

4 Tablespoons (½ stick)
  creamed butter
1 teaspoon dry mustard
1 teaspoon Worcestershire sauce

½ teaspoon grated onion
½ teaspoon minced chives
3–4 drops of Tabasco

LOBSTER BUTTER

4 Tablespoons (½ stick)
  creamed butter
Salt

2 Tablespoons lobster coral (roe),
  sieved

SHRIMP BUTTER

4 Tablespoons (½ stick)
  creamed butter

8 shrimp, cooked, shelled, and
  deveined, then ground to a paste

WATERCRESS BUTTER

4 Tablespoons (½ stick)
  creamed butter
2 Tablespoons minced watercress

1 teaspoon minced parsley
Worcestershire sauce to taste
Lemon juice to taste

MAÎTRE D'HÔTEL BUTTER

4 Tablespoons (½ stick) creamed
  butter (unsalted)
½ teaspoon salt
½ Tablespoon minced parsley

¾–1½ Tablespoons lemon juice
⅛ teaspoon pepper
⅛ teaspoon nutmeg

Tomato-Base Sauces

TOMATO SAUCE

1 medium onion, minced
½ cup diced carrot
½ cup chopped celery
2 cloves garlic, minced
3 Tablespoons salad oil
2 Tablespoons flour
At least 1 cup stock (chicken or beef)
4 cups fresh tomatoes, skinned and
  chopped; or 3 cups canned Italian
  plum tomatoes

1 teaspoon sugar
1 bay leaf
¼ teaspoon thyme
¼ teaspoon dried sweet basil,
    or 2 fresh basil leaves, minced
2 Tablespoons minced parsley
At least 1 teaspoon salt
Pepper to taste

Sauté onion, carrot, celery, and garlic slowly in oil until they begin to brown. Stir in flour and cook for 3 minutes. Mix in 1 cup of stock, then tomatoes, and add remainder of ingredients. Simmer about 1 hour, stirring often. Add more stock if sauce becomes too thick. (Tomato sauces scorch easily. To eliminate close supervision, you can cook sauce in a preheated 325°F. oven for 1½ hours.) Remove bay leaf, then purée cooked sauce in a food processor, reheat, and serve.

PORTUGUESE TOMATO SAUCE

2 onions, sliced
2 Tablespoons olive oil
2 cloves garlic, pressed

2 cups Tomato Sauce (p. 433)
Chopped parsley to taste, as a garnish

Sauté onions in olive oil until they yellow. Stir in pressed garlic, and Tomato Sauce, and heat slowly to a boil, stirring occasionally. Serve with a parsley garnish.

CREOLE SAUCE

2 Tablespoons (¼ stick) butter
1½ cups chopped onion
½ cup chopped celery
¼ cup minced green pepper
2 cups (28-ounce can) tomatoes
¼ cup minced parsley
2 cloves garlic, minced

1 teaspoon grated lemon rind
1 bay leaf
Pinch of clove
¼ teaspoon thyme
2 teaspoons Worcestershire sauce
Tabasco
Salt and pepper

Heat butter in a large, heavy skillet and sauté onion, celery, and green pepper until tender, about 10 minutes. Stir in tomatoes, parsley, garlic, lemon rind, bay leaf, clove, thyme, Worcestershire sauce, and Tabasco. Bring to a boil, then simmer slowly, stirring frequently, until thick, about 15 minutes. Add salt and pepper to taste.

TOMATO SOUR–SWEET SAUCE

½ cup minced onion
¼ cup minced parsley
¼ cup minced basil
3 Tablespoons olive oil
2 cups chopped tomatoes

1 small cinnamon stick
1 teaspoon sugar
1 Tablespoon wine vinegar
Salt and pepper to taste

Sauté onion, parsley, and basil in oil until tender, then add tomatoes and cinnamon. Cook sauce slowly until thick, stirring frequently. Mix sugar with vinegar; stir it into the sauce and season with salt and pepper. Serve with simply poached fish.

COLD MEXICAN TOMATO SALSA

1 1/2 cups fresh tomatoes, peeled and
    chopped; or 1 1/2 cups canned
    whole tomatoes, chopped
1/2 medium onion, chopped
1 clove garlic, pressed
1 Tablespoon vinegar

1/2 teaspoon oregano (powdered)
1 or more Tablespoons canned
    jalapeño peppers, chopped
Salt to taste
Chopped fresh cilantro to taste,
    as a garnish

Mix together all ingredients and serve at room temperature.

Other Sauces

COCKTAIL SAUCE I

Makes about 1 cup

1 cup chili sauce
Juice of 1/2 lemon
4 Tablespoons prepared horseradish

1/2 teaspoon Worcestershire sauce
Salt and pepper to taste

Mix all ingredients and serve cold over fish or shellfish.

COCKTAIL SAUCE II

Makes about 1 cup

1/2 cup catsup
1/2 cup chili sauce
1 Tablespoon prepared horseradish
1 teaspoon Worcestershire sauce

Several drops each of hot pepper sauce
   and lemon juice
Salt and pepper to taste

Combine all ingredients. Chill and serve with fish or shellfish.

COCKTAIL SAUCE III

Makes about 1 cup

1 cup chopped tomatoes
1/2 cup chopped onion
1/4 cup chopped cilantro or parsley
2 Tablespoons lime juice

1–2 canned green chiles, chopped
1 Tablespoon salad oil
1/2 teaspoon salt
Dash of pepper

Combine all ingredients. Chill and serve with cold shellfish or fish.

WHITE CLAM SAUCE

½ medium onion, chopped
2 cloves garlic, minced
1 Tablespoon each butter and
  olive oil
¼ cup dry white wine

½ cup clam broth
2 cups clams, cut in pieces; or 2 cans
  (8-ounce) minced clams, drained
2 Tablespoons minced parsley
Generous milling of pepper

Sauté onion and garlic in butter and oil until tender. Add wine and broth and cook, uncovered, over medium heat until sauce is reduced by half. Add clams and parsley and cook, stirring, only until clams are heated through. Season with pepper and serve at once.

CHEESE SAUCE

1 egg
1 cup milk
⅛ teaspoon garlic powder
¾ teaspoon salt
¾ teaspoon dry mustard

¼ teaspoon paprika
Dash of cayenne pepper
¾ pound (3 cups) grated
  Cheddar cheese

Beat egg with milk, add seasonings, and pour into the top of a double boiler. Cook, stirring, until hot, then add cheese and continue stirring until it melts. Serve cheese sauce hot.

GUACAMOLE SAUCE

Makes about 2 cups

2 large avocados
2-3 Tablespoons lemon or lime juice
1 clove garlic, pressed
½ small onion, minced

½ teaspoon salt
2 teaspoons minced fresh cilantro
Tabasco to taste

Mash avocados; combine with remaining ingredients and chill.

ORIENTAL FISH SAUCE

2 teaspoons minced fresh ginger
2 cloves garlic, minced
1 ½ Tablespoons fermented salted
   black bean, rinsed and mashed*
¼ cup ground pork
2 Tablespoons soy sauce
2 Tablespoons dry sherry or brandy
*See Glossary

1 teaspoon sugar
2 Tablespoons oil
½ teaspoon salt
2 cups fish or chicken stock
2 Tablespoons cornstarch
1 egg, beaten with 1 Tablespoon stock
   (optional)

Mix ginger, garlic, and black bean with pork and set aside. In another bowl, mix 1 tablespoon of the soy sauce, the sherry or brandy, and the sugar and set aside.

    Heat oil very hot in a skillet over high heat, then add salt and pork mixture. Stir-fry, breaking up lumps, until meat firms. Pour in soy-sherry and cook, stirring for another minute, then add stock. Bring sauce to a boil, cover, and simmer for 5–8 minutes. Moisten cornstarch with the remaining tablespoon of soy sauce and mix it into the sauce, stirring constantly, until sauce thickens. A beaten egg is sometimes poured into the scalding sauce. In this case, let eggs set without stirring for 1 minute before serving.

Marinades

Marinate fish in glass or enamel or plastic; anything but a metal container.
Prepared salad dressing of your choice can be used. Marinate fish for
10 minutes on each side.

WINE MARINADE FOR STEAKS AND FILLETS

¼ cup olive oil
1 cup dry white wine
2 teaspoons grated lemon rind

½ cup minced parsley
¼ teaspoon white pepper

Herbs of your choice may be added; for example, ½ teaspoon rosemary or
¼ cup chopped green onion, or both. Marinate fish for at least 1 hour.

BUTTER MARINADE FOR FILLETS AND STEAKS

12 Tablespoons (1½ sticks) butter,
  melted
Juice of ½ lemon

½ teaspoon onion flakes
1 clove garlic, minced
Salt and pepper to taste

Marinate for at least 30 minutes.

TERIYAKI MARINADE

⅔ cup soy sauce
¼ cup salad oil
1 Tablespoon minced fresh ginger
2 cloves garlic, pressed

1 teaspoon dry mustard
⅓ cup sugar
2 Tablespoons brandy

Marinate fillets for 1 hour.

COOKED TOMATO MARINADE

1 clove garlic, minced
1/4 cup chopped onion
8 Tablespoons (1 stick) butter
8-ounce can tomato sauce

2 teaspoons Worcestershire sauce
Pinch each of thyme, basil,
  and oregano
Salt and pepper

Sauté garlic and onion in butter until tender. Add remaining ingredients and season to taste. Cool sauce before using as a marinade.

MARINADE FOR FAT FISH

6 Tablespoons mirin
1/4 cup soy sauce

1 Tablespoon sake

Marinate small pieces of fish for 15 minutes. Skewer and grill.

Basting Sauces

Basting sauces are generally stronger than marinades. They are brushed on fish during cooking.

BUZZY'S SAUCE AND BASTE

1 onion, grated
2 teaspoons grated fresh ginger
Grated rind of 1/2 lemon
Juice of 1 lemon
2 Tablespoons molasses

1/2 cup soy sauce
1/2 cup dry white wine
1/2 teaspoon garlic powder
1 teaspoon sesame oil

Let sauce stand for 1–3 hours before brushing on fish.

GARLIC-BUTTER BASTE

4 Tablespoons (1/2 stick) butter, melted
2 cloves garlic, pressed
Juice of 1 lemon

1 teaspoon Worcestershire sauce
1/4 teaspoon black pepper

LEMON MUSTARD BASTE

4 Tablespoons (½ stick) butter, melted   1 teaspoon Dijon-type mustard
Juice of 1 lemon   Dash of cayenne pepper

SESAME-SOY BASTE

2 teaspoons sesame seeds   2 Tablespoons mirin
¼ cup peanut oil   2 Tablespoons lemon juice
2 Tablespoons rice vinegar   2 teaspoons soy sauce

Toast sesame seeds in a heavy iron skillet until they are brown and pop. Grind them to a paste by whirling in blender. Add all other ingredients and blend together. Brush on fish before and during grilling.

FISH CHART
GLOSSARY

Fish Chart

FISH THAT MAY BE SUBSTITUTED
FOR SIMILAR FISH IN A RECIPE

Group I

PANFISH — ANY EDIBLE FISH
ORDINARILY TOO SMALL TO BE CALLED A GAME FISH

Whole fish or fillets: butter sauté, pan fry, oven fry, or deep fry. Clean, scale, score each side — or skin if muddy tasting.

Freshwater

Black bass
Black bullhead
Bluegill
Crappie, black and white
Green sunfish
Pumpkinseed
Red breast sunfish
Rock bass
Shellcracker
Warmouth
White perch
Yellow bass
Yellow perch

Saltwater

Bluefish (snapper size)
Cunner
Grunt, bream, porkfish
Kingfish
Mojarras
Pinfish
Pompano, lookdown, moonfish
Porgy, scup, spadefish
Sailor's choice
Smelt, silversides, whitebait, grunion
Snapper (small)
Spot, croaker
Surf perch, halfmoon, opaleye

The following is a list of recipes to supplement basic cooking methods of panfish:

Sautéed Kingfish, page 61
Pan-fried Croakers, page 62
Broiled Fillet of Perch with Topping, page 98
Perch with Bananas in Grapefruit Curry, page 99
Pan-fried Flounder with Mushrooms and Almonds, page 123
Fried Scrod Niçoise, page 184
Barbecued Porgy, page 199

Pan-fried Porgy and Other Panfish, page 200
Rye-fried White Perch, page 202
Pan-fried Bass (and Other Panfish), page 295
Pan-fried Bass in Tomato Sauce, page 295
Pan-fried Small Trout with Mushroom Sauce, page 308
Deep-fried Small Trout with Green Peppers, page 309

Group II

THIN FLATFISH WITH DELICATE FLAVOR AND TEXTURE
(SOLE, FLOUNDER, TURBOT)

1. Classic "fillet of sole" dishes — Dover sole (European), winter flounder, summer flounder, or petrale sole (brill)

2. Whole fish or fillets to butter sauté, pan fry, oven fry, poach, or broil — American plaice, butter sole, curlfin sole, Pacific Dover sole, Pacific English sole, sand sole, southern flounder, starry flounder, witch flounder, yellowtail flounder

3. Whole fish to grill or sauté — Rex sole, sand dabs, hogchoker, windowpane flounder

Group III

SMALL TO MEDIUM-SIZE FISH
WITH MODERATELY DENSE TEXTURE

A. Lean Fish with Delicate to Mild Flavor

1. *Lean White Fillets* may be substituted in recipes marked *"Any Lean* White Fillets":

Bass, kelp, rock, sand, striped
Black drum
Blackfish
Catfish, bullhead
Codfish, cusk, haddock, hake, pollock
Greenling (California seatrout)
Halibut (California)
Ling cod
Monkfish
Ocean whitefish
Perch, ocean, seaperch, surfperch
Pike, muskie

Pompano, lookdown, permit
Porgy
Redfish (drum)
Rockfish
Sculpin, cabezon, Irish lord
Seabass, Atlantic black
Seabass, California black
Sea robin
Sheepshead, Atlantic, Pacific
Snapper, red or Pacific
Tilefish
White seabass

2. *Firm Lean Fillets* may be substituted in recipes marked *"Firm Lean* White Fillets":

Bass	Pollock
Black drum	Redfish
Black seabass, Atlantic	Rockfish
Black seabass, California (small)	Snapper, red or Pacific
Catfish	Striped bass
Codfish	Tilefish
Grouper	White seabass
Haddock	

3. *Lean Whole Fish* to bake, plank, or stuff alike

Bass, striped, etc.	Redfish
Codfish, pollock	Rockfish
Ocean whitefish	Sheepshead

4. *Lean Soft-textured Fish with Mild Flavor:* whole small fish or larger fish filleted: deep fry, pan or oven fry, butter sauté, broil, or bake

Corvina	Spot
Croaker	Weakfish
Kingfish	Whiting
Speckled seatrout	

B. Oily Fish with Rich or Distinctive Flavor

1. Whole fish, steaks or fillets to barbecue, broil, bake in sauce, poach, bake in foil, or pan fry.

Albacore	Mullet
Bluefish	Sablefish
Bonito	Salmon
Butterfish	Shad
Cisco	Smelt
Herring	Trout
Mackerel, small, king, cero	Whitefish
Mahi mahi (dolphin)	Yellowtail

2. Oily Whole Fish to bake and stuff alike:

Bluefish	Salmon trout
Mullet	Shad
Salmon	Whitefish

Group IV

BIG (GAME) FISH WITH DENSE, MEATLIKE TEXTURE
AND DISTINCTIVE MILD FLAVOR

Fish will not break up during cooking. All should be skinned and may be cut into small cubes to skewer; finger-size slices to fry or poach; 1–1½-inch-thick steaks to barbecue or bake in sauce. Chunks may be cooked in foil.

Cobia	Shark
Giant black seabass	Snook
Grouper	Sturgeon
Marlin	Swordfish
Northern halibut	Tuna

Glossary

Bok Choy is a thick-stemmed, green leaf vegetable, similar in appearance to Swiss chard.

Chinese Pickle Mixed Vegetables contain ginger, cucumber, carrot, scallions, and turnip in sugar and vinegar. A 12-ounce jar is processed by Tung Chun Soy Canning Co. (Chinese).*

Cilantro (Chinese parsley or coriander) looks much like parsley, but has a strong flavor.

Daikon is white radish, a root vegetable. It is used fresh.

Dashi-No-Moto is a dehydrated soup stock made of bonito shavings and kelp. It is packaged like teabags; the broth is made by steeping the bag in boiling water (Japanese).*

Garlic. An average-size clove fresh garlic is equal to 1/8 teaspoon dehydrated powdered garlic or 1/2 teaspoon garlic salt (decrease the amount of salt in a recipe when using garlic salt).

Ground Bean Sauce comes in a 1-pound can packed by Koon Chun Co., Hong Kong. It is made of soybean and lasts indefinitely when refrigerated (Chinese).*

Jicama is a crisp root vegetable, similar in taste to water chestnuts. Thin raw slices are often served with lime juice and chili powder.

Mirin is a sweet liquor (Japanese), obtainable at liquor stores on the East Coast.*

Miso, White (Shiro) is soybean paste, malt, and salt. It comes in a plastic container and lasts indefinitely, even without refrigeration (Japanese).*

Oyster Sauce is an oyster-flavored bottled sauce. It lasts indefinitely (Chinese).*

Sake is a sweet white wine (Japanese), obtainable at liquor stores on the East Coast.*

Salted Black Beans, Fermented, are fermented salted soybeans. They come in plastic bags and last indefinitely, even without refrigeration (Chinese).*

Tofu is a white cake of custard consistency, made of fresh soybean.

Wasabi is horseradish powder. It comes in a 2-ounce can (Japanese).*

*These products may be found in most Oriental food stores or supermarkets.

INDEX

Index